THE ORDER OF PENITENTS

THE ORDER OF PENITENTS
Historical Roots and Pastoral Future

Joseph A. Favazza

Foreword by James Lopresti, S.J.

THE LITURGICAL PRESS
Collegeville, Minnesota

Cover design by Don Bruno

Library of Congress Cataloging-in-Publication Data

Favazza, Joseph A., 1954–
   The order of penitents : historical roots and pastoral future /
Joseph A. Favazza.
   p. cm.
   The author's doctoral thesis, Katholieke Universiteit te Leuven,
1986.
   Bibliography: p.
   ISBN 0-8146-1542-2
   1. Penance—History of doctrines. 2. Penance. 3. Catholic
Church—Doctrines. I. Title.
BV840.F38 1988   88-10170
265'.6'09015—dc19   CIP

To the memory of
CARROLL THOMAS DOZIER
(1911–1985)
friend, bishop, prophet,
whose reconciling embrace
simply knew no limit

CONTENTS

FOREWORD

The only truly enduring human institutions are those that can
ceaselessly arise transformed by change. Such institutions are, in the
end, stronger than any present form. They retain a memory — that
is their continuity — but they also suffer the new, and that, paradoxically, is their life. The Church, born of the side of the dying
Jesus, is expected to be one of those enduring institutions. In fact,
it is expected to stand above all the rest. It is not some imagined
changeless form or shape or way of behaving that is the life promise
of the community of believers; it is the capacity of the community
to suffer renewal. That capacity can come only from the incessant
presence of the Resurrected One in our midst promising to be with
us until the end. Rather than fear any change of form, faith demands
the ready embrace of death genuinely inviting new life.

Historians serve today's Church very well whenever they enable
a new age to surface buried memories and see the practice of the
present rooted in the past. Such good work catalogues our collective wisdom, as it were. It helps us claim our past with deep and
full respect. It counsels caution about giving in to the urge to re-
invent, as if we were disconnected from our past. That is no small
contribution. But historians serve us even better when they enliven
our imagination with full awareness of the discontinuities as well.

Dipping into deep wells of the practice and the wisdom of the
churches of the first three centuries is an especially refreshing and
nourishing effort. Through the careful examination of the rich era
of Church life offered in this text, one cannot but marvel not only
at the lines of connection in practice but at the similarities of the

struggle to give birth to new ways of enfleshing the gospel. The churches of the subapostolic era, like the Church in our own age, were challenged to allow creative ways of giving voice to the ceaseless mercy of God. One thing we learn in the pages that follow is that the ancients did not shy away from the challenge. Brought alive for us once again in the way that good historical scholarship allows, they may well gift us with some of their fortitude.

Today's fruitful life, even the best of what we have, even our virtues and good deeds, become the seed that falls into the ground to sprout something new in undreamed-of springtimes. Now is a death-life intersection time, time for the seed to fall to the earth, a bittersweet time of death to the familiar inviting resurrection into the new. One harbinger of all that is the unsettled condition of the way we do penance. The crisis in penance is window into some of the most central issues about being Church.

Some very powerful shifts have been occurring in our perception of the way reconciliation is accomplished. The sacrament of penance, subset of the larger topic of reconciliation, is perceived differently than in former times as well. That is true not only for theologians but also for the average Church member. Those shifts have been occurring quite gradually over a number of years. Many people probably do not even pay much attention to them anymore. But just as a small shift in the continental plate under California can mean new shapes for the city limits of Los Angeles, so these shifts under the ground of the Church have already begun to shake up our once serene surface. Let us examine two of them.

THE FIRST SHIFT: FROM ACT TO PROCESS

Anyone over forty will remember our sincere efforts to "seek perfection." That usually meant picking out a particularly troublesome sin and then working against it. Little Pelagians that we were, we approached our "problems" with the modest expectation that we could surmount them. So we charged out into the world of ubiquitous temptations, practicing modesty of the eyes and counting on the power of endlessly chanted ejaculations. We shunned the proximate occasions of sin and kept on guard for the ever-lurking remote ones as well. Our efforts to avoid sin sometimes failed. Even if we didn't seek out the forbidden delights of the back seat of the Buick, we knew that we had allowed ourselves the brief pleasure of imagining we had. Rightly remorseful, we carried our failure to the dark confessional and admitted our impure thoughts. Counseled to take a few more cold showers or to busy ourselves about matters meant to distract our overly stimulated adolescent hormones, we left the Saturday rites relieved that we had another chance to get it right. I do not mean to mock by retelling this stereotypical story. For some, indeed many, the discipline of weekly confession was, and still is, a source and stimulus for conversion of life. That is especially true if it was done in the context of regular spiritual direction. I do mean, however, to paint a contrast of changing sensibilities in the most divergent tones in order to make a point.

Much is different today. Some lament that the reduced confession lines on Saturday afternoon are sure testimony that we have lost a sense of sin and entered upon an age of terrible moral decline. That may be true in part. One would be hard put to claim that moral uprightness has enjoyed a healthy resurgence in our day. But in every age the righteous have sounded the alarm of moral decline. If they are all to be believed, then we have been on a downhill slide for the past two thousand years. When do we hit bottom? But the absence of former adolescents from the confession line does not by itself mean either a loss of a sense of sin or a lack of the experience of reconciliation.

Perhaps people are even more aware of sin in our day. But their awareness is about something more evasive than identifiable forbidden acts and more pervasive than matters able to be accounted for in the usual examination of conscience. Of course, there are many who beg off responsibility for their destructive behaviors. There is no intent here to excuse scoundrels and charlatans. But they are not our concern. Struggling people trying to live well, suffering failures, facing uncertainties, and enduring the pains of brokenness are our concern. Undoubtedly they are aware of sin, or at least of its tread marks impressed upon their fractured lives. No one believes in marriage for life more than some who have suffered a tragic divorce. They know the pain, hurt, and even the death of that pledge of lifelong fidelity. It is time to relinquish the too often and too facilely stated claim that our age lacks a sense of sin. Such assertions beg the question, belittle the searching spirit of so many hurting people, and, what's more, they smack of cheap ascendancy.

People suffer confusion about which actions are sinful and which are not. That is true. There is also much confusion about where the responsibility lies when things go wrong. New understandings about the regular progression of moral development in individual lives and about the complexity of social relationships make ascribing guilt less certain. But all that confusion does not lessen the pain or the tragedy nor dispel the fear. In fact, for many the confusion makes the problem of sin, fault, failure, and evil in our world even more troublesome. The problem is not lack of a sense of sin; the problem is how to keep faith in the midst of a world in which sin seems all the more pervasive. The challenge is to find assurances that keep the morally confused from losing heart and giving up. Clarity is not the fundamental issue; hope is.

Furthermore, it is hard to avoid the deep suspicion that some new measure of God's loving spirit is at work in so many of the twelve-step programs that have arisen in recent years. Listen to a few stories of the levels of compassion, surrender, and hope generated in such groups as Alcoholics Anonymous, Alanon, Overeaters Anonymous, Debtors Anonymous, and you walk away with the compelling sense that serious and genuine reconciliation is going on in those gatherings. Only the crustiest institutionalist — and there are a few around — would decry such movements as lesser "secular" counterparts to Church practice. They may well be some of the best efforts of gospel-empowered people to be leaven in the world. They may be fashioning some of the best sacramental moments of reconciliation. Without such truly reconciling sacramental moments with the small "s," our celebration of sacrament with the capital "S" will remain rote and remote. Alcoholics Anonymous and the like may be telling us that Church may be happening, as Jim Dunning might say, without our permission. Imagine that!

If we have moved away from focus on acts to direction and quality of life as means for assessing our behavior, then forms of expressing and effecting change in a damaged life are also going to move away from judgment about acts to restorative processes. Curiously, many of the people who have opted out of the confessional line show up in large numbers whenever someone announces a healing service of any kind. Might it be that people are nurturing a changed imagination about what reconciliation is all about? While we have consistently, and in part rightly, used the metaphors of forgiveness of guilt to effect reconciliation in the sacrament, some people are actually using metaphors of healing to match their own experience of reconciliation. Reconciliation may well be happening in ways we have not paid attention to.

Let me comment on one special example of new means of experiencing reconciliation. Those who belong to twelve-step groups recognize that some particular dependency has exerted control over their lives. That is to say, they have experienced firsthand what it means to be held captive. That is what addiction is all about. So it is not only healing and strengthening that they seek, but also liberation or rescue from an enslaving power.

Anglican pastoral theologian Keith Miller, in his marvelous new book starkly titled *Sin*,[1] in fact claims that addiction is the raw and root power of sin and that liberation is the fundamental dynamic of reconciliation. Even a cursory look at the work of Sobrino, Gutierrez, Boff, and other Latin American theologians shows how convincing a claim that is. Many of us have heard the sometimes tragic and agonizing cry ''I can't help it; I seem to be unable to behave differently.'' Sometimes those words are not childish excuses whined to cover up unconscionable behavior in adults. Sometimes they do indeed express the truth of people looking for rescue, not only forgiveness — as necessary as forgiveness may be.

Should we be hearing in all these modern-day experiences that an announcement of forgiveness of guilt without concomitant liberation from captivity and without healing of debilitation is not enough? Surely that is true whenever a hurting member of the community has matured enough to understand that life patterns are revealed in our acts, and that those only partly visible life patterns are the underlying malaise that needs more than an effort to seek perfection, more than repeated mentioning in a court of judgment, more than a few minutes' attention from the presider at the end of the Saturday waiting line. Some of our people may be absenting

---

1. J. Keith Miller, *Sin: Overcoming the Ultimate Deadly Addiction* (New York: Harper and Row, 1987).

themselves from the reconciliation room (which too often is a confessional with the furniture but not the attitude rearranged), not because confession is too much to bear, but because it is too little to carry the weight of their need. What should be done about them?

Rather than lamenting, we need to seek the Spirit in what is happening. Historians of the liturgy of penance tell us that every significant change in the form of the sacrament happened because of grass-roots insistence. While schooled to seek reconciliation in one way, people found other ways of their own to experience new hope and promise in the midst of their brokenness. Sometimes it took a while for the leaders of the community to accept what the people had already done. Eventually they did.

Throughout the complex history of the sacrament of penance, however, one thing remains constant. Whatever the means by which one found rescue from sin and evil, people of all times have expected that somehow being a part of the Christian community is itself a sign of their being at peace with God. That awareness may have been more explicit in the ancient Church. Whenever we carefully examine the way third-century Christians perceived reconciliation and forgiveness as it showed up in their ritual practice, we find a group of people who knew that they were forgiven, healed, and rescued by God because they were at peace with the community. As Jesus said about the woman of bad reputation wiping his feet with her tears: "Her sins must have been forgiven her, for see how she loves much" (Lk 7:47).

THE SECOND SHIFT: THE PLACE OF THE COMMUNITY IN RECONCILIATION

What we once called "confession" we now (except, unfortunately, in the 1983 Code of Canon Law) call "reconciliation." What's in the change of names? It is a shift in understanding and imagination from Church as the place in which someone receives forgiveness to Church as the signal event of forgiveness itself. In certain, and increasing, numbers of believing communities in this country, people want to find belonging to the community itself to be a reconciling act of its own. Twenty-five years ago I know I was forgiven (the word reconciliation" was not yet in my vocabulary) because the priest used powerful words to tell me so. That was not only very comforting, but it was, and remains, true. But the priest's connection to the believing community was never apparent to me, nor did it seem to be anything of an issue. I was as sorry as I could be, and he said those words and it seemed that was all that mattered. That is not true. The community did matter; I simply was not able to advert to how much it mattered. In all likelihood, neither did the priest. I simply took it for granted that the Church, that is, the community, was the context in which the sacrament happened. I would not have been able to understand that the prior sacrament is the community itself.

The ancients would have known better. They knew that being at peace with the Church was the mystery, the sacrament, which somehow told me that I was at peace with God. Just how that was true was something they were content to leave quite ambiguous. They were more interested in the power of the mystery than in the clarity of its explanation. That provides a basis for a much different way to build an understanding of how this thing called the sacrament of reconciliation does what it does. My adolescent jaunts to the confessional were done in the anonymity of Saturday afternoon. My continuing search for reconciliation, although perhaps less well defined today, is nonetheless a bit more inclusive and holistic than that.

A powerful shift in understanding about what the Church is all about shows up when we take all this seriously. Without denying the essential, indeed indispensable, role of the priest as a main actor in this drama of reconciliation, we now must face, as a community of believers, the immense demands that such a shift makes of us corporately.

Paul identifies the Church's mission, indeed its very reason for gathering, with reconciliation. We, as a community, are "ambassadors of reconciliation," (2 Cor 5:20). Our way of life is meant to be an announcement to the world that all enmity between God and humankind is at an end. The peace that marks the life of the community is a sign of all that. That peace itself comes from the Spirit of God animating the community.

The *Rite of Penance* correspondingly asserts: "The whole church, as a priestly people, acts in different ways in the work of reconciliation that has been entrusted to it by the Lord" (no. 8). Somehow, then, gathering with these other believers is the sign par excellence of reconciliation for the world. If by gathering one means the mere physical juxtaposition of warm bodies, that doesn't make any sense. But if by gathering one means something radically deeper, then we're on to something.

I referred above to the change of names of the sacrament, that is, from confession to reconciliation, as sign of a shift in consciousness. I want to qualify that a bit. Along with some other liturgists, I find myself a little uncomfortable with that name. Yes, penance is *a* sacrament of reconciliation, but it is not really *the* sacrament of reconciliation. Even the document of the rite of penance, the more technical name, recognizes that. In fact, *the* sacrament of reconciliation is the event of Church itself. That should be clear from the above discussion. The journey of penance, including the ritual celebration, the liturgy of penance, is a road to reconciliation. Just as the RCIA, the journey of initiation, is a road to full membership in the Church, so penance is preeminently a road to return to full membership. It is the event of full membership that is the liturgy of reconciliation par excellence. And the fullest expression we have of that event is the Eucharist.

There is a crucial point to make about Eucharist, which is the keystone to everything attempted here. Our understanding about what happens when a community assembles to celebrate the Eucharist is often truncated. While many of us have a fully developed understanding about the Real Presence in the bread and cup, and we are gradually beginning to appreciate a little more what we mean when we speak of Christ present in the Word, we have least developed our understanding about presence in the community. Something happens that equals more than the sum of its parts when the community truly assembles. That something is at the heart of the matter of reconciliation. There is something about our being together that speaks more truth about human reconciliation than anything else we do. There is something profound and full of mystery in the act of coming together, something so easily missed because it is covered by the veil of ordinariness. Like the Nazarenes in the early days of Jesus' ministry, we are too close to see the mystery.

We need to take some time to fill that out. To do that we need to build a foundation of understanding about the mystery of being human. This is hard to talk about because it is so close. The philosopher Santayana once claimed that we do not know who first discovered water, but we can be sure it wasn't the fish. We need a fresh look at the waters our imagination swims in.

Most of us take for granted that being an individual precedes being in community. The really real is my isolated self. Sometimes when we allow ourselves to dwell on that unquestionable presupposition, we feel uneasy. Occasionally the isolation of it all wells up in lonely dissatisfaction. We sense that something is wrong. Accordingly, we struggle to connect with one another. Yet even our deepest experiences of being in love and the passionate attempt to cross over the boundaries to enter one another's hearts can seem to be futile attempts to break out of isolation. All the while we have left unquestioned the presupposition that we begin as disconnected subjective cells trying to bridge the insufferable gap between us. We seldom stop to ask ourselves whether we might have presupposed things to be opposite what they really are. It may well be that our fundamental imagination is at fault. Perhaps we have forgotten something so basic that our whole starting point is flawed.

What if the truth about us is that being in community is primary? What if the truth about us is that we are inseparably connected with one another? What if the truth is that being human means being one cell of a larger living organism? Imagine a world fashioned out of that imagination! Whatever diminishes you diminishes me. Whatever builds you up builds me up. Whatever makes you cry pains my heart. Whatever delights your spirit gives me joy. Your birth is new life for me. Your death is part of my dying. In a marvelous little poem entitled "A Prayer for the Secret Solidarity of the Human Race," John Shea puts it this way: "The man I did not notice yesterday died today and left me alone."[2]

When Paul speaks of Jesus as being like us in all things but sin, remember that he is speaking of Jesus' humanity. The difference between Jesus and the rest of us is that he never attempted to escape being human. His humanity is without that faulted imagination. He knew the deep connection in fullest measure. He never forgot that truth. He never did anything but live it out to the end.

2. John Shea, *The Hour of the Unexpected* (Allen, Tex.: Argus, 1977), p. 44.

He is more human than I am, because I spontaneously, infallibly, incessantly forget that deep connection. Every time I find myself feeling lonely and depressed, I've forgotten. Every time I find myself anxious about how many people are ahead of me in line, I've forgotten. Every time I feel the surge of envy, the meanness of ascendancy, or the steel of defensiveness, I've forgotten. It makes one wonder: whoever gave us that apple to eat? Who convinced and confused us so thoroughly that we have the whole world backwards from the very beginning of our imagination? from the very birth of our consciousness?

True, our imagination is narrowed by a kind of presupposition that the individual precedes the community. But the starting place for the Eucharist is just the opposite. The Eucharistic assembly is founded in the imagination of Jesus. It begins with our inescapable unity and will not let us forget it. In the Eucharistic liturgy we don't make human community happen, we discover it. Even our less than best efforts at assembling for worship on Sunday give us hints about this truth. We who assemble for Eucharist gather with no distinction according to class, rank, privilege, age, ideology, color, economic status, or even temperament. The only distinctions have to do with facilitating the service of the assembled body. We sing our prayer as much as possible, not because it sounds better that way, but because music unites our many voices into one continuous sound, the same notes in a thousand vocal cords. We hear one word proclaimed. We exchange the sign of peace with whoever is near. We process to one table to eat of one bread and drink the same wine. These are all corporate acts; they are acts done by a community as a community, not by a collection of juxtaposed individuals.

Just picture what kind of a world ours would be if the imagination that shapes our worship were the unquestioned foundation of our behavior! There would be no need to talk of reconciliation in a fractured world; there would be no more fracture. The Eucharistic assembly, then, is the model of what reconciliation is meant to accomplish. Now we can understand why Eucharist is *the* sacrament of reconciliation. The discipline and liturgy of penance is a process to regather around the table those who had not truly assembled, had absented themselves from the sign of reconciliation, had returned to the faulted imagination of isolation. Whenever one is freed from the captivity of the lie, healed of the maladies it generates, and has accepted forgiveness, then the festival of truth rises. "There is more rejoicing in heaven over one sinner who repents than over ninety-nine who have no need of repentance." (Lk 15:7)

Thank God we try our worship so often, at least once a week. Truth be told, our memory is very short. Perhaps for that brief one hour on Sunday we have a glimpse into the mysterious depths of our blessed connectedness. Perhaps for that one special hour we are able to allow deep conviction about our solidarity, especially with the poor, who have no other advocates. Perhaps we dare to speak the truth about ourselves in our prayer and embrace. But for some strange reason it all comes apart in the parking lot. We do need to gather in Eucharistic assembly often; we are too weak not to. We need very frequently not-to-forget, what the Greeks called *anamnesis.* Paradoxically, the truest Eucharistic assembly closely borders on hypocrisy. We don't look like that Eucharistic assembly when we are at battle in the expressway passing lane. Rightly we begin each Eucharistic celebration with an acknowledgment that we remain un- reconciled in so many ways, even as we sing the words of unity. True worship holds that paradox in perilous balance.

We have claimed that reconciliation is not merely a matter of taking care of personal sins; it means a holistic reform of life. We have claimed that the Church (read community) is not merely the context in which forgiveness is announced but the very center of it. We have shown that the Eucharistic assembly is the primary sign to the world about what being human means. There are some weighty pastoral implications inside all these theological ramblings. Allow me to tease out just a few of them. We will focus on the com- munity as a whole as means of reconciliation and then on specific ministries in a community of reconciliation.

1. *About the community as a whole:* Obviously, if what we have said about the theological importance of the community is true, then the community must be of a kind whose corporate life bespeaks reconciliation. It is true that many people are disappointed by the lack of community, especially in our large impersonal suburban par- ishes. But the very fact that people should express a disappointment shows that there has been a conversion of mind-set. Twenty years

ago most Catholics would not even have seen that as an issue at all. That there is disappointment is, strangely enough, a sign of growth in expectations. But there are also an increasing number of people who tell stories of communities of faith that have broken down the barriers of impersonalism. More people feel warm and welcome. In some cases that breakdown of impersonalism has led to a second step in building community, namely, a breakdown of individualism. There are communities in which the claims of people given to people have fashioned bonds too important and challenging to allow one to exclusively seek self-actualization. In some communities there are people who go out of their way for other people, not just because that makes them feel good, but because it is good in itself to do that. It feels natural to do that.

The fostering of such relationships in communities is probably the most important thing we can do to become ambassadors of reconciliation. Solidarity in community, shared life, common stories, willingness to be responsible to, and for, one another, is the only way of life befitting a Eucharistic people. Such solidarity acts as a beacon for those who feel lost, alone, isolated, rejected, trapped, sinful. Sometimes timid, often just beginning to feel enough freedom to voice pent-up angers that had no place to be aired and healed in faceless, anonymous parishes, the inactive will approach such communities with hesitant steps. A faithful, loving community does more to evangelize than many a slick ad campaign using Gospel texts and invitations to come home for Christmas.

But there is a trap in this. Communal involvement in the penitential journey of individuals is difficult to imagine as long as the name "penitent" carries with it the freight of judgment. A penitent is someone who has been naughty, so the popular imagination might say. Implied in that is the obviously false assumption that the nonpenitent is nice. Paradoxically it is an easy temptation for a warm and loving community of good and holy people to cozily curl in on itself and ice out others from the comfy hearth it has worked so hard to fashion.

There is the rub. Communal involvement in the reconciliation of the penitent is not "being received into an all-holy community"! The penitent is being welcomed into the fellowship of others who are able to acknowledge the ever-active power of the reconciling spirit of the victorious Christ in their midst. That is to say, all endure the pain and rubble of sin. There is no vine-covered cottage for the Catholic Prince Charming family to happy-ever-after in. But believers do recognize that the event of Christ has vanquished the power of sin to dominate their lives. They know themselves still to be subject to the buffeting and snares of their own compulsions, weaknesses, and addictions, yet they rejoice in the sure knowledge that the power of Christ is always greater than these demons. No buffeting need work fatal damage; no snare precludes release. Our lives can be changed. The goal of reconciliation, we remarked before, is not so much moral uprightness as it is faith and hope. Then it is that faith and hope, more than externally correct behavior that marks a community ready to be sign of reconciliation. The so-called Moral Majority has badly missed that point.

We will know we have begun to learn this lesson whenever the name penitent has as much honor attached to it as the name catechumen. The community of reconciliation truly rejoices over the journey of the penitent who becomes the sign about the truth of itself. It is a community reborn again and again, fashioned in its own healing. The rescue of each member is the enlargement of all. The penitent is sign of Christ alive in our midst.

2. *All ministries can grow out of that common soil of faith and hope in the loving journey of reconciliation for individuals.* Let's look at three: the companion, the spiritual director and the presider.

THE COMPANION: A community is not a mere collective. It is real people truly united in heart, mind, and resolve. The glue of communal life is the simple reality of true friendship. Such friendship leads members of a community to sponsor the best aspirations of their companions. Out of this most fundamental human relationship grows every ministry, bar none. Ministry, even — nay especially — when it is in a leadership role, begins with the capacity to accompany. When companionship is lacking, ministry becomes benevolent paternalism at best and autocratic rule at worst. When evaluating a candidate for ministry of any kind, one should first ask whether the candidate can be a good and faithful companion. Only following a positive response to that query should one pursue questions of job competency. That is true no matter the office, from parish secretary to archbishop, to mention two of the most powerful. The RCIA, for example, is built upon the foundation of the sponsor relationship. It should be no different for the journey of the penitent. Somehow, especially for someone who has been away from active identification from the Church community for a very long time, there has to be a way to provide understanding companionship. That precedes all other ministrations.

THE SPIRITUAL DIRECTOR: If all there were to ministry of penance was the judgment of the sincerity of one's contrition, then the ministry would end with a pronouncement of that judgment. Some people's imagination ends right there. But fewer people today are willing to be content with such a limited understanding of reconciliation. They will not accept such minimalism. But as judgment wanes discernment waxes. Discerning patterns and directions is a more formidable task than pronouncing judgment on acts. Hence the need for those schooled in discernment.

The role of the spiritual director in penance is at least as ancient as that of judge. Like their companions of former times, many people today who have rejected what they consider to be the "sterile" experience of the confessional have turned to wise counselors who are gifted with vision into the workings of the spirit. This is not a rejection of confession so much as a renewal of its meaning. The reform of the sacrament of penance has yet to fully engage the service of these wise ones because of an unwillingness to look beyond the presbyterate. Many gifted people of discernment have been overlooked, or "underlooked." That is not true of our larger tradition.

THE PRIEST: It sounds as though all this leads to the suggestion that responsibilities heretofore reserved for priests be taken away and given to others. That is not exactly true. The issue is not either/or; it is both/and. The full ministry of reconciliation makes demands on a community far exceeding what any group of priests could do, even were we to increase their number a hundredfold overnight. Any positive reading of the crisis in penance these days points that out with utmost clarity. People who truly hunger for reconciliation are not seeking less than confession; they are seeking more. More than the ministration of priests is needed, not less.

Specifically, we need priests to do what our tradition most often demands: to preside over actions done by the whole community and to give leadership in prayer and strong exhortation from the Word of God. A priest must preside over a reconciling community, but he should never pretend that he can ever replace it. Sometimes we get that confused.

These reflections have been both too long and too little. So much has yet to begin to happen before we come to understand all that is promised to the reconciling community and all that is needed from it. I have come to be more and more convinced that as a Church we haven't even begun the reform of the sacrament of penance. There probably are some more significant changes in the way we do important things coming down the road. Those changes are decisions for the whole Church to make. It has happened before. Unlike many who feel discouraged or even threatened by that, we ought to be of good heart. We are a living community, animated by no small spirit. And rather than trying to force change in any patterns, we need truly to read the signs of the times. Without relinquishing the responsibility to shine the gospel light on the dark parts of our modern life, we need also to see the good news peering out at us from the way ordinary people lead their lives. Such an exercise, done in humility and confidence, allows our God to raise us up anew.

There is more mystery to being God's people than we can ever grasp in any age. The deepest mystery of all is the ever-renewing miracle of reconciliation. It makes no end a dead end and no failure a last chance. That equals outrageous mercy, the kind the prodigal father willingly and recklessly lavished. We can do no less if we are to be ambassadors of reconciliation ourselves. And we can never count the cost.

—James Lopresti, S. J.

AUTHOR'S PREFACE

Like any worthwhile destination, this book can be approached in a variety of ways. The most determined will begin at the beginning and end at the end. I applaud you, for certainly the book is arranged with logical persons like you in mind.

Those more impatient may decide to skip Chapter One and move immediately into the witness of the first three centuries. Feel free to do so, with one caveat: At least read pages 57–66 for the sake of familiarizing yourself with the terminology; otherwise, it will prove confusing reading indeed!

Finally, the most pragmatic readers may skip immediately to Chapter Five, where the pastoral implications of a restored order of penitents is discussed. Do so with my blessing, but please heed the sage advice of the historian Owen Chadwick: "History . . . does more than any other discipline to free the mind from the tyranny of present opinion." I promise you that going back to read the earlier chapters will restore and reveal the whole picture rather than just a fragment.

Whatever approach into this book you take, I hope you also discover that it is written as a resource, a printed archaeological tool to be used to help us plumb the depths of our past, present, and future ecclesial penitential practices. To this end, I hope it will prove its worth for the journey that lies ahead.

Those who have made this book possible are legion. I wish to thank those professors, colleagues, and friends of the University of Louvain, Belgium, and of the American College, who helped to give this book its "first life" as a doctoral dissertation. In addition, I especially wish to thank Dr. Lambert Leijssen, who directed me in my work; Rev. Michel Dujarier, who offered me invaluable advice; Rev. James Lopresti, S.J., who offered the same as well as a pastorally challenging foreword; Sr. Catherine Galaskiewicz, O.P., who meticulously proofread the text; Mr. Stephen Duncan, who had the unglamorous job of preparing the Index; and Mr. Mark Twomey and the staff of The Liturgical Press who worked so long and hard on the innumerable details of publication.

I also wish to thank the people of the Diocese of Memphis, ordained and non-ordained, who never stop shaping and reshaping my pastoral perspective. And to my family and my friends scattered throughout the world: thank you. Your prayer and support over the years have been for me an amazing grace.

Memphis
28 August, 1988
Feast of Augustine, Bishop and Doctor

ABBREVIATIONS

AB	*The Anchor Bible*, W. F. Albright and D. N. Freedman (eds.), Garden City, New York, 1964ff.
ACW	*Ancient Christian Writers*, Westminster, Maryland, 1946–1960; New York, 1961ff.
AER	*American Ecclesiastical Review*, Washington, D.C. 1889ff.
AK	*Arbeiten zur Kirchengeschichte*, Berlin, 1922ff.
ANF	*Ante-Nicene Fathers* (American reprint), Grand Rapids, Michigan, 1978ff.
AuC	*Antike und Christentum*, Münster, 1929ff.
BBK	*Bonner Beiträge zur Kirchengeschichte*, Cologne, 1972ff.
BCSR	*Bibliothèque catholique de science religieuse*, Paris, 1928ff.
BFT	*Beiträge zur Förderung christlichen Theologie*, Gütersloh, 1897ff.
BHTh	*Beiträge historischen Theologie*, Tübingen, 1929–1936, 1950ff.
BLE	*Bulletin de littérature ecclésiastique*, Toulouse, 1899ff.
BSHTh	*Breslauer Studien zur historischen Theologie*, Breslau, 1934ff.
BTAM	*Bulletin de théologie ancienne et médiéval*, Louvain, 1929ff.
BTh	*Bibliothèque de théologie*, Tournai, 1958ff.
CCL	*Corpus Christianorum. Series Latina*, Turnhout, 1953ff.
CHR	*Catholic Historical Review*, Washington, D.C., 1915ff.
Coleti	*Illyrici sacri...Daniele Farlati/Jacopo Coleti*, 23 vols., Venice, 1751–1819.
CSCO	*Corpus Scriptorum Christianorum Orientalium*, Paris-Louvain, 1903.
CSEL	*Corpus Scriptorum Ecclesiasticorum Latinorum*, Vienna, 1866ff.
CTh	*Cahiers théologiques*, Neuchâtel, 1949ff.
CTT	*Chrétiens de tous les temps. Textes du Ier au XXe siècles*, Paris, 1963ff.
CUAT	*Catholic University of America. S. Facultas Theologica*, Washington, D.C., 1915ff.
DACL	*Dictionnaire d'archéologie chrétienne et de liturgie*, F. Cabrol and H. Leclercq (eds.), Paris, 1907–1953.
DCA	*A Dictionary of Christian Antiquities*, 2 vols., London, 1875–1880.

DicSp	*Dictionnaire de Spiritualité*, M. Viller, et al. (eds.), Paris, 1937ff.
DS	*Enchiridion Symbolorum*, H. Denzinger and A. Schönmetzer (eds.), 33rd ed., Freiburg, 1965.
DThC	*Dictionnaire de théologie catholique*, A. Vacant and E. Mangenot, continued by A. Amann (eds.), 15 vols., Paris, 1903–1950.
EeT	*Église et théologie*, Paris, 1958ff.
EL	*Ephemerides liturgicae*, Rome, 1887ff.
EThL	*Bibliotheca ephemeridum theologicarum Lovaniensium*, Louvain, 1948ff.
FC	*Fathers of the Church*, Washington, D.C., 1947ff.
FCLD	*Forschungen zur christlichen Literatur- und Dogmengeschichte*, Paderborn, 1900–1938.
FRLANT	*Forschungen zur Religion und Literatur des Alten und Neuen Testaments*, Göttingen, 1903ff.
GCS	*Die Griechischen christlichen Schriftsteller der ersten drei Jahrhunderte*, Leipzig/Berlin, 1897ff.
HDg	*Handbuch der Dogmengeschichte*, M. Schmaus, J. Geiselmann, and A. Grillmeier (eds.), Freiburg, 1951ff.
HThR	*Harvard Theological Review*, Cambridge, Massachusetts, 1908ff.
IER	*Irish Ecclesiastical Record*, Dublin, 1864ff.
IThQ	*Irish Theological Quarterly*, Maynooth, 1906ff.
JThS	*Journal of Theological Studies*, London, 1899ff.
Mansi	J. D. Mansi, *Sacrorum conciliorum nova et amplissima collectio*. 31 vols., Florence/Venice, 1757–1798.
MBTh	*Münsterische Beiträge zur Theologie*, Münster, 1923ff.
MD	*La Maison-Dieu*, Paris, 1945ff.
MSR	*Mélanges de science religieuse*, Lille, 1944ff.
MThZ	*Münchener Theologische Zeitschrift*, Munich, 1950ff.
NRTh	*Nouvelle Revue Théologique*, Louvain, 1869.
OCP	*Orientalia Christiana Periodica*, Rome, 1935ff.
PeL	*Paroisse et liturgie*, Bruges, 1946ff.
PG	*Patrologia Graeca*, J.-P. Migne (ed.), 161 vols., Paris, 1857–1866.
PL	*Patrologia Latina*, J.-P. Migne (ed.), 217 vols., Paris, 1844–1855.
PO	*Patrologia Orientalis*, Paris, 1907ff.
PS	*Patristic Studies of the Catholic University of America*, Washington, D.C., 1922ff.
PTS	*Patristische Texte und Studien*, Berlin, 1964ff.
QL	*Questiones Liturgiques*, Louvain, 1969ff.
RB	*Revue biblique*, Paris, 1892ff.
RDC	*Revue de droit canonique*, Strasbourg, 1951ff.
RET	*Revista Española de Teología*, Madrid, 1941ff.
RevSR	*Revue des sciences religieuses*, Strasbourg, 1921–1940, 1947ff.
RHE	*Revue d'histoire ecclésiastique*, Lyon, 1900ff.
RHLR	*Revue d'histoire et de littérature religieuse*, Paris, 1896–1907, 1910ff.

RHPR   *Revue d'histoire et de philosophie religieuse*, Strasbourg, 1921ff.
RHR   *Revue de l'histoire des religions*, Paris, 1880ff.
RSR   *Recherches de science religieuse*, Paris, 1910ff.
RSPTh   *Revue des sciences philosophiques et théologiques*, Paris, 1907–1940, 1947ff.
RThAM   *Recherches de Théologie ancienne et médiévale*, Louvain, 1929ff.
SAC   *Studi di antichita christiana*, Rome, 1929ff.
SC   *Sources Chrétiennes*, H. de Lubac and J. Daniélou (eds.), Paris/Lyon, 1941ff.
SCA   *Scuola Cattolica*, Milan, 1873ff.
SE   *Science et Esprit*, Bruges, 1968ff.
SGKA   *Studien zur Geschichte und Kultur des Altertums*, Paderborn, 1907ff.
SH   *Subsidia Hagiographica*, Brussels, 1886–1936, 1942, 1948ff.
SP   *Studia Patristica*, Berlin, 1957ff.
SR   *Science et religion*, Paris, 1900–1914.
SRTR   *Science religieuse. Travaux et recherches*, Paris, 1943–1944.
SSL   *Spicilegium Sacrum Lovaniense. Études et documents*, Louvain, 1922ff.
StCA   *Studies in Christian Antiquity*, Washington, D.C., 1941–1957.
STh   St. Thomas Aquinas, *Summa Theologiae*, Latin text and English translation, 60 vols., New Blackfriars edition, London, 1963–1965.
SuppNT   *Supplements to Novum Testamentum*, Leiden, 1958ff.
TDNT   *Theological Dictionary of the New Testament*, 10 vols., Grand Rapids, Michigan, 1964–76.
ThGl   *Theologie und Glaube*, Paderborn, 1909ff.
ThQ   *Theologische Quartalschrift*, Tübingen/Stuttgart, 1819ff.
ThRv   *Theologische Revue*, Münster, 1902ff.
TThS   *Trierer Theologische Studien*, Trier, 1941ff.
TThZ   *Trierer Theologische Zeitschrift*, Trier, 1947ff.
TS   *Theological Studies*, Baltimore, 1940ff.
TU   *Texte und Untersuchungen zur Geschichte der altchristlichen Literatur*, Leipzig/Berlin, 1882ff.
UCLDiss   *Universitas Catholica Lovaniensis Dissertationes ad Gradum Magistri in Facultate Theologica vel in Facultate Iuris Canonici consequendum conscriptae*, Louvain, 1935ff.
VC   *Vetera Christianorum*, Bari, 1964ff.
VigChr   *Vigiliae Christianae*, Amsterdam, 1947ff.
ZKG   *Zeitschrift für Kirchengeschichte*, Stuttgart, 1876ff.
ZKTh   *Zeitschrift für Katholische Theologie*, Innsbruck, 1877ff.
ZNW   *Zeitschrift für die neutestamentliche Wissenschaft und die Kunde der älteren Kirche*, Giessen/Berlin, 1934ff.

OTHER ABBREVIATIONS FOR WORKS FREQUENTLY CITED:

Ecclesiastical Authority	Campenhausen, H. von, *Ecclesiastical Authority and Spiritual Power in the Church of the First Three Centuries*, translated by J. Baker, Stanford, California, 1969.
L'Église	Galtier, P., *L'Église et la rémission des péchés*, Paris, 1932.
Busstufenwesens	Grotz, J., *Die Entwicklung des Busstufenwesens in der vornicänischen Kirche*, Freiburg, 1955.
Paenitentia Secunda	Poschmann, B., *Paenitentia Secunda*, Bonn, 1940.
PAS	Poschmann, B., *Penance and Anointing of the Sick*, translated by F. Courtney, New York, 1964.
Early Church	Rahner, K., *Theological Investigations*. Vol. 15: *Penance in the Early Church*, translated by L. Swain, London, 1983.

Biblical quotations are from the Revised Standard Version, London, 1966.

INTRODUCTION

One fact endures: Jesus ate and drank with sinners. He showed compassion to them and forgave them. He ultimately died for them. Jesus' ministry is at the very heart of the Church's own reconciling ministry. The Church's task is to continue the ministry of Jesus in the world. It is a serious task, one that evokes mercy and compassion balanced with a recognition of the reality of sin. Throughout the ages the Church has always responded to those living in grave sin after baptism. Sin changes something fundamental in the relationship between the sinner and God, and the Church, through its pastoral mission rooted in the ministry of Jesus, responds to the situation of the sinner.

The Second Vatican Council, in its Constitution on the Sacred Liturgy, called for the renewal of the ritual action specific to the Church's pastoral mission to sinners, namely, the sacrament of penance (*Sacrosanctum concilium*, 72). While no specific plan of reform was offered, other statements by the Council, though surprisingly few, speak clearly of the ecclesial essence of the sacrament. To be reconciled with God is to be reconciled with the people of God, the Church.[1] The affirmation of the ecclesial nature of the sacrament of penance was an assessment that this sacrament, like the others, had become too individualized and juridic. As far as possible, sacramental celebrations are to be communal rather than individual or quasi-private events (*Sacrosanctum concilium*, 27). More spe-

---

1. *Lumen gentium*, 11; *Presbyterorum ordinis*, 5.

1

cifically, some of the bishops wanted the Church's penitential practice to mirror more appropriately the communal nature of sin and penance.[2] This was part of the Church's ancient tradition, which the Church of the present has to rediscover.

The eventual result of the Council's call for renewal was the promulgation of the revised Rite of Penance, the *Ordo Paenitentiae*, in 1973. But the reform of the rite could not stem the tide of decline in the number of persons who availed themselves of the sacrament. Society was changing, along with its conception of morality and authority. Sin was no longer a black-and-white issue, as the ascendancy of the social and positive sciences resulted in the reinterpretation of actions previously considered morally wrong. The authority of the Church as the indisputable moral legislator came under question, nowhere more dramatically seen than in the dissenting response to the issue of birth control. The survival of the sacrament of penance in its past form was in grave doubt.

In response to the "crisis of penance," the theme of "Reconciliation and Penance in the Mission of the Church" was chosen for the 1983 Synod of Bishops. The outcome of the Synod remains open to interpretation; at best, it can be said that the resultant exhortation by Pope John Paul II does not appear harmonious with what is known of the bishops' discussions.[3] In any event, it is the 1983 Synod and the intervention by Cardinal Joseph Bernardin that give rise to the present study. At the Synod Cardinal Bernardin called for the restoration of the ancient order of penitents as another form of the rite of penance.[4] Fundamental to his suggestion is the process model of conversion adopted by the revised Rite of Christian Initiation of Adults (RCIA). It is his opinion that the model suggested by the RCIA is adaptable to the sacrament of penance, allowing for a long-term process of sacramental reconciliation in certain pastoral situations. This is in contradistinction to, but not in conflict with,

---

2. *Acta Synodalia Sacrosancti Concilii Oecumenici Vaticani II*, I, part 2 (Rome, 1962-). See the interventions during the *Congregatio Generalis XIII* by M. Mazier (pp. 174–75) and A. Barbero (p. 188).

3. See J. Dallen, "Reconciliatio et Paenitentia: The Postsynodal Apostolic Exhortation," *Worship* 59 (1985) 98–116.

4. See *Origins* 13 (1983) 324–26. Below, pp. 253–254.

the present forms, which compress the entire process of reconciliation into a single event.

The intervention by Cardinal Bernardin, as well as present experimentation with a restored order of penitents on the parish level in the United States, buttresses the appropriateness of reexamining the penitential experience of the early Church. Any desire on the part of the Church to restore a practice of the past demands a carefully studied historical foundation. This is especially true with regard to the Church's early penitential discipline, which the popular conception connects only with harshness and severity. Restoring the order of penitents solely on the basis of demonstrated pastoral need runs the risk of having no roots in the tradition and being vulnerable to the same mistakes of the past. Taking as one's starting point a thorough study of the tradition of the early Church can serve to inform the present pastoral need and transform future pastoral praxis. Laying the historical framework for a restored order of penitents is the first part of the working hermeneutic of the present investigation.

Without doubt, uncovering the difficult dossier of ecclesial penance during the first three centuries has already been undertaken by numerous authors. Therefore, it might be questioned why yet another study is needed. Besides the distinctiveness of the working hermeneutic mentioned above, there are two methodological distinctions between past studies and the present work. First, previous studies of the history appear to have an appreciation that the penitential experience of the third century is in some way distinguishable from the canonical discipline, which is well defined from the fourth century and beyond. The wide variety of interpretations of the early history points to this fact. Even so, there has not been an adequate definition of terms or a serviceable descriptive vocabulary of the early experience of penance that would take away from, rather than add to, the already existing ambiguity of the sources. Terms such as ''canonical penance,'' ''public and private penance,'' and ''excommunication'' are all interpretable in numerous ways. The present study, in an attempt to come to a more understandable and neutrally descriptive terminology, avoids such terms completely (except in the case of canonical penance, which is used only in a strictly circumscribed way). The experience of the early Church is intelligible enough to lend itself to the formulation of a new vocabulary.

A second methodological distinction lies in the fact that the present work approaches the sources thematically. It is not our intention to present an exhaustive treatment of all aspects of the patristic reflection on sin and penance during the first centuries. Indeed, the penitential teaching of the main early witnesses alone easily could be (and has been) the subject of entire dissertations. In searching for the roots of the order of penitents, the focus is on the practices of the early Church with regard to grave postbaptismal sinners. To be sure, these were exceptional cases, but they laid the foundation for the evolution of an order of penitents. In particular, exclusion from the Eucharist and the development of distinct penitential stages are practices at the heart of the early discipline, and we will return to them again and again. It is they which most adequately reflect the changed relationship between the sinner and God (and so the Church), and the altered status of such a one within the community.

Taken together, these distinguishing methodological approaches bring us to the second part of our working hermeneutic. Is it possible to discover the existence of an order of penitents prior to its being overcome by the stranglehold of canonical penance? In other words, does the experience of the third-century churches reveal a defined process of penance which, though less liturgically demarcated, is free from the harsh consequences of the canonical discipline? These are ultimately the questions which have led to the wide assortment of interpretations of the early experience of penance and which remain enough unanswered for the present study, far from being redundant, to be particularly appropriate.

The book is divided into five chapters. In the first chapter we enter into the world of interpretation and into dialogue with previous commentators on the history of penance during the first centuries. The work of these later authors provides access to the major points of controversy that have framed the interpretational history, especially in the nineteenth and twentieth centuries. A second section of the chapter sets the context of the present study. It specifies terms which, though used by past historians of penance, are no longer tenable and are avoided in this study. A new vocabulary of more neutrally descriptive terms is offered to guide the reader through the early experience of penance. The chapter concludes by briefly setting the development of penitential practices within the larger context of ecclesiological and sociological factors operative during the first three centuries.

The next three chapters present the patristic witness itself. In the second chapter we begin with the first two centuries. Though the testimony of the New Testament and the postapostolic writers does not offer a specific penitential discipline, we can detect certain practices that will later be incorporated into the Church's response to sinners, particularly the isolation of grave sinners from the community. Special attention is given to the *Shepherd of Hermas,* the most important witness of the second century, and to the late second-century writings of Irenaeus. The chapter concludes with three fragments from Eusebius's *Ecclesiastical History,* which are situated by him in the second century.

In the third and fourth chapters we examine the all-important witness of the third century. The third chapter begins in the East, looking at the penitential practices in the writings from Syria and Asia Minor, as well as Alexandria. Of special importance are the lucid testimony of the *Didascalia Apostolorum* and the more enigmatic writings of Origen. They reveal a developed process of penance, with penitents moving from being isolated from the Church (already seen in the witness from the first two centuries) to their being segregated within the community. In the fourth chapter we see this process more strongly confirmed in the writings from the West, especially those of Tertullian and Cyprian in North Africa and, to a lesser extent, Hippolytus and Novatian in Rome. It is appropriate that the patristic witness conclude with the unique clarity of Cyprian, who attests to a defined penitential *ordo* for the reconciliation of the *lapsi.*

After the patristic examination of the historical roots of the order of penitents, the last chapter serves as our conclusion by turning again to our twofold working hermeneutic. A first section brings together the evidence for the discovery of an order of penitents in the third century, prior to its life as one of the characteristic elements of the fourth-century canonical discipline. A second and final section shifts our attention from the historical roots to the pastoral future of the order of penitents, establishing the foundation upon which to base serious consideration of its future restoration. Though applicable in only certain pastoral situations, a process model of reconciliation offered by a restored order of penitents might hold the key for the future renewal of the sacrament of penance.

Chapter One

STATING THE QUESTION
AND SETTING THE CONTEXT

One who aspires to study the early history of ecclesial penance must first be prepared to enter the dangerous jungle of interpretation. Only through dialogue with the numerous authors who have studied and commented upon the development of penitential beliefs and practices in the Church can one be initiated into the major points of controversy that have formed the history of interpretation. It is impossible to begin any historical study in a vacuum; the insights of those who have gone before us must be both critiqued and built upon. For this reason the history is allowed to be self-referential for a moment, as we begin with an account of the interpretational history of the order of penitents.[1]

The interpretation of early penance has essentially revolved around two poles, both of which have had an impact, at least indirectly, on the history of the order of penitents. The first concerns the possibility of full readmission to the Church after one had fallen into grave sin after baptism. Were the early Christians elitists who

---

1. As will be seen, it is only recently that contemporary writers have begun to distinguish between the early experience of penance and the institution of public or "canonical" penance of the fourth century. Many authors have consolidated the entire experience of ecclesial penance in the first six centuries under the generic heading of canonical penance. This is an example of past terminology that can no longer be maintained. Yet, in the examination of the history of interpretation, one must be cognizant of this fact, recognizing that references by certain authors to canonical penance, even some very recent (for example, C. Munier, *Tertullien: La pénitence*, SC 316 (Paris, 1984), pp. 59ff.), include the experience of penance during the third century.

refused any contact with such contaminated persons, or could those guilty of sin, no matter how objectively serious, be once again admitted to the Church, provided they showed adequate repentance and internal conversion through the performance of external acts of penance? This is a question which has in the past served as a confessional battleground between Catholics and Protestants, but which now, at least since the publication of Poschmann's *Paenitentia Secunda*, has moved toward a more accepted consensus.

The second pole of interpretation concerns whether different forms of ecclesial penance existed in the early Church alongside the public actions that developed into the order of penitents. Earlier in this century, especially due to Galtier's influential *L'Église et la rémission des péchés*, the issue centered on the existence of a private form of penance more in continuity with present sacramental practice. This view has now been abandoned, as the results of historical-critical research have freed later historians from approaching the early history apologetically to find justification for a present practice. In addition, a terminological quagmire was created by the use of hopelessly ambiguous language, especially the terms "public" and "private." More recently, the publication of Grotz's *Die Entwicklung des Busstufenwesens in der vornicänischen Kirche* has shifted the question to the practice of exclusion from the Eucharist: Might there have been an older form of penance in the early Church that did not include exclusion from the community? Inasmuch as exclusion from the Eucharist will emerge as the essential "root" of an earlier order of penitents, might this mean that ecclesial penance and the embryonic order of penitents are not coextensive realities?

These are the major issues through which we will be able to trace the history of the interpretation of penance in the early Church. This task will be accomplished in the first section of the chapter, beginning with Thomas Aquinas and early scholasticism, and continuing through to the contemporary era. A second section will contextualize the present study in light of the previous interpretation and will set the historical stage for the examination of the patristic sources that is to follow.

I. THE INTERPRETATION OF THE EXPERIENCE OF PENANCE IN THE ANCIENT CHURCH

A. THE MEDIEVAL AND MODERN PERIODS

The numerous explications of the early history of penance until the nineteenth century are rooted in the thinking of Thomas Aquinas and the later development of scholastic theology, and in the controversies over nature and grace in the sixteenth and seventeenth centuries.

1. THE VIEW OF THOMAS AQUINAS AND THE LATER SCHOLASTICS

Thomas's integration of scholastic thought had a profound influence on the basic notion of sacrament.[2] With regard to ecclesial penance, he was more concerned to define the essence of sacramentality, constituted by the Aristotelian metaphysical categories of matter and form, than to deal with the historical questions. Since the predominant experience of penance in his day was individual confession and absolution, it was on this foundation that he built his thought. The penitential experience of the ancient Church, surviving in the obsolete medieval form of the *paenitentia solemnis* ("solemn penance"), is hardly mentioned in Thomas's writings.[3]

Thomas teaches that the "form" of sacramental penance is the absolution given by the priest, while the "quasi-matter" is the acts of the penitent: contrition, confession, and satisfaction.[4] There ex-

---

2. For a fuller treatment of Thomas's sacramental theology, see A. Teetaert, "Doctrine de Saint Thomas d'Aquin au sujet du sacrement de pénitence et de la confession aux laïques," *Miscellania Tomista* (Estudis Franciscans) 34 (1924) 302–325; P. Fransen, *Faith and the Sacraments*, Aquinas Papers 31 (London, 1958), pp. 11–22.

3. St. Thomas Aquinas, *Summa Theologiae*, Blackfriars Edition, Vol. 60: *Penance*, introduction and translation by R. Masterson and T. O'Brien (London, 1966), p. XX. Poschmann, *PAS*, p. 154, adds that only one question was devoted to the *paenitentia solemnis* in the *Supplementum*, and then after the treatment of indulgences. Though Thomas's authorship of the *Supplementum* is doubtful, this is a judgment on the relative unimportance of the almost forgotten ancient practice during Thomas's time.

4. STh, IIIa, q. 90. a. 2 (*Blackfriars* 60:166): "Sic igitur requiritur ex parte poenitentis, primo quidem voluntas recompensandi, quod fit per contritionem; secundo quod se subjiciat arbitrio sacerdotis loco Dei, quod fit in confessione; tertio quod recompenset secundum arbitrium ministri Dei, quod fit in satisfactione. Et ideo contritio, confessio et satisfactio ponuntur partes Poenitentiae."

ists an intrinsic connection between the contrition of the penitent and acts of satisfaction that express contrition, yet they are not the same reality. Both are necessary in the causality of the sacrament, whether the act of satisfaction occurs before or after the sacramental absolution.[5] For this reason, when the *paenitentia solemnis* is mentioned in the *Supplementum*, its sacramental effect is assumed, though the existence of some sort of private discipline in the ancient Church is likewise assumed.[6] Thomas also insists on the absolute power of the Church to forgive sins, demanding that the indicative form of absolution be used. Against later historical verification, he claims that the indicative form has been employed even from the first centuries.[7]

The influence of Thomas on the theological development of the sacrament of penance is inestimable. From his day until the Council of Trent, his understanding of the operation of the sacrament was the accepted explanation.[8] In fact, official Church teachings used

---

5. Without wishing to reopen the attritionist/contritionist controversy that raged in the centuries after Thomas, suffice it to say that Thomas understands the acts of the penitent, as well as absolution by the priest, as effecting a "dispositive" causality through which God is able to forgive sins. See especially Appendix I, *Blackfriars* 60:177-179; L. Leijssen, *Penance and Anointing of the Sick*, unpublished course notes, Katholieke Universiteit Leuven (1980), pp. 127-129.

6. P. Palmer, "Jean Morin and the Problem of Private Penance," *TS* 6 (1945) 317-357; 7 (1946) 281-308, p. 341, n. 83. (Hereafter, "Jean Morin" and "Jean Morin II"). Palmer believes that such an interpretation of the ST, *Supplementum*, q. 28, a. 1, is possible, while admitting that Thomas never directly affirms the sacramental character of public penance. Also, Thomas believed in the repeatability of penance (*STh*, IIIa, q. 84, a. 10), which could only mean that he is able to discern, in the ancient Church, a discipline of penance in continuity with the contemporary practice.

7. J. Jungmann, *Die lateinischen Bussriten in ihrer geschichtlichen Entwicklung*, Forschungen zur Geschichte des innerkirchlichen Lebens 3-4 (Innsbruck, 1932), pp. 258-259. Later scholastic theologians interpret Thomas's position to mean that the ancient supplications were *formaliter* indicative though *materialiter* deprecative. Not long after Thomas the deprecative form is no longer to be found except in some fourteenth-century manuscripts. The formula "Ego te absolvo" was proclaimed officially as the form of the sacrament at the Council of Florence (A.D. 1439). See F. Courtney, "The Administration of Penance," *The Clergy Review* 46 (1961) 10-27, 85-98, pp. 97-98; below, n. 9.

8. Concerning the development of the theology of penance from the beginning of scholasticism until Trent, the literature is vast. For a recent bibliography, see H. Vorgrimler, *Busse und Krankensalbung*, HDg 4,3, ed. M. Schmaus *et al.* (Freiburg, 1978), pp. 117-119.

Thomas's terminology almost verbatim.[9] The indirect result of Thomas's scholastic approach to the sacrament was that the historical preeminence of the contemporary practice of individual confession came more and more to the fore. At the time of the Reformation, this was one of Luther's objections to the scholastic approach to penance. It was Luther's feeling that it only served to justify an exaggerated need of the magisterium to exercise authority in the Church and separated the sacrament from the intention of its historical roots.[10]

Counter-Reformation theologians rose up against Luther, stressing, even more than Thomas himself, the efficacy of the sacrament as the indispensable element of salvific justification. So important did this stand become in defense of the Church's authority to forgive sin that the *ordo* of private penance came even more to be appreciated as an ancient institution of the early Church. By means of example, one can cite the writings of Melchior Cano, one of the contributing theologians in the discussion of penance at the Council of Trent. Cano states that the secret confession of secret sin is a divine institution, such that those who hold otherwise fall into heresy.[11] Trent itself confirmed the stand taken by Cano and others.[12]

---

9. For example, the *Decretum pro Armenis* of Pope Eugenius IV in A.D. 1439 (DS 1323:699): ". . .paenitentia, cuius quasi materia sunt actus paenitentis, qui in tres distinguuntur partes. Quarum prima est cordis contritio . . . Secundo est oris confessio . . . Tertia est satisfactio pro peccatis secundum arbitrium sacerdotis . . . Forma huius sacramenti sunt verba absolutionis, quae sacerdos profert, cum dicit: 'Ego te absolvo' . . . Effectus huius sacramenti est absolutio a peccatis."

10. M. Luther, "Disputatio pro declaratione virtutis indulgentiarum. 1517," in Vol. I: *D. Martin Luthers Werke. Kritische Gesamtausgabe* (Weimar, 1883–), p. 233: "Olim pene canonice non post, sed ante absolutionem imponebantur tanquam tentamenta vere contritionis." For an appreciation of Luther's attack of the scholastic thought concerning the sacrament of penance, see T. Tentler, *Sin and Confession on the Eve of the Reformation* (Princeton, 1977), pp. 349–362.

11. Cano states: "Quam ob rem ex revelatione et institutione Dei est, quod confessio sit secreta, alioquin non esset haeresis, ab Evangelica veritate penitus aliena, assertio contraria . . ." Text from W. Anderson, *Jus Divinum and the Sacrament of Penance in Two Tridentine Theologians: Melchior Cano and Ruard Tapper*, published doctoral dissertation, The Catholic University of America, Washington, D.C. (Ann Arbor, Mich., 1969), p. 130.

12. Council of Trent (A.D. 1551), sess. 14, *Decretum de Sanctissimo Poenitentiae*, c. 6 (Coleti 20:100): "Si quis negaverit confessionem sacramentalem vel institutam, vel ad salutem necessariam esse jure divino; aut dixerit modum secrete confitendi soli

With the historical eminence of canonical penance called into question by the Tridentine theologians, later scholastic theologians used Thomistic categories to deny the sacramental efficacy of the public aspects of ancient penance. Suarez, for example, speculated that the only true penance of the ancient Church was a private discipline, in continuity with contemporary practice. Canonical penance affected only the penitents' relationship with the Church, leaving their relationship with God untouched. In this way these later scholastics were able to reconcile the rigorism of the ancient practice, especially centered on the teaching of a single penance, by holding that it only applied to the extrasacramental public practice. Private sacramental reconciliation could be obtained more than once.[13]

The later scholastics' historical explanation of the experience of penance in the first centuries was that it involved two absolutions: one given when the penitent confessed his/her sin (private and sacramental absolution), and one given at the end of the entire process, when the purely external "excommunication" was lifted and the penitent was readmitted to the Church (public and extrasacramental absolution). In this way the later scholastics developed a tight dogmatic system, one based on speculative theology rather than sound historical data, and one that attempted to put to rest once and for all any controversy concerning the penitential practice of the early Church. It was perfectly in accord with the contemporary sacramental experience of penance. Even against the works of the great positive historians of the seventeenth century, it was this later scholastic perspective that influenced historical investigations of penance into the twentieth century.[14]

---

sacerdoti, quem ecclesia catholica ab initio semper observavit & observat, alium esse ab institutione & mandato Christi, & inventum esse humanum, anathema sit."

13. F. Suarez, *Opera Omnia*, Vol. 22: *Commentarii et Disputationes*, ed. C. Berton (Paris, 1861), p. 134, on the question of canonical penance: "Respondetur, in illis decretis non esse sermonem de poenitentia, ut est virtus, vel sacramentum, et ad internam peccati remissionem ordinata; sed de quadam poenitentia solemni, quam possumus caeremonialem appellare, quoniam peculiari ritu ab Ecclesia instituto olim fiebat ad publicam satisfactionem et aedificationem . . ." (Text cited by Palmer, "Jean Morin," p. 341, n. 83).

14. *Ibid.*, pp. 341–342. For a list of nineteenth- and early twentieth-century authors who disclaim the sacramental efficacy in the public actions surrounding the early experience of penance, see Rahner, *Early Church*, p. 380, n. 141. Other authors hold-

2. THE JANSENIST MOVEMENT OF THE SEVENTEENTH CENTURY

The followers of Jansenius reacted against the speculative theology of the scholastics, insisting that it was a cause for the laxity in faith and morals prevalent in the society of their day. Their dissatisfaction was found particularly in their call for a renewal of the practice of penance. Of singular importance were the writings of A. Arnauld, but his rigorist thinking also found expression in the writings of C. Leutbrewer, G. Huygens, and J. Van Neercassel.[15] Here the more rigorist aspects of the penitential practice in the ancient Church are seen as an ideal, while the individual and private practice of the day is interpreted as a perversion of the sacrament. Arnauld argued that the contemporary practice of sacramental penance was in reality a relaxation of needed penitential discipline, which was the cause of many other disciplinary problems for the Church. The ancient Church had no such problems. It was a communion of saints, remaining pure in a sinful world, largely due to hard penitential procedures, including even refusal of ecclesial reconciliation for certain serious sins. This was the practice the Church should restore, Arnauld believed, in order to bring under control the widespread lapse in morals.[16]

---

ing the same position are cited by G. Rauschen, *L'Eucharistie et la pénitence*, trans. M. Decker and E. Ricard (Paris, 1910), p. 200, n. 2. Palmer, "Jean Morin," p. 348, 353, adds: S. Harent, "La Confession," *Études* 80 (1899) 577–605, pp. 585ff; L. De San, *De Poenitentia* (Bruges, 1900), p. 193.

One can easily see the great influence later scholastic thought had on the historical interpretation of penance in the early Church.

15. A. Arnauld, "De la fréquente communion," in *Oeuvres de Messire Arnauld*, Vol. XXVII (Paris, 1779), pp. 181–673, esp. pp. 343–350.

C. Leutbrewer, *Industria spiritualis in qua modus traditur praeparandi se ad confessionem aliquam plurimorum annorum* (Cologne, 1639); G. Huygens, *Methodus remittendi et retinendi peccata* (Louvain, 1674); J. Van Neercassel, *Amor poenitens, sive de divini amoris ad poenitentiam necessitate et recto clavium usu* (Emmerich, 1683).

16. Arnauld, "De la fréquente communion," pp. 321–365, where he outlines seven proofs for the necessity of the ancient discipline of exclusion from the Eucharist "pour des crimes énormes." However, his understanding of such an exclusion was purely penal, which, as shall be seen in the following chapter, was not the original intention of the action. On the Jansenist reaction, see: G. Voorvelt, "L'Amor Poenitens de Neercassel," in *Jansénius et le Jansénisme dans les Pays-Bas*, ed. T. Van Bavel and M. Schrama, EThL 56 (Louvain, 1982), p. 78; H. Rondet, *The Grace of Christ*, trans. T. Guzie (New York, 1966), pp. 340–364; K. Hargreaves, *Cornelius Jansenius and the Origins of Jansenism*, published doctoral dissertation, Brandeis University, Waltham, Mass. (Ann Arbor, Mich., 1974), *passim*.

3. THE REACTION OF THE SEVENTEENTH-CENTURY POSITIVE THEOLOGIANS

The Jansenist position regarding the history of penance evoked a strong reaction among Catholic positive historians. These authors argued in favor of the clemency of the early Church, insisting that their position was based on a historical study of the patristic authors, not on the speculation of the scholastic theologians. This was the position taken in the writings of D. Pétau.[17] Pétau believed that, prior to the famous Edict of Callistus at the end of the second century, the Church did not offer ecclesial reconciliation to those who had committed one of the three capital sins (idolatry, murder, or adultery); yet, neither did it cut them off from the possibility of final reconciliation with God.[18] Based on the thirteenth canon of Nicaea, Pétau held that the Church has always had a tradition of reconciling repentant sinners on their deathbed, no matter how objectively serious their sin.[19]

The interpretation by J. Morin was similar to that of Pétau but differed on the explanation of the edict of toleration.[20] He held that, against a creeping rigorism that began with Novatian's schism, the edict was an attempt by Church leaders to return to the apostolic tradition of showing tolerance toward postbaptismal sinners. He writes:

---

17. D. Petavius (Pétau), *De poenitentiae vetere in Ecclesia ratione diatriba* (1622); *De poenitentia et reconciliatione veteris ecclesiae moribus recepta Diatriba ex notis in Synesium* (1633); *De paenitentia publica et praeparatione ad communionem* (1644). These writings are collected in his *Opus de theologicis dogmatibus*, Vol. 6, ed. F. Zachariae (Venice, 1757).

18. It was Tertullian, in his Montanist treatise *De pudicitia*, who referred to an edict from the hand of the "Pontifex Maximus." The interpretation of his words has been vigorously debated by historians of penance for centuries, due to its enormous bearing upon whether the tradition of the early Church was one of rigorism or clemency. While most historians would date this decree around the end of the second century, it is generally agreed today that the famous edict was not from the hand of Pope Callistus. For this reason subsequent references will be to its more neutral designation, the edict of toleration. Below, pp. 30–33.

19. A. d'Alès, *L'Édit de Calliste* (Paris, 1914), pp. 3–4, pointed out that it was only in his later works that Pétau came to this position on the reconciliation of those on their deathbed. See also Poschmann, *PAS*, p. 85, n. 128.

20. J. Morinus (Morin), *Commentarius historicus de disciplina in administratione sacramenti paenitentiae* (Antwerp, 1682). Palmer, "Jean Morin," p. 321, insists that, while Morin's classic is not a polemic against Jansenism, the weight of historical scholarship is able to disprove their position. However, Morin can hardly be said to be neutral with regard to the Jansenists.

Before the heresy of Novatus [sic], much more so than afterwards, the penalties imposed for sin were of shorter duration and administered with much more clemency. One might consider this statement rather difficult to believe. However, if we consider the fragments that remain from the writings of the most ancient fathers, the truth of the statement will be immediately evident.[21]

His was a radical thesis that did not receive wide acceptance until the beginning of this century.

While both Pétau and Morin, as well as their contemporaries, defended the sacramental efficacy of the ancient discipline against the later scholastics, they also reacted against the position of the Jansenists that there was no private discipline of penance in the ancient Church.[22] As noted above, Pétau believed that all classes of sins could be forgiven on the deathbed; such reconciliation lacks public actions, such as exclusion from the Eucharist. Morin, on the other hand, based his defense of the existence of a discipline of sacramental private confession on the argument of "illation" rather than on the meager and fragmentary sources.[23] His position rested on his ability to prove that penitents underwent the discipline of canonical penance only if they were guilty of one of the capital sins. If this was the case, which he attempted to demonstrate through

---

21. "Poenae peccatis impositae, quas Poenitentias vulgo & antonomastice dici demonstratum est, quae antonomastica appellatio etiam nunc perseverat, ante Novati haeresim, multo quam postea & breviores fuerunt, & clementius inflictae. Hoc forsan quis difficile in animum suum inducet: Verum si consideremus quae de iis nobis supersunt antiquissimorum Patrum fragmenta, hujus pronuntiari veritas statim elucescet" (Morin, *Commentarius historicus*, p. 182; translation by Palmer, "Jean Morin," p. 324).

22. D'Alès, *L'Édit*, p. 6, lists those authors from the seventeenth and eighteenth centuries who share the position of either Pétau or Morin: J. Sirmond, *Historia paenitentiae publicae* (Paris, 1651); G. de l'Aubespine, *De veteribus Ecclesiae ritibus Observationum*, Vol II. (Paris, 1623); N. Alexandre, *Historia ecclesiastica* (Paris, 1699); and later, Cardinal Orsi, *Dissertatio historica qua ostenditur catholicam Ecclesiam* (Milan, 1730).

To these Palmer, "Jean Morin," p. 345, adds: B. Francolini, *De disciplina poenitentiae*, Vol. III (Rome, 1708); and later, H. Tournely, *Praelectiones theologicae* (Paris, 1728).

Neither author makes mention of L. Thomassin, *Ancienne et nouvelle discipline de l'Église*, Vols. I and II, *passim*.

23. Palmer, "Jean Morin II," pp. 282, 285–286, is of the opinion that Morin is referring to a "private satisfaction," since he recognizes that confession of sin was private and absolution was public.

appropriate texts from the Fathers, then there must have been another model of ecclesial reconciliation for those who had committed serious sin, but not one of the canonical triad. Inasmuch as Morin believed that it had always been the practice that all serious sins had to be submitted to the "power of the keys" for forgiveness, he upheld a private discipline of penance for these "intermediate" types of sin.[24]

The work of the positive theologians was only truly "discovered" when the scholastic interpretation of the ancient experience of penance began to wane around the beginning of the twentieth century. Unquestionably, theirs was a significant contribution to the study of penance; yet, their perspective of the first six centuries was seriously unnuanced. There was no clear distinction between the practice of the third century and the later development of canonical penance. The blurring of historical lines continued into the contemporary period.

B. THE EARLY CONTEMPORARY PERIOD

The nineteenth century, dominated by the growth of modern historical research, ushered in a new era in the study of the history of penance. From the immense amount of material that appeared from the last part of the century until the beginning of the First World War, it is clear that it was an apologetical age. What was at stake was the fundamental question of the development of dogma, specifically expressed in the meaning of grace, the efficacy of the sacraments, the authority of the magisterium, even the proper understanding of revelation itself. Within this context, the interpretation of the early history of penance became one of the focal points of this debate.[25]

---

24. Morin, *Commentarius historicus*, pp. 249–250, believes there were three classes of sins defined by the Fathers: "gravissima," which were the canonical triad for which public penance was demanded; "levissima," lighter sins that were forgiven without sacramental reconciliation; and "minus gravia," which were mortal sins not grave enough for the public discipline. It is these that he says were submitted to a private form of penance. Obviously, Morin attempted to interpret Tertullian's division of the classes of sin (wrongly) and to apply the experience to the entire early Church.

25. Rahner, *Early Church*, p. 18.

From the Catholic perspective, the history of ecclesial penance was a bulwark protecting the sacramental authority of the Church from the insidious influence of German Protestant liberal theology. For the Protestants, the history served as demonstrative proof that the Catholic claim on the "power of the keys" had little historical basis in the experience of the ancient Church. Over and above these basic camps, there were different approaches taken between Catholic and Catholic and between Protestant and Protestant, which only served to further confuse the issue.

1. ATTACK OF THE PROTESTANTS

As has been indicated, the influence of the seventeenth-century positive theologians could not stem the tide of the later scholastic interpretation of the ancient experience of penance. By the end of the nineteenth century, it was generally accepted by Catholic scholars that the discipline of canonical penance in the ancient Church was nonsacramental. This opened the door for Protestant historians of penance. If they could prove from the patristic sources that there was no regular private practice of absolving sinners in the Church during its first centuries (the view of the later scholastics), then it would be apparent that the sacramental practice of penance was not so much a mandate from the Lord as a later ecclesial practice worked out by Church leaders. In the eyes of their Catholic counterparts, such a conclusion would have grave doctrinal implications for the sacramental character of the Church itself.

A. von Harnack was the first Protestant theologian in contemporary times to draw out such a conclusion.[26] He was the most influential historical theologian of the last century. He came out of the German liberal philosophical tradition, most essentially expressed in the thinking of Hegel and Schleiermacher, with its stress

---

26. A. von Harnack, *History of Dogma*, Vol. II, trans. N. Buchanan (London, 1896), pp. 94–127.

J. Pelikan, *Historical Theology: Continuity and Change in Christian Doctrine* (London, 1971), pp. 58–67, and J. Pelikan, *Unfolding Revelation: The Nature of Doctrinal Development*, Theological Resources (London, 1972), pp. 230–235, both ascribe a central role to Harnack in the development of historical theology. Rahner, *Early Church*, p. 18, specifies his importance in the field of penance.

on science and reason.[27] In his methodology, he attempted to approach Christian tradition, not from any theological presuppositions, but rather from the critical standpoint of history alone. Only from a proper understanding of the bare facts of history could one hope to understand the process of dogmatic development.[28]

Harnack's position on the history of penance cannot be separated from his historical perspective of the ancient Church. The first Christians were a communion of saints who expelled from their community any person who had committed one of the capital sins after baptism. Harnack interpreted the edict of toleration as an innovation not only because of its offer of reconciliation to adulterers but also because it includes the first instance of reference to the "power of the keys." This was a new theological self-reflection by the Church of its own power. Suddenly the bishops, as the successors of the apostles, claimed to have the power to loose and bind sin on earth. As a negative result, Harnack felt it was this understanding that led to the schism by Novatian, the fury of Tertullian (in the *De pudicitia*), and even to the underemphasis of ecclesial office in the writings of Origen.[29] And it was upon this claim that Cyprian admitted the *lapsi* after the Decian persecution some fifty years later. Harnack claimed that it was this act that sounded the death knell to a more compassionate approach to sinners by the confessors:

> The confusion occasioned by the confessors after the Decian persecution led to the non-recognition of any rights of "spirit-filled" persons other than the bishops. These confessors had frequently abetted laxity of conduct, whereas, if we consider the measure of secularization found among the great mass of Christians, the penitential discipline insisted on by the bishops is remarkable for its comparative severity. The complete adoption of the episcopal constitution coincided with the introduction of the unlimited right to forgive sins.[30]

Harnack saw the growing institutionalization of the power of the bishop as giving rise to the notion that ecclesial penance effected

---

27. Walgrave, *Unfolding Revelation*, pp. 226, 232.
28. Pelikan, *Historical Theology*, pp. 66–67.
29. Harnack, *History of Dogma II*, pp. 108–112.
30. *Ibid.*, p. 112.

the sinner's reconciliation with God. If this is so, then the process of penance must not encourage laxity. The bishops' recognition of their own power over sin led them to create the harshness associated with the penitential process of the early Church.[31]

H. Lea was the next major Protestant author to attack the sacramental efficacy of penance in the ancient Church, though his historical approach did not have the precision that was uniquely Harnack's.[32] The tenor of his writing made it clear that he was developing an anti-Catholic polemic. One might sum up his position in the following way: The ancient Church knew only the institution of canonical penance; canonical penance was not sacramental; therefore, there was no sacramental reconciliation in the first centuries of the Church's life.[33] The historical basis of the Catholic Church's authority to forgive sin was negated, which in turn negated all present claim to sacramental authority by the Catholics. Lea's historical analysis prompted more of an outcry from Catholics than Harnack's and forced the Church to rethink its position.[34]

Another important contributor from the Protestant camp was H. Koch.[35] Koch, picking up an idea proposed by H. Windisch, was a strong defender of what has come to be known as the "postbaptismal theory" concerning the interpretation of the *Shepherd of Hermas*.[36] In the tradition of Harnack, Koch stated that there was no

---

31. Harnack, *History of Dogma II*, pp. 118–127.

32. H. Lea, *A History of Auricular Confession and Indulgences in the Latin Church*, Vol. 1: *Confession and Indulgence* (Philadelphia, 1896), pp. 20–76. Prior to Lea, E. Rolffs, *Das Indulgenz-Edict des römischen Bischofs Kallist*, TU 11,3 (Leipzig, 1893); *Urkunden aus dem Antimontanistischen Kampfe des Abendlandes*, TU 12,4 (Leipzig, 1895), took basically the same position as Harnack. However, Rolffs played an important role in the question of the authorship of the edict of toleration. See below, pp. 31–32.

33. For a summation of Lea's position, see E. Vacandard, "Le Pouvoir des clefs et la confession sacramentelle. A propos d'un livre récent," *Revue du clergé français* 18 (1899) 142–157, p. 156. See also Palmer, "Jean Morin," p. 350.

34. *Ibid.*, pp. 350–353.

35. Among the many contributions by H. Koch, see especially "Die Bussfrist des Pastor Hermä," in *Festgabe von A. von Harnack*, ed. K. Holl (Tübingen, 1921), 173–182; *Kallist und Tertullian*, Sitzungsberichte der Heidelberger Akademie der Wissenschaften, Philosophie-historische Klasse 10 (Heidelberg, 1919); *Cyprianische Untersuchungen*, AK 4 (Bonn, 1926), pp. 211–285.

36. H. Windisch, *Taufe und Sünde im ältesten Christentum bis auf Origenes* (Tübingen, 1908), pp. 356–382.

reconciliation in the early Church for those who had committed one of the capital sins. What was extraordinary about the witness of Hermas was that, for the first time, the possibility of forgiveness was offered, if only but one time.[37] Seen in this context, Tertullian was no innovator in his protestations over the famous edict. Koch's argument depended on the edict having a Roman origin, borne out in his staunch support of authorship by Callistus, against the arguments of K. Adam and others.[38] As the support for such a position more and more declined, so did Koch's argument.

Later Koch attacked the sacramentality of the early practice of penance based on the writings of Cyprian. He was against any notion of reconciliation resulting from the power of the bishop or priest. Rather, it was only the hard work of the penitent in fulfilling the obligations of the *paenitentia satisfactionis* that accomplished his or her being readmitted to the Church. He contended that the reconciling ''power'' of the clergy was a later theological development and was not found in the original tradition of the Fathers.[39]

The last major Protestant author to be examined is O. Watkins.[40] Watkins joined the previous authors in holding that the ancient Church was a Church only for saints, resulting in a rigorist cult. There was no forgiveness of capital sins prior to the edict of toleration.[41] However, unlike his Protestant predecessors, Watkins viewed the action of the author of the edict as a positive step, one that ''cast to the winds the long obsession of the rigorist tradition.''[42] Though not as polemical in his views as previous authors from the Protestant camp, Watkins did indicate that there is no continuous history of the sacramental reconciliation of sinners.[43]

---

37. Koch, ''Die Bussfrist des Pastor Hermä,'' *passim*.

38. Koch, *Kallist und Tertullian*, pp. 47–59.

39. Koch, *Cyprianische Untersuchungen*, pp. 281–285.

40. O. Watkins, *A History of Penance*, Vol. I: *The Whole Church to A.D. 450* (London, 1920), especially pp. 109–125.

41. *Ibid.*, p. 109.

42. Watkins, *History of Penance I*, p. 119.

43. Other Protestant authors who shared similar positions include R. Haslehurst, *Some Account of the Penitential Discipline of the Early Church in the First Four Centuries* (London, 1921); M. Dibelius, *Der Hirt des Hermas* (Tübingen, 1925); K. Kirk, *The Vision of God* (London, 1932). A similar position was taken by the Catholic A. Vanbeck (a pseudonym for J. Turmel), ''La pénitence dans les premières générations chré-

2. THE FIRST CATHOLIC REACTION

The situation of Catholic theology in the nineteenth century was one of isolation and entrenchment. The result of the First Vatican Council was a strong reaffirmation of the doctrines defined by the Council of Trent and of the absolute authority of the Church (best exemplified in its teaching on papal infallibility). The Council perpetuated a dialectical philosophical system operative totally within the confines of the Church itself in order to keep the tradition of faith free from the insidious influences of modern culture and thought. The Church looked upon itself as a bedrock against the floods of change, its position maintained only through a certain theological rigidity. It was a time of a hardened defensiveness.[44]

The Protestants had declared war on the Church's entire sacramental system in their attack on the history of penance. The watertight approach of the scholastics had begun to leak badly. The Church had to defend itself, and it was on the fortress of the sacramentality of penance in the early Church that a stand had to be taken.

About the same time that Harnack was articulating the Protestant synthesis, F. Funk began to rethink the Catholic scholastic tradition.[45] It was his clear intention to preserve the sacramental efficacy of the sacrament of penance during the first centuries of the Church. His was a definite polemical stand against the Protestant position. He explained that the power of the keys did indeed reside in the Church from its earliest tradition, but that the Church itself decided not to offer ecclesial reconciliation for those who had committed one of the capital sins. Why? He answered:

> The rigor had without doubt, from a disciplinary and pedagogical
> point of view, a certain signification. It could and had to serve to

---

tiennes," *RHLR* 1/new series (1910) 436–465. Turmel played one of the more notorious roles of the Modernist crisis when, as an avowed atheist, he remained a priest in order to fight the Church from within. His many articles all uphold the position that penance in the ancient Church was nonsacramental.

44. Walgrave, *Unfolding Revelation*, pp. 153–56.

45. F. Funk, *Kirchengeschichtliche Abhandlungen und Untersuchungen*, Vol. I (Paderborn, 1897), pp. 155–209; *Histoire de L'Église*, Vol. I, trans. M. Hemmer (Paris, 1911), pp. 102–106; "Das Indulgenzedikt das Papstes Kallistus," *ThQ* 88 (1906) 541–567.

give to one's conscience the sense of the gravity of sin and to awaken a strong and serious spirit of penance.[46]

Funk believed that Callistus issued the edict of toleration because of the large number of Christians who were excluded from the Church and who were subsequently falling into disbelief and sinful lifestyles. This situation was the result of the stringent penitential discipline. As such, Funk understood this action as a reform and a genuine shift in the penitential practice of the Church. But against the Protestants, this shift did not affect the Church's self-understanding of its power to forgive sins in the name of the Lord. It only further specified in which instances sacramental reconciliation was to be offered.[47]

Since Funk had protected the power of the Church over sins, he could agree with the Protestants that it is impossible to interpret a private penitential discipline, analogous to contemporary practice, from the patristic sources. He held that a private discipline, which did not include Eucharistic exclusion, developed at different times for different local churches in the West, but nowhere before the fifth century.[48]

After the appearance of Lea's work in 1896, a veritable army of Catholic authors came to the defense of the Church's position. The first was A. Boudinhon, who made a blistering attack on Lea's conclusions that there was no sacramental efficacy in the canonical dis-

---

46. "Die Strenge hatte zwar in disciplinärer und pädagogischer Hinsicht eine gewisse Bedeutung. Sie konnte und sollte dazu dienen, die Schwere der Sünde recht zum Bewusstsein zu bringen und einen starken und ernsten Bussgeist zu wecken" (Funk, *Kirchengeschichtliche*, p. 158). See also D'Alès, *L'Édit*, p. 10.

47. Funk's interpretation of the edict of toleration was founded on his interpretation of Tertullian. He argued that Tertullian, as a Montanist, obviously shifted his position in the *De pudicitia* from what he said earlier in the *De paenitentia*, while still a Catholic. But the importance of such a shift is not whether Tertullian moved from being tolerant towards postbaptismal sinners to being a rigorist, but whether, even in his earlier work, he held open the power of the Church to grant ecclesial reconciliation for the canonical triad, even if, in fact, it did not. Obviously, Funk believed he did. See P. Batiffol, "L'Édit de Calliste d'après une controverse récente," *BLE* 10 (1906) 339–348.

48. Poschmann, *Die abendländische Kirchenbusse im Ausgang des christlichen Altertums*, Münchener Studien zur historischen Theologie 7 (Munich, 1928), p. 207.

cipline of penance.[49] Yet on the question of when the private discipline appeared, Boudinhon was much less exact, seeming to hold to the clearly antihistorical position that ancient Christians could choose either the canonical discipline or a private penance without exclusion.[50]

Other key authors who entered the controversy at this time included P. Batiffol,[51] E. Vacandard,[52] J. Tixeront,[53] and G. Rauschen.[54] With very few minor points of difference, these authors lined up behind Funk and Boudinhon in upholding the sacramentality of public penance, while affirming that the Church denied sacramental reconciliation for the three capital sins on disciplinary grounds. The edict of toleration represented a new practice for the Church but not a new theology. These later authors also denied the existence of an ecclesial penitential practice outside of the canonical discipline.[55] Along with Funk, they admitted the evolution of a pri-

49. A. Boudinhon, "Sur l'histoire de la pénitence à propos d'un livre récent," *RHLR* 2 (1897) 306–344, 496–524. Boudinhon states: "Il est facile de retrouver dans cette pratique de la pénitence solennelle les éléments qui constituent encore le sacrement: aveu, absolution et satisfaction; la contrition, alors, comme aujourd'hui, était une condition nécessaire, une disposition du pécheur manifestée dans tous les actes que comportait le rite pénitentiel." His appreciation of the ancient practice as sacramental was based on whether it could be fitted into the contemporary experience of penance.

50. This was the assessment by Palmer, "Jean Morin II," pp. 331–333.

51. P. Batiffol, *Études d'histoire et de théologie positive* (Paris, 1902; 7th ed. 1926), pp. 45–144.

52. E. Vacandard, *La confession sacramentelle dans l'Église primitive*, SR 224 (Paris, 1903), pp. 5–61; *La pénitence publique dans l'Église primitive*, SR 223 (Paris, 1903), pp. 9–61; "Absolution des Péchés au temps des Pères," *DThC* I,1 (1903) c. 145–161; "Confession du I^e au XIIIe siècle," *DThC* III (1908), c. 838–894, Vacandard was not sure that the tradition of excluding capital sinners from the community was from apostolic times, though he felt that there is no strong evidence to the contrary. See the review of his works by M. Jacquin, "Bulletin d'histoire des doctrines chrétiennes," *RSPTh* 2 (1908) 383–387, p. 384.

53. J. Tixeront, *History of Dogmas*, Vol. I: *The Antenicene Theology*, trans. H.L.B. (St. Louis, 1930), pp. 337–346; *Le sacrement de pénitence dans l'antiquité chrétienne*, Questiones théologiques 691 (Paris, 1914).

54. G. Rauschen, *L'Eucharistie et la pénitence*, pp. 133–240.

55. There is a question of whether or not grave sinners were reconciled on their deathbeds prior to the edict of toleration, which would have necessitated a private reconciliation. There is much variation among the different authors on this point, though most would only admit this in exceptional cases and not as a generally accepted practice.

vate practice around A.D. 400, when Augustine appeared to allow those who had committed serious sin in secret to be exempt from the public exomologesis and Eucharistic exclusion. In such a case, penitents were reconciled after secret confession and secret absolution.[56]

With these authors, the foundation of the scholastic interpretation began to crumble.[57] No longer was the nonsacramentality of public penance a sacrosanct conclusion; indeed, in the viewpoint of these authors, such a conclusion could have put the Church in a doctrinally precarious situation with regard to its entire sacramental system. Yet, at the same time, no longer could the Church build its case on a patristic practice of private penance; the evidence was at best fragmentary and inconclusive. It was a point of doctrinal crisis.

The assailable position of these authors is a good demonstration of how the Church approached questions of dogma at the beginning of this century. One could study the history of the sources, as long as the history did not alter the immutable status of dogma. One senses from the writings of these authors that what was first and foremost in their thinking was the defense of the Church's possession of the power of the keys against the Protestant attack. They gave ready assent to the Protestant argument that there was no forgiveness of capital sins in the first two centuries of the Church's life, yet at the same time they attempted to preserve the Church's mandate to mediate the forgiveness of sins, stating that in cases involving capital sins, the Church chose to bind rather than to loose. It was an interpretation based on the primacy of dogma rather than the early witnesses, and it would not withstand the test of time. Nonetheless, the work of these historians of penance was a move toward a better appreciation of the early experience of the Church.

---

56. Poschmann, *Die abendländische Kirchenbusse*, p. 208. See also Palmer, "Jean Morin," p. 353. For the first two centuries, these authors would hold, only those capital sins known to the community incurred automatic exclusion from the Eucharist.

57. Other authors who held similar views included P. Kirsch, *Zur Geschichte der katholischen Beichte* (Würzburg, 1902), pp. 5ff.; P. De Labriolle, *Tertullien. De paenitentia, De pudicitia* (Paris, 1906), p. XVIIIff.; J. Pohle, *Lehrbuch der Dogmatik in sieben Büchern*, Vol. III (Paderborn, 1905), pp. 482ff.; J. Kirsch, *Handbuch der allgemeinen Kirchengeschichte*, Vol. I: *Die Kirche in der antiken Kulturwelt* (Freiburg, 1911), pp. 345ff.

They formed a bridge for later, more historically based lines of interpretation.

3. THE SECOND CATHOLIC REACTION

In the early part of this century, the floodwaters of the historical-critical method were surging against the Church's dam of theological isolation. Harnack's positivist critique, the historical interpretation of all theology, was a direct cause of Alfred Loisy's response on the proper role of historical exegesis.[58] What is called the Modernist crisis raised its head for the first time.

Those who undertook the study of the early history of penance found themselves in a very difficult position indeed. With the Protestant liberal synthesis pressing in on one side, the Catholic dogmatic critique of Funk and others pushing from another side, and the growing consternation in Rome over the role of historical exegesis exerting pressure on yet another side, there seemed to be little room to maneuver.[59] Yet the work on penance moved forward cautiously, as a second group of Catholic scholars, committed to historical honesty, turned their attention to the controversy.

a) *From dogma to history: A new Catholic direction*

Unlike the dogmatic interpretation of their Catholic counterparts, the interpretation of this group of authors disagreed with the Protestant position that there was no sacramental reconciliation for capital sins during the first two centuries. Their interpretation of the patristic sources allowed them to posit that, in fact, no sin was excluded from the possibility of ecclesial reconciliation in the ancient Church. So while agreeing with the school led by Funk that there

---

58. A. Loisy, *The Gospel and the Church*, ed. and introduction by B. Scott, trans. C. Home, Lives of Jesus Series (Philadelphia, 1976), pp. xxii–xxiii.

59. The growing consternation in Rome became an explicit condemnation on 3 July 1907, when Pius X issued the decree *Lamentabili sane exitu* against Modernism. Among his condemnations, note Proposition XLVI: "Non adfuit in primitiva Ecclesia conceptus de christiano peccatore auctoritate Ecclesiae reconciliato; sed Ecclesia nonnisi admodum lente hujusmodi conceptui assuevit. Imo etiam postquam poenitentia tanquam Ecclesiae institutio agnita fuit non appellabatur sacramenti nomine, eo quod haberetur uti sacramentum probrosum" (*Actes de S. S. Pie X*, Vol. III [Paris, 1905–1910], p. 232).

was a sacramental efficacy of the canonical discipline from apostolic times, they disagreed on the major point that some sins were excluded from reconciliation. This line of interpretation was basically a rediscovery of the positions taken by Petau and Morin over two hundred years before.

G. Esser was the first modern author to hold that the edict of toleration was no innovation in any sense of the word.[60] The Church regularly granted pardon to those who had committed one of the three capital sins and who manifested sincere repentance. This position seemed to fly in the face of overwhelming evidence, especially the witness of Hippolytus and Tertullian.[61] But at the heart of Esser's argument was his careful comparison of the texts of Tertullian's *De paenitentia* and *De pudicitia*. From a technical evaluation of these works, he was able to draw some conclusions. First, the *paenitentia secunda* mentioned in the *De paenitentia* is a clear reference to the possibility of ecclesial reconciliation of all sinners. Second, the term *restitutio* is used in both works to connote a specific action of ecclesial reconciliation. Therefore, the author of the edict was confirming a present practice, not introducing a new one.[62] Esser writes:

> On the disciplinary question, the Edict rendered a decision described by Tertullian himself as preemptive and which had a deep effect on the communities. Callistus did not introduce a new practice but defended a present one which was both disputed and not a general practice, but one which he helped towards its victorious breakthrough.[63]

---

60. G. Esser, *Die Busschriften Tertullians "De paenitentia" und "De pudicitia" und das Indulgenzedikt des Papstes Kallistus* (Bonn, 1905); "Nochmals das Indulgenzedikt des Papstes Kallistus und die Busschriften Tertullians," *Der Katholik* 8–9 (1907) 184–204, 297–309; 1–2 (1908) 12–28, 93–113; *Der Adressat der Schrift Tertullians "De pudicitia" der Verfasser des römischen Bussediktes* (Bonn, 1914).

61. Instead of assuming Tertullian's credibility as a witness, Esser took as his starting point the dubiety of the African's testimony, in light of his turn toward Montanism. This enabled him to perceive that it was the author of the edict rather than Tertullian who had the force of tradition on his side.

62. Esser, *Die Busschriften*, pp. 20–21.

63. "Das Edikt gab eine von Tertullian selbst als peremptorisch bezeichnete Entscheidung in einer disziplinären Frage, welche die Gemeinden tief bewegte. Kallist hat nicht eine neue Praxis eingeführt, sondern eine bestehende, aber nicht unwider-

After Esser had opened the possibility of this interpretation, the next to develop it was P. Stufler.[64] Stufler was a strong supporter of Esser in his main thesis that the Church never refused ecclesial forgiveness for those who undertook the stringent demands of canonical penance.[65] There was no distinction in the Church's practice or theology concerning the possibility of ecclesial reconciliation. He based his argument on the same interpretation of Tertullian as Esser, as well as on texts from the *Shepherd of Hermas*, Eusebius's *Ecclesiastical History* (particularly concerning the tolerance of Dionysius of Corinth), and other patristic sources.[66]

On the question of the existence of a private form of penance in the early Church, Stufler was the last modern author to maintain a vestige of the old scholastic viewpoint, maintaining that there was a secret sacramental reconciliation of the sinner prior to the performance of the exomologesis. This was followed, after the completion of the penance, by a second, nonsacramental absolution, which lifted the ban from the Eucharist and signified the sinner's return to the community.[67] After Stufler, this interpretation, which has a questionable historical foundation, had few proponents.

In France, A. d'Alès was the most important historian of penance to expostulate the view that all postbaptismal sinners had the possibility of ecclesial reconciliation in the early Church.[68] D'Alès critiqued the Protestant position by situating the historical circumstances of Hippolytus and Tertullian. Given their growing dissatisfaction with the Church, they were most interested in finding points of controversy, from which they could circulate their own positions.

---

sprochene und nicht allgemein eingeführte verteidigt und ihr zum siegreichen Durchbruch verholfen" (*Ibid.*, p. 28).

64. P. Stufler, "Die Bussdisziplin der abendländischen Kirche bis Kallistus," *ZKTh* 31 (1907) 433–473; "Zur Kontroverse über das Indulgenzedikt des Papstes Kallistus," *ZKTh* 32 (1908) 1–42; "Einige Bemerkungen zur Busslehre Cyprians," *ZKTh* 33 (1909) 232–247.

65. Stufler, "Die Bussdisziplin," p. 437. See also Rauschen, *L'Eucharistie et la pénitence*, pp. 136–137, as well as Stufler's review of Rauschen's work in *ZKTh* 32 (1908) 536–544.

66. Stufler, "Die Bussdisziplin," pp. 471–73; "Zur Kontroverse," pp. 16, 21.

67. Stufler, "Einige Bemerkungen", p. 245.

68. A. d'Alès, *L'Édit, passim; La théologie de Tertullien* (Paris, 1905), pp. 339–355, 478–491; *La théologie de saint Cyprien* (Paris, 1922), pp. 272–302.

Therefore, they could hardly be considered objective witnesses.[69] D'Alès went on to list the writings of the first three centuries which mention the necessity of seeking pardon from the Church: Dionysius of Corinth, Gregory Thaumaturgus, and Firmilian of Caesarea. Such thinking even finds expression in the more anti-institutional works of Origen and in the polemical writings of Tertullian and Hippolytus themselves.[70]

D'Alès was strong in his critique of Funk, Batiffol, and their followers. To say that the Church always had the power to remit sins but chose not to exercise this power is to "spiritualize" the power of the Church and rob it of any historical application. That is exactly what the Montanist Tertullian himself did (De pudicitia 21,7) when he granted the power of forgiveness to the "Church of the Paraclete" and not to the concrete historical Church of the bishops. D'Alès quotes from Cyprian, who reaffirmed the power of the keys, given by God so that sinners could be saved. To have a God who closes the door on sinners is to take away the very purpose of the Church. Therefore, d'Alès concluded, this power must have been more than a theological possibility. It must have been rooted in historical reality.[71]

Staying true to the tradition of the seventeenth-century positivists, d'Alès believed that there is enough patristic evidence to support a regular practice of penance in the early Church that did not include Eucharistic exclusion. His viewpoint is not to be confused with the later scholastic conception; that is, he did not say that there were two absolutions given within the framework of the public discipline. However, given the example of reconciliation granted in extremis, one cannot ignore the fact that it was an accept-

---

69. D'Alès, L'Édit, p. 399.

70. Ibid., pp. 399–400.

71. Ibid., pp. 402–404. D'Alès admitted that in the conscience of the Church, the sins of the flesh were the object of a special reprobation, which probably further confused the controversy over the edict of toleration. He states: "L'exercice ordinaire du pouvoir des clefs étant admis par tous, les dénégations ne pouvaient se produire qu'en vue d'un cas extraordinaire, à l'égard d'un de ces péchés particulièrement graves devant lesquels les pasteurs de l'Église avaient dû hésiter bien des fois et sur le traitement desquels leur pratique avait dû osciller entre la sévérité et l'indulgence" (p. 404).

able practice for sacramental forgiveness to be effected outside of public exomologesis.[72]

The views of d'Alès were shared by K. Adam.[73] Adam believed that the churches of North Africa must have had some sort of practice of excluding those guilty of capital sins; otherwise Tertullian's displeasure in the *De pudicitia* makes little sense. However, for Adam, one of the important keys to understanding the penitential practice of the churches during the first two centuries is the proper identification of the author of the edict of toleration. If indeed the author was a local bishop in North Africa rather than a Roman bishop, then it is possible that the edict was not intended to be a general teaching but a response to a specific case. Therefore, Adam felt justified in holding for a more rigorist tradition in Africa (perhaps seen in Cyprian's initial, more stringent stance toward the reconciliation of the *lapsi*). Yet he did not feel that this was the universal experience of the local communities.[74]

In a rather prolonged debate with B. Poschmann, Adam outlined his belief in a private discipline of penance from the time of Augustine.[75] It was his contention that Augustine clearly witnesses to a sacramental forgiveness of less serious ''mortal'' sins outside of canonical discipline. In most cases Augustine followed the rule that sins known to the community were to be submitted to the exomologesis and Eucharistic exclusion, while private sins could be reconciled outside of these more public penitential actions. Whereas Augustine stayed faithful to the rule of a single reconciliation

---

72. D'Alès, *L'Édit*, pp. 453–455. D'Alès's view differed from that of the first Catholic group, inasmuch as they understood deathbed reconciliation as an exception and not a regular practice. But one senses that d'Alès here is speaking of a later moment in the history when penance *in extremis* had become the normative experience.

73. K. Adam, *Der Kirchenbegriff Tertullians*, FCLD 6,4 (Paderborn, 1907), pp. 148–151; *Das sogenannte Bussedikt des Papstes Kallistus*, Veröffentlichungen aus dem Kirchenhistorischen Seminar München 4,5 (Munich, 1917); *Die kirchliche Sündenvergebung nach dem hl. Augustin*, FCLD 14,1 (Paderborn, 1917); ''Die abendländische Kirchenbusse im Ausgang des christlichen Altertums. Kritische Bemerkungen zu Poschmanns Untersuchung,'' ThQ 110 (1929) 1–66.

74. Adam, *Das sogenannte Bussedikt*, pp. 63–64. See below, pp. 32–33.

75. For a list of the periodical literature of this debate, see Poschmann, *Die abendländische Kirchenbusse*, p. 5, n. 1.

through canonical penance, the ecclesial pardon effected for private sins could be repeated.[76]

The authors examined here are representative figures of this position; there were other contemporary commentators on the early history of penance who held the basic elements of this view.[77] Yet it is appropriate that we conclude this period of the interpretation of early penance with the position of Adam. His work played a pivotal role in shaping the thought of two of the most significant historians of penance in this century, Paul Galtier and Bernard Poschmann. Not only did he take on the role of "devil's advocate" against the position of Poschmann in their debates over the appearance of private penance, but he also served as the harbinger before Galtier, who became the most forceful and articulate spokesman in favor of an early appearance of a private form of ecclesial penance.[78]

b) *The authorship of the edict of toleration*

Before proceeding to the work of the most recent commentators, it is necessary to examine the question of the authorship of the edict of toleration. It is a question that all major figures who have contributed to the study of the history of penance have had to consider,

---

76. Adam, *Die kirchliche Sündenvergebung*, pp. 132–158.

77. D'Alès, *L'Édit*, pp. 238–240, n. 2, lists those authors who would essentially be in agreement with this position, including: P. Monceaux, *Histoire littéraire de l'Afrique chrétienne*, Vol. I: *Tertullien et les origines* (Paris, 1906), pp. 432ff.; O. Bardenhewer, *Patrologie*, 3rd ed. (Freiburg, 1910), p. 195; E. Preuschen, "Die Kirchenpolitik des Bischofs Kallist," *ZNW* 10 (1910) 134–160, p. 135; F. Loofs, *Leitfaden zum Studium der Dogmengeschichte* (Halle, 1906), p. 207; R. Seeberg, *Lehrbuch der Dogmengeschichte*, Vol. I: *Die Anfänge des Dogmas im Nachapostolischen und alt katholischen Zeitalter*, 2nd ed. (Leipzig, 1908), p. 496. Loofs, Seeberg, and Preuschen were Protestant theologians who, while admitting that the Church never excluded the possibility of reconciliation to grave sinners, held that such a reconciliation was only the necessary means for reconciliation with God and was not an automatic guarantee of a divine pardon. This view was also shared by the Protestant historian of dogma G. Bonwetsch, *Grundriss der Dogmageschichte*, 2nd ed. (Munich, 1919), pp. 71ff. To this list we add: J. O'Donnell, *Penance in the Early Church with a Short Sketch of Subsequent Development* (Dublin, 1907); F. Hünermann, *Die Busslehre des heiligen Augustinus*, FCLD 12,1 (Paderborn, 1914), pp. 149ff.

78. Referring to Galtier's work, *L'Église et la rémission des péchés*, Adam states: "Es scheint dass Galtier mit dieser Schrift das letzte entscheidende Wort über das Bestehen einer Privatbusse gesprochen hat" (*ThQ* 144 (1933) 149). On this point Adam is hardly prophetic.

and how they do so profoundly affects their entire perspective of the history. Furthermore, the edict's authorship had a bearing on the shift that occurred in historical studies in the early part of this century. For this reason, it is important to briefly examine its development, especially in light of its relationship with later interpretation.

Until the middle of the nineteenth century, most historians favored the Roman bishop Zephyrinus (A.D. 199–217) as the author of the famous edict.[79] There were exceptions, such as S. Morcelli in 1817 and J. Gieseler in 1844, who chose Cyrus as the author, preferring as they did an African origin and believing he would have been the primate of Carthage at the time of the edict.[80] However, such alternative theories of authorship found little support.

The question shifted into a new stage of inquiry with the discovery in 1850 of Hippolytus's *Refutatio omnium haeresium*, otherwise known as the *Philosophoumena*. In 1866, J. de Rossi was the first to identify Callistus (A.D. 217–222/23), the successor of Zephyrinus, not only as Hippolytus's adversary in the newly discovered work but also as the "pontifex maximus" in Tertullian's *De pudicitia*.[81] This identification was picked up by Harnack in 1878 and Funk in 1884, and became almost unanimously accepted by historians of penance.[82]

E. Rolffs, in 1894, was the first author after de Rossi to question whether the Roman bishop who was the object of Hippolytus's wrath was really the same bishop who was scorned by Tertullian as the author of the edict. The very fact that Hippolytus, Cyprian,

---

79. These included Pétau, Morin, Sirmond, as well as J. Döllinger, *Hippolytus und Kallistus, oder die römische Kirche in der ersten Hälfte des dritten Jahrhunderts* (Regensburg, 1853).

80. D'Alès, *La théologie de Tertullien*, p. 217, n. 3, informs us of this position taken by S. Morcelli, *Africa christiana*, Vol. II (Brescia, 1817), p. 81; and J. Gieseler, *Lehrbuch der Kirchengeschichte*, 4th ed. (Bonn, 1844), p. 287.

81. J. de Rossi, "Esame archeologico e critico della storia dei S. Callisto narrata nel libro nono dei Filosofumeni," *Bulletino di archeologia cristiana* 4 (1866) 1–33, p. 26.

82. G. Bardy, "L'édit d'Agrippinus," *RevSR* 4 (1924) 1–25, p. 21. See Poschmann, *Paenitentia Secunda*, p. 350, n. 2, and J. Quasten, *Patrology*, Vol. 2: *The Ante-Nicene Literature after Irenaeus* (Utrecht, 1953), p. 235, for lists of those authors who have defended the authorship of the edict by Callistus.

and Origen make no mention of the edict is in itself an indictment against its universal application. For this reason, Rolffs held that the edict was not meant for the universal Church, but was intended solely for the local church in Rome and was probably written by Zephyrinus. It was then distributed in other places, such as Africa, perhaps as a solution to the problems created by the growing numbers of postbaptismal sinners excluded from ecclesial reconciliation.[83] Esser and Rauschen were the last modern authors to hold that Zephyrinus was the author of the edict.[84] Esser qualified his stand, stating that Tertullian was reacting not just against the author of the edict (Zephyrinus) but also against the local bishop of Carthage for implementing it.[85]

As seen above, Adam was the first modern author to posit the theory that the author of the edict was Agrippinus of Carthage. He based his opinion on a reexamination of the terms employed by Tertullian to describe the author of the edict in the *De pudicitia:* "pontifex maximus," "episcopus episcoporum" (1,6), and "bonus pastor et benedictus papa" (13,7). Such titles could have been used to describe any local bishop during Tertullian's time, insofar as the primacy of the bishop of Rome had not yet developed to a point where such descriptions would have been applicable only to him. Since Cyprian explicitly makes mention of Agrippinus twice in his correspondence (*Epp.* 71.4.1; 73.3.1), both times as a man of clemency, he would seem to be a natural choice as the author of the famous edict.[86] Based on Adam's insight, both Galtier and Poschmann agreed that the edict was African in origin and not from the hand of a Roman bishop. Tertullian was responding to a local decree by an African bishop whose identity is not so important, but who prob-

---

83. Rolffs, *Das Indulgenzedikt-Edikt des römischen Bischofs Kallist,* pp. 135–138.

84. Esser, *Der Adressat der Schrift Tertullian "De pudicitia" und der Verfasser des römischen Bussedikts,* p. 31; Rauschen, *Tertullianus, Quintus Septimus Florens: De paenitentia et De pudicitia recensio nova,* Florilegium Patristicum 10 (Bonn, 1915), p. 7.

85. D'Alès, "Zéphyrin, Calliste ou Agrippinus?," *RSR* 3–4 (1920) 254–256, p. 255. Similar positions were adopted by D. Franses, "Das 'Edictum Callisti' in der neueren Forschung," in *Studia Catholica* 1 (Roermond, 1924), pp. 248–259; and A. Vellico, " 'Episcopus episcoporum' in Tertulliani libro 'De pudicitia,' " *Antonianum* 5 (1930) 25–56, pp. 25–26.

86. Adam, *Der sogenannte Bussedikt des Papstes Kallistus,* pp. 12–22, 47ff.

ably was Agrippinus, considering the chronology and his prestige in the African Church.[87]

It is generally accepted today that the famous edict of toleration was not from Callistus or any other Roman bishop but had a North African point of origin.[88] This consensus has had a great impact on the study of the history of penance, especially in relation to the argument of Funk and the traditional Catholic interpretation prevalent at the turn of the century. For if it can be construed, based on the edict, that certain local churches in North Africa refused ecclesial reconciliation for certain grave sins, at least at the end of the second century, this can hardly be interpreted as an indication of the practice of all other Christian communities. The experience of the early churches cannot be so easily universalized. The result is that it becomes possible to admit that the mainline tradition may have allowed for the reconciliation of all serious offenders, a conclusion that robs from the Catholic disputers at the turn of this century the grounds upon which they based their polemicizing. As more and more Catholic scholars accept an African point of origin for the edict, the curtain is drawn on the apologetical phase of the early history of penance. A fundamental shift of direction is on the horizon.

C. THE MOST RECENT INTERPRETATION

After the First World War the study of theology was shaken to its foundations. The prewar status quo, as well as the optimistic belief in the inexorable progress of all human history, were all but destroyed.[89] Theological reflection had to redefine its purpose in light of the experience of the war. As a result, the Catholic Church found itself more open to the formerly suspect historical-critical method

---

87. Galtier, *L'Église*, pp. 143–168; Poschmann, *Paenitentia Secunda*, pp. 348–367.

88. For lists of other authors who hold this position see Poschmann, *Paenitentia Secunda*, p. 349, n. 7, and Quasten, *Patrology*, Vol. 2, p. 235. To these we add C. Daly, ''The 'Edict of Callistus','' SP 3 [=TU 78] (1959) 176–182. However, the theory of authorship by Callistus still has its adherents. See A. Hamel, *Kirche bei Hippolyt von Rom*, BFT 49 (Gütersloh, 1951), pp. 59ff.; F. Volkes, ''Penitential Discipline in Montanism,'' SP 14 [=TU 117] (1971) 62–76, p. 75.

89. Walgrave, *Unfolding Revelation*, p. 253.

in search of such a redefinition. Total reliance upon scholastic categories and dialectic methodology was no longer adequate.

Studies of the evolution of ecclesial penitential practices profited from the growing openness to critical historical analysis. In both the Protestant and Catholic camps, there emerged a certain separation from the confessionally based controversies that had dominated past studies. The opportunity for more precise research into specific questions presented itself.[90]

It is important to trace the essential lines of interpretation by the authors who after the First World War led the study of penance into the historical-critical age. The first part of this survey begins with four authors whose works are of major importance, and with whom any student of the early history of penance must engage in dialogue. Paul Galtier and Bernard Poschmann brought a scientific knowledge of the patristic sources and a comprehensive acquaintance with the previous literature to raise the historical study of penance to a new level of development. Their work made possible a fresh approach to the origin and practice of penance in the early Church. Later, the work of Joseph Grotz and especially Karl Rahner added clarity and a note of further preciseness to the historical picture of penance. In a second part, the work of other influential contributors to the ongoing research will be surveyed.

1. MAJOR CONTRIBUTORS

a) *Paul Galtier*

Of Galtier's many writings, none had the impact of his best-known work, *L'Église et la rémission des péchés.*[91] Here Galtier accepted and elaborated the main insights of d'Alès and Adam. Throughout the first part of the book, he was in fundamental agreement with these earlier authors that there is no irrefutable proof from the patristic sources of any sin being outside the reconciling power of the Church, except in cases where the sinner was not open to repent-

---

90. Rahner, *Early Church*, p. 19.

91. Much of Galtier's work formed an apologetic against Poschmann's *Die abendländische Kirchenbusse*. General points of divergence in the viewpoints of the two authors will become clearer after the next section.

ance.[92] Galtier went through most of the important witnesses of penance in the first six centuries to show that this position harmonized with the great concern of the early Church for efficacious penance. He went so far as to argue in favor of a continuity between the patristic and present-day experience of absolution. Sin is not merely forgiven due to works of penance but also involves the supplication by the Church. For Galtier, the experience of penance in the ancient Church, just as in contemporary times, necessitated a concrete involvement on the part of the bishop/priest.[93]

But it is the second part of Galtier's work that is the best known and most controversial. Here he attempted to demonstrate the existence in the early Church of a private form of penance that was clearly distinct from the canonical discipline. If such an attempt was not ambitious enough, Galtier also wanted to show that it was this private discipline rather than canonical penance that was the more ancient practice in the early Church. Such a radical thesis deserves careful consideration.

Galtier made it clear that he was not advocating a private penitential discipline operating alongside the public aspects of canonical penance (the exomologesis and excommunication), as if people could choose one or the other. He admitted that there is no direct mention of a private discipline in any of the juridical or liturgical texts of the first centuries.[94] But he was undaunted. The reason why contemporary historians of penance (particularly Poschmann) could not find proof of a private form of ecclesial penance in the ancient Church was because the early Christians knew no such categories as "public" and "private."[95] To say that only the canonical discipline existed in the Church during the first six centuries is to be unwilling to admit

---

92. Galtier, *L'Église*, p. 137. Part of Galtier's position concerning the Church's willingness to reconcile all sinners, even those who had committed capital sins, was founded on his acceptance of K. Adam's theory that the edict of toleration was not from the hand of the bishop of Rome but rather of African origin. See above, pp. 32–33.

93. Galtier, *L'Église*, pp. 3–28. Here Galtier's perspective reveals his desire to demonstrate the continuity between the efficaciousness of ecclesial reconciliation in the early Church and present practice.

94. *Ibid.*, p. 221.

95. *Ibid.*, p. 231. Even Augustine rarely makes use of the designation "public" penance.

the clear patristic evidence that some sinners were reconciled in other ways. Certainly if there were private elements in public penance (such as confession to the bishop), why was it not possible to conclude that there could be public elements in a private discipline?[96]

Galtier's argumentation for this private discipline turned on his ability to define his terms. On the one hand, everything that was true about the public discipline was equally true of the private: the same difficult penitential practices needed for expiation, the same exclusion from the Eucharist, the same expectation that the assigned penance be completed prior to reconciliation, and the same reconciliation allowing one to be readmitted to communion.[97] So what was distinguishable about Galtier's private discipline? He states:

> [In the private discipline] nothing then is missing from the public penance except the enrollment in a category of the faithful subject to having special liturgical rites and contracting, therefore, for all their lives, a certain number of obligations or juridical incapacities.[98]

Therefore, according to Galtier, the private form of penance was any experience of ecclesial penance in the early Church that did not include the liturgical ceremony of enrollment in the order of penitents and the imposition of juridic restraints upon the newly reconciled penitents.[99]

Galtier rejected the later scholastic notion of the two absolutions in the canonical discipline: one private and sacramental, the other public and nonsacramental. Nor did he attempt to build his case on what was actually private and public in the practice itself. Rather, his argument first and foremost was a liturgical one: canonical penance, from the time of Tertullian, necessarily included special litur-

---

96. Galtier, L'Eglise, p. 230.

97. Ibid., p. 244.

98. "Rien donc ne manque de la pénitence publique, que l'enrôlement dans une catégorie de fidèles soumis a des rites liturgiques spéciaux et contractant, de ce chef, pour toute leur vie, un certain nombre d'obligations ou d'incapacités juridiques" (Ibid., pp. 244–45).

99. As will become apparent in the following chapters, these signs of Galtier's public penance are, in fact, not found in the witness of the first three centuries. Therefore, he was correct in distinguishing this experience from canonical penance. However, the problem with his interpretation resulted chiefly from his working hermeneutic, expressed in his controversial choice of terms.

gical rites. When these rites were not celebrated for whatever reason, this meant that the penitent was not engaged in the demands of canonical penance. Still, the sinner was reconciled outside such liturgical rites and without the juridic restraints. There was an efficacy to the deviation. This, for Galtier, was private penance.[100]

Starting then with the postapostolic writings, Galtier attempted to prove that, at best, canonical penance was not a hard and fast rule. In fact, since these writings lack any reference to its liturgical character, so well attested in Tertullian (and possibly Irenaeus), any reference to ecclesial penance prior to this time can be said to be private.[101] Galtier showed that by the third century Origen, Tertullian, and Cyprian all witness to the possibility of reconciliation outside the public discipline for less grave sins. What this discipline entailed is unclear; yet to Galtier it was clear that it was not canonical penance. Therefore, it must have been private.[102]

The rest of Galtier's work was concerned with proving the presence of such a private experience of penance in the witness of the later patristic authors, particularly Augustine, Leo the Great, and Gregory.[103] In all, the greatest contribution of Galtier's historical investigation of ecclesial penance was to bring to light that the experience of penance in the first six centuries of the Church's life cannot simply be brought together under the all-inclusive designation of canonical penance. There were other experiences, ones that did not include a formal enrollment in the order of penitents and the harsh consequences of the canonical discipline. However, his terminology "public" and "private" was ambiguous and connoted too many other meanings. Nonetheless, his was a step in the right direction. Before the clear historical development of the canonical discipline, there were distinguishable elements in the Church's penitential practice.

---

100. Galtier, *L'Église*, pp. 246, 251–52.

101. *Ibid.*, pp. 258–260.

102. *Ibid.*, pp. 265–295. Central to Galtier's argumentation was his exegesis of the words *castigatio* and *damnatio* in Tertullian. The latter always referred to canonical penance, whereas the former was used more as a repeatable reprimand. It is in this sense that Galtier believed that the word reveals a penitential practice outside of public penance. See especially pp. 277–280.

103. Galtier, *L'Église*, pp. 303ff.

b) *Bernard Poschmann*

It is impossible to study any aspect of the history of penance and not be confronted with the extensive work of Bernard Poschmann. Most notable of many writings is the *Paenitentia Secunda*, which, more than any other single study, brought toward a resolution the question concerning the possibility of ecclesial reconciliation for postbaptismal offenses in the early Church.[104] His exhaustive examination of each of the sources of the first three centuries led him to hold (in agreement with Galtier and earlier penance historians, such as d'Alès and Adam) that there was no sin, not even capital sins, outside the possibility of ecclesial readmission and reconciliation. Of course, this was dependent on the sinner's willingness to undertake the necessary penance. What was most important was the accomplishment of the penance itself, which included penitential works, confession of sin, and excommunication. It was the penance that expressed genuine conversion and the readiness of the sinner for pardon.[105]

Poschmann, like Galtier, saw in all the early writings an emphasis on the role of Church leaders in the punishment and pardon of sin. It was not just the work of the penitent that effected pardon; reconciliation also required the judgment of the bishop.[106] However, Poschmann expressed doubt about the presence of an actual rite of reconciliation in the readmission of sinners to the community after the completion of their penance. The bishop only judged if a sinner had successfully completed the penance and was ready for readmittance. It was the Eucharist itself that was the instrument of forgiveness, not the direct intervention of the minister.[107] Without

---

104. Poschmann's work on the history of penance is also treated in summary fashion in *Busse und Letzte Ölung*, HDg 4,3 (Freiburg, 1951). The English translation is cited here: *Penance and the Anointing of the Sick (PAS)*, trans. F. Courtney (New York, 1964).

105. Poschmann, *Paenitentia Secunda*, pp. 481ff.

106. Poschmann, *PAS*, p. 25.

107. Poschmann, *Paenitentia Secunda*, pp. 398ff. Poschmann admitted that this position is most easily defendable from the witness of Cyprian, and even admitted that Tertullian may speak of some sort of absolution formula (p. 345). This is also the view of the recent study by W. Swann, *The Relationship Between Penance, Reconciliation with the Church and Admission to the Eucharist in the Letters and the 'De Lapsis' of*

question, there were intercessory prayers by the ministers and the laying on of hands by the bishop, but these cannot be construed as absolution formulas. In this, Poschmann laid more stress on the ecclesial aspect of penance than did Galtier. Just as it was the community that excluded a sinner from their midst, so it was the entire community, in conjunction with the ministry of the bishop, that granted the *pax Ecclesiae* to the repentant sinner.[108]

The clearest disagreement between Galtier and Poschmann lay in their interpretation of the sources in connection with the appearance of a private penitential discipline.[109] It is on this point of debate that their understanding of an order of penitents is most clarified. Poschmann agreed that the rite of enrollment in the order of penitents was the most characteristic element of canonical penance.[110] He even went so far as to agree that when the enrollment was not present, it is possible to make a distinction between canonical penance in a strict sense and other forms of penance. But against Galtier's position, Poschmann remained adamant in his belief that such expressions of penance could not in any way be considered a private discipline.[111]

Just as with Galtier, Poschmann's position turned on his ability to define the meaning of the terms. He disagreed with Galtier's definition that any experience of penance in the early Church that was not public in every sense was private. Poschmann wanted private to mean private, defined as "a secret procedure *in foro interno* which is outside of external ecclesiastical law."[112] Given this definition as

---

Cyprian of Carthage, published doctoral dissertation, The Catholic University of America, Washington, D.C. (Ann Arbor, Mich., 1980), pp. 451–459.

108. Naturally, this is not equally clear in all the ancient authors. Yet Poschmann did distance himself from Galtier's emphasis on the ministry of the bishop. The latter believed that Poschmann only saw the minister as an "exhorter" to penance (*L'Église*, p. 49).

109. Even though Poschmann's *Die abendländische Kirchenbusse* (1928) was published four years before Galtier's *L'Église* (1932), Poschmann knew of Galtier's position from the latter's *De Paenitentia* (Paris, 1923), pp. 186–233 and "La rémission des péchés moindres dans l'Église du troisième au cinquième siècle," *RSR* 13 (1923) 97–129. See also Poschmann's review of *L'Église* in *ThRv* 7 (1933), pp. 263–267.

110. Poschmann, *PAS*, p. 87.

111. Poschmann, *Die abendländische Kirchenbusse*, pp. 148–149, 211.

112. Poschmann, *PAS*, pp. 119–120.

a starting point, it is impossible to regard the early experience of penance as "internal forum." Though aspects of it were private, it was a public event, involving the whole community. In this, Poschmann attempted to lay to rest the strong Catholic desire to root present-day confessional practice in the early Church experience.[113]

But negating Galtier's argument for a private discipline does not mean that Poschmann was unable to distinguish different experiences of penance during the first six centuries. Canonical penance in the strict sense necessitated an enrollment in the order of penitents to which there is no witness before the fourth century. Therefore, Poschmann had the basis on which to make a distinction between the experience of penance in the third century and the canonical practice of the fourth and following centuries.[114] Yet, against the distinctions created by Galtier, he believed that the later experience of penance was only a further development of what had gone before. It was certainly more severe, but it was a severity caused by the Peace of Constantine, which effected a profound change in the external life of the Church, including its penitential system.[115] The severity did not develop suddenly; there were severe elements in the third century as well.[116] And already in Tertullian, penitential procedures had taken a fixed form, centered on exclusion from the community, the central practice of the later canonical practice.[117] Even in the absence of an enrollment in the order of penitents, the basic elements of the canonical discipline were left intact.[118] To call it private penance is to accentuate the differences

---

113. Poschmann, *PAS*, p. 120. Poschmann held that the first clear evidence of any sort of private penitential discipline is to be found in canon 11 of the Council of Toledo (A.D. 589). For him, to hold for an earlier appearance of private penance was to listen too much to one's own opinion rather than to the silence of the sources. However, his interpretation of this canon and his theory concerning the appearance of private penance on the Continent has come under recent attack. See below, p. 55, n. 173.

114. *Ibid.*, pp. 81–82.

115. *Ibid.*, p. 82.

116. Poschmann cited Tertullian's complaint (*De paenitentia* 10,1) that many guilty of serious postbaptismal sin "shrank" from undertaking penance.

117. Poschmann was able to draw such a conclusion from his interpretation of Tertullian's use of *castigatio* and *damnatio*, which differed from Galtier's interpretation. See Poschmann's review of *L'Église*, in *ThRv* 7, pp. 264–265.

118. Poschmann, *Die abendländische Kirchenbusse*, pp. 215–229, 269–278.

rather than the similarities in the two experiences. For Poschmann, the similarities were more fundamental.[119]

c) *Joseph Grotz*

In 1955, Joseph Grotz published his controversial work *Die Entwicklung des Busstufenwesens in der vornicänischen Kirche*, which is described by Rahner as a "frontal assault on the thesis [of penance] . . . generally accepted today by Catholic historians of dogma."[120] Indeed, Grotz took up the role of a revisionist and played the part well.

Grotz was no "postbaptismal theorist." He agreed with the predominant viewpoint that the Church had always offered ecclesial reconciliation for those who undertook penance. He even agreed with Poschmann and others that the structure of penance in the early Church eventually came to be founded on the exclusion of the sinner from the community (what he called "exkommunikationbusse"), the exomologesis, and the eventual readmission of the penitent to the Church. However, Grotz's understanding of the connection between excommunication and ecclesial penance lay at the heart of his controversial thesis.[121]

Grotz held that it was only during the second century, from the testimony of the *Shepherd of Hermas* in the West and Clement of Alexandria in the East, that a link can be seen between the practice of excommunication and ecclesial penance, and then only for limited sins and situations. For example, in the *Shepherd of Hermas* there was official exclusion only for apostates and those who fell again into grave sin. This had nothing to do with penance but was a "natu-

---

119. In actuality, the debate between Poschmann and Galtier over the appearance of a private form of penance was most intensive over the witness of Augustine, especially the *Enchiridion* 65 and *Sermon* 351. The central point is over the proper interpretation of *correptio*. See Poschmann, "Die kirchliche Vermittlung der Sündenvergebung nach Augustinus," *ZKTh* 45 (1921) 497–526; and *Kirchenbusse und correptio secreta bei Augustinus* (Braunsberg, 1923), pp. 41–53, as compared with Galtier, *L'Église*, pp. 360–372, 380–89.

120. Rahner, *Early Church*, p. 59.

121. Grotz, *Busstufenwesens*, pp. 437ff. Distancing himself from other authors such as Poschmann and Rahner, who admitted to different degrees of exclusion from the Eucharist, Grotz held that anything less than an absolutely total exclusion from the community was, in fact, not a true excommunication. See below, n. 130.

ral attitude'' of a young Church toward those who deserted the ranks.[122] Other sinners could be readmitted to the ''Tower'' by undertaking ecclesial penance without first being officially excluded. However, these sinners were expected to voluntarily separate themselves from the community and do works of penance before undertaking official ecclesial penance. In this way, excommunication, even though voluntary, came to be experienced as a kind of ''pre-step'' to ecclesial penance.[123]

With Cyprian, exclusion became a part of the discipline of ecclesial penance, but only for serious sins of action (the capital sins). These required the *paenitentia plena* (''full penance''), the first step of which was the *paenitentia satisfactionis*. This was a formal excommunication during which the sinner prepared for admittance to exomologesis through personal works of penance. It was outside the communion of the Church, while the exomologesis was inside. Excommunication was now part of the system of penance, though with Cyprian its purpose was always to lead a stubborn sinner to accept the official ecclesial penance of the exomologesis and so to eventually receive the *pax* of the Church.[124]

By the time of Origen the development was further along. Exclusion from the community was now a necessary part of the penance discipline, and for offenses other than the capital sins. At the same time, less and less stress was laid on the power of the exomologesis, without exclusion, to heal sin. Also, Origen introduced to the penitential discipline an objective element that was never so clear before. Sins could be objectively heavy enough to demand exclusion, the subjective disposition of the sinner notwithstanding.[125] What had begun as a pastoral remedy to sin had now grown into a vindictive punishment.[126]

---

122. Grotz, *Busstufenwesens*, p. 69.
123. *Ibid.*, pp. 69, 438–439.
124. *Ibid.*, pp. 169–170, 444.
125. *Ibid.*, pp. 308, 444.
126. Grotz believed that this change resulted from the rigorist influence of Montanism on the Church, expressed through the writing of Tertullian: ''So zeigt sich, dass es vorzüglich der Montanismus war, der die katholische Kirche zu einer neuen Auffassung der exkommunikation drängte. Allmählich wird aus der medizinalen eine vindikative Strafe'' (*Ibid.*, p. 365).

Grotz overviewed the penitential discipline of Tertullian, the *Didascalia Apostolorum*, Hippolytus (and Callistus), as well as the witness of Gregory Thaumaturgus from the East and the early Greek councils. In each of these he could see a gradual linking between excommunication and the more original ecclesial penance. For Grotz, it was a clear unilinear development, traceable through all these ancient authors.[127] And it highlighted the development of the ancient grades of Church penance made explicit in the writings of Gregory Thaumaturgus.[128] Grotz's success in demonstrating such an evolution is questionable. His detractors were many.[129] Yet his thesis brought a new approach to the history of the order of penitents. He maintained that excommunication was the "binding" of the sin by the Church; this occurred before admission to penance (or, in the fourth century, before the liturgical enrollment as a penitent). The admission to penance itself "loosed" the sin and granted the sinner the *pax Ecclesiae*. This brought the sinner back into *communio*, began the period of exomologesis, and led him or her toward eventual readmission to the Eucharist and the *pax divina*. Seen in this light, excommunication was not an integral element of the order of penitents.[130]

---

127. Grotz, *Busstufenwesens*, pp. 343–437 and *passim*. Grotz's historical perspective was, in fact, too unilinear for Rahner (*Early Church*, p. 60).

128. *Ibid.*, pp. 424–425. At the risk of oversimplifying Grotz's position, exclusion from the community developed into the stage of the "listeners," while exomologesis eventually framed the stage of the "prostrators."

129. Those with strong critiques of Grotz's thesis include: S. Hübner, "Kirchenbusse und Exkommunikation bei Cyprian," *ZKTh* 84 (1962) 49–84, 171–215; A. Matellanes Crespo, *El tema de la 'Communicatio' en los escritos penitenciales y bautismales de San Cipriano de Cartago*, UCLDiss 41 (1965) 5–92, pp. 23–70; *id.*, "Communicatio. El contenido de la comunión eclesial en San Cipriano," *Communio* 1 (1968) 19–64, 347–401, pp. 36–50; Rahner, *Early Church*, pp. 57–64, 108–113; Swann, *Relationship*, pp. 477–478.

130. Grotz appears to have lacked precision when he spoke of excommunication. Clearly, when an excommunicated sinner underwent the process of exomologesis, he or she was still excluded from the Eucharist, though while being segregated within the community rather than being isolated from it. (These terms will be further explained in the next section of this chapter). It is hard to imagine, as Grotz suggested, that to be excluded from the central act of communion, even if one had already been admitted to the exomologesis, was to be considered as being "in communion" with the Church. Even the existence of different penitential stages, with one class of penitents being "nearer" to being readmitted to the Eucharist than another, did not negate the altered status within the Church of any baptized Christian guilty of serious

Grotz was grappling with the same historical questions about the experience of penance in the early Church as Galtier had. There was something about it that did not quite fit the description of canonical penance. Galtier answered the question by designating any experience of penance that did not include the liturgical action of enrollment in the order of penitents as a private discipline. Grotz, on the other hand, said that excommunication was a later addition to an older, repeatable penitential discipline, which eventually came to be known as the exomologesis.[131] In any event, both authors highlighted the basic fact that the experience of penance in the first three centuries was a reality distinct from the later institution of canonical penance. Their arguments touched on the essential questions: What were the foundational elements of an order of penitents? Was its existence in the early Church absolutely coextensive with the canonical discipline?

d) *Karl Rahner*

Throughout the entire course of his lifework, Karl Rahner maintained an acute interest in the historical evolution of penance. His culminating work on the subject appeared in 1973 as the eleventh volume of his *Schriften zur Theologie: Frühe Bussgeschichte in Einzeluntersuchungen.*[132] In broad strokes, it can be said that Rahner was close to Poschmann in his interpretation of the historical evidence concerning penance. Even his methodology of studying the relevant patristic authors until the third century paralleled Poschmann's approach in the *Paenitentia Secunda.* Yet Rahner's presentation revealed some basic differences between the two authors.[133]

---

sin, expressed through Eucharistic exclusion. See Rahner's critique, *Early Church,* pp. 61–62, 110–113.

131. Though Grotz's approach was comparable to Galtier's, it is important to recognize that he himself never referred to this older experience of penance ("einfache Kirchenbusse") as a private penance.

132. References here make use of the English translation: *Theological Investigations,* Vol. 15: *Penance in the Early Church,* trans. L. Swain (London, 1983). Though a collection of previous articles on the development of ecclesial penance during the first three centuries, it remains a fundamental contribution to the field of study.

133. Rahner was much more hermeneutical in his approach than Poschmann. Whereas Poschmann offered an abundance of historical data, Rahner, also making use of the fruits of his research, was more sensitive to the dogmatic implications in

Rahner added his name to the growing list of contemporary authors who recognized that the Church, even from apostolic times, held no sin as objectively outside the possibility of reconciliation.[134] Even in the face of evidence of individual local churches refusing reconciliation to seemingly repentant sinners, such occasions were due to a more rigorous view of conversion rather than a denial of the principle that the Church had a right to reconcile even capital sinners.[135] Yet the tolerant treatment of sinners was tempered by the tradition, especially in the West, of the practice of a single penance after baptism. This was taken over from the testimony of the *Shepherd of Hermas* and remained in force throughout the life of canonical penance.

Rahner held that the early Church acknowledged the sacramental nature of penance. The subjective penance of the sinner was not enough; reconciliation with the official Church was necessary.[136] It was the bishop who had the final authority as to when a person might be admitted to penance and eventually be reconciled. And it was he who reconciled a sinner through prayer and the laying on of hands, but only when joined with the efficacious prayer of the whole Church.[137] Whether this was a direct forgiveness of sin or sin being removed by the communication of the Holy Spirit is unclear; yet the sinner's reconciliation with the Church in some way influenced his or her reconciliation with God, and so was necessary for salvation. There was no experience of a mere ecclesial reconciliation.[138]

---

the historical development of the sacrament. For example, his reflection of the historical development of penance as a visible reality of the Church in all its phases was particularly insightful (*Early Church*, pp. 316–318).

134. Rahner, *Early Church*, pp. 65–66, the exception remaining the unrepentant sinner.

135. *Ibid.*, p. 9. Rahner cited examples from Cyprian (*Ep.* 55.21) and the early fourth-century synods of Elvira and Saragossa.

136. *Ibid.*, p. 11.

137. *Ibid.*, p. 140. Tertullian especially developed this notion: the power of the bishop acting *with* the whole Church to effect reconciliation. Rahner interprets the prayer of the bishop as complementary to the intercessory prayers of the whole Church. While neither took away God's freedom to offer forgiveness to the sinner, the prayer of the Church will not go unheard by God.

138. *Ibid.*, p. 11. See also his interpretation of Cyprian and the meaning of reconciliation with the Church, pp. 189–199.

Rahner insisted that ecclesial penance in the ancient Church was the penance of excommunication.[139] From the time of Hermas, even from the apostolic age, there is no evidence of sacramental penance that did not include at least a temporary exclusion from the Eucharist.[140] In this, Rahner took a strong polemical stand against Grotz's thesis. Every experience of penance involved the "binding" of the sin through excommunication and its "loosing" through reconciliation. It was only later, in the sixth century, that excommunication began to be separated from the discipline of penance, developing into an ecclesiastical sanction.[141]

Rahner saw clearly that excommunication took different forms in the writings of the ancient authors. For example, he agreed that in some cases public excommunication for scandalous sins preceded the "partial" liturgical excommunication of those who had been allowed to begin the process of exomologesis.[142] However, in cases where excommunication was not imposed, he preferred to see these as examples of a nonsacramental practice. Rahner, then, made a distinction between different experiences of penance in the early Church based on the different forms of excommunication; yet, to his thinking, they remained examples of one public discipline of penance.[143]

On the question of private penance, Rahner was in full agreement with Poschmann that there is no witness of a private discipline of penance prior to the sixth century. But the basis for his response was different. In attempting to identify a private penance, Rahner did not believe that it was possible to take as one's starting point the experience of penance today. Present-day auricular confession occurs within the *forum internum* and so appears to omit many of the elements of the ancient discipline.[144] Yet this picture is deceiving, inasmuch as all the characteristics of public penance—

---

139. Poschmann, *PAS*, p. 87, also agreed that excommunication and reconciliation were the linchpins of the early discipline.

140. Rahner, *Early Church*, pp. 63–64, 86–97.

141. *Ibid.*, p. 13.

142. *Ibid.*, pp. 229–233. This distinction is especially evident in the *Didascalia*.

143. *Ibid.*, p. 62.

144. *Ibid.*, p. 216. Here was an implicit parting of the ways with Poschmann, who defined private penance along these lines. See above, pp. 39–40.

admittance to penance (later, the rite of enrollment as a penitent), exomologesis (confession), excommunication, public works of penance, prayer by the bishop (and the Church), and reconciliation— can either still be seen in a less public form today or could have been seen in a more private form in the ancient Church.[145] Rahner states:

> . . . although church penance remains exactly the same in its essence, with regard to the degrees in which it is expressed publicly, it is susceptible to an extraordinary number of variations. This variety of degrees and levels in the public character of penance is such that it would be purely arbitrary to dub certain forms of it "public" and others which evince hardly any differences making them at all or only occasionally less public, on the contrary, "private."[146]

Throughout the history of the Church, the public character of penance has become less evident, while its private character has become more obvious.

As far as Rahner could ascertain, the only element that was fundamental to the public discipline of the first six centuries not present in the later private penance was the aspect of unrepeatability. And it is on this that he built his case that no matter what the degree of publicity or secrecy that surrounded the penitential practice of the ancient Church, sacramental penance was always an unrepeatable experience.[147] Based on this fact, he suggested that penance no longer be distinguished by the terms "public" and "private," but by the more precise expressions "unrepeatable" and "repeatable."

Rahner was not denying that an order of penitents was the most fundamental feature of penance in the early Church. It was the belonging to a distinct class of penitents that allowed penance to be

---

145. Rahner, *Early Church*, pp. 216–217. For example, there is still excommunication today for serious sin, though in a less public form. And in the ancient Church, the reconciliation of heretics and of those on their deathbed necessarily minimalized the publicity normally connected with the rite.

146. *Ibid.*, p. 217.

147. *Ibid.*, p. 217. This was certainly true for the West. In the East, the law of a single penance is witnessed to only in the Alexandrian Church (Clement and Origen). The Syrian *Didascalia Apostolorum* does not mention such a custom. See below, p. 143.

what it was: a transitional order through which one guilty of post-baptismal sin moved from limited to full baptismal stature in the community. Nonetheless, it is arbitrary to pick out one part of the order of penitents as that which, in an absolute sense, made a sinner part of this special class (so Galtier and Grotz).[148] Adaptations in the ancient Chruch were numerous, but they were exactly that—adaptations and not a different discipline of penance existing alongside the one unrepeatable penance (so Poschmann). One could even build a case to show that the earliest evidence of repeatable penance includes all the elements of the order of penitents.[149] For Rahner, the actual process of penance cannot reveal the real difference between "public" penance and another distinct discipline known as "private" penance. The difference is only unlocked by the number of times such a process was allowed to occur.

2. OTHER RECENT CONTRIBUTORS

In addition to the principal authors, there have been other recent contributors to the question of the early history of penance. It would be an impossible task to speak of every historian and theologian who has, to a greater or lesser extent, studied the penance of the ancient Church. Yet, with a hope for further clarification of the issues involved and for the sake of completeness, it is necessary that the work of the more significant authors be mentioned.

---

148. Rahner, *Early Church*, pp. 213–214.

149. *Ibid.*, pp. 13–14. It remains a disputed point as to whether the early Irish penitential books, when speaking of the elements of penance, such as the penitential stages and Eucharistic exclusion, are in fact speaking of a public, unrepeatable discipline; viz., the *Pontifical of Egbert*, the *Dialogue*, and the canons attributed to the Second Synod of Patrick. The question of whether the Celtic Church ever had a tradition of practicing canonical, unrepeatable penance is an important one; yet in this context it is a moot point for Rahner. Elements of the order of penitents found expression in private repeatable penance so that a continuity between the two disciplines is clear. See T. Oakley, *English Penitential Discipline and Anglo-Saxon Law in Their Joint Influence*, Studies in History, Economics, and Public Law 107 (New York, 1923), pp. 78–88; J. McNeill and H. Gamer, *Medieval Handbooks of Penance*, Records of Civilization 29 (New York, 1938), pp. 80–86; C. Dooley, "Devotional Confession: An Historical and Theological Study," unpublished doctoral dissertation, Katholieke Universiteit Leuven (1982), pp. 67–81.

In the 1930's the works of E. Amann, J. Hoh, and R. Mortimer all made an impact on the historico-dogmatic situation of the question. Amann held that, while there were rigorist elements in the Church prior to the fourth century, all sin had the possibility of ecclesial reconciliation. After the appearance of Montanism and Novatianism, the rigorist element inside the Church grew stronger, leading to the harshness connected with the canonical discipline in the fourth century. Amann, more than later authors, was cognizant of the external factors that aided in the shift toward rigorism, particularly the situation of the mass conversions after the Peace of Constantine. Yet he indicated that, in fact, the practice of the third century only blossomed in the centuries that followed; there was really no fundamental difference in the practice of penance.[150] Finally, Amann held that the appearance of a repeatable penance certainly did not occur before the fifth century and probably not before the sixth.[151]

Hoh ambitiously attempted a study of the practice of penance during the first two centuries. Essentially, he held that the development of a penitential discipline in the early Church was in response to the harsh practice of some local churches that excluded grave sinners from any possibility of forgiveness after baptism. As yet, in these first centuries, there was no specific discipline of penance, though what was to develop in the next century was present in embryonic form.[152] Mortimer, on the other hand, wrote specifically against the conclusions of Galtier. He appeared to agree with Galtier's definition of what constituted canonical penance in a strict sense: liturgical enrollment in the order of penitents, the unrepeatability of penance, and the juridic restraints imposed upon the reconciled. Yet he went on to reject the conclusion of the existence of a private penance before the sixth century.[153]

---

150. E. Amann, "Pénitence," *DThC XII, 1 (Paris, 1932)* 749–846, c. 773–775, 779–783, 789; "Novatien et novatianisme," *DThC XI, 1* (Paris, 1931) 816–849, c. 832.

151. Amann, "Pénitence," c. 837–40.

152. J. Hoh, *Die kirchliche Busse im zweiten Jahrhundert*, BSHTh 22 (Breslau, 1932), pp. 129–131, *passim*.

153. R. Mortimer, *The Origins of Private Penance in the Western Church* (Oxford, 1939), pp. 4–5, 22, 30–31, 44, 188–190. Mortimer's view was severely criticized by G. Joyce, "Private Penance in the Early Church," *JThS* 42 (1941) 18–42.

In the mid-1940's the two previously cited articles by P. Palmer appeared.[154] Palmer upheld the position first taken by Morin in the seventeenth century: not only did the Church always exercise the power of the keys for the sins of apostasy, murder, and adultery through the discipline of public penance, but other serious sins were also reconciled through a private form of penance. However, his work was clearly apologetical, with his stated purpose to preserve the Catholic Church from doctrinal embarrassment through the "rediscovery" of Morin's conclusions.[155] As a result, his commitment to historical criticism was brought into question. Influenced by Morin's perspective, Palmer was the last modern author to agree with Galtier in upholding the existence of a private form of penance prior to the fifth or sixth century.

In 1953 H. von Campenhausen published his fundamental work *Kirchliches Amt und geistliche Vollmacht*.[156] In this study, von Campenhausen understood the roots of the Church's penance practice in two experiences of the apostolic and postapostolic Church: the act of excommunication used against serious sinners in the second century, and the Church's own procedure for judgment and the resolution of civil cases involving Christians. These factors witnessed to a sectarian, somewhat rigorist Church that may or may not have extended reconciliation to those guilty of the three capital sins.[157]

Von Campenhausen believed that the explicit development of an actual discipline of penance, involving liturgical rites and based on pastoral reflection, occurred only with the strengthening of the

---

154. Palmer, "Jean Morin" and "Jean Morin II." Palmer is also noted for his publication of a source book on the history of penance: *Sacraments and Forgiveness*, Sources of Christian Theology 2 (Westminster, Md., 1959).

155. Palmer, "Jean Morin II," pp. 306–308.

156. References here make use of the later English translation: *Ecclesiastical Authority and Spiritual Power in the Church of the First Three Centuries*, trans. J. A. Baker (Stanford, Calif., 1969).

157. *Ibid.*, pp. 215–16, 218, n. 21. One should not try to reconcile the refusal to reconcile those who had committed one of the capital sins "with the supposedly fundamental principle that all sins can be forgiven." It could be that these sins occurred so rarely that there was no set procedure for them—until Tertullian claimed that there was. Also, Von Campenhausen pointed out that the rigorism seen in the writings of the New Testament and the postapostolic period was much more "paraenetic" than legal or disciplinary.

episcopal office in the third century. It was this factor that opened the way for ecclesial forgiveness to be offered for all sins, relaxing the sectarian rigorism of the first two centuries.[158] Part of this development was the movement from an indirect (the community avoiding the sinner) to a direct (imposed upon the sinner) excommunication during the first three centuries. Von Campenhausen not only further amplified the nineteenth-century theory of Harnack that the practice of penance was substantially a development of episcopal authority, but served as a forerunner to Grotz, who, as has been seen, posited the existence of some form of excommunication prior to its being linked to ecclesial penance.

In the late 1950's the work by P. Anciaux upheld the point that the Church offered forgiveness for all sins from its earliest tradition. He agreed with the now near universal position that truly private penance developed later in the life of the Church.[159] But what was most striking about Anciaux's work was his struggle to define canonical penance. On the one hand, he said that canonical penance existed in the first three centuries of the Church's life but was not organized; on the other hand, he affirmed that one cannot really speak of canonical penance until after the Peace of Constantine.[160] Anciaux pointed out that there were definite differences between the practice of penance in the first three centuries and the "stabilization of canonical rules that began in the fourth century," but these differences were not different enough to speak of them as anything but forms of canonical penance.[161]

---

158. Von Campenhausen, *Ecclesiastical Authority*, pp. 236–37.

159. P. Anciaux, *The Sacrament of Penance* (London, 1962), pp. 56, 58–59, 70 (n. 11), 71 (n. 17). This is a translation of the second edition of the author's earlier work, *Le sacrement de la pénitence* (Louvain, 1960).

160. "Canonical penance . . . certainly existed in the first centuries, with its essential meaning and basic structures" (Anciaux, *Sacrament of Penance*, p. 55); "To obtain a clear idea of ecclesiastical penance during its early period it is necessary to discover what form it took in the fourth century" (p. 47).

161. *Ibid.*, p. 55. In fact, Anciaux mentioned differences that will be shown later in the present study to form the very basis for making a distinction between the earlier order of penitents and canonical penance, including the late development of the juridic restraints on the reconciled, and the shift in the practice of a single penance from custom to law (pp. 56–60).

Perhaps the most prolific author of the recent era was C. Vogel.[162] Vogel came very much under the influence of Poschmann, holding the same position with regard to the possibility of forgiveness in the ancient Church and the sixth-century appearance of a private discipline.[163] Vogel did not speak of the penitential discipline of the third century as canonical penance; on this point he exhibited a greater preciseness than Anciaux. However, he did not feel that the Peace of Constantine absolutely altered the institution of penance. Its essential elements remained intact, and the only real distinguishable characteristic of the penitential practice of the fourth century in comparison to the century before was a greater rigorism due to the influx of new converts.[164]

A short but significant article by M.-F. Berrouard appeared in 1974.[165] Berrouard clearly distinguished different periods within the Church's penitential practice of the first six centuries, based not only on historical but on sociological factors. He was one of the first authors to do so.

Berrouard agreed that there were no absolutely irremissible sins in the first centuries. Yet in the third century the Church was influenced by an evolving rigorism, resulting from its growing institutionalization. This rigorism was a reaction against what was perceived as a relaxation of ethical and moral norms, counterpointed by the ethical fervor of Montanism and Novatianism. Berrouard pointed out that two conflicting ecclesiologies were at work here: the rigorist model, which sought to keep the Church pure from sin, and the more tolerant model of the bishops, who saw the Church as the mediator between the sins of humanity and the grace of God. With the growing authority of the episcopate, it would be the latter

---

162. In his lifetime Vogel devoted over twenty-five books and articles on the subject of penance. See A. Faivre, "Bibliographie de Cyril Vogel," *RDC* 34 (1984) 390–395. Special attention is given to: *Le pécheur et la pénitence dans l'Église ancienne*, CTT 15 (Paris, 1966); "Le péché et la pénitence," in *Pastorale du péché*, ed. P. Delhaye, BTh II, Théologie Morale 8 (Tournai, 1961) 147–235.

163. *Ibid.*, pp. 147–148, 188–189.

164. *Ibid.*, pp. 176–177.

165. M.-F. Berrouard, "La pénitence publique durant les six premiers siècles: Histoire et sociologie," *MD* 118 (1974) 92–130. Berrouard himself admitted that it has been very rare for historians of penance to consider the impact of the shifting relationship between the Church and society on the development of penitential practice.

model that would eventually win the day, but not without being affected by the rigorism of the other.[166]

With the Peace of Constantine in the fourth century and the beginning of mass conversions, the Church lost its ethical fervor of the earlier period. Councils and individual bishops attempted to confront this new sociological experience of the Church through canonical legislation on penance. The growing size of the local churches encouraged a shift to impersonalism, from decisions being made based on particular cases, as in the earlier centuries, to general norms being legislated that tended to be stricter, in order to cover the widest possibility of action. For Berrouard, the new situation of the Church in society made for a new situation with regard to penitential practice.[167]

In 1978 H. Vorgrimler published his revised edition of Poschmann's study in the *Handbuch der Dogmengeschichte*.[168] Vorgrimler fell very much in line with the position of Poschmann but was most influenced by Rahner. The possibility of reconciliation for all sins was offered in the early Church, and the first witness to a private experience of penance was the Synod of Toledo (A.D. 589).[169] Vorgrimler also affirmed that the experience of penance in the fourth century was a continuation of the penitential practices that developed in the third century. He agreed that it was in the third century that one can perceive a growing rigorism in the Church, inspired by the same reaction against laxism that inspired the Montanists and Novatianists. This led to the inflexibility of penitential procedure in the later centuries. This analysis allowed him, along with Berrouard, to lay greater stress on the subjective nature of penance in the earlier centuries as opposed to the more objective legislation from the fourth century onward.[170]

The last author to be mentioned is L. Orsy. Orsy's work was not so much a study of the history of penance as an investigation into the causes of change in the Church, seen through the development

---

166. Berrouard, "La pénitence publique," pp. 109, 114–116.

167. *Ibid.*, pp. 116–125.

168. H. Vorgrimler, *Busse und Krankensalbung* (hereafter *Busse*). This is a revision of Poschmann's 1951 work in the same series, *Busse und Letzte Ölung*.

169. Vorgrimler, *Busse*, pp. 68–69, 89.

170. *Ibid.*, pp. 68–69, 70–73.

of penance. As a result, while giving assent to the basic points that forgiveness was offered for all sins in the ancient Church, and that there was no private form of penance before the sixth century, he did not distinguish any points of difference in the practice of the first five centuries, which he refers to generically as the "Mediterranean system."[171] Orsy's work may be historically unspecific for the early period, yet his appreciation of the factors that effect change in society has contributed to an understanding of the history of penance that goes beyond the external witness of the sources.

This has been but an overview of some of the more prominent recent works that examine the experience of ecclesial penance in the ancient Church. Certainly this list is not exhaustive; there are other studies that could have been included in this survey.[172] However,

---

171. L. Orsy, *The Evolving Church and the Sacrament of Penance* (Denville, N.J., 1978), pp. 31–34.

172. Other recent works that touch on the early history of penance include: H. Rondet, "Esquisse d'une histoire du sacrement de pénitence," *NRTh* 80 (1958) 561–584; K. Baus, *From the Apostolic Community to Constantine*, Vol. I of *Handbook of Church History*, ed. H. Jedin and J. Dolan (New York, 1965), pp. 318–345; F. Courtney, "The Administration of Penance," *Clergy Review* 46 (1961), pp. 10–27, 85–98; B. de Vaux Saint-Cyr, *Revenir à Dieu. Pénitence, conversion, confession*, CTT 26 (Paris, 1967); J. Ramos-Regidor, " 'Reconciliation' in the Primitive Church and Its Lessons for Theology and Pastoral Practice Today," *Concilium* 1 (1971) 76–88; J. Steinruch, "Busse und Beichte im ihrer geschichtlichen Entwicklung," in *Dienst der Versöhnung*, TThS 31 (Trier, 1974), pp. 45–65; M. Nicolau, *La reconciliación con Dios y con la Iglesia* (Madrid, 1976), pp. 61–125; N. Mitchell, "The Many Ways of Reconciliation: An Historical Synopsis of Christian Penance," in *The Rite of Penance. Commentaries*, Vol. 3: *Background and Directions*, ed. N. Mitchell (Washington, D.C., 1978), pp. 20–37; M. Hebblethwaite and K. Donavan, *The Theology of Penance*, Theology Today 20 (Dublin, 1979), pp. 21–28; L. Hamelin, *Reconciliation in the Church*, trans. M. O'Connell (Collegeville, Minn., 1980), pp. 32–39; M. Hellwig, *Sign of Reconciliation and Conversion. The Sacrament of Penance for Our Times*, Message of the Sacraments 4 (Wilmington, Del., 1982, rev. ed. 1984), pp. 27–44; R. Gula, *To Walk Together Again. The Sacrament of Reconciliation* (New York, 1984), pp. 187–201; J. Dallen, *The Reconciling Community*, (New York, 1986), pp. 5–55.

General works on the sacraments that include significant sections on the historical development of penance include: W. Bausch, *A New Look at the Sacraments* (Notre Dame, Ind., 1977; rev. ed. 1983), pp. 160–171; J. Martos, *Doors to the Sacred* (Garden City, N.J., 1981), pp. 313–328.

Works on the history of the rites of penance include: J. Jungmann, *Die latienischen Bussriten; id., The Early Liturgy to the Time of Gregory the Great*, trans. F. Brunner, Liturgical Studies 6 (Notre Dame, Ind., 1959), pp. 240–248; P.-M. Gy, "Histoire liturgique

the representative authors presented here, it is hoped, will allow one to appreciate the development in the interpretation of penance over the course of this century and the growing preciseness in the identification of the experience of penance within the first six centuries.

CONCLUSION

It is apparent that a variety of factors have influenced the interpretation of the early history of penance. There is the vagueness of the sources during the first three centuries, which itself has stimulated much speculation and many theories concerning the origins of ecclesial penance. Also, later commentators were necessarily affected by the historical context within which they lived and wrote, reflecting in their work the controversies and concerns of their day. At the turn of the century, the chief concern was the protection of Catholic dogma against the Protestant attack. Later, thanks to the ascendancy of the historical-critical method, this was replaced by a sole dedication to the positive facts of historical research. And in the recent era, the influence of sociological factors in the ancient Church has begun to be more appreciated as a factor in the development of the penitential discipline.

Nonetheless, progress has been made toward a more precise understanding of the experience of the early Church. First, there seems to be common agreement on a definition of private repeatable penance. This has allowed for a consensual verdict among historians that such a practice cannot be discovered (at least in the West) from the sources until the late fifth or sixth century.[173] Second, it is gener-

---

du sacrement de pénitence," *MD* 56 (1958) 5–21; J. Gunstone, *The Liturgy of Penance*, Studies in Christian Worship 7 (London, 1966), pp. 17–40.

From the perspective of the history of canon law, see G. D'Ercole, *Penitenza canonico-sacramentale dalle origini alla pace Costantiniana*, Communio 4 (Rome, 1963).

Collections of texts on penance during the first three centuries, besides the previously cited work by Watkins, *A History of Penance* and Palmer, *Sacraments and Forgiveness*, include: H. Karpp, *La pénitence. Textes et commentaires des origines de l'ordre pénitentiel de l'Église ancienne*, Traditio Christiana 1, trans. A. Schneider, W. Rordorf, and P. Barthel (Neuchâtel, 1970).

173. The history of the rise of private repeatable penance is certainly outside the scope of the present study. But there have been recent challenges to the traditional opinion that the practice only came to the Continent with the Celtic mission-

ally concluded by contemporary authors that the majority of the local churches during the first three centuries acted upon their mission to offer reconciliation to any sinner who sincerely repented of sin. This does not deny the presence of more rigorist perspectives and practices but only indicates the mainstream of the tradition. One can conclude that, on these two former points of controversy, dogma no longer has to be defended. Through historical freedom, there is now a convergence of opinion.

This leads us back to our focus, the order of penitents. It is difficult to isolate its existence in the thinking of the later interpreters within the larger controversies surrounding the early history. Yet it is this very point that is telling. Certainly it is beyond debate that the order of penitents was one of the most characteristic features of the harsh canonical discipline by the fourth century. But did it have a life prior to this? Is there evidence of its existence, at least in a less liturgically guised form, during the third century, when the witnesses to ecclesial penance are more demonstrative in their testimony than in the prior two centuries? These are the questions still to be answered.

To be sure, most later interpreters recognized a distinction between the penitential experience in the early centuries and the canonical discipline that appeared after the Peace of Constantine. It was this fact that contributed to Galtier's thesis concerning the existence of a private penance in the early centuries. It was this fact that formed the basis for Grotz's distinction between ecclesial penance and excommunication. It was this fact that led both Poschmann and Rahner to argue that variations in the experience of penance were still experiences of the one discipline of public (and in Rahner's case, unrepeatable) penance. It is this fact that has allowed for a more precise nuancing by recent authors in their appreciation of penance during the first six centuries, with the third-century experience being more and more distinguished from the experience of the fourth century and beyond. And it is this fact that forms the

---

aries. It may have had a life previous to their coming, therefore earlier (fifth century?) than has been commonly accepted (late sixth or early seventh century). See the excellent presentation of the documentation by C. Dooley, ''Devotional Confession,'' pp. 81-95.

foundation of the present study. A reexamination of the early sources of ecclesial penance may well reveal the existence of an order of penitents in the third century, distinct from the later institution of canonical penance.

II. THE CONTEXTUALIZATION OF THE PRESENT STUDY

It is necessary to contextualize the present study within the larger framework of the previous interpretation, especially with regard to the use and nonuse of the customary language. In addition, following the example of the most recent interpreters, the examination of the early witnesses to ecclesial penance must first be briefly set within the broader ecclesiological and sociological context of the first three centuries.

A. THE PRESENT STUDY IN THE CONTEXT OF PREVIOUS INTERPRETATION: THE ISSUE OF TERMINOLOGY

In examining the works of previous historians of penance, it becomes apparent that one of the key stumbling blocks to a fruitful discovery of the early Church's penitential experience is their often-times bewildering use of a wide variety of terms. It becomes the student's task not only to discern the working hermeneutic that a particular author brings to the subject but also to understand in what way the terminology is being employed. Only after learning how the customary vocabulary has been used in the past might one have the courage to aid in the development of a new language to describe the early experience of penance.

1. THE PROBLEM OF PAST TERMINOLOGY

The vocabulary used to speak of the experience of penance in the local churches during the first three centuries has often been used uncritically, and often with the result of adding to the ambiguity of the already ambiguous sources. Certain terms in particular stand out as being more culpable in this regard.

a) *Canonical penance*

It has been seen that many later interpreters used the term "canonical penance" to denote the entire experience of ecclesial penance during the first six centuries. Even in cases where authors perceived a distinction between the practice of the third century and that of the fourth century and after, more often than not they highlighted the similarity of the two experiences rather than what distinguishes them from one another. Yet when one examines the canonical legislation of the fourth century, reasons that serve to highlight a distinction come to light.[174]

i) *The appearance of distinct liturgical stages*

By the fourth century in the West, distinct stages in the order of penitents were marked by liturgical actions.[175] Appearing for the first time was a distinguishable rite of enrollment of penitents through the imposition of the hand. This rite was not seen in the third-century witness, and occurred after a private confession of faults to the bishop or his representative. This began the period of segregation within the community, during which penitents were excluded from the Eucharist, took special places in the assembly, performed works of penance, and, at least in certain communities, were clothed in special penitential garb. Throughout this period there were prayers and the imposition of the hand. Penitents, though allowed to remain for the *missa fidelium,* had to assume penitential postures, such as kneeling or prostration, even on joyful feast days. This was unlike the graded discipline in the East, where "hearers" and "prostrators" were both dismissed after the Liturgy of the Word.

Once the bishop decided that the penitents' contrition for sin was sufficient and their penance complete (in accord with the canonical legislation), a solemn prayer and imposition of the hand by the bishop, along with intercession by the whole community, reconciled them to the Church. This opened the way for their readmission to

---

174. Beginning with the Councils of Elvira (c. 300 A.D.), Arles (314 A.D.), Ancyra (314 A.D.), Neocaesarea (320 A.D.), and especially Nicaea (325 A.D.). To this list might also be included the *Canonical Epistle* of Peter of Alexandria (306 A.D.), the writings of Basil († 379 A.D.) and Gregory of Nyssa († 394 A.D.) and the fourth- (and fifth-) century letters from the bishops of Rome.

175. For a detailed description of the organization of canonical penance during the fourth and fifth centuries, and for the relevant patristic references, see Poschmann, *PAS,* pp. 87–99.

the Eucharist. Thus, the rites framing the institution of penance in the fourth century were much more liturgically specified than what appears in the documentation from the third century.

ii) *The indivisible connection with the juridical consequences of penance*

With the clearer liturgical definition of the order of penitents came the juridic imposition of the consequences of ecclesial penance: the unrepeatability of ecclesial penance and juridic lifelong restraints imposed upon the reconciled. Certainly the practice of unrepeatable penance predated the fourth century, as will be seen in the following chapters. However, what began as a custom arising out of a desire to aid a penitent to experience genuine conversion evolved into canonically prescribed law by the fourth century. Also, the status of penitents ceased to be transitional as obligations were demanded of penitents for the rest of their lives, even after their reconciliation. (Except for one passage in Origen, there is no mention of such restraints in the first three centuries.) They were intended as penal actions to stigmatize penitents for the rest of their lives due to the gravity of their sin and to serve as a warning to others in the community. Though reconciled, penitents remained second-class citizens of the Church. It was the harshness of these consequences that led to ecclesial pardon being delayed until one's deathbed, thus making canonical penance less and less pastorally effective in the life of the Church.

Based upon these reasons, the term ''canonical penance'' will be used in the present study only in reference to the experience of ecclesial penance resulting from the canonical legislation of the fourth century and afterward.[176] Though having roots in the third-century experience, it was a distinct discipline.

---

176. This is not to give the impression that every experience of penance described by the fourth-century witnesses includes all these elements. For example, Augustine does not mention the juridic restraints imposed upon penitents; indeed, his witness to the abundance of penitents (*Sermon* 232, 7–8) would seem to rule them out (Poschmann, *PAS*, p. 106). However, the number of occurrences where these elements were linked to the experience of ecclesial penance gives a certain appropriateness to the application of the term ''canonical penance'' to the penitential discipline from the fourth century onwards.

b) *Public and private penance*

Hopelessly used beyond recognition by the later interpreters of early penance are the terms "public" and "private" penance. Countless meanings have been assigned to these expressions, making them unusable to the present student for all practical purposes. It is agreed that there were private elements in a public rite of penance (even as there are public elements in the private ritual of today, as Rahner pointed out). Rahner's distinction between repeatable and unrepeatable further clarified the situation, yet his distinction also had its limitations.[177] Therefore, the present study will assiduously avoid the use of the terms "public" or "private," and "unrepeatable" or "repeatable," penance. Rather than attempting to overclassify ecclesial penance in the early Church, terms more neutrally descriptive will be employed here.

c) *Excommunication*

It is agreed among the historians of penance that the experience of excommunication played a fundamental part in the development of the penitential discipline of the early Church. However, the term "excommunication" connotes an immediate juridic sense, devoid of a connection with penance and conversion. This is due to the term's later canonical usage. One could be excommunicated from the Church as a disciplinary action and then readmitted when the objective obstacle that had evoked the excommunication was removed. In this way the juridic action of excommunication was completely separated from the sacramental event of reconciliation.

This was not the experience of the local churches of the first three centuries. A grave sinner was isolated from the community and/or segregated within the community for the predominant purpose of conversion. While both actions included the penitent's being barred from partaking of the Eucharist, this was hardly a juridic or merely disciplinary action. The Church mirrored in an external way the internal situation of the sinner's damaged relationship with God. It

---

177. For example, if one identifies repeatable penance with the tariff system of the sixth or seventh century (or perhaps earlier?), what is to be made of the penitential discipline of the *Didascalia*, where no mention is made of the custom of unrepeatability?

had everything to do with the guilty individual's seeing the seriousness of the sin committed, doing penance, and returning to the fold. Therefore, due to the juridic image evoked because of its later usage and the inappropriateness of such an application to the early Church, the term "excommunication," even though used by the major interpreters of early Church penance, is avoided in this study.

2. TOWARD A NEW TERMINOLOGY

After distancing ourselves from some of the more customary, though problematic, terminology, our attention shifts to the use of a new language by which one might more appropriately speak of the early experience of penance. It is an ambitious endeavor, yet the sources themselves cry out for a more understandable and descriptive interpretation. Though admittedly fragmentary and often vague, the sources are not unintelligible. Hence, foreshadowing the following chapters on the patristic witness of the first three centuries, we present here a glossary of the descriptive terms used throughout this study.

a) *The order of penitents*

Used in its strictest sense, the designation order of penitents refers to the most characteristic feature of canonical penance. However, if part of our working hermeneutic is to examine the sources from the first three centuries in hopes of discovering the existence of an order of penitents prior to the fourth century, and if it is agreed that canonical penance cannot be spoken of before the fourth century, then the definition of an order of penitents must necessarily be broader. For this reason the term is employed here more generically, not being limited to the practice following a liturgical enrollment rite. This is possible due to the transitional nature of the "order" itself.[178] As will be further elucidated in the final chapter, the existence of a transitional and organized order of penitents was founded upon the actions of excluding the sinner from the Eucharist

---

178. It must be clear that *ordo*, used in the sense of the *ordo paenitentium* or the *ordo catechumenorum*, does not imply a hierarchical order. They are transitional orders, organized so that those enrolled in their ranks may pass from one status within the Church to another. See below, pp. 234–238.

and demanding that he or she move through clearly delineated steps toward ecclesial reconciliation. On this basis there is sufficient justification for the use of the term prior to the fourth century.

b) *Indirect and direct coercive penance of isolation*

In the hope of moving away from the perplexing terms "public" and "private" penance, and from the overly juridic "excommunication," a new language is employed to describe more neutrally the penitential actions of the first three centuries. By the term "coercive penance of isolation" is meant an action that isolated a grave postbaptismal sinner from all interaction with the community, including, but not exclusively, participation in the Eucharist. It was an isolation imposed for a variety of reasons. Certainly it was purgative (to preserve the purity of the community) and didactic (to instruct others in the community on the serious effect of sin). But its central purpose was coercive, namely, to coerce the transgressor to turn away from sin in order to be received back into the fold of the Church. In the first two centuries this action was usually indirect, imposed indirectly by the community, whose members simply avoided the sinner. With the development of hierarchical order, this action became direct, imposed directly on the sinner, who was simply expelled from the community.

c) *A penance of segregation*

With the witness of the third century, an intermediate penitential step appeared between the coercive penance of isolation and readmittance to the community. This step is described here as a "penance of segregation," a term more adequately describing the fundamental situation of the sinner. Such a one was segregated within the community, indicative of the member's status within the Church. This status was evidenced in the accepted penitential actions that organized penitents as a specific group within the life and worship of the Church: a designated location within the assembly, special liturgical garb, penitential actions such as kneeling or prostration, and, most important, exclusion from the Eucharist.

For some of the third-century witnesses, the exomologesis included the entire period during which penitents were segregated within the community; for others, the exomologesis formed only the concluding ritual action at the end of their segregation.[179] Yet, segregation within denoted a definite progression from isolation outside the community. In the fourth century it was the penance of segregation that was more liturgically specified to form the order of penitents within the institution of canonical penance.

B. The Early History of Penance Within the Broader Context of Early Church History

The major historians of penance in this century have been accused of being too positivistic in their approach to its history.[180] They did not take enough into account the forces of change that occurred within the Church during the early centuries or the shifting relationship of the Church vis-à-vis society. These factors indirectly influenced the development of the Church's penitential discipline. They are mentioned here as necessary background to the present study.

1. THE ECCLESIOLOGICAL CONTEXT

The mediating nature of the Church is a theme that runs throughout nearly all the patristic texts of the first three centuries.[181] This is based on the mysterious relationship with Christ, to whom the Church is inseparably joined through the bond of the Holy Spirit. The image of the Church as *mater* finds expression in many of these early witnesses, a sign of the maternal role that the Church plays in the care of her children. Her prayer is efficacious in the eyes of the Father because it is a prayer joined with the prayer of Christ. For this reason, those within her fold experience a unique relationship to God, while the salvation of those outside her embrace is in grave doubt.[182] This is particularly evidenced in the Church's inter-

---

179. Tertullian's use of "exomologesis" coincides with the former meaning, while Cyprian's use of the term indicates a further evolution, with exomologesis being only a specific concluding rite within the entire process of ecclesial penance.

180. See the critique by Dallen, *Reconciling Community*, pp. 356–357.

181. K. Delahaye, *Ecclesia mater chez les Pères des trois premiers siècles*, Unam Sanctam 46 (Paris, 1964), pp. 204–206.

182. As will be seen in the later chapters the internal relationship between the Church and Christ was the basis on which the early writers implied the ecclesiological maxim: *Salus extra Ecclesiam non est.*

cession for grave sinners. Though not infringing upon the freedom of God, who alone forgives the sinner, the mediating prayer of the Church is confidently expected to be granted a divine hearing. It is of salvific importance to sinners.[183]

That not everyone had such a strong sense of the Church's mediating power is seen in the early schisms. These rocked the local churches to their foundations. This resulted in a time of crisis, which forced Church leaders to define and redefine the position of the local communities with regard to dogmatic belief and disciplinary action. In particular, the rigorism of Montanism and Novatianism affected the Church's position with regard to postbaptismal sinners. They effected two fundamental results. First, the efficacy of the Church's prayer for grave sinners was asserted against the schismatics, who held that the Church did not have the authority to offer reconciliation to such transgressors. The image of the Church as *mater* won out over those who preferred other, more disciplinarian images of the role of the Church.

A second, more negative result was that the churches were influenced by the rigorism of the schismatics. If those who separated themselves from the Church, and so from God, could live austere and moral lives, should not faithful Christians within the fold of Mother Church, whose salvation is more assured, be willing to do the same? The accusation made by the schismatics that the Church had grown lax in her commitment to Christ was heard by Church leaders. Postbaptismal pardon, though possible through adequate penance, demands more and more stringent requirements.[184]

The ability of the churches to handle the dogmatic and disciplinary challenges raised by the schisms revealed a development in the role of ecclesial leadership. By the third century the charismatic elements that affected the direction of the churches in the first two centuries had given way to a clearly defined hierarchical structure. The authority of the bishop in the communities increased, a development that came to its climax with the strong monarchical episco-

---

183. Delahaye, *Ecclesia mater*, pp. 239–241.

184. The previous examination of the later historians of penance reveals a consensus that the rigorism of the Montanists and Novatianists played a role in the evolution toward harshness in the Church's penitential discipline.

pate of Cyprian. The further defining of ecclesial office led to a further defining of the discipline of ecclesial penance. The latter cannot be truly appreciated without being cognizant of the former.[185]

2. THE SOCIOLOGICAL CONTEXT

The development of ecclesial practices cannot be isolated from the effect of societal events that influenced the life of the Church. With regard to penance, the procedural approach taken by the Church was necessarily affected by Roman society, within which the Christian communities lived their life. Of foremost importance were the persecutions of the third century. Much pain and confusion were unleashed upon the young communities by these violent purges from the hand of the emperor. Yet they introduced the conditions that forced the churches to deal much more specifically with the situation of serious postbaptismal sin (especially apostasy in order to escape torture and death). This is nowhere more graphically seen than in the unfortunate circumstances of the *lapsi* in Carthage during the Decian persecution.

But as much as Roman violence against the Christians forced the development of the penitential discipline, the Christians appear to have adopted a Roman approach to societal offenders in their penitential practice. The Romans did not forgive societal transgressions easily; they demanded juridical satisfaction for wrongs committed.[186] This is especially evident in the Roman class of the *infamia*, who, because of grave morally wrong actions or participation in morally wrong professions, were considered to be on the fringes of society.[187] In like manner, the Church also demanded specific rectifying actions of those whose grave sin had put them on the margins of the Church's life and worship. In the West the Roman legal tradition clearly affected the development of ecclesial penance.[188]

---

185. This is the position held by Von Campenhausen, *Ecclesiastical Authority, passim,* to which the present study makes numerous references.

186. A. Wilhelm-Hooijbergh, *Peccatum. Sin and Guilt in Ancient Rome,* published doctoral dissertation, Rijksuniversiteit te Utrecht (Groningen, 1954), p. 101.

187. J. Thomas, *Textbook of Roman Law* (Amsterdam, 1976), p. 410. The influence of Roman law on the penitential discipline of the early churches is in need of further examination.

188. This statement is further supported if one considers the juridical backgrounds of both Tertullian and Cyprian.

The most important sociological event for the evolution of ecclesial penance was the Peace of Constantine, which occurred at the beginning of the fourth century. Once it became socially, or even economically, advantageous to be a Christian in the empire, the communities grew quite rapidly. One of the results was that bishops came less and less into personal contact with the flock to whom they were to minister. They were forced to rely more on the objective legislation of the Church than on subjective interaction in the governance of the communities. This led to a stifling casuistic approach to penance, evidenced in the canonical witness. The size of the communities forced an institutionalization of ecclesial penance that was distinctly different from the experience of the third century. Canonical penance was born.

CHAPTER SUMMARY

In undertaking a reexamination of the early sources of the Church's penitential discipline, one immediately senses a methodological tension. On the one hand, the student may not presume to attempt such a study without first entering into dialogue with previous historians and interpreters of penance during the first centuries. It is their work that sheds light on the many-sided contours of the controversial issues. The fruit of their research must not be overlooked or rejected outright; rather, it must be built upon in the continual task of uncovering the great wealth that is the Church's tradition.

Yet, on the other hand, one cannot be paralyzed by the previous interpretation of the early history of penance. Though the sources remain constant (except for the fact that more critical text editions are available at the present time), those who study the penitential practices of the first three centuries bring to such an undertaking their own hermeneutic, their own tool by which interpretation is fashioned. Against previous perspectives and in the face of popular (mis)conceptions, the present study generally takes as its starting point a positive approach toward the history, believing it to be useful in informing and transforming present practice. This unbinds us from the constrictions of a customary vocabulary that is no longer useful, and allows for the evolution of a new language with which to speak of the penitential experience of the early Church. Further, it obliges us to consider the ecclesiological and sociological forces that influenced the early procedures of penance. After stating the question and setting the context, it is time to move from the jungle of interpretation to discover the treasure of the sources themselves.

Chapter Two

THE WITNESS
OF THE FIRST TWO CENTURIES

Any serious attempt to research the ancient origins of ecclesial penance must begin by allowing the early sources to speak for themselves. As valuable as the later interpretations are, and as necessary for an orientation into the present state of the research, it is upon the patristic witnesses themselves that the present study must be built.

Unquestionably, the documents of the first two centuries do not allow a precise picture of the practice of penance in the primitive Church. Not only do remarks concerning penance and the remission of sin reveal different attitudes and practices in the varying local churches, but such remarks are often more paraenetic than descriptive. Even the use of the term *metanoia* is ambiguous, referring at the same time to an attitude of conversion and to concrete acts of repentance.[1] Yet, these early sources do reveal approaches in the treatment of the sinner that will not be inconsistent with the more vivid descriptions of penitential practices in the writings of the third century.[2] While the literature of the third century will pos-

---

1. J. Behm, "*metanoeō, metanoia*," *TDNT* IV, ed. G. Kittel, trans. G. Bromiley (Grand Rapids, Mich., 1967) 975–1008, pp. 999–1008; A. H. Dirksen, *The New Testament Concept of Metanoia*, CUAT 34 (Washington, D.C., 1932), pp. 109ff. For an appreciation of the Hebrew roots of the term, see P. Adnès, "Pénitence," in *DicSp* 12,1 (1984) 943–1010, c. 943; for the Greek roots, R. Joly, "Note sur *metanoia*," *RHR* 140 (1961) 149–156.

2. There are those who take this point somewhat too far and who border on the anachronistic, such as E. Amann, "La pénitence primitive," *DThC* 12,1 (1933) 749–845, c. 754, who states that while it is impossible to determine how the primi-

sess a welcome degree of clarity after the abstruseness of the texts about to be examined, it is only within the context of the witness of these first centuries that it will be possible for us to fully appreciate the testimony of the third century to be presented in the following chapters.

This chapter will be divided into four major sections. The first will examine the witness of the New Testament writings; the second will look at the relevant works of the postapostolic writers; the third will focus specifically on the most significant work concerning ecclesial penance in the second century, the *Shepherd of Hermas*; and the final section will examine the testimony of the late second century, including Irenaeus as well as three other witnesses taken from Eusebius's history.

I. THE WITNESS OF THE NEW TESTAMENT

The Gospels attest to one fact with extreme clarity: Jesus forgave sinners.[3] His was a forgiveness that manifested the beginning of a new era, the beginning of the reign of God. In the face of the rabbinic tradition that demanded an external personal purity in conformity to the law of Moses, Jesus embraced sinners and called them to an internal repentance and reconciliation for the sake of the Kingdom.[4]

The apostles not only personally experienced Jesus' ministry of reconciliation but came to believe in his dying and rising as having universal significance for the reconciliation of a sinful world. At its apostolic origins, the Church took seriously its pastoral mission to preach the saving power of faith in Christ, continuing Jesus' ministry of reconciliation and calling all persons to turn away from sin and to believe in the gospel.[5] It is a call to radical conversion, involving personal sorrow for sin and a willingness to be created anew

---

tive Church exercised ecclesial forgiveness, the penitential practices of the New Testament were consistent with later developments based on the "principe de continuité."

3. Some examples include Mt 9:2, 6; 18:21-35; 26:28; Mk 2:15-17; 11:25-26; Lk 1:77; 7:34-50; 15:1-2, 7, 10, 11-32; 18:9-14; 19:1-10; 23:34; 24:27; Jn 1:29; 5:14; 8:3-11.

4. A. Lefévre, "Péché et pénitence dans la Bible," *MD* 55 (1958) 7-22, pp. 8-13.

5. J. Murphy-O'Connor, "Péché et communauté dans le Nouveau Testament," *RB* 74 (1967) 161-193, pp. 161-168.

through participation in the two experiences that defined the limits of membership in the early Church: baptism and Eucharist. Through baptism a person is cleansed from sin and empowered to put on the new garment of faith. Through the Eucharist believers are formed into the Body of Christ and strengthened against relapse into sin. Only within the framework of these foundational faith encounters can the penitential practice of the entire New Testament be fully appreciated.[6]

For the primitive Church, the occurrence of sin after baptism was unexpected. Since baptism and Eucharist joined persons to Christ and made them partakers of the reign of God, there could be no possibility of sin. Yet sin was an existential reality, having consequences that were impossible to ignore.[7] Attempts to deal with this reality were not a matter of following predetermined rituals or patterns of behavior but of balancing the mission to forgive "not seven times but seventy times seven" (Mt 18:22) with the call of Jesus to "be perfect, as your heavenly Father is perfect" (Mt 5:48). It is this tension that serves as the background to a much debated question: Did the churches of the New Testament, as elite groups of believers, intolerant of sin, designate certain grave sins as irremissible? Or did they take a more lenient attitude in their pastoral practice and choose to remit all sins, regardless of their gravity?[8] Certainly, there are passages in the New Testament where sin appears irremissible: Mt 12:31-32; Mk 3:28-29; Lk 12:10; Heb 6:4-6; 10:26-31; 12:15-17; 1 Jn 5:16b). While such texts may reveal intolerant elements in the primitive Church, the primary stress is to induce a Christological deci-

---

6. Adnès, "Pénitence," c. 944.

7. Rahner, *Early Church*, pp. 24–28, sees an evolution in the Church's understanding of the consequences of sin. From the time of the New Testament until the middle of the third century, the effect of sin was spoken of in mainly juridical-ethical language (the sinner being a morally inferior person) or in eschatological language (the sinner incurring God's eternal judgment). The notion of sin affecting the interior life of grace received through baptism was a later development.

8. As seen in Chapter One, the former position was the interpretation of certain Jansenist theologians such as Arnauld, the Protestant school led by Von Harnack, and the Catholic camp led by Funk and Batiffol. The latter position was taken by Morin in the sixteenth century, picked up again by the Catholic camp led by Esser and Stufler at the beginning of this century, and confirmed by Poschmann, Galtier, and Rahner, to name but a few more contemporary historians of penance.

sion: The measure to which one accepts or rejects Christ is the measure one shares in the salvation he offers.[9] Therefore it is not a question of the emphasis being on any sort of an objectively irremissible sin or even on a demand for radical ecclesial purity, but on the subjective willingness of the sinner to be open to genuine conversion.[10] The overwhelming evidence of the New Testament confirms the willingness of the Church to offer the possibility of penance and reconciliation to all sinners.

The New Testament offers neither a clear nor uniform picture of penitential procedures used in the treatment of postbaptismal sinners. Certainly there are many references to the necessity of prayer for the forgiveness of sin. Not only must the sinner pray for forgiveness (Mt 6:12; Acts 8:22), but the community must also join its prayer to that of the sinner and so intercede with God on his or her behalf (Jas 5:16; 1 Jn 5:16). The efficacy of the community's prayer is based on love for one another, which is the sign of their underlying connection with Christ.[11] Also, the sinner must work for God's mercy through the performance of acts of charity (Mt 3:8; Lk 7:47; Acts 26:20; Jas 2:25; Rev 2:5). These works signify to the community the good intention of the offender to make amends for the transgression. The community helps only after they have judged that the sinner has done everything possible to obtain forgiveness and is truly contrite.[12]

Yet prayer and good works as solutions to everyday sin are enjoined on all those who are serious about following Christ (Mt 6:1-6, 16-18). As for the situation of very grave sinners, ecclesial procedures evolved only gradually, developing from the penitential liturgies of postexilic Israel, the institutional discipline of rabbinic Judaism, as well as the more charismatic practices of groups such

---

9. Adnès, "Pénitence," c. 954–955.

10. Poschmann, *Paenitentia Secunda*, pp. 13–14, 38–52, 71–80; Murphy-O'Connor, "Péché et communauté," pp. 170–173.

11. Poschmann, *Paenitentia Secunda*, p. 80.

12. Murphy-O'Connor, "Péché et communauté," pp. 168–169. Penitential practices found in the Old Testament find a place in the good works of the early Christians: fasting, taking care of the poor, laments to God. See Behm, *"metanoeð, metanoia,"* pp. 980–982.

as the Essenes.[13] Whatever the source, the purpose is clear: that the Church might reflect by its practice the sinner's relationship with Christ, damaged or broken through sin. Certain penitential practices are discernible in the Gospels and the Acts of the Apostles, as well as the Pauline Epistles and later New Testament writings, practices that will be foundational in a developed order of penitents in the following centuries.

A. THE GOSPELS AND THE ACTS OF THE APOSTLES

1. *EXOMOLOGEISTHAI TAS HAMARTIAS* ("CONFESS YOUR SINS")

The term *homologeō* (and its derivatives, including *exomologēsis*) is employed with a variety of meanings throughout the entire New Testament. While its secular Greek meaning, "to promise," "to agree," appears (Acts 7:17), the more properly Christian usage of the term has been more influenced by its Old Testament and Septuagint roots, "to bear witness," "to praise," 'to make solemn statements of faith" (Mt 10:32; 16:16; 27:54; Mk 8:29; 14:62; 15:39; Lk 12:8; Jn 11:27).[14] The public confession of Christ before all people

---

13. A detailed study of the Old Testament roots of *metanoia* and penance would take us beyond the limits of this study. For penitential liturgies of postexilic Israel, see E. Lipinski, *La liturgie pénitentielle dans la Bible*, Lectio Divina 52 (Paris, 1969); A. Marcen Tihista, "Liturgias penitenciales en el Antiguo Testamento," in *El sacramento de la Penitencia, XXX Semana española de teología, Madrid, 1970* (Madrid, 1972), pp. 85–104; R. Koch, "La rémission et la confession des péchés selon l'Ancien Testament," *Studia Moralia* 10 (1972) 219–247. For post-temple Judaism, see M. Arranz, "La liturgie pénitentielle juive après la destruction du Temple," in *Liturgie et rémission des péchés*, Bibliotheca Ephemerides Liturgicae, Subsidia 3 (Rome, 1975), pp. 39–56. For rabbinic discipline, especially the synagogal ban, and the manuscripts from Qumran, see P. Galtier, *Aux origines du sacrement de pénitence* (Rome, 1951), pp. 1–32; J. Schmitt, "Contribution à l'étude de la discipline pénitentielle dans l'Eglise primitive à la lumière des textes de Qumran," in *Les manuscrits de la Mer Morte*, Colloque de Strasbourg, Mai 1955, (Paris, 1957) 93–109; W. Doskocil, *Der Bann in der Urkirche. Eine rechtsgeschichtliche Untersuchung*, MThZ 11 (Munich, 1958) 4–25; H. Thyen, *Studien zur Sündenvergebung im Neuen Testament und seinen alttestamentlichen und jüdischen Voraussetzungen*, FRLANT 96 (Göttingen, 1970); G. Forkman, *The Limits of the Religious Community. Expulsion from the Religious Community within the Qumran Sect, within Rabbinic Judaism, and within Primitive Christianity*, Coniectanea Biblica 5 (Lund, 1972).

14. O. Michel, "*Homologeō, exomologeō, anthomologeomai, homologia, homologoumenōs*," *TDNT* V, ed. G. Friedrich, trans. G. Bromiley (Grand Rapids, Mich., 1968) 199–220, pp. 207–212.

is related to the liturgical profession of faith at baptism, both being acts in praise of God. Yet prayer and praise are closely linked to confession of sin, which, from the time of John the Baptist, was a sign of true conversion of life (Mt 3:6; Mk 1:5).[15] It requires a true humility (Lk 15:17-21) that justifies the sinner more than any outward show of holiness (Lk 18:13). Though obviously a postbaptismal practice cannot be ascertained from the witness of the Gospels or the Acts of the Apostles, the roots of such a practice are already to be found here.

2. EXCLUSION FROM THE COMMUNITY

Traditionally, the power of the Church over all sin has been interpreted as stemming from the authority given by the Lord to Peter (Mt 16:19) and to the Twelve (Mt 18:18): ''. . . whatever you bind on earth shall be bound in heaven, and whatever you loose on earth shall be loosed in heaven.''[16] While these passages on their own can hardly be cited as proof texts for the Church's power to remit postbaptismal sin, they do indicate that all serious sin necessarily involves an ecclesial dimension.[17] The latter passage is of particular

---

15. Michel, *"Homologeō"* p. 215.

16. Dogmatic and exegetical studies of these passages, along with Jn 20:23, are voluminous. Of special note is B. Rigaux's excellent article: '' 'Lier et Délier'—Les ministères de réconciliation dans l'Église des temps apostoliques,'' *MD* 117 (1974) 86-135. Other recent studies include: Poschmann, *Paenitentia Secunda*, pp. 4-12; Von Campenhausen, *Ecclesial Authority*, pp. 125-141; J.-D. Didier, "D'une interprétation récente de l'expression 'lier-délier,' '' *MSR* 9 (1952) 55-62: T. Worden, "The Remission of Sins," *Scripture* 9 (1957) 65-79, 115-127; J. Emerton, "Binding and Loosing—Forgiving and Retaining," *JThS* 13 (1962) 325-331; H. Vorgrimler, "Matthieu 16, 18s. et le sacrement de pénitence," *Théologie* 56 (1963) 51-62; *id., Busse*, pp. 12-21; G. Bornkamm, "Die Binde- und Lösegewalt in der Kirche des Matthäus," in *Die Zeit Jesu* (Festschrift H. Schlier), ed. G. Bornkamm and K. Rahner (Freiburg, 1970), pp. 93-107; J. Burgess, *A History of the Exegesis of Matthew 16:17-19 from 1781 to 1965* (Ann Arbor, Mich., 1976); J. Mantey, "Distorted Translations of John 20,23; Matthew 16,18-19, and 18,18," *Review and Expositor* 78 (1981) 409-416.

17. It may be objected that the texts cited could in fact only refer to sins remitted at baptism rather than to the Church's having authority even over postbaptismal sin. Certainly Worden, "The Remission of Sins," pp. 65-68, affirms the fact that in the first three centuries, the Fathers used these texts in reference to baptismal forgiveness rather than the power to forgive sins committed after baptism (with the possible exception of Origen, *De orat.* 28,9). For a dated yet inclusive study of the patristic interpretation of these texts, see H. Bruders, "Matt. 16.19; 18.18 und Jo. 20.22-3 in frühchristlicher Auslegung," *ZKTh* 34 (1910) 659-677; 35 (1911) 79-111,

importance because it is perhaps more specifically concerned with the sin of those who already are full members of the community and comes as the climax to a definite procedure for how to manage an erring brother (or sister):

> If your brother sins against you, go and tell him his fault, between you and him alone. If he listens to you, you have gained a brother. But if he does not listen, take one or two others along with you, that every word may be confirmed by the evidence of two or three witnesses. If he refuses to listen to them, tell it to the church; and if he refuses to listen even to the church, let him be to you as a Gentile and a tax collector (Mt 18:15-17; see also Lk 17:3-4).

This passage further defines what is meant by the power of binding granted to the Twelve: the right to correct and exclude any from the community who remain obstinate in their wrongdoing.[18] It demonstrates that the early Church could not stand by idly if some of its members stood convicted of sin; it had an obligation to seek such persons out, convince them of the sin that separated them from the community, and lead them back to the life of the Church. It was the sin itself that separated the sinners from the community; the community only recognized this separation either by working to lead sinners back or by stepping away from them if they remained unwilling to change the error of their ways.[19] That such a procedure

---

292-346, 466-481, 690-713. R. Brown, *The Gospel According to John*, Vol. II: *Chapters XIII-XXI*, AB 29A (New York, 1970), pp. 1039-1045, agrees with Worden but goes on to say that there is not enough exegetical evidence to prove only a baptismal remission of sin in Jn 20:23. The Church's authority over all sin, including postbaptismal sin, is implied here. It is this interpretation that has come to be most strongly affirmed in Christian tradition.

18. È. Cothenet, "Sainteté de l'Église et péchés de chrétiens. Comment le N.T. envisage-t-il leur pardon?" *NRTh* 96 (1974) 449-470, pp. 467ff., rather than connecting Mt 18:18 to verses 15-17 (which has led to the interpretation that "binding" and "loosing" included a disciplinary action of excluding and readmitting to the community erring sinners), prefers to connect 18:18 to verses 10-14, the parable of the lost sheep. In this way 18:18 would only refer to an institution of salvation to "win" the sinner rather than a specific action taken by the community. However, as will be seen below, the close parallel to rabbinic practice (Lev 19:17; Deut 19:15) and the Qumran documents (CD IX,2-8; 1QS V,24-26; VI,1) must at least keep one open to the possibility of the texts' having both a disciplinary and eschatological intent.

19. J. Bernhard, "Excommunication et pénitence-sacrement aux premiers siècles de l'Église," *RDC* 15 (1965) 265-280, 318-330; 16 (1966) 41-70, pp. 269-272.

was not solely juridical but possessed an eschatological dimension affecting the sinner's relationship with God is confirmed by the post-resurrection words of Jesus found in John's Gospel: "If you forgive the sins of any, they are forgiven; if you retain the sins of any, they are retained" (20:23). The effect of sin vis-à-vis one's relationship with the community confirmed one's ultimate relationship with God. Therefore, it can be said that Matthew's terminology of "binding and loosing" and John's "forgiving and retaining" are complementary notions that express both the internal and external reality of the relationship with God and the Church of one who sins after baptism.[20]

The procedure of fraternal correction and the banning of obstinate sinners from the community was not without precedent in the religious milieu of the time. In the writings of rabbinic Judaism and in the Qumran manuscripts, similar disciplinary procedures are found. In the case of a synagogal ban, action against an erring member could be taken for either a set period of time (usually thirty days) or, in cases of heresy or very grave faults, indefinitely. Such measures not only preserved the purity of Israel as God's chosen people but served as a disciplinary action to coerce the sinner to repent and return to the synagogue.[21] However, while the primitive Christians might have taken the practice over, the emphasis seems to have been more decisively on the side of coercing an erring brother or sister to repent. Though sin was not expected after baptism, the fact that Christians wished to "win back" the sinner indicates that the ideal of a "pure community" remained an ideal and was not the primary purpose of disciplinary action taken against those who sinned after baptism.[22]

---

20. P. Adnès, "Les fondements scripturaires du sacrement de pénitence," *Esprit et Vie: L'ami du clergé* 93 (1983) 305–310, 385–392, 497–508, pp. 387–392, who demonstrates the basic similarity of meaning in both Matthew and John. See also C. Dodd, *Historical Tradition in the Fourth Gospel* (Cambridge, 1963), pp. 347–349, who maintains that John conserved a variant of a common oral tradition.

21. Forkman, *The Limits of Religious Community*, pp. 124–128; Galtier, *Aux origines du sacrement de pénitence*, pp. 26–30; Adnès, "Pénitence," c. 947–948. See above, n. 18; below, n. 31.

22. Bernhard, "Excommunication et pénitence," p. 274, who cites numerous passages from the New Testament to show that the early Christians saw themselves as a Church of both saints and sinners.

In the Acts of the Apostles, two instances of grave postbaptismal sin are especially noteworthy: the story of Ananias and Sapphira (5:1-11) and the account of Simon the magician (8:20-24). In the first, two members of the community are struck dead as a result of their selfishness. Though the story could be seen as a justification of the purity of the early Christian community, which allowed no sin after baptism, it is better interpreted with an eschatological message: The future result of sin is death. The fact that the persons involved had no chance to repent points to the paraenetical purpose of the passage.[23] In the case of Simon the magician, who wants to "buy" the power of conferring the Holy Spirit, Peter's stern correction leads him to seek repentance. It shows, as has been seen in Matthew's threefold correction, that the Church's role is to coerce the sinner through chastisement to turn from sin and repent. For those who do so, no sin is too grave for forgiveness.[24]

B. THE PAULINE LETTERS AND LATER NEW TESTAMENT WRITINGS

1. CONFESSION OF SIN

As in the Gospels and the Acts of the Apostles, there is witness in these writings to *exomologēsis* as a practice that has been defined as "a contrite consciousness of guilt, linked to a desire and prayer for forgiveness."[25] However, that this practice was closely linked to postbaptismal sin is clearer in the later works of the New Testament. According to Jas 5:16, it is an individual and personal act through which the sins of the members of the community are made known to one another: "Confess your sins to one another, and pray for one another, that you may be healed."[26] This mutuality of confession is also intimated in 1 Jn 1:9, where the author seems to make

---

23. Bernhard, "Excommunication et pénitence," 274–275, against Doskocil, *Bann in der Urkirche*, pp. 47–49, who maintained that the early Christians took over the Old Testament notion of physical death as punishment for sin.

24. Adnès, "Les fondements scripturaires," p. 498.

25. Poschmann, *PAS*, p. 17.

26. Koch, "La rémission et la confession," pp. 243–244, points out that confession in the Old Testament was normally a collective recognition of the sin of the nation. However, there is evidence, although scant, of individual confession in postexilic texts, such as Ps 51:5-6.

the practice a prerequisite for reconciliation: "If we confess our sins, he is faithful and just, and will forgive our sins and cleanse us from all unrighteousness."[27]

It has been debated whether confession of sin in the primitive Church was public or private. At particular moments in history this debate was clearly anachronistic, born out of a desire to find justification or fault in a current practice.[28] It appears that the confession practice of the apostolic Church was public, at least to some extent, in order to allow the community to pray for the sinner. Yet, what is more notable for the present study is that the practice of confession itself receives testimony from later New Testament texts as a remedy for postbaptismal sin.

2. EXCLUSION FROM THE COMMUNITY

In agreement with the tradition of the Gospels, the Pauline Epistles and later New Testament writings witness to the practice of disciplinary exclusion of the grave sinner from the community, leading Rahner to state that "the original biblical notion of church penance is that of a penance of excommunication."[29] The term "excommunication" is misleading here if it leads one to believe that an action is being directly incurred against the sinner.[30] Only in 1 Cor 5:1-13 might such an interpretation be possible; there the community is told to "drive out the wicked person from among you"

---

27. While some have interpreted *homologeō* here to mean confession of faith (as it is used in 1 Jn 2:23; 4:2ff., 15), most commentators see it as a reference to a confession of sins, either before God (R. Bultmann, *The Johannine Epistles*, Hermeneia, trans. R. O'Hara [Philadelphia, 1973], pp. 21-22), or before the community (R. Brown, *The Epistles of John*, AB 30 [New York, 1982], pp. 207-208).

28. It is not surprising that the Council of Trent (1551), Session 14, *De Sacramento Poenitentiae*, c. 6 (Coleti 20:100), found justification in 1 Jn 1:9 for a private sacramental confession in the New Testament Church. This position, held by Catholic exegetes since that time, has, for the most part, been abandoned today.

29. Rahner, *Early Church*, p. 63. Rahner is correct to such a degree as he is referring to the new status of a believer in relationship to the community due to sin, and the need to restore the sinner back to his or her original status in the community prior to sin. However, as has been stated previously, the use of the term "excommunication" may confuse the necessary distinction between a modern juridic understanding of excommunication and the biblical practice of isolating a sinner from the community.

30. Von Campenhausen, *Ecclesiastical Authority*, pp. 142-144.

(5:13). Authority of the Apostle Paul passes authority to the community, which in turn has the power to expel the sinner (5:3-5).[31] Yet, even here the primary action is to be taken by the community indirectly rather than directly by the sinner; it is they who must effect the sinner's isolation.[32]

The tone of this text might be interpreted to emphasize the spiritual danger the community would be exposed to from association with such a sinner (5:6-11). It cannot be denied that Paul fears the contagion of sin. However, the key concern of the text is for the sinner: ". . .you are to deliver this man to Satan for the destruction of the flesh, that his spirit may be saved in the day of the Lord Jesus" (5:5).[33] The term *paradounai tō satana* seems to be almost a technical term used by Paul to connote an isolation of the offender from the community so that such a one might be led to repentance.[34] It is a connotation not inconsistent with 1 Tim 1:20 concerning the fate of the blasphemers Hymenaeus and Alexander. Though it is peculiar that Paul would have implied a partnership with Satan in

---

31. This interpretation might also apply to 1 Tim 1:18-20; however, Forkman, *Limits of the Religious Community*, pp. 186–187, sees a development in the New Testament in the form of expulsion practiced by the community from the charismatic (1 Cor 5:5) to the juridical (1 Tim 1:19-20). In the latter case, the leaders of the community would be forced to admit that the authority of their word only extended to the community itself and had no direct effect on the sinner.

32. This idea might be better understood by the use of an analogy. If an entire Christian community was lined up side by side, directly isolating a sinner would be tantamount to asking him or her to take one step forward away from the group, whereas indirectly isolating a sinner would be equivalent to asking the community to take a step back away from the sinner. It is the latter action that is more usually found in the New Testament and the postapostolic writings. The designation of this action as an "indirect" coercive penance of isolation is more descriptive and less clumsy than Hoh's nomenclature for the same procedure as a "Christian boycott" (*Die kirchliche Busse*, pp. 75ff.).

33. J. Dauvillier, *Les temps apostoliques, Ier siècle*, Vol. II of Histoire du droit et des institutions de l'Église en Occident, ed. G. LeBras (Paris, 1968), pp. 585–586, and Hein, *Eucharist and Excommunication*, pp. 92–96, see both the purgative (for the purity of the Church) and medicinal (for the sake of the sinner) dimensions in Paul's action. However, Bernhard, "Excommunication et pénitence," pp. 276–280, sees the emphasis much more clearly on the medicinal.

34. Against the position of Doskocil, *Bann in der Urkirche*, pp. 62ff., Bernhard, "Excommunication et pénitence," pp. 277–280, understands Paul to be giving a Christian interpretation to the Jewish conception of death: isolation from the community, which meant isolation from God. See above, n. 23.

the ultimate salvation of the sinner, it may well have been a common term in antiquity and one that had precedent even in the torment of Job in the Old Testament.[35] Therefore, if it is possible to maintain that Paul's words are first and foremost directed to the community rather than to the sinner, and that it is the repentance of the sinner that is the primary purpose of the action, then the description of 1 Cor 5:1-13 is an example of what we have designated as an indirect coercive penance of isolation.

Other passages that speak of a separation of a sinner from the community echo the threefold fraternal correction of Mt 18:15-17 and, in the most serious cases, lead to the indirect isolation of the sinner by the community for the sake of his or her own salvation (2 Thess 3:6, 14-15; 1 Tim 5:19-22; Titus 3:10-11). This isolation is total. The faithful not only close their Eucharistic gatherings to the sinner but also treat the person as a social outcast, an untouchable. Such an isolation can be temporary if the sinner repents and expresses a desire to be reconciled. In this way a sin is considered "bound," not as a punishment, nor even solely for the sake of the purity of the community, but as a measure of clemency. It is through the indirect coercive penance of isolation that the sinner has the possibility of being "loosed" from sin and so come once more into right relationship with the Church. Given the prevailing New Testament ecclesiology of *extra Ecclesiam nulla salus*, being in right relationship with the Church is the only way one could be assured of the possibility of being in right relationship with God.[36]

3. RECONCILIATION WITH THE CHURCH

There remains a question as to whether there is any clear text in the New Testament referring to a specific action of reconciliation with the community of one guilty of postbaptismal sin. Commentators from the patristic era until the present have interpreted 2 Cor 2:5-11 as a reference by Paul to the incident of exclusion mentioned in 1 Cor 5:1-13. However, present opinion has generally abandoned this view, preferring instead to see in the passage from 2 Corinthians a reference by Paul to someone by whom he has been personally

---

35. Hein, *Eucharist and Excommunication*, pp. 94–95.
36. Lefévre, "Péché et pénitence," p. 21

attacked and who, as a consequence, has been rejected by the Corinthian church.[37]

Much debate has occurred concerning the text of 1 Tim 5:22: "Do not be hasty in the laying on of hands, nor participate in another man's sins; keep yourself pure." The question centers on whether this passage refers to the ordination of presbyters or to the reconciliation of sinners.[38] Certainly there is evidence that makes it possible to construe the meaning of the text in either direction. Yet even in the face of strong evidence that the laying on of hands is in reference to the ordination of presbyters, this conclusion is not totally adequate in light of the unusual phrase *mēde koinōnei hamartiais allotriais*.[39] Due to the ambiguity created by this phrase, it is impossible to know with certainty the original historicity of this verse. Therefore, it would not be imprudent to leave open the possibility that 1 Tim 5:22 is the earliest reference to an actual reconciliation rite through the imposition of hands.[40]

---

37. See the excellent discussion of this question in V. Furnish, *II Corinthians*, AB 32A (New York, 1984), pp. 160–168; also, C. Barnett, *A Commentary on the Second Epistle to the Corinthians*, Black's New Testament Commentaries (London, 1973), pp. 89–93, 212–214.

38. The former position has most recently been taken by N. Adler, "Die Handauflegung im NT bereits ein Bussritus? Zur Auslegung von I Tim. 5,22," in *Neutestamentliche Aufsätze* (Festschrift J. Schmid), ed. J. Blinzler, O. Kuss, and F. Mussner (Regensburg, 1963), 1–6; J. Kelly, *A Commentary on the Pastoral Epistles*, Black's New Testament Commentaries, ed. H. Chadwick (London, 1963; reprint 1972), pp. 127–128. The latter position has been held by P. Galtier, "La réconciliation des pécheurs dans la première épître a Timothée," *RSR* 39 (1951) 317–320; M. Dibelius and H. Conzelmann, *The Pastoral Epistles*, Hermeneia, trans. P. Buttolph and A. Yarbro, ed. H. Koester (Philadelphia, 1972), p. 80; Von Campenhausen, *Ecclesiastical Authority*, pp. 147–148, n. 133, who also lists earlier authors who have taken either one or the other position.

39. The evidence in favor of such an interpretation lies not only in the fact that there are other instances in the New Testament where the imposition of hands is a clear reference to ordination (Acts 6:6; 1 Tim 4:14; 2 Tim 1:6), but also that prior to the witness of the *Didascalia*, Origen, and Cyprian in the third century, there is no other undisputed testimony to the reconciliation of sinners through the imposition of hands.

40. Murphy-O'Connor, "Péché et communauté," pp. 173–175. Von Campenhausen, *Ecclesiastical Authority*, p. 148, makes the point that "the composition of the Pastoral Epistles was at the very end of the sub-apostolic period," composed after some of the writings of the postapostolic writers. In this way, they are not as far away from the third-century witnesses as first appears. This position is confirmed by Dibelius/Conzelmann, *The Pastoral Epistles*, pp. 4ff.

CONCLUSION

In the New Testament witness to penitential procedures, no uniform discipline is practiced by the Church toward postbaptismal offenses. The apostles knew only that the Church must somehow continue the mission of Jesus, who forgave sinners. However, in addition to the constant exhortations to pray and perform works of mercy for the forgiveness of sin, specific practices that will form the backbone of later penitential procedures imposed upon, and/or undertaken by, those guilty of grave postbaptismal sin can be identified: mutual confession of sin as an external sign of contrition; the indirect isolation of the sinner by the community (if the offender, following upon the procedure of Mt 18:15-17, refused to heed private fraternal correction), in order to coerce him or her to turn away from sin and experience conversion; and, possibly, a specific action of reconciling the sinner back to the Church. In all such practices the role of the community is paramount, constantly exhorting the transgressor to repentance (Gal 6:1ff.; 2 Tim 2:25) so that such a one might die to sin and have life again in Christ.

II. THE WITNESS OF THE POSTAPOSTOLIC WRITERS

Contemporary with the end of the New Testament era and extending to the middle of the second century, the works of the postapostolic writers can hardly be classified as a homogeneous collection. These writings originated in all corners of the Roman Empire and treat very different concerns of the young, struggling communities, particularly the preservation of the churches from false prophets and doctrines in the light of an imminent eschatological expectation. Yet their content and style echo the literature of the New Testament.[41] This fact is no less true in their witness to penitential practices for postbaptismal sinners. Following the principle announced in 1 Pet 4:8 that "love covers a multitude of sins," there are a plethora of references to the necessity of prayer, fasting, and the giving of alms as remedies for sin (*I Clem.* 40; *Did.* 4,6; 7,1; 8,2; Justin's *Dial.* 90,141, *Apol.* 1,61; *Barn.* 19,10; *II Clem.* 16,14). These

---

41. Quasten, *Patrology* I, p. 40.

are necessary for the day-by-day conversion of life that every Christian must be willing to undertake.[42]

As much as these writings call the early communities to holiness, they are not unaware of the presence of sin among Christians. It is not just the daily faults that the above references treat but even grave offenses such as apostasy, adultery, pride, and hatred (*I Clem.* 30,1; Ignatius' *Philad.* 7,2; 8,1; *Trall.* 8,2; Polycarp's *Phil.* 11,4), all found among the Christians. As in the New Testament, the postapostolic writings maintain the ideal of holiness while at the same time allowing for the possibility of conversion and forgiveness of those guilty of any postbaptismal sin. It is the responsibility of the community to intercede for the sinner through their prayers and fraternal correction (*I Clem.* 56,1-2; 59,4–60,3; *Did.* 4,3; *II Clem.* 17,1-2). Repentance is never solely personal; it necessarily involves the cooperation of the entire Church. As we shall see, only in cases of obstinacy on the part of the sinner is the possibility of reintegration into the community to be denied.[43]

These writings also attest to the gradual rise of the authority of specific elders in the local churches; they play a more centralizing role in the development of the communities' life and worship.[44] In regard to penitential practices for postbaptismal sinners, the role of bishops and presbyters comes more into focus than in the New Testament (*I Clem.* 57,1; Ignatius' *Phil.* 3,2; 8,1; *Did.* 10,6; Polycarp's *Phil.* 6,1). This fact serves to highlight the inseparable connection between the growth of institutional ministry in the early Church and the development of the Church's penitential practices. As the former becomes more clearly defined and structured, so will the latter.[45]

---

42. Poschmann, *PAS*, pp. 21–22.

43. *Ibid.*, pp. 20, 23–24.

44. Von Campenhausen, *Ecclesiastical Authority*, pp. 184ff., who posits that the balance between the authority arising from the charismatic gifts of the whole community and the more institutional authority of bishops and presbyters, maintained in the New Testament, begins to tilt toward the latter group in the postapostolic writings.

45. *Ibid.*, pp. 124ff. Along with Von Campenhausen, it could be said that the controversies surrounding the Church's power to remit postbaptismal sin, especially poignant in the rise of Montanism and Novatianism in the first three centuries, will be a strong contributing factor in the eventual rise of a monarchical episcopacy by the end of the third century.

Yet, with regard to specific procedures for grave sinners, the witness of the writers of the postapostolic era is as undefined as the testimony of the New Testament. In a general way it can be said that two actions emerge that seem to be distinctly connected to serious postbaptismal sin, both of which have already been attested to in the New Testament: confession of sin (*exomologēsis*) and the coercive isolation of the sinner by the community.[46] In the examination of the specific postapostolic writings to follow, these penitential actions will form the focus of our study.[47]

A. CLEMENT OF ROME (C. 95–98 A.D.)

In his *Epistle to the Corinthians*, Clement hopes to restore peace to the Corinthian community, divided by bitter internal rivalries and dissension.[48] Throughout the work he pleads for the reestablishment of integrality based on the natural order: the precepts of the Old Testament, the work of the Spirit, and the authority of the apostles.[49]

---

46. Bernhard, "Excommunication et pénitence," p. 41, held the position that the two experiences were two different expressions of the "power of the keys": confession (*exomologēsis*) was properly sacramental, while isolation (excommunication) was juridical. While we agree that the two are not connected in either the New Testament or in the postapostolic writings, his appreciation of the practice of confession as medicinal for all sins, no matter how grave, seems to assign too much to what Poschmann called "an everyday act of repentance" (*Paenitentia Secunda*, pp. 92ff.). Further, if Grotz had treated these works in detail, he would have applauded Bernhard's position, which drew a distinction even from the time of the New Testament, between exclusion of the sinner and ecclesial penance. We prefer to maintain, with Poschmann and Rahner, that while confession of sin was a penitential expression in the early Church, practiced by *all* sinners, including grave ones, the isolation of sinners from the community was an action that recognized the fundamentally changed status of the offender in the community and therefore was more integral to the development of the later order of penitents.

47. As stated previously, there is no pellucid witness in the first two centuries to any specific action of reconciling a sinner to the Church, save for the tenuous evidence of 1 Tim 5:22. However, it seems probable that for those who were isolated from the community and subsequently repented, the presbyters had the responsibility of reintegrating (informally?) the sinner into the community (*I Clem.* 57,1; Polycarp's *Phil.* 6,1-2).

48. A. Jaubert, *Clément de Rome: Epître aux Corinthiens*, SC 167 (Paris, 1971), pp. 23ff. Direct citations will be from this edition and will be indicated by page number.

49. A. Faivre, "Le 'système normatif' dans la lettre de Clément de Rome aux Corinthiens," *RevSR* 54 (1980) 129–152.

Those who have been the cause of divisions in the community must be willing to change their ways:

> It is better for one to confess his sins than to harden his heart, as the heart of those who rebelled against Moses, the servant of God, was hardened . . .(51,3).[50]

The confession of sin could suggest a general liturgical expression of offenses, similar to the penitential liturgies of Judaism. This position is supported by Clement's use of the penitential Psalm 51 (18,16; 52,4) and his inclusion of solemn liturgical prayers (59–61). Both references reflect the strong Hellenistic-Jewish influences present in the entire work.[51] How such a liturgical confession of fault might have taken place is described by Clement:

> Let us act quickly to remove this [evil]; and let us fall down before the Master, beseeching Him with tears, that he become merciful and be reconciled to us and reestablish us in the honored and holy practice of fraternal love (48,1).[52]

In this way the practice of confession could be seen in relation to the liturgical assembly of the Christians.

Clement witnesses to the need for Christians to practice fraternal correction with one another (56,2). This is perhaps a reference to at least the first stage of Matthew's threefold process. He exhorts those who have caused dissension to be humble and submit to the authority of the legitimate leaders of the community:

---

50. *Kalon gar anthrōpō exomologeisthai peri tōn paraptōmatōn ē sklērynai tēn kardian autou, kathōs esklērynthē hē kardia tōn stasiasantōn pros ton theraponta tou theou . . .* (Jaubert, pp. 182, 84; trans. F. Glimm, *The Apostolic Fathers*, FC 1 [Washington, 1947], pp. 48–49).

Poschmann, *PAS*, p. 22, n. 23, believes that this is the only use of *exomologēsis* by Clement where the confession of sin is explicitly meant. Other references have the more scriptural meaning of "praise" (26,3; 48,2; 52,1.2; 6,3). However, Bernhard, "Excommunication et pénitence," p. 49, may be correct in adducing a penitential meaning in 52,1.2.

51. Jaubert, pp. 35–41, 46–52. Even the use of Old Testament figures (7,5–8,5) could be a reference to the postexilic liturgies of penance. See also Behm, "*metanoeō, metanoia,*" pp. 981–982.

52. *Exarōmen oun touto en tachei kai prospesōmen tō despotē kai klausōmen iketeuontes auton, hopōs hileōs genomenos epikatallagē hēmin kai epi tēn semnēn tēs philadelphias hēmōn hagnēn agōgēn apokatastēsē hēmas* (Jaubert, p. 178). To Bernhard, "Excommunication et pénitence," pp. 49–50, this is a foundational reference to a specific rite of exomologesis.

. . . for it is better for you to be found among the smallest of the elect of the flock of Christ, than to be highly exalted and be rejected from His hope (57,2).[53]

Yet, in point of fact, Clement does not make any reference to an explicit discipline of isolating an unrepentant sinner; rather, he pleads with those guilty of schism to leave the community so that peace may once again reign (54). To volunteer such an action would prove their love for their brothers and sisters. For it is only genuine love of neighbor that restores a sinner to life.[54]

B. IGNATIUS OF ANTIOCH (C. 110 A.D.)

The seven letters of Ignatius manifest a concern over the situation of those who had gone over to the heresy of the Judaizers and the Docetists, exhorting them to submit once again to established ecclesiastical authority. A developed picture of hierarchical ministry is in evidence, especially in the central role of the bishop in the life of the community (*Phil.* 7,1; *Smyrn.* 8,2).[55] It is he who enforces the primary place of the Eucharist, around which revolves all ecclesial discipline (*Trall.* 7,2). Yet even with such a strong emphasis on the Eucharist, there is no direct mention of any confession practice in any of the letters, certainly not within a liturgical context.[56]

Ignatius is a much stronger witness to the scriptural practice of an indirect coercive penance of isolation. Heretics who have disrupted the unity of the Church must be shunned:

---

53. . . . . *ameinon gar estin hymin, en tō poimniō tou Christou mikrous kai ellogimous heurethēnai, ē kath' hyperochēn dokountas ekriphēnai ek tēs elpidos autou* (Jaubert, p. 190). While this has been interpreted as an explicit reference to an ecclesial disciplinary exclusion, it is too imprecise to warrant such a strict interpretation. The same can be said of 28,1; 46,8; 59,1.

54. Hein, *Eucharist and Excommunication*, pp. 205–206; S. Hall, "Repentance in I Clement," SP 8 [=TU 93] (1963) 30–43, pp. 39–42; Doskocil, *Bann in der Urkirche*, pp. 131–132.

55. P. Hamell, *Handbook of Patrology* (New York, 1968), pp. 29–30. Direct citations will be from J. Fischer, *Die Apostolischen Väter* (Darmstadt, 1970), pp. 142–225, and will be indicated by page and line numbers.

56. Though the term *exomologēsis* is not used by Ignatius, Bernhard, "Excommunication et pénitence," p. 52, insists that his use of *metanoia* implies a penitential institution connected with the Eucharist. If this implies a liturgical confession rather than the isolation of the sinner, this seems to read too much into the text.

I warn you beforehand against wild beasts in the shape of men;
not only must you not receive them but, if possible, not even to
meet them. . . (*Smyrn.* 4,1).[57]

While the isolation is to keep the sin of the offender from contaminat-
ing the faith of the Church, its proper purpose is to gain the repentance and conversion of the sinner. The above passage continues:

. . . only you must pray for them, so that they might repent, as
difficult as this is. Yet Jesus Christ has such a power, Himself who
is our true life.[58]

Such a repentance reunites the sinners with the Church and allows
the peace of Christ to reign once more (*Phil.* 3,2; 8,1). Yet it is not
an exclusion imposed directly upon the sinner. Ignatius only exhorts
the communities to avoid the heretic due to the serious nature of
the offense. In this sense it is an indirect isolation that Ignatius hopes
will coerce the wrongdoers to experience a change of heart.[59]

C. THE *DIDACHE* (C. 100–120 A.D.)

The earliest extant Christian text that can be classified as a
"Church order," the *Didache,* allows a unique glance into the disciplinary and liturgical life of the primitive Church, while perhaps
raising as many questions as it solves. Its many different literary
styles and the shift from the paraenetic "Two Ways" in the first
six chapters to its more practical exposition of rules of worship and

---

57. *Prophylassō de hymas apo tōn thēriōn tōn anthrōpomorphōn, hous ou monon dei hymas mē paradechesthai all' ei dynaton mēde synantan* . . . (Fischer, 206:11-12). See also *Ephes.* 7,1; *Smyrn.* 7,2).

58. . . . *monon de proseuchesthai hyper autōn, ean pōs metanoēsōsin, hoper dyskolon. Toutou de echei exousian Iēsous Christos, to alēthinon hēmōn zēn* (Fischer, 206:12-14. See also *Ephes* 10,1.

59. Hein, *Eucharist and Excommunication,* p. 217. Von Campenhausen, *Ecclesiasti-cal Authority,* pp. 142–144) rightly points out that a bishop of the apostolic period, after the example of 2 Jn 10–11; Tit 3:10-11; *Did.* 11,1; 12,1, realized that all he could do in this matter was to instruct his people to stay away from those who fell into heresy because "any sentence he may pass on the heretics will have no significance for them" (p. 143). Even when Ignatius instructs Polycarp to beware of heretics, he does not instruct him to exclude them but only to stand firm in his own faith (*Poly-carp* 2,1-2).

community life in the following chapters make it hardly possible to accept the text as a literary unit. More likely it is the result of a redactor who combined different texts that could well date from different periods.[60] The place of the work's origin is difficult to pinpoint—perhaps Syria, Palestine, or Egypt.[61]

Less equivocally than other contemporary works, the *Didache* calls for confession of sin when the Eucharistic assembly is gathered:

> In the assembly, you will confess your sins and not come to prayer with a bad conscience (4,14).

> And on the day of the Lord, assemble for the breaking of the bread and the Eucharist, after having first confessed your sins, so that your sacrifice may be pure" (14,1).[62]

The expression *ou proseleusē epi proseuchēn sou* used in the first text evokes a picture of Jewish cultic prayer, resonant with the "place of prayer" found in Acts 16:13. In addition, the literary similarity between *syneidēsei* and "synagogue" gives further credence to this picture.[63] It might be imagined that the communal confession of sin within the context of the Christian liturgy (14,1) is rooted in and developed from Jewish cultic practice. As was noted in the letter

---

60. J. Audet, *La Didachè. Instructions des apôtres* (Paris, 1958), pp. 104–120; W. Rordorf and A. Tuilier, *La doctrine des douze apôtres (Didachè)*, SC 248 (Paris, 1978), pp. 17–21. While both authors have different theories concerning the composition of individual sections of the work, both agree that chapters 1–10 are earlier than chapters 11–16. Direct citations will be from the latter edition and will be indicated by page and line numbers.

61. Hamell, *Handbook*, p. 24.

62. 4,14: *En ekklèsia exomologèsē ta paraptōmata sou kai ou proseleusē epi proseuchēn sou en syneidēsei ponēra* (Rordorf/Tuilier, (164:27-29);

14,1: *Kata kyriakēn de kyriou synachthentes klasate arton kai eucharistēsate, prosexomologēsamenoi ta paraptōmata hymōn, hopōs kathara hē thysia hymōn ē* (Rordorf/Tuilier, 192:1-3). The latter text might well have been composed later in the second century as a more precise directive to the liturgical instruction of 9–10. See Audet, *La Didachè*, pp. 459–463. Further, parallel texts of 4,14 in *Barn.* 19,12, *Can. apost.* (short version, 11), and *Const. apost.* 14,3; 17,1 exclude *en ekklēsia*, which may point to its being a later addition in the *Didache*. See S. Giet, "Pénitence ou repentance dans le Pasteur d'Hermas," *RDC* 17 (1967) 15–30, pp. 26–29; W. Rordorf, "La rémission des péchés selon la Didachè," *Irénikon* 46 (1973) 283–297, p. 286, n. 1.

63. S. Giet, *L'énigme de la Didachè*, Publications de la faculté des lettres de l'université de Strasbourg 149 (Paris, 1970), p. 88; Rordorf/Tuilier, p. 165, n. 6.

of Clement of Rome, such a liturgical confessional practice might even have been expressed through a set formula.[64]

The practice of confession found in these passages from the *Didache* reflects a concern to call believers to true *metanoia*, to take seriously the demands of the gospel. Not only is it a conversion that goes beyond the Eucharistic meal to touch on all aspects of life, but it is a requirement especially grave in relation to Christian worship (10,6).[65] The Eucharist stands at the center of the primitive experience of Church. Here Christ is truly present. Only those who are disposed to his presence, who are at peace with each person in the community, can draw near to him in worship (14,2).[66] This repentance might involve a temporary self-exclusion from the Eucharist until a person's offense could be rectified. Therefore, the liturgical setting of the confessional action first and foremost sets in relief the purity demanded of any who would partake of the Eucharist. It is how the members of the community remind themselves and one another of the serious *metanoia* necessary to enter the presence of the Lord.[67]

In the case of those whose sin is known to the Church but who refuse to take the necessary measures to redress the wrong com-

---

64. Poschmann, *Paenitentia Secunda*, pp. 90ff., perhaps along the lines of the *Confiteor*. Rordorf/Tuilier, p. 68, suggests the prayer of *I Clem* 60,1-2 as an example of a communal confession of sin. See also Rordorf, "La rémission des péchés," p. 287.

65. A. Vööbus, *Liturgical Traditions of the Didache* (Stockholm, 1968), pp. 73–74, maintains that the exhortation of 10,6 ("If someone is holy, let them come; if someone is not, let them do penance") was a call to conversion and was not at all within a liturgical context. Those unworthy of the Eucharist would not have been present to hear the exhortation in the first place.

66. Hein, *Eucharist and Excommunication*, pp. 197–198, n. 17, who convincingly argues that the conversion required of Christians in the *Didache* is more in line with Mt 5:23, which bids the Christian to do whatever is necessary to make peace with one's brother or sister rather than allow a liturgical separation between the baptized and nonbaptized. Rordorf/Tuilier, pp. 69–70, further identifies the reference to Mk 11:25, which enunciates a general principle rather than the specific context of Mt 5:23, which concerns temple sacrifice in Jerusalem.

67. Rordorf, "La rémission des péchés," pp. 286–288; Hein, *Eucharist and Excommunication*, pp. 197–198. Bernhard, "Excommunication et pénitence," pp. 46–48, is correct in his criticism of Poschmann, who held that only light sins were submitted to the practice of liturgical confession. However, it is not so much a question of the degree of sins but their publicity and the attitude of the sinner that determined whether such a person would be further subject to fraternal correction and even isolation from the community. See 1 Cor 11:28.

mitted, fraternal correction is necessary, in imitation of at least the first stage of Matthew's threefold process (*Did.* 2,7; 4,3; 15,3). However, in the most serious cases the community is to isolate the sinner:

> Correct one another, not in anger but in peace, as you have it in the gospel, and do not speak to that person who has harmed a neighbor, nor is such a one to hear a word from you until he has repented (15,3).[68]

The action described here is reminiscent of the isolation demanded in the New Testament and in the other postapostolic writers, where it is indirectly asked of the community rather than directly imposed upon the transgressor. And as the corrective action is to be taken "not in anger but in peace," it appears more coercive than hard, penal medicine for the salvation of the erring member of the community.[69] In the tradition of the early Church, the *Didache* can be said to witness to the discipline of an indirect coercive penance of isolation.

What is unique about the testimony of the *Didache* concerning penitential practices for those guilty of postbaptismal sin is its apparent connection between the absolute necessity of conversion and one's readiness to partake of the Eucharist. The liturgical confession of faults serves as a reminder that if one is not ready to draw near to worship, then one should repent, meaning a temporary self-exclusion until one's sin is rectified, or even an indirect coercive penance of isolation if the person remains recalcitrant. It cannot be said that the *Didache* definitively connects the practice of a liturgical confession of faults with the procedure of being isolated from the community. Nonetheless, the purpose of both practices points to a dual emphasis: the Eucharist is central in the life of the community, and true worship demands that the members of the community live up to the standards set down by the gospel.[70] The status of the offender, vis-à-vis the Church, is somewhat more defined through the public

---

68. *Elengchete de allēlous mē en orgē, all' en eirēnē, hōs echete en tō euangelio kai panti astochounti kata tou heterou mēdeis laleitō mēde par' hymōn akouetō, heōs hou metanoēsē* (Rordorf/Tuilier, 194:8-10). See above, n. 57.

69. Bernhard, "Excommunication et pénitence," pp. 323–324; Rordorf, "La rémission des péchés," pp. 294–295.

70. Vööbus, *Liturgical Traditions*, pp. 109–110.

worship of the community. This fact will be fundamental in the history of the order of penitents.[71]

D. THE EPISTLE OF BARNABAS (C. 130–140 A.D.)

Once thought to have been authored by Barnabas, the companion of Paul, this anonymous document develops a polemic against the radical Judaizers (2–17) and shares with the *Didache* the common source material known as the "Two Ways" (18–21). Like the *Didache*, its point of origin is thought to be either Alexandria, Syria, or Palestine.[72] As for practices connected with postbaptismal sin, the letter repeats the command of *Did.* 4,14: "You will confess your sins and not come to prayer with a bad conscience" (19,12).[73] However, this text is missing the *en ekklēsia* found in the verse from the *Didache*, which may argue for the epistle's priority but does not allow one to apprehend in it a Christian practice of a liturgical confession of faults.[74]

As for evidence of a disciplinary procedure of isolating postbaptismal sinners from the community, references tend to be exhortatory and paraenetic, like the overriding allegorical style of the work itself. It emphasizes the need to avoid serious offenders in order to escape contamination in the last days (4,1-2.13; 10,5; 19,4).[75] Only once does the letter hint at the practice of fraternal correction: "You will not show partiality toward persons you rebuke for their faults" (19,4).[76] Yet this command seems to be part of a group of ethical exhortations addressed to the everyday life of Christians rather than proof of some sort of juridical procedure. It is not intended to solve the situation of an erring member of the commu-

---

71. Doskocil, *Bann in der Urkirche*, pp. 116–123; Rordorf/Tuilier, pp. 179–180.

72. P. Prigent and R. Kraft, *Epître de Barnabé*, SC 172 (Paris, 1971), pp. 9–24. Direct citations will be from this edition and will be indicated by page numbers and verses.

73. *Exomologēsē epi hamartiais sou. Ou prosēxeis epi proseuchēn en syneidēsei ponēra* (Prigent/Kraft, 210:12b-c).

74. See above, n. 62. Prigent/Kraft, p. 210, n. 2, agrees that the question of a Christian confessional practice cannot be decided by this meager reference.

75. Hein, *Eucharist and Excommunication*, pp. 222–224.

76. *Ou lēmpsē prosōpon elēgxai tina epi paraptōmati* (Prigent/Kraft, 200:4c).

nity but to instruct the Church on what is to be avoided if one is to live the "way of light."[77]

E. POLYCARP OF SMYRNA (C. 135 A.D.)

Venerated because of his link with the Apostle John, who appointed him bishop of Smyrna (Eusebius, *Eccl.Hist.* V,20,5ff.), Polycarp was asked by the Philippian church for his guidance because of dissension created there by the presbyter Valens, who was accused of idolatry (3,1; 11). What resulted was his *Epistle to the Philippians*, presently considered to be in fact two letters, both authored by Polycarp, which were later incorporated into one work.[78] Like his contemporary Ignatius, Polycarp witnesses to a somewhat developed hierarchical ministry in the Church, though it would be much too overstated to contend that he knew of a monarchical episcopacy.[79] Like Ignatius, the bishop of Smyrna testifies to the growing connection between the official ministry of the Church and the ministry to postbaptismal sinners, exhorting presbyters "to lead away from wandering" those who are lost, even while being aware of their own sinfulness (6,1).[80] Yet there is no mention in the letter of any Christian practice of a liturgical confession of faults.

Consistent with other postapostolic writers, Polycarp urges the community to avoid the company of false teachers (6,3). However, in the specific case of Valens and his wife, his harsh paraenesis is tempered:

> Therefore, I am very sorry for him [Valens] and his wife; may the Lord give to them true repentance. Therefore, be very moderate yourselves in this; and do not look upon them as enemies, but

---

77. Hein, *Eucharist and Excommunication*, p. 222.

78. This is the thesis of P. Harrison, *Polycarp's Two Epistles to the Philippians* (Cambridge, 1936), *passim*, which sees the first letter as being chapter 13 (and possibly 14) of the present work and the second letter as being formed by chapters 1–12. The Greek text is extant only up to 9,2. Direct citations will be from Fischer, *Die Apostolischen Väter*, pp. 248–264, and will be indicated by page and line number.

79. P. Camelot, *Ignace d'Antioche, Polycarpe de Smyrne: Lettres, Martyre de Polycarpe*, SC 10 (Paris, 1969), p. 170, especially evident in the fact that no bishop of Philippi is mentioned, which is unusual even if the see was vacant.

80. . . . *epistrephontes ta apopeplanēmena* (Fischer, 256:3-4). See Poschmann, *Paenitentia Secunda*, pp. 101–102.

call them back as suffering and erring members, in order to save your whole body. Doing this, you edify one another (11,4).[81]

That Valens and his wife must be "called back" makes it apparent that they are outside of the community, either due to voluntary separation or to isolation by the community, or both. Yet of all the authors of the period, Polycarp is perhaps the most clear that such an isolation is not to punish the offender or to be permanent; it is undertaken by the community only to coerce such a one, no matter how serious the sin, to come to true repentance and so once more be included in the Body of Christ, the Church.[82] In suggesting how the Philippian Christians are to behave toward Valens, Polycarp witnesses to an indirect coercive penance of isolation.

F. EPISTOLA APOSTOLORUM (C. 140–160 A.D.)

Originating in either Asia Minor or Egypt, this apocryphal letter relates a series of revelations made by Christ to his disciples after his resurrection. Though epistolary in its opening chapters, the work as a whole tends to be apocalyptic in style and is an important early witness to both a developed Christology and the history of the liturgy.[83] On the question of postbaptismal sin, an exposition of the parable of the wise and foolish virgins offers the possibility of repentance for any who have sinned (Ethiopic, 54-56). There remains a question of whether the letter allows such an "indulgence" as a general principle or if it is due to the imminent end-times (along the same lines as the *Shepherd of Hermas*).[84] However, the fact that post-

---

81. "Valde ergo, fratres, constristor pro illo et pro coniuge eius, quibus det dominus paenitentiam veram. Sobrii ergo estote et vos in hoc: et non sicut inimicos tales existimetis, sed sicut passibilia membra et errantia eos revocate, ut omnium vestrum corpus salvetis. Hoc enim agentes vos ipsos aedificatis" (Fischer, 262:2-7).

For chapters 10–12, 14 we must rely on the ancient Latin manuscript. See the close parallel of 2 Thess 3:15.

82. See above, nn. 62 and 74.

83. Quasten, *Patrology* I, pp. 150–152. Editions consulted include C. Schmidt and I. Wajnberg, *Gespräche Jesu mit seinen Jüngern nach der Auferstehung*, TU 43 (Leipzig, 1919); L. Guerrier and S. Grébaut, *Le Testament en Galilée de Notre-Seigneur Jésus-Christ*, PO 9,3, ed. R. Graffin and F. Nau (Paris, 1913). The original Greek text is not extant. There is a Coptic version (incomplete), a complete Ethiopic version, and fragments of a Latin version.

84. Poschmann, *Paenitentia Secunda*, pp. 105ff., who argues from the work's imminent eschatology that the *Epistola* allows for postbaptismal forgiveness, against

baptismal repentance is allowed is what is most significant to the witness here.

The text goes on to warn the disciples of the necessity of extending correction to those who have sinned rather than repaying sin with sin. Such correction demands just judgment, which is to show favoritism to neither rich nor poor (Ethiopic, 58).[85] While this charge might at first appear as strictly paraenetic, it is immediately followed by a repetition of Matthew's threefold process of correction and isolation of the sinner (Ethiopic, 59). This may indicate that a procedure of isolating grave sinners for the sake of their own conversion is not only simply a teaching passed down from the apostles but is practiced in the life of the local churches. However, the *Epistola Apostolorum* does not connect this action with the Christian liturgy.

G. The Second Epistle Ascribed to Clement of Rome (c. 150–160 A.D.)

The oldest extant Christian homily, this pseudo-Clementine work was probably composed in Corinth, though it also contains elements that suggest an Alexandrian origin.[86] The epistle speaks of general themes of Christian life and offers a rebuttal against those who would deny the resurrection of the body (9ff.). Those who are saved by the flesh of Christ and who are to be rewarded in the last days through the resurrection of the flesh must live lives in the flesh that keep pure the *sphragis* ("seal") of their baptism, even amidst temptation (6,1-3.8-9; 7,1-2.6). Those who fail to do so will be lost (7,6). Therefore, beginning in the eighth chapter, the author frequently reminds his listeners of the necessity for repentance now, before the endtimes, while the possibility still exists.[87]

---

the earlier positions of Schmidt, pp. 380ff., and Hoh, *Die kirchliche Busse*, pp. 66ff., who argue for the work's rigorism. Poschmann's interpretation of this text has more recently been supported by Doskocil, *Bann in der Urkirche*, pp. 154–157, and attacked by M. Hornschuh, *Studien zur Epistula Apostolorum*, PTS 5 (Berlin, 1965), pp. 121–124.

85. See above, n. 76. Also, *Barn.* 19,4.

86. Quasten, *Patrology* I, pp. 53–54. Direct citations will be from K. Bihlmeyer (ed.), *Die Apostolischen Väter* (Tübingen, 1956), pp. 71–81, and will be indicated by page and line numbers.

87. See 8,1-3; 9,8; 13,1; 15,1; 16,1.4; 17,1; 19,1. K. Donfried, *The Setting of Second Clement in Early Christianity*, SuppNT 38 (Leiden, 1974), pp. 129–130, argues against

While we are still on earth, let us repent. For we are as clay in the hand of a potter. Just as the potter, if he misshapes or breaks a vessel in his hands while he is making it, shapes it over again if he has not already put it into the fiery oven, when he can do nothing more; let us as well, while we are still in the world and have the time to repent of the evil we have committed with our flesh, let us do so with our whole heart, that the Lord will save us while there is time for repentance (8,1-2).[88]

Without doubt, such references affirm the author's concern for those who have sinned after baptism and open the way to a sort of "second baptism," that is, penance.[89]

The passage above continues, speaking of confession of sin: "Because after going out from the world, you can any longer neither make confession nor penance" (8,3).[90] While such a confession is advised for eschatological reasons, namely, to obtain eternal life (8,4ff.), it seems nonetheless to be a reference to the practice of confessing faults within the context of the Christian liturgical assembly. The very fact that the homily itself is occasioned by such a gathering makes this conclusion possible.[91]

The letter does testify to the practice of communal correction:

So let us aid one another and guide those who are weak in goodness, that we might all be saved; and let us convert and bring back one another (17,2).[92]

---

earlier authors who see a shift in audience from chapter 7 (addressed to the community), to chapter 8 (addressed to the unbaptized). He shows that the entire letter is addressed to the baptized, so that the repentance spoken of in chapters 8ff. is necessarily postbaptismal. V. Pavan, "Battesimo e Incorruttibilità nella *II Clementis*, catechesi ai neofiti," VC 14 (1977) 51–67, has recently countered that the whole homily was addressed to catechumens.

88. *Hōs oun esmen epi gēs, metanoēsōmen. Pēlos gar esmen eis tēn cheira tou technitou; hon tropon gar ho kerameus, ean poiē skeuos kai en tais chersin autou diastraphē ē syntribē, palin auto anaplassei, ean de prophthasē eis tēn kaminon tou pyros auto balein, ouketi boēthēsei autō, houtōs kai hēmeis, heōs esmen en toutō tō kosmō, en tē sarki ha epraxamen ponēra metanoēsōmen ex holēs tēs kardias, hina sōthōmen hypo tou kyriou, heōs echomen kairon metanoias* (Bihlmeyer, 74:22-28).

89. Poschmann, *Paenitentia Secunda*, pp. 124ff.

90. *Meta gar to exelthein hēmas ek tou kosmou ouketi dynametha ekei exomologēsasthai ē metanoein eti* (Bihlmeyer, 74:28-30).

91. Donfried, *Setting of Second Clement*, p. 132. See also *I Clem.* 51,3; *Did.* 4,14; 14,1.

92. *Syllabōmen oun heautois kai tous asthenountas anagein peri to agathon, hopōs sōthōmen hapantes kai epistrepsōmen allēlous kai nouthetēsōmen* (Bihlmeyer, 79:8-10).

Though there is no explicit reference to total isolation by the community in cases of recalcitrance, the fact that the offender must be "brought back" hints at such a situation. It is a medicinal action taken by the Church to save those guilty of postbaptismal sin, done only for their own good. *Second Clement* witnesses then to a liturgical confession of sin and an indirect coercive isolation of the sinner, both being acts of the repentance necessary for those who have not kept "the seal" pure. Though not as evident as in the *Didache*, these acts of penance are more closely connected with the celebration of the Eucharist.[93]

CONCLUSION

The witness of the postapostolic writers with regard to grave postbaptismal sinners can generally be seen as being in continuity with the witness of the New Testament. All the works testify in some form to the procedure of isolating an offender from the community, by the community, in order to convince such a one to repent and return to the Lord and the Church. In addition, the Jewish practice of confession of sin within a cultic setting is further witnessed to, most clearly in Clement, the *Didache,* and *Second Clement.* In both cases the role of the community continues to be central, though with Ignatius and Polycarp the hierarchical ministries of the Church can be seen as having a more prominent place in the treatment of erring members of the community.

If there is any point of development in the postapostolic writings from the New Testament witness, it is in the apparent link between the public worship of the Church and both the practice of confession and the isolation of the sinner. The status of postbaptismal offenders, vis-à-vis the Church, is fundamentally changed due to their sin, a fact the community is reminded of each time they gather and communally confess their faults. If a sinner does not respond to the correction of his or her brothers and sisters, then such a one can be isolated more or less along the lines of the Matthean three-step process. However, there is a slight and subtle shift here,

---

93. Hein, *Eucharist and Excommunication,* pp. 226–227.

from the emphasis being on isolation from all social interaction with the community to a greater emphasis on the liturgical isolation of the sinner. To be sure, the former is still predominant in these writings, yet the latter development is also discernible and will become more prominent in the next century.

III. THE *SHEPHERD OF HERMAS* (c. 150 A.D.)

There is no document more significant for the study of penitential practices in the second-century Church and none more controversial than the *Shepherd of Hermas*.[94] Its allegorical form and Roman origin open the way for a plethora of interpretations by later authors, serving as foundation stones of numerous theoretical reconstructions of the origins of the Church's penitential discipline.[95]

A. The Possibility of Postbaptismal Forgiveness: A Window to Later Interpretations

The work makes it clear that the core of the revelation given to Hermas concerns the possibility of repentance (*metanoia*) for those who have sinned after baptism.[96] In broad strokes, there have been three basic approaches to explain this proclamation of repentance.[97]

---

94. Editions consulted: R. Joly, *Hermas le Pasteur*, SC 53 bis (Paris, 1968); M. Whittaker, *Die Apostolischen Väter: Der Hirt des Hermas* GCS 48/2 (Berlin, 1967). Direct citations will be from Joly's edition and will be indicated by page numbers. Other references to Joly's work will be similarly cited, while other works by him will include an abbreviated title. The numerical references used here are based on the system developed by R.A.B. Mynors and adopted by both Joly and Whittaker.

95. How the interpretation of the *Shepherd of Hermas* has influenced the work of selected contemporary authors has already been seen in Chapter One.

96. See 6,4-5; 13,5; 17,5; 31,3-6; 86,4; 96,2; 97,4; 98,4; 103,6; 114,4.

97. In examining the different theories of interpretation, it is necessary to keep in mind the important works of S. Giet, *Hermas et les pasteurs* (Paris, 1963); "Les trois auteurs du *Pasteur d'Hermas*," SP 8 [= TU 93] (1963) 10–23. Giet has posited the theory that the work is the composition of three separate authors, based upon inconsistencies in both style and content: 'Hermas'' (Visions I-IV), "le Pasteur'' (Sim. IX), and "le Pseudo-Pasteur'' (Mandatums + Sim. I-VIII, X). This flies in the face of other contemporary authors (such as Poschmann, Rahner, Fischer, and Joly) who hold that the work was either from one author writing at different times or a final redactor who drew material from different sources.

The first understands the *Shepherd of Hermas* as offering an entirely new revelation of reconciliation of sins committed after baptism, which up until that time were unforgivable. Those authors who hold such an interpretation have come to be known as the "postbaptismal theorists."[98] However, following upon the previous examination of New Testament and other postapostolic writers, this theory seems untenable. There is a clear tradition of tolerance in the Church, allowing for the return of grave sinners if true repentance is present. Certainly the work makes reference to certain sins of apostasy that are regarded as outside the possibility of *metanoia* (103,5). But as in other Christian writings from the first two centuries, such references speak of those who refuse repentance and remain obstinate in their sin (72,2-6). There is no sin so objective as to exclude the sinner from forgiveness if a genuine desire on the part of the offender to repent and return to the Lord is present.[99]

A second approach understands *Hermas* as not proclaiming a first reconciliation but a last one, in light of the impendent end-times. It is this aspect of his preaching that is new, inasmuch as reconciliation for grave sin is attested to since the beginning of the Church.[100] In this way Hermas is fully within the lenient tradition of the primitive Church, which did not exclude forgiveness to all who repented.

Those who posit this line of interpretation are not unaware that the Shepherd seems to both affirm and deny a second repentance after baptism. In the fourth Mandatum, Hermas asks whether it is

---

One point is clear: the apocalyptical style of the work makes interpretation difficult. It is not so important for us here to make a decision concerning authorship, except to admit that, without doubt, different traditions have been imprinted onto the work, allowing one to perceive a development in theological reflection in the second-century Roman Church.

98. For a list of authors who hold this position, see Poschmann, *Paenitentia Secunda*, p. 134, n. 1; p. 135, nn. 1-2. Catholic dogmatic theologians such as Adam, Rauschen, Hoh, and Amann modify this approach with regard to the extent of the proposed rigorism prior to Hermas and to whether this rigorism applied only to penitential discipline or was characteristic of all aspects of Church life.

99. Rahner, *Early Church*, pp. 67–69; Hein, *Eucharist and Excommunication*, pp. 231–234.

100. For a list of authors who hold this position, see Poschmann, *Paenitentia Secunda*, p. 134, n. 2. To this list we add Poschmann himself (pp. 140ff.), Rahner, *Early Church*, pp. 64ff., and Doskocil, *Bann in der Urkirche*, pp. 165ff.

true that there is no other repentance than that given at baptism, to which the Shepherd replies:

> . . . that which you have heard is correct; it is the case. Indeed, the one who has received pardon of his sins must no longer sin, but remain in holiness (31,2).[101]

But immediately afterward he goes on to affirm:

> . . . if, after this great and solemn call, someone, seduced by the devil, commits a sin, he has opportunity of only one repentance (31,6).[102]

However, the fact that the fourth Mandatum is addressed to catechumens must form the context of its interpretation. The first two verses could well be more paraenetic expressions addressed to the catechumens, exhorting them not to sin after their gift of baptism, rather than a description of an actual practice. The latter verses could then be seen to speak of the true teaching of repentance offered a second time to all the baptized.[103] Further, these same verses (along with 32,4) use the terms *metanoia* (repentance) and *aphesis* (remission) in a most unclear manner. While *Hermas* sees the effects of both being admission to the "tower" (72,6), the forgiveness of sin through penance is conceived as a long and difficult process, whereas the remission of sin through baptism is an easier and more rapid process. The work seems to assume that the distinction is well known already, another reason why a postbaptismal forgiveness of sin might well have been a custom predating this work.[104]

A third approach has been proposed. It holds that *Hermas* proclaimed a "jubilee period" of reconciliation, beginning with the pub-

---

101. *Kalōs ēkousas houtō gar echei. Edei gar ton eilēphota aphesin hamartiōn mēketi hamartanein, all' en hagneia katoikein* (Joly, 158).

102. *meta tēn klēsin ekeinēn tēn megalēn kai semnēn ean tis ekpeirastheis hypo tou diabolou hamartēsē, mian metanoian echei* (Joly, 160).

103. This is the position taken by Rahner and Galtier against Poschmann and d'Alès, who hold that Hermas's strong eschatological expectations did not allow reconciliation to be offered to the newly baptized; there was simply not enough time (Rahner, *Early Church*, pp. 69–71, 350, n. 27).

104. Rahner, *ibid.*, pp. 77–78. Of course, Giet, *Hermas et les pasteurs*, pp. 269–271, will dispute this point, based on his three-author theory, holding that the confusion between the two terms is an example of the conflict of the different traditions employed in the work.

lication of the first four visions by Hermas and ending on "a certain day which has been fixed" (6,5).[105] As such, *Hermas* harmonized the current practice of the rigorists (forgiveness only through baptism) with that of the more tolerant (postbaptismal forgiveness possible through penance). This theory of interpretation attempts to reconcile the first two approaches inasmuch as it admits the presence of a rigorist element in the Church alongside the more lenient tradition.[106]

This interpretation justifiably brings to attention (along with the "postbaptismal theorists") that there might well have been a rigorist faction operative in ecclesial life from the beginning. As such, penitential discipline may not have had a constant continuous line of tolerance in all places, a position that has been defended by more recent historians.[107] However, its basic thesis remains insupportable in the face of strong evidence that *Hermas* preached the time of penance as beginning from a person's baptism and not from the time of the revelation itself.[108] And the strong apocalyptic flavor of the work suggests that "the certain day" on which penance ended is none other than the day of Christ's return, a day close at hand for Hermas.[109]

---

105. . . . *hōrismenēs tēs hēmeras tautēs* (Joly, 92). This is Joly's own position (pp. 22ff.; "La doctrine pénitentielle du Pasteur d'Hermas et l'exégèse récente," *RHR* 147 (1955) 32–49, pp. 37ff.

106. Joly, *ibid.*, pp. 48–49, based on 31 (Mand. IV,3).

107. Joly, *ibid.*, p. 49, against Poschmann, who goes on to say that the rigorist element, which eventually faded out of the mainstream of ecclesial life, was adopted later by extremist groups such as the Novatianists and Donatists. See below, pp. 184–185.

108. Rahner, *Early Church*, pp. 350–351, n. 29, reminds the reader of the convincing argument put forth by d'Alès (*L'Édit de Calliste*, pp. 73–78) on this point. See especially 31,6 and 77,1, where the "call" (*klēsin*) of baptism gives one the possibility of repentance.

109. Giet, *Hermas et les pasteurs*, pp. 123ff. While admitting a development from a more radical eschatology in Vis. I-IV to one more moderate in Sim. IX, the eschatological vision of Hermas and his preaching on repentance are intimately linked. See Giet's "L'Apocalypse d'Hermas et la pénitence," SP 3 [= TU 78] (1959) 214–218; A. O'Hagan, "The Great Tribulation to Come in the Pastor Hermas," SP 4 [=TU 79] (1959) 305–311.

B. The Practice of Postbaptismal Penance

Having examined the question of the possibility of postbaptismal penance in *Hermas*, we must answer a second question: What can be discovered about the actual practice of ecclesial penance? As with other aspects of the work, many answers have been posited.[110]

Throughout the work there are abundant references to the efficacy of good works, fasting, and prayer in the forgiveness of sin (56,6-7). Of particular note, however, is *Hermas's* testimony concerning confession (*exomologēsis*) of sin: 1,3; 9,5; 42,2; 51,5; 100,4.[111] Though the liturgical context of confession is not immediately apparent, these references could be seen to reflect the practice taken over from Hellenistic Judaism of confessing one's faults before God prior to offering sacrifice. In this sense the work is consistent with the witness of other postapostolic authors, though any explicit link with confession and the purity demanded of those present at the Eucharist is not evidenced.[112] Nor is there any connection between the action of confession and being excluded from the "tower." To confess one's faults was required of all Christians in any situation, but most especially when gathered together for liturgy.[113]

As for the status of the sinner due to grave postbaptismal offenses, the work confirms that serious sin puts one outside the

---

110. Both Von Campenhausen, *Ecclesiastical Authority*, pp. 141ff., and Giet, "De trois expressions: *Auprès de la tour, la place inférieure, et les premiers murs*, dans le *Pasteur d'Hermas*," *SP* 8 [=TU 93] (1963) 24-29; "Pénitence ou repentance," pp. 29-30, do not see any specific references to an ecclesial institution of penance. Grotz, *Busstufenwesens*, pp. 15-70, sees *Hermas* as the first author to begin connecting the practice of excommunication with the more original ecclesial penance. Poschmann, *Paenitentia Secunda*, pp. 185ff.; Rahner, *Early Church*, pp. 85ff.; Joly, pp. 28ff.; Doskocil, *Bann in der Urkirche*, pp. 169ff.; Bernhard, "Excommunication et pénitence," pp. 55-62; and Hein, *Eucharist and Excommunication*, pp. 234-235, can see a somewhat developed penitential discipline, including "excommunication," involvement of Church leaders, and (except for Joly, who reserves judgment) reference to special places that penitents occupied in the community.

111. The use of *exomologēsis* in 42,2 and 51,5 might more properly have the meaning of praise rather than confession of faults; however, the latter meaning need not necessarily be excluded. See Joly, p. 433, note on p. 217, 1. 6.

112. The Eucharist is not mentioned at all in the work. However, in 1,3 and 9,5 confession in proximity to the "old woman" (the Church) might indicate the ecclesial dimension of the practice.

113. Joly, pp. 78-79, n. 3.

relationship with God and the Church. In the third vision the author uses the image of the stones being "cast out" (*rhiptō*) far from the tower, in contrast to those that are "lying around the tower" (*kyklo tou pyrgou ekeinto*) (10,7-9). In the ninth parable the same imagery of stones being rejected from the tower is used (81,83-86,95,107,108). If indeed, as it seems, only those stones used to construct the tower or placed within the tower are the ones that form the Church (and so the ones who will be saved), then the stones outside the tower, whether far away or near its walls, are outside the Church.[114] These sinners, in order to gain access to the tower, must do penance (91,1-3).[115]

While one can agree that every serious sin necessitates a separation from the Church, what remains unclear is whether this separation is coercive; that is, is it done for the sake of the sinner? Or might the purpose of the action be first and foremost to preserve the purity of the Church? Certainly the central place of the Church is difficult to ignore. Throughout the Visions it is allegorized as "beautiful," "wise," "strong," and "pure," images echoed in the ninth parable in the description of the tower, which is made acceptable by the Master (83,84).[116] Yet, while it cannot be denied that the separation of the sinner from the Church is purgative, done to prevent the contagion of sin to its members, this emphasis does not overshadow the fact that all correction of the sinner, no matter how difficult, is carried out ultimately so that the sinner might repent and have life again (7,1; 17,10; 63,6). In this way, being placed outside

---

114. There has been much discussion over the meaning of the location of certain stones in attempting to discover a developed penitenial discipine in Hermas; see below, pp. 102–103.

115. One can clearly distinguish here different layers in the composition of the work. In 15, 5-6 those rejected from the tower can do penance but cannot be readmitted to the tower: theirs will be a lesser place (*poly elattoni*). However, in 91,1-3 those rejected are given the possibility of entering the tower.

116. A question much debated is whether *Hermas*'s vision of the Church includes both an eschatological perspective of the heavenly Jerusalem as well as the earthly Church, which has to deal with the situation of the sin of its members (Rahner, *Early Church*, pp. 85–86), or if the work speaks only in eschatological images (Giet, "Pénitence ou repentance," p. 22). If we accept that the work was compiled in stages, and if the Visions were of an early stage with a more imminent eschatological perspective, then Giet's position may be correct for the Visions, whereas Rahner's view could be said to prevail in terms of the work as a whole.

the tower (isolation), except in cases where the sinner remained obstinate in his or her sin, is to ensure that adequate penance is accomplished in order that the former status of the transgressor can be restored.[117] Hermas, though strongly allegorical, is consistent with other writings of the period in witnessing to a coercive penance of isolation.

As to whether this isolation is indirect (an action taken by the community) or direct (imposed directly upon the sinner), it must be noted that the work does not speak of the role of a single Church authority, such as a bishop, having control of any sort of a penitential process. All references to Church leaders are in the plural (8,3; 17,7-10; 108,5).[118] While one could maintain that there is evidence of the developing role of leaders under whom the discipline of the Church is maintained (especially in the ninth parable, with its emphasis on the exclusion of sinners), even here it cannot be held that these leaders manifestly exercised authority over sin.[119] The entire community is involved in keeping the sinner separated from the Church. It is an indirect action, taken in order to at least open the possibility of such a one being forgiven only by God.[120]

It has been argued that beyond the normative postapostolic procedure of isolating the sinner, a more developed expression of pen-

---

117. Here we take issue with Giet, *ibid.*, pp. 22–23, who insists that the purification of the Church is the focus over and against the repentance of sinners, even though such a conclusion follows logically from his ecclesiological perspective. See above, n. 116.

118. Joly, "La doctrine pénitentielle du Pasteur d'Hermas," pp. 32–33. The position of Rahner, *Early Church*, p. 99, that the work witnesses to a high degree of activity on the part of Church leaders does not seem justified by the text. The relative silence of *Hermas* on the identification of Church leaders would seem to point to a less active role rather than vice versa.

119. Von Campenhausen, *Ecclesiastical Authority*, pp. 95–96, has pointed out that there is no rivalry between Church leaders and the man of the Spirit (Hermas). Both have a place in the community. However, this very collaboration between the hierarchical and the charismatic might be an indication of the decline of the charismatic function. See Joly, p. 29, 40.

120. Von Campenhausen, *ibid.*, pp. 95–96, 141–142, who holds that in *Hermas* there is not as yet a clear recognition by Church leaders of their authority over sin. This will develop synonymously with the development of a monarchical episcopacy. Once again, this is why we prefer the designation of an "indirect coercive penance of isolation" rather than the misleading "excommunication," which implies such a hierarchical authority.

ance is operative in this work, apparent from occasional references to certain sinners being closer to the tower than others: "near the tower" (10,8; 13,5; 81,8; 83,5,8; 84,1); "an inferior place" (15,6); "the first [exterior] walls" (72,6; 73,3; 74,3). Such terminology could refer to an actual process of penance through which offenders are admitted back by degrees into right relationship with the Church according to the sincerity of their conversion and penance.[121] These might even be allusions to specific places to which penitents are assigned when the community gathers for the Eucharist, indicating a definite evolution in the penitential discipline seen heretofore.[122]

To be sure, given the figurative style of *Hermas*, one may not deny the possibility of such an interpretation. However, the missing witness to a developed clergy as well as the homiletic nature of the work itself appear to clash with this explication. The Shepherd offers a new revelation concerning the possibility of forgiveness: it can be done only once. Hence he exhorts those guilty of postbaptismal sin to undertake penance before Christ returns and it is too late. These vague allusions, then, might be better understood from the experience of the individual sinners themselves rather than from the perspective of the Church: they are closer to being saved than others, a definite advantage in light of Hermas's imminent eschatology.[123] Consequently, beyond the testimony to a confession of sin that is probably liturgical and to the practice of an indirect coercive penance of isolation, the *Shepherd of Hermas* is too allegorical and too influenced by its own eschatology for one to say with certainty anything further concerning its penitential witness.

C. Readmittance of the Sinner to the Church

Like other contemporary writings, *Hermas* does not mention any rite of reconciliation of sinners. Yet, there are indications that those who are isolated from the Church and show adequate repentance are once again admitted to the "tower." For example, a warning

---

121. Rahner, *Early Church*, pp. 98–106. While certainly not advocating a developed order of penitents, Rahner does believe that a "fairly improvised" structure of penance did exist. For others who held similar positions, see above, n. 110.
122. *Ibid.*, pp. 99–100.
123. Giet, "De trois expressions," pp. 24–29.

is issued to a certain Maximus not to deny the faith again (*palin*), because persecution is coming (7,4). Such a one could be a believer who has "lapsed" once in faith but has since been reintegrated into the community. The action of readmittance is probably informal, with a person simply moving from being "quarantined" by the community to being able once again to interact with them, including Eucharistic communion. This would be done whenever the whole assembly decides that the person is sincere in his or her repentance.[124]

Perhaps the most controversial passage with regard to the question of the role of the Church in the readmission of the sinner comes in the fourth Mandatum. There Hermas asks the Shepherd if a man should receive back his adulterous wife, whom he has divorced, if she repents:

> "Certainly," he said. "If the husband does not receive her, he sins, and he loads upon himself a heavy sin, because it is necessary to receive those who have sinned and who have repented . . ." (29,8).[125]

If the interaction between the husband and his wife is looked upon as a model of the interaction between the Church and the sinner, then there does seem to be some type of "receiving back" (*paradechthēnai*) of the offender into the community.[126] Further on, the fact that one might again be brought back into the "tower" (72,6; 110,2-3) allows that there must be some definitive end to the period of isolation, leading to the person's being returned to full status in

---

124. Joly, p. 29.

125. *Kai mēn, phēsin, ean mē paradexētai autēn ho anēr, hamartanei kai megalēn hamartian heautō epispatai, alla dei paradechthēnai ton hēmartēkota kai metanoounta* . . . (Joly, p. 154).

The passage has been cited by Grotz, *Busstufenwesens*, pp. 30ff., as an example of ecclesial penance without "excommunication," but Rahner, *Early Church*, pp. 90–94, successfully maintained that the woman's "excommunication" was a necessary part of her penance, revoked through her readmission. Giet, "Pénitence ou repentance," pp. 16–20, refused both interpretations, holding that the situation in question speaks only of a moral imperative in the private domain of marriage and, as such, cannot be interpreted as a model of Church discipline.

126. The same term is employed by Ignatius, *Smyrn.* 4,1, in the negative sense of not "receiving" false teachers, implying that they were not to be allowed readmittance into the Church until they had repented. See above, n. 57.

the Church. How such a "receiving back" occurs remains a mystery; that it occurs is supported by the text.[127] It is only back within the "tower" that the sinner has the possibility of attaining divine forgiveness for his or her transgression and having the marks of former sins forever hidden (110,3).[128]

D. THE CONSEQUENCE OF POSTBAPTISMAL PENANCE: THE TEACHING OF A SINGLE POSSIBILITY OF PENANCE

What is more "new" about the revelation contained in the *Shepherd of Hermas* is not the possibility of penance as much as the teaching that penance can only be undertaken one time:

> For the servants of God, there is only penance (29,8):
>
> . . . if, after this great and solemn call, someone, seduced by the devil, commits a sin, he has opportunity of only one repentance (31,6).[129]

The rule of a single opportunity for postbaptismal penance will become one of the most characteristic features of the Church's penitential discipline during the first six centuries. Prior to *Hermas*, there is no evidence for it; however, the matter-of-fact way in which it is postulated here suggests that "the Shepherd" may not have been the originator of this custom.[130]

What is behind such a teaching? First and foremost, it must be seen within the context of eschatology: There simply is not going to be enough time left in the world to complete the "hard" process of penance. But in addition, the Shepherd believes that repeated

---

127. Rahner, *Early Church*, pp. 106–108. Also, one must not overlook the witness of Tertullian (*De pud.* 10,12; 20,2), who speaks of Hermas as the "pastor of adulterers," due to his willingness to reconcile them.

128. Whether readmission to the Church was the gauge (so d'Alès) or the condition (so Poschmann) for reconciliation with God has long been a point of controversy. In light of the New Testament and postapostolic witness, the latter position seems more defendable for *Hermas*.

129. . . . *tois gar doulois tou theou metanoia estin mia* (Joly, p. 154). For the text of 31,6, see above, n. 102. For a discussion of the proper sense of these passages, see Joly, p. 430, note on p. 155, 1. 20-21.

130. At least, this is the position of Rahner, *Early Church*, pp. 81–82, against Poschmann, *PAS*, p. 35, who holds that the work is indeed the initiator of the practice based "strictly on pastoral and psychological grounds."

acts of repentance are ultimately indicative of an unrepentant heart. If true repentance is present, once is enough. This highlights a pastoral, indeed almost a psychotherapeutic, dimension to the teaching. The author is concerned with true conversion toward Christ and genuine healing of the soul rather than punishment for the sinner. The principle of a single penance best suits this purpose, being both pastorally sensitive yet offering necessary guidelines.[131]

In addition, there is a certain parallel that the Shepherd makes between the act of repentance and baptism (31,3). As the rule of a single baptism is known from the earliest Church tradition, this practice is now applied by the author to penance. Though *Hermas* clearly makes a distinction between the remission of sin at baptism and postbaptismal penance, their points of differences do not overshadow the basic element of their similarity: both take away sin and lead one to new life. Therefore, both must be exercised only once.[132] Later patristic writers, particularly in the West, will further develop this comparison as the basis for a single postbaptismal remission of sin.[133]

As for the fate of those who sin after the completion of penance, *Hermas* is consistent: those who are unrepentant are lost (73,5). However, if they repent, the author is less clear. The passage above continues:

> . . .but if he sins again and again, even if he repents, penance will not benefit such a man: for with difficulty he will live (31,6).[134]

On the one hand, penance will do no good for such a person; on the other hand, there is still a chance the recidivist will live.[135] In another passage seen earlier (29,8), the adulteress is to be forgiven her sin and be welcomed back by her husband "but not many times" (*mē epi poly de*). While the Shepherd does not want to give an ap-

---

131. Rahner, *Early Church*, pp. 79–80; Hein, *Eucharist and Excommunication*, p. 231, n. 14.

132. Rahner, *Early Church*, pp. 78–81. See above, pp. 97–98.

133. Especially the writings of Jerome, Ambrose, Pacian, and Augustine.

134. . . . *ean de hypo cheira hamartanē kai metanoēsē, asymphoron esti tō anthrōpō tō toioutō; dyskolōs gar zēsetai* (Joly, p. 160).

135. Poschmann, *Paenitentia Secunda*, p. 169, n. 2, relates the study by d'Alès, who convincingly has shown that it is textually unjustifiable to interpret *dyskolōs* as "impossible." Though little hope exists for the recidivist, a little is better than nothing.

pearance of being too "soft" on sinners, he does not entirely shut the door on recidivists if they are sincere in their repentance.[136]

In *Hermas*, the teaching of a single opportunity for repentance after baptism is based on eschatological and pastoral grounds. From the argument of silence, it cannot be said that the practice, as a universal custom, predates the work. However, there may have been some precedent for it, especially in light of the parallel with baptism. But from the author's ambiguity in the treatment of recidivists, this teaching does not appear to be a "law" or a "doctrine." This development will come later.

CONCLUSION

The above analysis of the *Shepherd of Hermas* reveals four points that might be offered by way of summary. First, there is no evidence from the work that the Church universally denied the possibility of repentance for postbaptismal sin, even though such a practice may have been a custom within certain local communities. What is new with *Hermas* is a last rather than a first possibility of penance after baptism. Second, the clearest expression of any penitential discipline, as in other postapostolic works, continues to be the connection between serious sin and the coercive penance of isolation of the sinner by the community. The recognition that postbaptismal sin creates a different relationship between the Church and the sinner is confirmed by the community's stepping back from the sinner in hopes of leading him or her to true repentance. Though the latest parts of the work can be said to witness to an increase in hierarchical order and a decrease in the authority of the "charismatic" element, the act of isolation continues to be indirect rather than directly imposed upon the sinner by the leaders of the community. Third, though *Hermas* does not witness to a reconciliation rite, there appears to be a recognition of the possibility of a sinner's readmission into the community after adequate penitential works. And fourth, the teaching that penance after baptism is unrepeatable is the most novel aspect of the revelation. It is based on eschatologi-

---

136. Joly, p. 161, n. 7. This may be yet another example of both rigoristic and tolerant elements being present in the work. See above, p. 97.

cal and pastoral grounds and is, at this stage of development, far from being a juridically binding law.

IV. THE TESTIMONY OF THE LATE SECOND CENTURY

A. IRENAEUS OF LYON († c. 180 A.D.)

The most important theologian of the second century, Irenaeus brings together the experiences of two local churches: that of his native church in Asia Minor, where as a youth he is alleged to have been a disciple of Polycarp (III,3,4), and that of the church of Lyon, where, near the end of his life, he ministered as presbyter and bishop.[137] He is considered to be the first truly dogmatic theologian due to his systematic refutation of Gnosticism, which is the subject of his main work, *Adversus haereses*.[138] In spite of a later fourth-century tradition claiming that Irenaeus died a martyr, the date and cause of his death remain unknown.[139]

Irenaeus's references to penitential practices are comparatively few and are sprinkled throughout the *Adversus haereses*.[140] Recent studies are in general agreement that Irenaeus held no sin as objectively unforgivable, though such a position does not belie the fact

---

137. Eusebius, *Eccl. Hist.* V,20,5-7; Jerome, *De vir. illust.*, 35.

138. Only most of the first book and some few other fragments remain extant in the original Greek, causing innumerable textual problems. Fortunately the majority of the most important texts for our study here are to be found in the Greek. Editions of the *Adversus haereses* consulted include: A. Rousseau and L. Doutreleau, *Irénée de Lyon: Contre les Hérésies*, Book I, SC 263/264 (Paris, 1979); Book III, SC 210/211 (Paris, 1974); id. with B. Hemmerdinger and C. Mercier, Book IV, SC 100 (Paris, 1965); A. Rousseau, L. Doutreleau, and C. Mercier, Book V, SC 152/153 (Paris, 1969). Direct citations will be indicated by SC volume, page, and line number.

139. A. Houssiau, *Le christologie de S. Irénée*, UCLDiss 3,1 (Louvain, 1955), pp. 1-3.

140. There has been discussion concerning the ending of Irenaeus's *Regula fidei* (*Adv. haer.* I,10,1) as to whether his use of *ek metanoias* refers to postbaptismal sinners. After carefully considering the positions of Poschmann, *Paenitentia Secunda*, pp. 220ff., and Rahner, *Early Church*, pp. 114ff., F. van de Paverd, "The Meaning of *ek metanoias* in the *Regula fidei* of St. Irenaeus," *OCP* 38 (1972) 454–466, concludes that the reference is eschatological, having to do with how the Lord will treat all the faithful at the end of time, those "with Him from the beginning, called by Him during his earthly existence, or whether they were called by Him through the words of the preachers" (p. 464).

of his harsh paraenetic treatment of those who sinned after baptism (III,11,9; IV,27,2).[141] Yet, following the tradition of the Letter to the Hebrews, the only truly irremissible sin results from the obduracy of the impenitent heart (III,23,3; V,26,2). For those who repent of their apostasy and sinful lives, the possibility of salvation is open (I,31,3; III,14,4; 23,5; IV,40,1). In this manner Irenaeus, while a rigorist in his teaching due to his vigorous attempt to defend the integrity of the faith, could be said to be more pastorally lenient in his practice.[142]

Perhaps what is most intriguing about Irenaeus's penitential references is his use of the now familiar term *exomologēsis*. Including the verb form (*exomologeisthai*) and its Latin transcriptions (*exhomologesin, exhomologesin facere*), the word appears in six texts of the *Adversus haereses*: I,6,3; 13,5; 13,7; III,4,3; IV,27,1; 36,8.[143] While the use of some form of this term in reference to a confession of sin is not novel with Irenaeus, there is something about his usage which hints that he might have assigned to this expression a wider connotation.[144]

In each case the meaning of the term has to do with some sort of public confession or recognition of a public fault. In the case of David (IV,27,1) and the publican (IV,36,8), the confession recalls the

---

141. Debate has raged over this point. Poschmann, whose own work convincingly argued against Irenaeus's supposed rigorism (*Paenitentia Secunda*, pp. 211ff.), lists those who interpreted Irenaeus as not allowing postbaptismal penance, including H. Koch, "Die Sündenvergebung bei Irenäus," ZNW 9 (1908) 36–46, p. 45; H. Windisch, *Taufe und Sünde imältesten Christentum bis auf Origenes*, p. 104; G. Bonwetsch, *Die Theologie des Irenäus* (Gütersloh, 1925), pp. 131ff. Those who hold the more tolerant interpretation with Poschmann include J. Stufler, "Die Sündenvergebung bei Irenäus," ZKTh 32 (1908) 488–497, pp. 488ff.; d'Alès, *L'Édit de Calliste*, p. 123; Hoh, *Die kirchliche Busse*, p. 93; Rahner, *Early Church*, p. 118; H. Karpp, *La pénitence*, p. 115, n. 2.

142. Irenaeus's penitential teachings and exhortations cannot be separated from his theological and ecclesiological perspective. This point is well made by M. Mügge, "Das Bussverständnis in der Theologie des Irenäus," ThGl 67 (1977) 393–405, pp. 394ff.

143. Though the Greek *homologēsis* would properly be transcribed as "homologesis," *exomologēsis*, since it drops the rough breathing mark over the "o," is transcribed "exomologesis." It is this transcription that is used throughout the present study.

144. The use of the term has already been seen in Mt 3:6; Mk 1:5; Jas 5:16; I Clem. 51,3; 52,1-2; Barn. 19,12; Did 4,14; 14,1; Shepherd of Hermas 1,3; 9,5; 111,4. Other possible references with a penitential sense include Acts 19:18; Hermas 42,2; 51,5.

Judaic practice of admitting one's faults before God. It is what a sinner has to do in order to receive divine pardon. However, in the other references, the pardon of the sinner is not the central point of exomologesis, based strictly on what is found in the texts. In the case of the defiled women (I,6,3), the wife of Asiates (I,13,5), the other women defiled by Marcus (I,13,7), and in the case of the heretic Cedron (III,4,3), exomologesis seems to be almost a fixed action done for the sake of the publicity itself. Its purpose is not disclosive, inasmuch as the sin of the persons involved is already known to the community, as much as it is a public expression of contrition on the part of the sinner. What then appears most important is the publicity of the action rather than the action itself.[145]

It remains unknown what exactly is involved in the practice of exomologesis as described by Irenaeus. As has been seen in other writings from the first two centuries, most probably the confession took place within the context of the Christian liturgy when the transgressor(s) "returned to the Church of God."[146] The willingness to openly confess one's fault appears as the criterion by which one is allowed to come back to the Church.[147] Yet the emphasis on the necessity of confessing what is already known takes the experience beyond the postapostolic witness. Also, here specific persons are required to perform exomologesis, whereas the earlier witness tends to exhort believers to confess their sins as a general rule. In addition, two of the texts indicate that the exomologesis is not accomplished as one event but is ongoing. For example, once the wife of the deacon Asiates is convinced by the community to leave the company of the heretic Marcus:

> . . . for all of her time she remained making confession, weeping and lamenting over the defilement she had received from this magician (I,13,5).[148]

145. H. Holstein, "L'exhomologèse dans l'Adversus Haereses de Saint Irénée," RSR 35 (1948) 282–288, p. 286.

146. . . . epistrepsasai eis tēn Ekklēsian tou theou (264, 97:644-645; 200:83-84). See also the similar reference in III,4,3 (211, 51:50).

147. Holstein, "L'exhomologèse," pp. 285–286.

148. . . . ton hapanta chronon exomologoumenē dietelese, penthousa kai thrēnousa eph' hē epathen hypo tou magou diaphthora (264, 201:92-94).

Also, when the heretic Cedron came to Rome:

> . . . [and] coming to the church and there he remained making confession, [yet] ever teaching [heresy] in secret and ever again making confession (III,4,3).[149]

Generally, while there are similarities to the earlier practice, there is a uniqueness by what is implied in Irenaeus' use of the term.

It must also be noted that Irenaeus speaks more definitely than any text hereto of the office and succession of the bishop-presbyter. This fact gives the *Adversus haereses* a more institutional flavor. If it is remembered that the entire work is dedicated to the polemical task of detecting (Book I) and refuting (Books II–V) the Gnostic heresy, then the context of his "institutionalizing" of Church leadership becomes evident. It is the authoritative platform from which his attack is made.[150] That the practice of exomologesis, whatever it entailed, might have been influenced by such an evolution is not an inconsistent conclusion to draw. As has been said, a more developed postbaptismal penitential process looks to be an indication of a more developed hierarchical structure of ministry. This conclusion is further borne out by the fact that all faults requiring exomologesis in the texts cited above are exterior acts against the faith. With Irenaeus one has the feeling that there is a certain tightening of the dogmatic boundaries of the Church.[151]

It would be wrong to impose upon Irenaeus's exomologesis what is later known about the order of penitents, in the hope of proving the existence of an established institution of penance in Lyon by

---

149. . . . *eis tēn ekklēsian elthōn kai exomologēsamenos houtōs dietelese, pote men lathrodidaskalōn, pote de palin exomologoumenos* . . . (211, 51:50-52). The Greek fragment of this text is taken from Eusebius's *Eccl. Hist.* . IV,11,1. Though Eusebius only specifically uses the term *exomologeō* in the second instance where it appears in the text above, his use of *palin* makes it clear that Cedron's confession occurred on more than one occasion.

150. Von Campenhausen, *Ecclesiastical Authority*, pp. 170–173, who insists that the power assigned to the clergy in the *Adversus haereses* is always in relation to Irenaeus's apologetic and polemical intention. See also the discussion on the much discussed passage concerning the apostolic succession of the Roman bishops (III,2,3) in A. Rousseau/L. Doutreleau, SC 210 (note on p. 33, n. 1), pp. 223–236.

151. Holstein, "L'exhomologèse," pp. 287–288.

the close of the second century.[152] Conversely, as much as one would want to be cautious and hold that his use of the term implies first and foremost a spiritual attitude, there is something that defies a purely spiritualist interpretation.[153] Given this state of affairs, perhaps all that can be admitted is that there is a development in the practice of exomologesis in the writings of Irenaeus. The consistency with which the term is employed hints at the beginnings of an accepted discipline undertaken by those who have sinned against the faith. Yet, it remains impossible to interpret the indistinctness of his witness as a disclosure of a fully developed institution of penance.[154]

Concerning evidence in the *Adversus haereses* for the procedure of isolating one guilty of serious sin, Irenaeus does remind the local church of the apostolic tradition of not even having verbal contact with those who hold false doctrines (I,16,3; III,3,4; V,20,2).[155] He conveys this teaching in order to forestall any possible Gnostic contamination of the "Church of God." Nonetheless, as seen in the passages previously cited, those who perpetrate false teaching (III,4,3) as well as those who follow them (I,6,3; 13,5.7) might be coerced back and saved, but only if they "openly confess their

---

152. For example, Poschmann's careful explanation (*Paenitentia Secunda*, pp. 221ff.) that Cedron was admitted numerous times to exomologesis but never received reconciliation with the Church may assume a too developed institution of penance. Though Irenaeus considers the *Shepherd of Hermas* as part of the Scriptures (IV,20,2), there is no mention of an unrepeatable penance. Nor is there any absolute evidence that exomologesis necessarily led to ecclesial pardon (see below, n. 156). Nonetheless, the point is well taken that the action of exomologesis, however it is envisioned, is more specifically connected as a remedy for grave postbaptismal sin.

153. Holstein, "L'exhomologèse," pp. 286–287.

154. One is a bit mystified at Holstein, *ibid.*, pp. 287–288, who, after going to great lengths to warn against reading into Irenaeus the existence of a penitential institution, ends his article by affirming the very same! M. Mügge, "Das Bussverständnis bei Irenäus," pp. 402ff, is more cautious but holds the same conclusion. Their quandary is understandable: one cannot but see a development of Irenaeus's use of exomologesis in the *Adversus haereses*.

155. Here references are made to Is 48:22; Titus 3:10; 2 Jn 10-11. That all social intercourse is broken with the sinner is signified by refusing such a one even the traditional greeting of peace. See Rousseau/Doutreleau, SC 263, p. 260 (note on p. 263, n. 1).

faults."[156] For it is possible, though not easy, for those who have given in to false doctrines to come back to "truth" (I,31,3; III,2,3); indeed, the Church must continue to pray for them and love them (III,25,7). But the coercion does not seem to be in the act of isolation of the sinner but is done through actual contact with him or her by certain members of the community (as in the case of the wife of Asiates). In fact, Irenaeus implies that the separation of heretics and schismatics is not necessarily first imposed by the community but by the sinners themselves (V,27,2). The Church then only ratifies such self-imposed ecclesial exile, avoiding the sinner but also vigilant for opportunities to lead such a one back to salvation.[157]

In the story of Cedron, after the heretic is finally denounced after his many confessions:

> . . . [he] ever at last was convicted of his erroneous teaching and separated [separated himself] from the community of the brethren (III,4,3).[158]

The word *aphistamenos* can be translated here either in the active or passive voice, referring either to Cedron separating himself or being separated from the community.[159] In the active sense it would point to a voluntary separation on the part of Cedron, consistent with Irenaeus's belief that heretics isolated themselves from the Church by their own sin. However, the passive interpretation would imply a direct act of exclusion of the sinner emanating from the authority of the bishop-presbyter. In the latter case this would be one of the earliest witnesses to such an action. In the light of Irenaeus's testimony to the development of the authority of the

---

156. Irenaeus does not witness to any specific act of readmission of sinners to the Church, even those who made exomologesis. His silence on this matter is admitted by Hoh, *Die kirchliche Busse*, pp. 94ff.; Poschmann, *Paenitentia Secunda*, pp. 224ff. (while admitting that there is no evidence against this and that Irenaeus probably knew of such a practice); Von Campenhausen, *Ecclesiastical Authority*, p. 217; Rahner, *Early Church*, p. 118.

157. Hein, *Eucharist and Excommunication*, p. 256.

158. . . . *pote de elegchomenos eph' hois edidaske kakōs kai aphistamenos tēs tōn adelphōn synodias* (211, 51:52-53).

159. Rousseau/Doutreleau, SC 210, pp. 244-245 (note on p. 51, n. 3).

clergy and their emergence as a separate professional body, this interpretation has a certain appropriateness.[160]

B. THE WITNESS OF THE *ECCLESIASTICAL HISTORY* BY EUSEBIUS OF CAESAREA

Most probably writing at the beginning of the fourth century, Eusebius compiled a massive amount of documentation concerning the early Church in his *Ecclesiastical History*. Though his style of composition is less than pleasing at times, he has conserved excerpts of ancient Christian and pagan writings, many of which are no longer extant.[161] Yet, for all his prominence as a Church historian, he also plays the role of an apologist, defending orthodox tradition against those who assail it.[162] In this respect, there are limits to the historical accuracy of the work.[163] Having stated this, one cannot overlook the witness of the fourth and fifth books pertaining to certain practices connected with the treatment of those who fell away from the faith. The vivid descriptions of Eusebius shed further light on the second-century roots of the order of penitents.

1. LETTER OF DIONYSIUS OF CORINTH TO THE CHURCHES OF AMASTRIS AND PONT (c. 170 A.D.) = *Eccl. Hist.* IV,23,6

There is a startling directness in this letter by Dionysius, bishop

---

160. Von Campenhausen, *Ecclesiastical Authority*, p. 145, n. 122, who prefers the active tense interpretation. However, could it not be possible that Cedron separated himself from the community on his own accord but under pressure from Church leadership? In this way both voluntary isolation from the community and direct exclusion would be at work to achieve the same end: the recognition of the fundamental alteration of Cedron's ecclesial status due to his sin.

161. Quasten, *Patrology* III, pp. 311, 314-315. Direct citations from the *Ecclesiastical History* are taken from G. Bardy, *Eusèbe de Césarée. Histoire Ecclésiastique* (Books I-IV), SC 31 (Paris, 1952); (Books V-VII), SC 41 (1955), and will be indicated by SC volume and page number. For the Greek text, Bardy admits his heavy dependence on the classic edition by E. Schwartz, GCS 9 in 3 vols., (1903-1909).

162. J. Sirinelli and E. des Places, *Eusèbe de Césarée. Le préparation évangélique*, SC 206 (Paris, 1974), pp. 17-20. To Eusebius, history and apology are neither separate nor opposing disciplines; one serves the other. Though he was to eventually be excommunicated for his Arian sympathies, at the time of his writing of the *Ecclesiastical History* he was fiercely dedicated to orthodoxy.

163. T. Barnes, "Eusebius and the Date of the Martyrdoms," in *Les martyrs de Lyon (177). Colloques internationaux du centre national de la recherche scientifique, 20-23 Septembre, 1977* (Paris, 1978) 137-141, pp. 137-139.

of Corinth, who speaks strongly in favor of the pastoral tolerance that is to be shown to postbaptismal offenders. About Dionysius's ministry in his local church, Eusebius writes:

> . . . he gives them much counsel regarding marriage and on continence and he commands them to receive those who are converted after any fall, whether through negligent conduct or the error of heresy.[164]

That such sinners are "to be received" is an indication of some action that restores to these persons their former status in the Church.[165] Yet, Dionysius offers no further details on any procedures of penance or reconciliation.[166] In this light, his brief witness could be said not to be absolutely essential to the history of the order of penitents; yet, he is included here because of the stress he places on the fact that no sin, no matter how serious, could keep one out of the fold of Christ's flock. His letter might well have been in response to those with a more rigoristic approach to postbaptismal sin.[167] While rigorism may have had a life in certain local churches, the evidence of the first two centuries shows clearly that it is not the predominant tradition.

---

164. . . . *polla de peri gamou kai hagneias tois autois parainei, kai tous ex hoias d' oun apoptōseōs, eite plēmmeleias eite mēn hairetikēs planēs, epistrepontas dexiousthai prostattei* (31, 204).

165. As has been seen, a similar use of the verb *dechomai* (or a derivative) appears in Ignatius's *Smyrn.* 4,1 and the *Shepherd of Hermas* 29,8. Those who believe that this is a reference to some sort of ecclesial reconciliation rather than admittance to penance include Hoh, *Die kirchliche Busse*, p. 88; Poschmann, *Paenitentia Secunda*, pp. 267ff.; Von Campenhausen, *Ecclesiastical Authority*, p. 219, n. 25; Bernhard, "Excommunication et pénitence," p. 63.

166. In the history of interpretation, Dionysius's silence has been interpreted as proof of an ecclesial penance without a prior isolation of the sinner (d'Alès, *L'Édit de Calliste*, pp. 128ff.; Galtier, *L'Église*, pp. 257ff.). However, this obviously reads too much into the text.

167. Both Bardy, SC 31, p. 204, n. 10, and P. Nautin, *Lettres et écrivains chrétiens des IIe et IIIe siècles*, Patristica 2 (Pais, 1961), pp. 16–18, believe that Dionysius's counsel concerning marriage and continence makes it possible to understand the whole passage as an apologetic against the rigorism of the Encratites, who were known in Asia Minor at the time and whose negative anthropological conceptions led them to deny the possibility of marriage. See G. Blond, "L'hérésie encratite vers la fin du IVe siècle," *SRTR* 2 (1944) 157–210. On the other hand, Poschmann, *PAS*, pp. 35ff., and Vogel, *Le pécheur et la pénitence*, p. 19, interpret the leniency of Dionysius as more directed against the intolerance of the Montanists.

2. LETTER FROM THE CHURCHES OF LYON AND VIENNE TO THE CHURCHES OF ASIA AND PHRYGIA AFTER THE PERSECUTION OF 177 = *Eccl. Hist.* V,1,45-46.48; 2,5

One of the most moving of the ancient Acts of the martyrs, this account raises the question of the role of early Christian martyrs and confessors in the forgiveness of postbaptismal sin.[168] Though it will become an explosive issue in the next century, even seen by Cyprian (in his dealings with the *lapsi*) as a threat to established hierarchical authority, the present letter stands as a simple testimony to the prestige that the martyrs and confessors enjoyed in the local community. Their suffering for the faith gives them an authority to intercede with God on behalf of those who have sinned by denying Christ in the midst of persecution.[169] This account implies that their status in the community allows them to exercise this ministry, which is later to become more and more reserved to the clerical office. It is their intercession alone that is sufficient to reconcile apostates to God, enabling them to stand firm in the faith in the midst of troubled times.[170]

As in the witness of Dionysius of Corinth, this letter from the churches of Lyon and Vienne confirms that no sin objectively is able

---

168. Tertullian was the first to make any distinction between confessors and martyrs, with confessors being those who suffered for the faith, while martyrs were those who died for it (*De corona*, 11). See H. Leclercq, "Martyr," in *DACL* 10,2 (1932) 2359-2511, c. 2263-2266; J. Ruysschaert, "Les 'martyrs' et les 'confesseurs' de la lettre des églises de Lyon et de Vienne," in *Les martyrs de Lyon (177)*, pp. 155-164.

169. See Tertullian, *Ad martyres* I, 4-6 and, for a negative affirmation, *De pud.* 22. Catholic theologians such as d'Alès, Galtier, Palmer, and Poschmann have held that such an intercession was either to aid the sinner in recognizing the need to make repentance and to begin the process of exomologesis or to intercede with the bishop on behalf of the sinner. But true ecclesial pardon was ultimately reserved to the bishop. See W. LeSaint, *Tertullian: Treatises on Penance*, ACW 28 (Westminster, Md., 1959), pp. 291-292, n. 669; also, G. Jouassard, "Le rôle des chrétiens comme intercesseurs auprès de Dieu dans la chrétienté Lyonnaise au second siècle," *RevSR* 30 (1956) 217-229.

170. M. Lods, *Confesseurs et martyrs. Successeurs des prophètes dans l'Église des trois premiers siècles*, CTh 41 (Neuchâtel, 1958), pp. 69-72. It seems admissible to hold that at least during times of persecution martyrs pardoned sinners. See Bardy, *Ecclesiastical History*, p. 18, n. 52; Von Campenhausen, p. 219, n. 27; E. Dassman, *Sündenvergebung durch Taufe, Busse und Martyrerfürbitte in den Zeugnissen frühchristlicher Frömmigkeit und Kunst*, MBTh 36 (Münster, 1973), pp. 171-178.

to keep one outside the Church. It speaks of the tolerant approach of the martyrs:

> They humbled themselves under the mighty hand by which they are now highly exalted. They defended all and accused no one; they loosed all and bound no one (V,2,5).[171]

The use of "binding" and "loosing" here shows that the authority of the martyrs includes the apostolic authority to minister to those once guilty of denying the faith, enabling them to now confess Christ (V,1,45-46.48). It is probable that the author of the letter had an apologetic purpose in mind, to prove that indulgence toward those who sinned after baptism is no sign of an indulgent faith that could not withstand the rigors of persecution.[172] The martyrs of Lyon are living proof that a lenient approach to sinners strengthened rather than weakened the Church.[173] In the midst of being tested in the faith, those who failed a first time are given a second chance through the intercession of the martyrs.

3. WRITINGS AGAINST THE CATAPHRYGIAN (MONTANIST) HERESY = *Eccl. Hist.* V,16,10; 18,5-7

The Church in Asia Minor found itself confronted with the spreading heresy of Montanism and its rigoristic discipline.[174] Eusebius relates an anonymous letter that witnesses to synodal gatherings in Asia condemning the utterances of Montanus and his followers. It is a decision that will eventually be extended to Rome

---

171. . . . *etapeinoun heautous hypo tēn krataian cheira, hyph' hēs hikanōs nyn eisin hypsmenoi. tote de pasi men apelogounto, kategoroun de oudenos; elyon hapantas, edesmeuon de oudena* (41, 25).

172. Nautin, *Lettres et écrivains*, pp. 54–59, presents strong evidence in favor of Irenaeus's authorship of the letter.

173. *Ibid.*, p. 35. Nautin sees the letter as having apologetic overtones directed toward the Encratites, while Von Campenhausen, *Ecclesiastical Authority*, p. 220, and H. Kraft, "Die Lyoner Märtyrer und der Montanismus," in *Les martyrs de Lyon (177)*, pp. 233–244, believe the account is directed more against the Montanists.

174. It is beyond the scope of our study here to give a detailed explanation of the origins and influence of Montanism, though at the same time admitting that the Church's attack on Montanist rigorism aided it in clarifying its own position of tolerance toward postbaptismal sinners. The classic works by J. De Labriolle, *La crise Montaniste* (Paris, 1913) and *Les sources de l'histoire du Montanisme*, Collectanea Friburgensia 15 (Fribourg, 1913), continue to be indispensable.

and North Africa.[175] Those who remain in heresy are to be ''driven
out from the Church and cut off from communion.''[176] The word
eirchthēsan gives an indication that the delegates of the synod saw
themselves as having the authority to impose upon the heretics a
direct exclusion from the Eucharist. It is done not to coerce the sinners to undertake penance but to keep safe the Church's own doctrine and life. Therefore, it is an action that cannot properly be called
a penance; yet, for our purposes here, it is important, due to the
directness of the procedure. There is a definite development in the
perception on the part of the Church as to the authority that could
be exercised over postbaptismal sinners themselves and not just indirectly through the community.[177]

Two chapters later Eusebius relates excerpts from an apologetical work against Montanism, supposedly from the hand of the
bishop Apollonius (V,18).[178] He speaks of two Montanist disciples,
Themiso, a prophet yet covetous of possessions, and Alexander, a
robber ''and worse'' but also a martyr.[179] He then asks:

> Who, then, forgives the sin of whom? Does the prophet [forgive] the
> robberies of the martyr, or the martyr the covetousness of the prophet?
> (V,18,7)[180]

---

175. Theories of authorship of this account abound, but none are as convincing
as the position that the work is genuinely anonymous. See De Labriolle, *Sources du
Montanisme*, pp. xx–xxiv. The dating is difficult but probably comes some years after
Eusebius's witness to the origin of the heresy (c. 171–173 A.D.) in his *Chronicle*. As
to the further identity of such ecclesial synods, see De Labriolle, *La crise Montaniste*,
p. 30; J. Lebreton, ''Le développement des institutions ecclésiastiques à la fin du
second siècle et au début du troisième,'' *RSR* 24 (1934) 129–164, pp. 158–161; J. Deferrari, *Eusebius Pamphili. Ecclesiastical History* (Books 1–5), FC 19 (Washington, 1953;
reprint, 1965), p. 316, n. 16.

176. . . . *houtō de tēs te ekklēsias exeōsthēsan kai tēs koinōnias eirchthēsan* (41,49).

177. However, there is no evidence that such action necessarily meant permanent banishment. From the previous evidence, it is best to suppose that the decree
against the Montanists remained in effect until such time as they confessed their error and returned to the Church.

178. This text is probably later than the excerpts of V,16-17, closer to A.D. 200.
See Bardy, SC 41, p. 55, n. 1.

179. Though the term ''martyr'' was applied to those who died for the faith, it
could be used in anticipation, for example, after one had received his or her sentence. Leclercq, *DACL*, c. 2365–2366.

180. . . . *tis oun tini charizetai ta hamartēmata; poteron ho prophētēs tas lēsteias tō mar-
tyri ē ho martys tō prophētē tas pleonexia* (41,57).

Once again, the question of the power of the martyrs, confessors, and now prophets to pardon sins is raised.[181] If the Church had not had a tradition of reconciling sinners through the intercession of the martyrs, the irony of Apollonius's question would have been lost.

CONCLUSION

Irenaeus is a stronger witness to the practice of exomologesis as a specific action undertaken by those guilty of public sins against the faith after baptism. While this was not a defined discipline, his use of the term hints at the beginnings of some sort of "institutionalizing" of the practice. He is less clear regarding the procedure of isolating transgressors from interaction with the community. In Irenaeus's writings, unlike earlier ones, the act of isolation seems neither coercive nor (necessarily) indirect, and comes to an end when a person returns to the Church and undertakes exomologesis. The linking of the two actions is significant: the action of exomologesis appears important in convincing the sinner of his or her transgressions and leading such a one to true conversion. Yet, for all the evolution in penitential practice suggested in the *Adversus haereses*, it is only possible for one to be outside (via isolation) or inside (via readmission) the Church, even if one is engaged in ongoing exomologesis. As in other writings from the first two centuries, Irenaeus does not witness to any intermediate stage of penance through which one might be gradually reconciled to the "Church of God."

The testimony of the witnesses from the pages of Eusebius's *Ecclesiastical History* does not offer much in the way of description of actual procedures connected with those guilty of postbaptismal offenses. They are included here mainly as proof of an attitude of tolerance toward sin existing in the Church. Yet they also witness to one aspect that will be even more clearly seen in the develop-

---

181. The scant evidence (outside of Tertullian) concerning Montanist practices leaves open the question as to whether they allowed a certain efficaciousness through the intercession of the martyrs/confessors/prophets (the position of Poschmann, *Paenitentia Secunda*, pp. 264ff., and F. Vokes, "Penitential Discipline in Montanism," pp. 62–63) or refused such a possibility (the view of W. Schepelern, *Der Montanismus und die Phrygischen Kulte* (Tübingen, 1929), and Von Campenhausen, *Ecclesiastical Authority*, p. 220, n. 30).

ment of the order of penitents in the following century: the authority of ecclesial leadership to directly impose penitential action upon sinners themselves. Also, the intercession of the martyrs forms an eloquent testimony to a belief seen throughout the first two centuries, namely, the absolute necessity of the community's prayer in seeking God's pardon for sinners.

CHAPTER SUMMARY

The Christian communities of the first two centuries were small sects filled with evangelical fervor and eschatological hope. Faith in the saving Word of God, Jesus, was lived through the strong bonds of relationship among the members, the source and summit of which was the celebration of the Eucharist. Grave postbaptismal sin was an unforeseen experience, but one that the early communities knew altered in some way the relationship between the sinner and the Church. This reality had to be externally expressed through some response on their part.

Early penitential procedures were localized and informal, influenced by both rigorist and tolerant elements. However, the predominant tradition allowed for repentant transgressors to be able to be readmitted to the *koinōnia*. Two penitential practices were especially in evidence: the liturgical confession of faults (analogous to the confession of sin found in postexilic Israel), and, in cases of unrepentant offenders, the isolation of the sinner by the community (having its roots in the synagogal bans of Judaism). With the gradual institutionalization of the hierarchical ministry, a parallel development occurred in penitential procedures. They too became more established and less informal (evidenced in the shift from an indirect to a direct coercive isolation of the sinner). Yet an accepted penitential *ordo* was not in evidence before the very end of the second century. For grave sinners, to be reconciled to the Church required that some penance be done and the intercession of the entire Church be given. Penitents were not yet an organized class of persons in the Church, since a defined process of ecclesial penance was only in the initial stages of birth into the tradition.

Chapter Three

THIRD-CENTURY WITNESSES IN THE EAST

The examination of the second-century witness in the preceding chapter has set the stage for the more unequivocal testimony of the writers of the third century. It was during this period that the ecclesial actions undertaken by the Church and those guilty of sin after baptism were more systematically brought together in such a way that one can see more definitively an outline of an order of penitents. Though more lucid than the ambiguity of the earlier writers, the testimony of the patristic writers here can hardly be said to be cohesive on this point. It was the needs of the local church that determined the development of the process employed to deal with the situation of erring members of the community. Yet there is a surprising degree of consonance arising from the pages of the witnesses about to be surveyed. This is due, at least in part, to the ascendancy of an established hierarchical ministerial order by the middle of the third century, opening the way for a more institutional yet more effective development of penitential procedures. The fact remains that the churches of the East and West felt a need to make some response to grave postbaptismal sinners.

This chapter will examine the relevant third-century witness from the East.[1] Less influenced by the controversies over penance that

---

1. Though most systematic presentations of the penitential experience of the third century start with the witness from the West (Vorgrimler, *Busse*, pp. 42–68; Baus, *The Apostolic Community to Constantine*, pp. 324–345), the order is inverted here so that the Eastern testimony is not overshadowed by the more obvious Western attestation. Also, by ending with the West, the points of similarities between East and West are brought into sharper focus.

will be seen in the West, the Eastern writers highlight the pastoral dimension of postbaptismal penance. This is especially apparent in their advice concerning the need to seek out "someone of God" to whom a person could speak about his or her sins and from whom one could receive direction. It is a practice that will profoundly influence the entire development of penance in the East. Though somewhat later than the important Western testimony, especially Tertullian, the Eastern witness is presented first in order to display more demonstratively the substantial amount of agreement among the varied sources, even those geographically and chronologically distinct. The first section of the chapter will examine the witness of Syria and Asia Minor; the second section will present the testimony from Alexandria.

I. SYRIA AND ASIA MINOR

A. THE *DIDASCALIA APOSTOLORUM* (C. 200–250 A.D.)

A church order of Syrian origin and an invaluable source for a picture of the organization of early Christian life and worship, the *Didascalia* dates most probably from the first half of the third century.[2] One is immediately impressed with the hierarchical tone of

---

2. The controversy surrounding the dating of the work remains unresolved. B. Altaner, *Patrologie* (Freiburg, 1938), p. 26, was the first to hold that the entire work dates from the first decades of the third century. Galtier ("La date de la Didascalie des Apôtres," *RHE* 42 (1947) 315–351; reprinted in *Origines de pénitence*, pp. 189–221) staunchly defended this position, and it has received wide support (Quasten, *Patrology* II, p. 147; Grotz, *Busstufenwesens*, p. 371; Rahner, *Early Church*, p. 226; Vorgrimler, *Busse*, p. 65). However, Von Campenhausen (*Ecclesiastical Authority*, pp. 239–240, n. 7) is not so sure and seems to lean toward the argument set forth by H. Achelis/ J. Flemming (*Die syrische Didaskalia*, TU 25,2 [Leipzig, 1904], pp. 369–379) for the second half of the third century. For earlier authors who held this position, see Galtier, "La date de la Didascalie," p. 317. Though a more in-depth study of this work, in order to formulate a position as to its date, goes beyond the bounds of this study, it is included as the first witness from the East in agreement with the dating assigned it by the majority of later commentators.

The edition used in this study is the recently published Syriac text with English translation by A. Vööbus, *The Didascalia Apostolorum in Syriac*, CSCO 401–402, 407–408 (Louvain, 1979). All references including direct citations will be to the English text and will be indicated by page and line numbers. Other editions and translations consulted include the reconstructed Greek text by F. Funk, *Didascalia et Constitutiones*

the work, obviously written by one who gives strong assent to the central role of a monarchical episcopacy.[3] Of all the tasks that the bishop is instructed to perform, certainly one of the most important is the wise use of his authority to bind and loose sin (52:21-27; 67:7-69:3).[4] He is the doctor who must determine what measures must be taken in order for the soul to be healed of its sinfulness (78:9-79:1; 114:17-115:9).[5]

1. THE POSSIBILITY OF POSTBAPTISMAL PARDON

In paraenetic fashion, the author of the *Didascalia* reminds the Church that sin after baptism is an extremely serious matter:

> For we do not believe, brethren, when [once] a man has gone down into the water that he will do again the abominable and defiled works of the wicked heathen. For it is manifest and known to everyone, that whosoever does evil after baptism, the same is already condemned to the Gehenna of fire (50:20-51:5).[6]

Yet for all its juridic concern, the work is surprisingly pastoral in its approach, constantly exhorting the bishop to show compassion in the treatment of sinners (53:11-62:18). Just as the bishop is to be unafraid in imposing penance on sinners for the sake of their con-

---

Apostolorum, Vol. I (Paderborn, 1905); R. Connolly, *Didascalia Apostolorum. The Syriac Version Translated and Accompanied by the Verona Latin Fragments* (Oxford, 1929); E. Tidner, *Didascaliae apostolorum, Canonum ecclesiasticorum, Traditionis apostolicae versiones Latinae*, TU 75 (Berlin, 1963), pp. 1-103.

3. P. Beaucamp, "Un évêque du IIIe siècle aux prises avec les pécheurs: Son activité apostolique," *BLE* 50 (1949) 26-47, p. 30.

4. Von Campenhausen, *Ecclesiastical Authority*, p. 240.

5. Such an image, used by numerous patristic writers, underscores the fact that no matter how harsh the penance, its purpose was medicinal rather than penal. See J. Janini Cuesta, "La penitencia medicinal desde la Didascalia Apostolorum a S. Gregorio de Nisa," *RET* 7 (1947) 337-362, pp. 338-344. Might the bishop have been a physician? See Vööbus, p. 115, n. 32.

6. This passage raises the question of whether the work was originally more rigorist and only later redacted to include the more pastorally lenient passages concerning the pardon of postbaptismal sin as an anti-Donatist or anti-Novatian polemic, the position of E. Schwartz, "Busstufen und Katechumenatsklassen," in *Gesammelte Schriften*, Vol. 5: *Zum Neuen Testament und zum frühen Christentum* (Berlin, 1963; reprinted from 1911) 274-362, pp. 297-308. Presently, however, the consensus of scholarship accepts the work as a unity (Connolly, *Didascalia*, pp. xxxvi-xxxviii; Galtier, "La date de la Didascalie," *passim*; Von Campenhausen, *Ecclesiastical Authority*, p. 245, n. 54; Rahner, *Early Church*, pp. 226-227).

version (76:1-9), so must he never be too harsh toward them; if he drives them away with no hope of receiving them back into the community, he runs the risk of driving them into the hands of heathens or heretics (79:1-24). The author goes to great lengths to use examples from the Scriptures to prove that even the grave sins of idolatry and murder (80:20-88:14), as well as adultery (89:6-13), are able to be pardoned if one is willing to undertake penance. Only the sin of Amon, who was unwilling to repent of his sin, is unpardonable (88:14-89:3). Though harsh in its teaching, the *Didascalia* is consistently tolerant in its practice of offering hope to postbaptismal sinners.[7]

2. THE PROCESS OF ECCLESIAL PENANCE

The explicit description of the process of Church penance makes the *Didascalia* important for the historical development of the order of penitents. One is able to discern two exclusions of those guilty of grave sins after baptism. The first is an isolation of the transgressor from the Church, either voluntarily (52:7-10) or through being "cast forth" by the authoritative word of the bishop:

> But when you have seen one who has sinned, be angry at him, and command that they cast him out. And when he is cast out, let them be angry at him, and contend with him and keep him outside the church (64:14-17).[8]

Though distinct from the indirect coercive penance of isolation of the earlier period, insofar as this action could be directly imposed upon the sinner, it has a similar purpose: to coerce sinners to undertake the necessary penance and return to God's Church. Yet, the *Didascalia* testifies that this isolation is not total. The sinners are entrusted to the care of others in the community who carefully ob-

---

7. Poschmann, *Paenitentia Secunda*, pp. 476–480; Galtier, *Origines de pénitence*, p. 167, agreeing with Achelis/Flemming, *Die syrische Didaskalia*, pp. 306–307, and against the position of J. Bartlet, *Church-Life and Church-Order During the First Four Centuries*, ed. C. Cadoux (Oxford, 1943), pp. 83–85, who interprets the work as more rigorist than pastoral. As in other patristic witnesses, it could once again be an example of how both tolerant and rigorist traditions existed side by side in some of the early Christian communities.

8. See also 52:10-20; 117:1-2.

served their penitential works and attitude so as to be in a position to intercede on their behalf before the bishop (64:17-21).[9] These persons enable the bishop to exercise his ministry in the care of these "sick" members of the community (76:20-78:9).

It might be maintained that this practice is in fact different from what has been seen heretofore, inasmuch as the sinner, though separated from the life of the community, continues to have regular contact with at least some of its members. In this way one is tempted to invest the procedure with a designation other than "penance of isolation" so as to better express its distinctiveness from the earlier practice of totally quarantining the sinner. Yet, at the same time, it is necessary to keep before us the fact that the purpose of both remains the same: to bring to conversion one whose full status as a Christian, gained through baptism, is lost through sin. It is then the coercive intention of the isolation rather than its quantitative amount that leads us to maintain the same designation of this practice as for the earlier period. Now directly imposed upon the sinner, it is a coercive penance of isolation, through which one is led to an intermediate stage of the penitential process, seen clearly for the first time: the penance of segregation.[10]

When the sinner is ready to undertake ecclesial penance, a readiness affirmed by those who have cared for him or her in testimony before the bishop, the bishop calls the sinner back to the Church in order to examine him/her. If the bishop is satisfied that the per-

---

9. Galtier, *Origines de pénitence*, pp. 170-171. Galtier admits that references to such persons in the *Didascalia* are vague, though it may have been a ministry reserved to deacons (101:19-25). In any event, the use of the third person in 64:17-21 leads one to suspect the involvement of persons other than the bishop.

10. Rahner, *Early Church*, pp. 227-233, designates this first exclusion as a "real excommunication" to distinguish it from the "liturgical excommunication" that followed. Not only do we object to his use of the term "excommunication" for reasons previously cited, but such a designation does not adequately reflect the necessary place of the coercive penance of isolation in the entire penitential process. These grounds also form the basis of our disagreement with Galtier, *Origines de pénitence*, p. 180, and Grotz, *Busstufenwesens*, p. 391, who hold that the former experience was solely penal and was not a part of ecclesial penance. The ecclesial reality of the coercive penance of isolation must be seen in the fact that sinners continued to be cared for by the bishop and the community, even in their absence. Both this experience and the penance of segregation that followed were two moments of an ecclesial process expressing a sinner's new relationship with God and the Church due to sin.

son is truly repentant and honest in his or her desire for ecclesial reconciliation, a penance of segregation is assigned the person:

> And then, O bishop, command [the sinner] to come in, and ask him whether he repents. And if he is worthy to be received into the church, appoint him days of fasting according to his transgression, two weeks, or three, or five, or seven. And so dismiss him that he may go, saying to him all that is right for admonition and instruction (64:21–65:4).

The *Didascalia* is the first of the witnesses presented here to offer a picture of a step of penance intervening between the coercive penance of isolation and the ecclesial readmittance of the penitent.[11] Its duration is surprisingly brief, a mere matter of weeks. While continuing to remain under the special care of the bishop as a sign of a not-yet-restored ecclesial status, it is during this period that the penitent is drawn again into the life of the community (114:5-8). Though still barred from the Eucharist, penitents have a place in the worship of the Church as they are admitted to the liturgy of the Word (113:23–114:1; 220:6-7). They may even have been assigned a particular place within the assembly (112:16-17), a practice also to be seen in the witness of Tertullian.[12] They are continually to be admonished by the bishop and must constantly beg for his intercession and the intercession of the whole community so that pardon might be granted (65:4-16). Yet, for all the hardships, they are not isolated from the community but segregated within it.[13]

---

11. Unlike the third-century witness of the West and of the Eastern witness originating in Alexandria, the *Didascalia* does not use any term comparable to "exomologesis" to refer either to this intermediate period as a whole or to any external penitential actions that might have occurred during this period.

12. Tertullian, *De paen.* 7,10; *De pud.* 3,5; 5,14. Rahner, *Early Church*, p. 386, n. 36, sees the "bringing in" of 114:12 as an explicit reference to the act of leading a sinner back to his or her previous place in the community prior to ecclesial penance. This would confirm that penitents were segregated into a separate place during the time of penance. Given the strict instructions concerning the exact placement of members of the community within the church (130:8-134:18), this would not be inconceivable.

13. As explained in the first chapter, the term "penance of segregation" is chosen here to highlight this very fact: Penitents during this period were within the life and worship of the community, though with certain limitations. This is existentially quite different from the preceding coercive penance of isolation.

3. THE RECONCILIATION OF THE SINNER

After the penitent has successfully completed the weeks of the assigned penance and the bishop has seen the fruit of his or her repentance, such a one is reconciled to the Church. The *Didascalia* is most explicit on how such an ecclesial pardon is effected:

> And when he who has sinned has repented and wept, receive him. And while the whole people pray over him, lay [your] hand upon him, and allow him from henceforth to be in the church (68:23-25);

> And so as you baptize a heathen and receive him, so also lay the hand upon this man while everyone is praying for him, and then bring him in and let him communicate with the church. Indeed, the laying on of the hand shall be to him instead of baptism— indeed, whether by the laying of the hand, or by baptism, that they receive the fellowship of the Holy Spirit (114:10-16).[14]

It is the pouring out of the Holy Spirit upon the person that opens the way for readmittance to the Eucharist and reinstatement to his/her former status in the Church.[15] Though the involvement of the entire community is spoken of, the stress is clearly on the action of the bishop. It is ultimately he who decides on the readiness of the penitent for ecclesial pardon, and it is his authority, expressed in the imposition of the hand, that restores the sinner to spiritual health. The performance of penance serves only as the precondition for reconciliation by the bishop, whereas readmission to the Church appears almost as a mere postcondition to the bishop's action. Due to the heightened role that the *Didascalia* assigns to the monarchical bishop in the pardon of sin, the earlier emphasis on

---

14. See also 117:4-5. Rahner, *Early Church*, p. 386, n. 35, assumes that the imposition of the hand was accompanied by a prayer said by the bishop; however, the text is silent on this point.

15. Galtier, *Origines de pénitence*, pp. 177–178; Rahner, *Early Church*, pp. 234–238. Rahner shows that the imposition of the hand in 114:10-16 cannot be considered a mere repetition of the postbaptismal imposition of the hand which formed part of the initiation rite which could not be repeated. Neither can the rite be closely tied to the imposition of the hand in the exorcism of 156:17-18, since the effect of the action after penance was clearly the outpouring of the Holy Spirit. He sees the rite here as an imitation of the laying on of hands at the postbaptismal anointing (confirmation), yet a distinct rite in itself.

being reincorporated into the Body of Christ as the way a sinner is saved is somewhat diminished.[16]

4. THE CONSEQUENCES OF ECCLESIAL PENANCE

It is interesting to note that nowhere in the entire work is there any mention of ecclesial penance being unrepeatable as a consequence of the penitential process.[17] At first sight this stands in stark contrast to the circle of patristic witnesses in the West and in Alexandria who, following the teaching of the *Shepherd of Hermas*, will pass on the custom of a single possibility of reconciliation for sins committed after baptism. There is doubt whether the author of the *Didascalia* even knew of *Hermas*, and if so, dependency is slight and does not include Hermas's teaching of a single penance.[18] And there is no direct reference to either Clement of Alexandria or Origen.[19] Therefore, the "surprising" omission by the work on this point may in fact not be surprising at all, especially if one remembers that the only Eastern witnesses to an unrepeatable penance in the first three centuries come from Alexandria. The question can then be justifiably raised: In the East, could it not be the Alexandrians rather than the Syrian church or the churches of Asia Minor that are unique in their limitation of postbaptismal penance?[20]

---

16. Rahner, *Early Church*, pp. 238–239. Such an exercise of power by the bishop causes both Rahner and Galtier, *Origines de pénitence*, pp. 176ff., to see in the *Didascalia* evidence of a truly sacramental system of penance. Von Campenhausen, *Ecclesiastical Authority*, p. 243, n. 44, agrees with Rahner's assessment that the episcopal forgiveness of sins is more detached from incorporation into the Church as a means of salvation, but thinks that his insistence on the sacramental characer of reconciliation in the *Didascalia* is "somewhat overstated."

17. Rahner, *Early Church*, pp. 240–242, who bases this conclusion on 117:6–118:27, where a long justification is given for the permanent exclusion of the recidivist from the community. If a custom of a single penance was known, it would have been invoked here. Here Rahner is not as cautious as Grotz, *Busstufenwesens*, p. 385, who states that while unrepeatable reconciliation was not a rigid principle in the *Didascalia*, there is equally no witness to a repeatable penance.

18. Vööbus does see slight allusions to *Hermas*: p. 54, n. 15; p. 183, n. 128; p. 194, n. 163.

19. Rahner, *Early Church*, p. 241, agreeing with Connolly, *Didascalia*, pp. lxxix, lxxxiii.

20. Rahner, *Early Church*, pp. 241–242, who points to numerous similarities between the *Didascalia* and Jewish teachings and practices (p. 390, n. 64), so as to make the case that the penitential exclusions found in the Christian document are closely

5. AN ORDER OF PENITENTS IN THE *DIDASCALIA*

It can be said that the *Didascalia* allows for the reconciliation of all sin, even though sin committed after baptism is considered extremely serious. The role of the bishop is central in overseeing the care of those who find themselves in such a situation. It is he who leads them through the necessary penitential process by which they might once again recover their full Christian status. There are three discernible moments in this process.

The first is a coercive penance of isolation (either voluntarily undertaken or directly imposed by the bishop), which means a radical, though not total, separation from the sacramental and social life of the community. Sinners remain connected to the Church through those under whose care they are entrusted, who exhort offenders to do works of penance and who eventually intercede with the bishop on their behalf.

Upon this recommendation the bishop examines the sinner to gauge his or her readiness to undertake a second moment of the penitential process: the intermediate step designated as a penance of segregation. This includes a limited period of intense fasting and prayer, admonitions by the bishop, and being admitted to the assembly, but only to segregated places where penitents are able to be present, though forbidden to partake of the Eucharist.

Afterward, the penitent is pardoned of sin by the prayer of the community and the laying on of the hand by the bishop. In this way the person is reconciled once more to the Church (and so to God), readmitted to communion and, as in baptism, again given the gift of the Holy Spirit. Finally, the *Didascalia* does not witness to any further consequences resulting from the process of penance, not even to the custom of penance being unrepeatable.

---

related to the repeatable Jewish procedure of the synagogal ban (pp. 243–244). Also, the fact that the *Constitutiones apostolorum*, of which the *Didascalia* has traditionally formed the first six books, makes no mention of an unrepeatable penance even though they are from a later date. Finally, Rahner concludes that if indeed the practice of the Eastern Church (with the exception of Alexandria) did not include an unrepeatable ecclesial *metanoia*, ''it is possible to explain much more easily why the passage from public church penance to sacramental (repeatable) private penance was able to be achieved in a less striking and a less reflexive way than in the West'' (p. 244).

B. GREGORY THAUMATURGUS († C. 270–275 A.D.)

Born in Neocaesarea in the province of Pontus to a pagan family between 210 and 213 A.D., Gregory and his brother Athenodorus were classically educated in their own town.[21] Prior to setting out for Berytos in Phoenicia to continue their education, they were invited to Caesarea by their sister. While there, they attended some of the lectures of Origen, an event that was to change the direction of Gregory's life. He and his brother remained in Caesarea (231/233–238) as students of Origen's catechetical school and were eventually baptized. Some years later he was appointed the first bishop of Neocaesarea and soon had the reputation of one zealous in the proclamation of the gospel. He took part in the Council of Antioch (265 A.D.) and died a few years later during the reign of Aurelian. After his death, legends concerning the events of his ministry sprang up and were set down in a number of biographies, the best known being that by Gregory of Nyssa. It is the retelling of these "miracle stories" that has earned him the title of "Thaumaturgus."[22]

Gregory is an important witness to the penitential discipline in the East due to his so-called *Canonical Epistle*.[23] Here he is writing to an unknown bishop who has asked Gregory for advice concerning difficulties occasioned by an invasion of the Boradi and the Goths into Pontus. Pagan food has been eaten, women raped, and some Christians have collaborated with the barbarians in stealing from, and even killing, their fellow citizens. Can Christians responsible for such acts ever hope to come to pardon? And if so, what is the penitential procedure to be followed?

---

21. What is known of the life of Gregory comes principally from Eusebius's *Eccl. Hist.* (VI,30), from Jerome's *De viris illus.* (65), and most especially from Gregory's own *In Origenem oratio panegyrica* (V,48-72), an oration given upon the occasion of his taking leave of Origen's catechetical school in Caesarea.

22. H. Crouzel, *Grégoire le Thaumaturge: Remerciement a Origène suivi de la lettre d'Origène a Grégoire*, SC 148 (Paris, 1969), pp. 14–27.

23. Direct citations are from the recent edition by M. Phouska, "*Grēgoriou Thaumatourgou hē kanōnikē epistolē. Eisagōgē–kritikē ekdosis keimenou–metaphrasē scholia,*" *Ekklēsiastikos pharos* 60 (1978) 736–809, pp. 763–771. Though earlier editions of the *Epistle* usually cite eleven canons, Phouska numbers twelve, believing as he does that the first canon is in fact two separate canons. References in the text will follow his numerical order.

In response to the bishop, and ostensibly without precedent, Gregory outlines consecutive "grades" or steps of penance through which one guilty of postbaptismal sin must pass if there is to be any hope of eventual readmission to the Church. Four such grades are described in the twelfth canon:

> Mourning occurs outside the gate of the place of prayer; standing there, the sinner should beg the faithful as they enter to offer prayers on his behalf. Listening happens inside the gate of the forecourt, where the offender should stand until the departure of the catechumens, and then go forth. It is said, when he [the offender] has heard the scripture and the instructions, let him be put forth as one not deserving of the prayer. Prostration occurs when such a one stands within the gate of the nave, and goes forth along with the catechumens. "Standing together with" occurs when he [the sinner] stands beside the faithful and does not go forth with the catechumens. Last is that of participant in the Holies.[24]

No previous patristic author has witnessed to such a system of penance. The most developed penitential order seen till now has been in the *Didascalia*, where a two-step process seems to have been in place: the older coercive penance of isolation followed by what has been described as a penance of segregation leading to pardon. With Gregory, there is a further division of the penitential process. The coercive penance of isolation could be said to correspond roughly to the initial period of total isolation, that is, those who must stand outside the Church and "mourn" (*prosklausis*). Not only are these unfortunates unable to enter the Church at all, but the existential reality of isolation appears from the fact that the community is under no obligation to recognize their presence.

The next grade of "listeners" (*akroōmenoi*) falls somewhere between isolation and a penance of segregation, with penitents being allowed some contact with the community. The assembly still does

---

24. *Hē prosklausis exō tēs pylēs tou euktēriou estin. entha hestōta ton hamartanonta chrē tōn eisiontōn deisthai pistōn, hyper hauto euchesthai. Hē akroasis endothi tēs pylēs en tō nartheki, entha hestanai chrē ton hēmartēkota heōs tōn katēchoumenōn, kai enteuthen exerchesthai. Akouōn gar, phēsi, tōn Graphōn kai tēs didaskalias, ekballesthō, kai mē axiousthō proseuchēs. Hē de hypoptōsis, hina, esōthen tēs pylēs tou naou histamenos, meta tōn katēchoumenōn exerchētai. Hē systasis, hina synistatai tois pistois, kai mē exerchētai meta tōn katēchoumenōn; teleutaion hē methexis tōn hagiasmatōn* (Phouska, 770:14–771:5).

not seem to recognize the presence of the penitents, even though they are now allowed to at least be present for the liturgy of the Word.

The status of penitents is improved when they are allowed to become "prostrators" (hypopiptontes), being admitted to the nave and asked to go forth with the catechumens, a group possessing a definite status within the Church. Penitents are no longer considered outsiders to the community but segregated within it.

This penance of segregation continues through the last grade of "standing together with" (synistatai), which is the immediate step prior to what might be called a final step: the reconciliation of the sinner through participation in the Eucharist. As this process is to be found in the canons of the early Eastern councils, including Nicaea, and in the writings of the later Cappadocian Fathers, it is not without reason that certain contemporary authors have regarded Gregory as standing at the inceptive point of its development.[25]

Yet, before such a conclusion can be drawn, there are serious reasons to doubt the authenticity of the twelfth canon. First, the earliest commentators are in disagreement as to whether to include this canon in Gregory's Epistle.[26] Second, the canon bears remarkable resemblance to canon 75 of the third Canonical Epistle of Basil to Amphilochios, causing many recent authors to see the canon as a fourth-century emendation, added to the Epistle to explain Gregory's unexplained references to "listeners" and "prostrators" (in canons 8,

---

25. References to the four-stage penitential system may be found among the canons of the Councils of Ancyra (314 A.D.), Neocaesarea (320 A.D.), and especially canons 11-14 of Nicea (325 A.D.). Also, numerous references may be found among the Canonical Epistles of Basil and Gregory of Nyssa. Unlike the present work by Gregory Thaumaturgus, these later witnesses specify the length of time to be spent in each grade leading to readmittance to Eucharist, highlighting the fact that by the fourth century the process had become much more casuistical. Generally, the four-stage process has been interpreted as one of those historical peculiarities which, prima facie, appear to have enormous ramifications for a particular subject, whereas, in point of fact, its influence is relatively minor.

One author who sees Gregory as the "father" of the graded system is Watkins, A History of Penance I, pp. 242–246, 327.

26. The Byzantine jurist Zonaras (twelfth century) ignores the canon in his Apostolic Constitutions. He is followed in this by his contemporary Aristenos, while another contemporary, Balsamon, includes the canon in his commentary on the Epistle. Compare in Phouska, p. 786 with p. 798.

9, and 10).[27] Finally, if the purpose of the canon is explanatory (which seems clear from the fact that, unlike the previous eleven canons, it is not given in reference to some concrete situation of the community), it also reveals a certain confusion in its explanation of the stages of those who "mourn" and those who "stand together with" the community, neither of which is mentioned in the first eleven canons.[28] While this bespeaks the congruity between the highly revered bishop of Neocaesarea and the later Cappadocian Fathers, it may also be proof that such a congruity has been created anachronistically to justify the penitential experience of the Cappadocian Fathers themselves. In any event, doubts concerning the canon's authenticity are too strong to be overlooked.[29]

If canon 12 is deemed spurious, what remains of Gregory's penitential witness? In his ninth canon, on the treatment of Christians who had trespassed on the private property of others, he mentions both "listeners" and "prostrators":

> Now those who have been so audacious as to invade the houses of others should not be considered fit even to be listeners in the public assembly, if they have once been tried and convicted. But if they have denounced themselves and made restitution, they should be returned to the rank of the prostrators.[30]

Among the authentic canons from Gregory, only the grades of "listeners" and "prostrators" are designated. From his usage, the

---

27. Crouzel, *Grégoire le Thaumaturge*, p. 28.

28. Grotz, *Busstufenwesens*, pp. 406–408, while admitting that the grades of those who "mourn" and those who "stand together with" the community were later developments of the Eastern penitential discipline, maintains their implicit presence in the first eleven canons. It is possible to agree with Grotz only insofar as these grades are implicit in the basic actions of isolating sinners from, and segregating them within, the community, but not if he is implying that they are explicit as distinct actions in themselves.

29. Contemporary authors who hold the canon as spurious include: S. Salmond, *Fathers of the Third Century*, ANF 6 (Edinburgh, 1861; reprinted, Grand Rapids, Mich., 1978), p. 20, elucidations I; Palmer, *Sacraments and Forgiveness*, p. 63; Grotz, *Busstufenwesens*, pp. 406–408; M. Geerard, *Corpus Christianorum Clavis Patrum Graecorum*, Vol. I: *Patres Antenicaeni* (Turnhout, 1983), p. 239, n. 1765.

30. *Tous de oikois allotriois epelthein tolmēsantas, ean men katēgorēthentes elengchthōsi, mēde tēs akroaseōs axiōsēs; ean de heautous exeipōsi kai apodōsin, en tē tōn hypostrephsontōn taxei hypopiptein* (Phouska, pp. 769:13–770:3). Canon 8 (below) also mentions "listeners," while canon 10 speaks of "prostrators."

former conveys the sense of a sinner remaining on the fringes of the community, yet being allowed to be present to "listen" to something, most probably the Liturgy of the Word. This cannot properly be called a penance of isolation inasmuch as "listeners," though seemingly possessing the lowest rank in the Church, can still be admitted to the assembly. Also, canon 8 relates that those who have cooperated with the barbarians are to be "excluded even from being listeners."[31] This is an indication that the only worse fate that could befall a Christian would be to be excluded entirely, further distancing the grade of "listener" from being identified as a penance of isolation. In point of fact, it appears to combine elements of being isolated from and being segregated within the community to form a distinct stage of penance not seen in the *Didascalia*.

On the other hand, "prostrators" appear to have a closer relationship with the community, the result of a personal admission of guilt and the doing of whatever external action is necessary to heal the wrong committed.[32] Without wishing to paint too neat a picture, Gregory's witness to "prostrators" is likened to the penance of segregation seen in the *Didascalia* as an intervening step of penance following a coercive penance of isolation and immediately preceding readmission to the Eucharist.[33]

This examination of the penitential witness of Gregory Thaumaturgus reveals that he may not be the extreme innovator that he appears to be at first glance. While the origin of the four-stage process remains unknown, it will not be until the fourth century that the stages of those who "mourn" and those who "stand together with" the community will be unequivocally witnessed to as part of the accepted penitential discipline of the East. The authentic canons of Gregory's *Epistle* (1-11) make allusion only to the grades of

---

31. . . . *kai tēs akroaseōs apeirxai dei* (Phouska, 769:10).

32. Though Gregory does not use the term *exomologēsis*, his use of *exeipon*, here in the reflexive sense meaning "to denounce oneself," may also be a reference to some sort of confession of sin. See also canon 10. G. Lampe, *A Patristic Greek Lexicon* (Oxford, 1961), p. 495, s.v. *exeipon*.

33. As will be seen, a fragment of a letter by Dionysius of Alexandria may be the only other third-century testimony to the penitential grades of "listeners" and "prostrators," though the authenticity of his witness has come under serious attack (see below, pp. 165–166 and n. 137).

"listeners" and "prostrators." While not absolutely in step with the two-stage process of penance seen previously, neither is his witness inconsonant with the developing penitential practices at the roots of an order of penitents.[34]

The very purpose of Gregory's *Canonical Epistle* is to address the issue of what to do with those who had committed grave postbaptismal sin during the time of the barbaric invasions of Pontus. It is not meant to be a descriptive account of the liturgical life of his local church. For example, there is no reference to any rite of reconciliation and readmission to the Eucharist except the mention that certain sinners, "if they have denounced themselves and made restitution, are deemed worthy of the prayer" (canon 10).[35] Neither is any allusion made to the consequences of the penitential process, e.g., whether such an event is unrepeatable.[36] Yet, in what can be discerned from the *Epistle*, Gregory shows himself to be both a man of order and a man of clemency, opening a way of forgiveness for those guilty of grave sin after baptism. The way that is opened is consistent with other contemporary witnesses of the day who outline a penitential process that recognizes the changed status of postbaptismal offenders due to their sin.

C. METHODIUS OF OLYMPUS († c. 312 A.D.)

So little is known about the life of Methodius that he has been called the "most mysterious of the Greek Fathers who wrote before the peace of the Church."[37] The earliest source of information concerning his life is Jerome, who writes in chapter 83 of his *De viris*

---

34. Such a conclusion obviously goes against Grotz (see above, n. 28).

35. . . . *ean de heautous exeipōsi kai apodōsi, kai tēs euchēs axiōsai* (Phouska, 770:7-8). Later usage in the East confirms that reference to "the prayer" (*tēs euchēs*) meant the liturgy of the Eucharist (see below, p. 156). Grotz, *Busstufenwesens*, pp. 405–406, sees here an implicit reference to those who "stand together with" the community (see above, n. 28). In the nonauthentic canon 12 the terminology changes to reflect a later, more precise usage of reconciliation as being the participation in the "holies" (*tōn hagiasmatōn*) following the completion of a four-stage penitential process.

36. It must be reiterated that the experience of unrepeatable penance is only indisputably seen in the third century in the East with Clement of Alexandria and Origen.

37. H. Musurillo and V.-H. Debidour, *Méthode d'Olympe: Le Banquet*, SC 95 (Paris, 1963), p. 9.

illustribus that Methodius was bishop of the small town of Olympus in the region of Lycia in Asia Minor but later moved to Tyre in Phoenicia.[38] He authored several works, including the dialogue on virginity (*Symposium*), his only entirely extant work, and a polemical work against the Neoplatonic philosopher Porphyry, now lost. In his work *De resurrectione*, Methodius opposes Origen's teaching on the preexistence of the soul and what he considered to be an overly spiritualistic approach regarding the resurrection of the body. He is believed to have suffered martyrdom at Chalcis in Greece, probably around 312 A.D. during the persecution of Diocletian.[39]

Methodius offers a picture of ecclesial penance as it existed in Asia Minor at the very end of the third century.[40] His thought reflects an ascetic fervor for the gospel and a renunciation of worldly values, which only impede one's ability to embrace the means of all salvation—the cross of Christ. In his fervor, his teaching at times

---

38. Jerome's witness is essentially confirmed by Socrates (*Historia ecclesiastica* VI,13), though both accounts contain such inconsistencies that it is probable that they were composed from several contradictory traditions. See Musurillo/Debidour, *Le Banquet*, pp. 10–11. From his own writings there may be reason to believe that Methodius was in fact not a bishop but rather one who lived an ascetical life and taught the Scriptures. See F. van de Paverd, "Confession (*Exagoreusis*) and Penance (*Exomologēsis*) in De lepra of Methodius of Olympus," *OCP* 44 (1978) 309–341, pp. 312–313.

39. Socrates situates Chalcis in the Orient, most likely in Syria, a more likely site of his martyrdom, since it is nearer to Tyre. Against the argumentation presented by F. Diekamp, "Ueber den Bischofssitz des hl. Märtyrers und Kirchenvaters Methodius," *ThQ* 109 (1928) 285–308 (who, in accepting the correctness of Jerome's testimony, believes that Methodius most probably ended his episcopal career as bishop of Philippi in Macedonia rather than Tyre), most authors place the locus of his ministry in Asia Minor.

On the question of during which persecution Methodius was martyred, both Jerome and Socrates speak of his death near the end of the persecutions of Decius (249–250) or Valerian (259). However, this would have been impossible if indeed Methodius was the first to refute Porphyry's polemical books *Against the Christians*, written about the year 270. For this reason, most authors place his death around 312 A.D., near the end of the persecution by Diocletian, the last major persecution of Christians prior to the Peace of Constantine.

These discussions concerning the details of the life and death of Methodius serve merely to highlight the fact that very little reliable biographical information is available.

40. Direct citations are from the edition by N. Bonwetsch, *Methodius*, GCS 27 (Leipzig, 1917), and will be indicated by page and line numbers.

appears harsh and uncompromising toward those who have fallen into grave postbaptismal sin. Certain texts have even been interpreted to show that, at the very least, Methodius possesses a certain ambivalence toward the possibility of reconciling such sinners.[41] Yet, as seen in the writings of other patristic writers, paraenetic exhortations against the destructiveness of sin do not necessarily mean that sinners are excluded from the possibility of being restored to the Church and reconciled to God. It is no different with Methodius who, though fervent, is no rigorist and is very much within the tradition of offering a "second penance" to all who repent of their sin.[42] The clearest witness to an actual penitential procedure is to be found in the small work *De lepra*. Written as a dialogue between Sistelius and Eubulius (Methodius), it allegorizes the thirteenth chapter of the Book of Leviticus, concerning the treatment of those marked by leprosy, by speaking of the treatment of those who sin after baptism.[43] In the sixth chapter, those who know themselves to be guilty of evil temptations are exhorted to pray and abstain from communion until they are sure that the enticement has been overcome (VI,7). Only then might they, with a free conscience, once again draw close to the altar of God (VI,8).[44] What is related here is a voluntary separation from the Eucharist out of a desire to advance in spiritual and moral development. It is a personal rather than an ecclesial act.[45] But in the event that the temptation persists and develops into a

---

41. This is the position of L. Fendt, "Sünde und Busse in den Schriften des Methodius von Olympus," *Der Katholik* 3, no. 31 (1905) 24–45, based on *De resurrectione* I,11,2-3; 38,2; 41,4; 61,2; II,5,1; 13,8-10; *De lepra* X,3; *De cibis* XIII,1.3; XIV,2.5.

42. This is demonstrated most convincingly by F. van de Paverd, "*Paenitentia secunda* in Methodius of Olympus," *Augustinianum* 18 (1978) 459–485, refuting the earlier position of Fendt.

43. Only fragments of the work survive in Greek, the rest being translated by Bonwetsch, *Methodius*, pp. 449–474, into German from Slavonic. Fortunately the passages most concerned with the penitential process are, for the most part, found in the Greek.

44. Van de Paverd, "Confession and Penance," p. 318, believes that Methodius makes a distinction between *enthymēsis* (thought) and *epithymia* (desire). *De lepra* VI,7-8 is in reference to the former, described here as temptation. Unlike other authors, Methodius does not attempt to draw distinctions between sins/temptations that necessitate ecclesial penance.

45. J. Farges, *Les idées morales et religieuses de Méthode d'Olympe* (Paris, 1929), p. 152.

full-fledged desire to sin or into an act of sin, the person must be willing to involve the community:

> But if [the evil] does not stop and cease, he must go to the chastisers, in order to show his spot to the bishop . . . he must not feel ashamed to confess [*exagoreusai*] the truth (VI,9).[46]

It remains a question as to whether Methodius is saying that only a personal *desire* to commit a sinful act is grounds for a person's admission into a public and ecclesial penitential process. Certainly this position finds support in the following chapter, where he speaks of the "leprosy" of a person being found in the *hēgemonikon* (the principle part of the soul, the intellect) rather than on the body (VII,4).[47] If this is the case, then it is necessary for one guilty of a sinful act or even of a grave desire to commit sin which persists after prayer and voluntary abstention from the Eucharist, to present himself or herself to the "chastisers" and truthfully admit the need for help and guidance.[48]

For his part, the bishop must play the role of the skilled physician (an image reminiscent of the *Didascalia* and, as shall be seen, Origen), acting with firmness so as to lead the spiritually sick back to health:

---

46. . . . *ei de mē pausoito kai lōpha, prositō pros tous sōphronistas, deixōn heautou tēn haphēn tō episkopō* . . . . *exagoreusai mē aidesthētō to alēthes* . . . (Bonwetsch, 459:9-10,12; trans. Van de Paverd, "Confession and Penance," p. 319).

47. This is the position of Van de Paverd, "Confession and Penance," pp. 325–339, who argues that the use of *hēgemonikon* proves that Methodius has in mind the faculty of knowledge, so that its leprosy "signifies an inner disposition, not a sinful act . . ." (p. 339). This position has much to recommend it, especially in light of Methodius's ethical fervor. However, the description of the penitential process (VII,5-6) and the use of the term *exomologēsis* (VII,5; X,2), which by the end of the third century had become an expression closely identified with postbaptismal ecclesial penance, makes one unable to rule out that Methodius also had in mind the act of sin itself. It may well have been that, given his ethical perspective, the desire to accomplish sin and the accomplishment of sin were inseparable.

48. It remains a question whether "the chastisers" would have been the bishops themselves referred to as a group or some sort of college headed by the bishop and consisting of presbyters and deacons. The text is not explicit enough, except to make it clear that some sort of truthful admission of the person's need for spiritual aid was made to the bishop. See Farges, *Les idées morales*, p. 148, n. 2; Van de Paverd, "Confession and Penance," pp. 322–324.

. . . he [the bishop] must separate him [and put him] into the exomologesis. He has to pronounce him unclean and restrain him from
communion. He must weep and pray for him. . . . And if he
ceases, after he has been kept one and a second week from the
assembly, then he will be examined again, whether he mourned
and felt a godly grief which produces a *metamelon* which leads to
salvation, then he is hopeful, he is clean, for the evil has not spread
(VII,5).[49]

The description of exclusion of the person and his/her admittance
to the exomologesis is comparable to descriptions of penance found
in the *Didascalia* as well as other third-century writings yet to be seen.
It involves a brief time during which the penitents are segregated
within the liturgical assembly, abstention from the reception of communion, the intense engagement of the bishop, personal and difficult penitential works by the persons themselves, and, finally,
readmission to communion after the person is examined and deemed
worthy.[50] In short, it is similar to the penance of segregation seen
heretofore.[51] Though it is uncertain whether the process here
described by Methodius is intended simply as a means of spiritual
healing or is actually the process of ecclesial penance, its purpose
could be said to be comparable in both cases: to aid the sinner in
changing his or her inner disposition so as to experience true Christian conversion.[52]

---

49. . . . *aphorisatō auton eis tēn exomologēsin, mianatō auton tēs koinōnias epischōn,*
klausatō, parakalesatō hyper autou. . . . *kai ei men pauoito, mian kai deuteran hebdomada*
tou synagelazesthai kratētheis, episkephthēsetai palin, ei epenthēsen ē elypēthē "lypēn" tēn
"kata theon," hētis metamelon "eis sōtērian katergazetai," euelpis estin, katharos estin; ou
gar diedothē to kakon (Bonwetsch, 460:4-11; translation by Van de Paverd, "Confession and Penance," p. 339; "Confession and Penance" II, p. 60).

50. Nothing in the description of this process by Methodius would imply that
it was anything but public, against the position of Galtier, *L'Église*, p. 282, who sees
this time as a period of isolation and so a witness of a private penance.

51. Van de Paverd, "Confession and Penance," II, *OCP* 45 (1979) 45-74, pp. 51-57,
sees the exclusion that Methodius describes here as a "ritual" rather than a "penitential" *akoinōnia* because "it is an acknowledgment of a spiritual illness" rather than
"public penance . . . intended to heal a culpable attachment to sin" (pp. 56-57).
Yet, even if he is correct, this does not lessen Methodius's witness to the penitential
process but only affirms that he has adapted it for a different purpose. See below,
pp. 141-142.

52. *Ibid.*, pp. 60-63. Obviously, if Van de Paverd is correct in saying that the
purpose of the process was to change the person's inner disposition and so root out

However, if at the end of the time of the exomologesis such a person "continues to be careless and to pay no heed," then he or she must be "thrown out of the Church" (VII,7).[53] It seems strange that after undertaking not only a voluntary abstention from the Eucharist but also the involved process of exomologesis, Methodius could consider a person "careless" in the obligation to take seriously the call to live a holy and sinless life. Yet in light of the text of Leviticus 13, which he closely parallels here, if the spot of "leprosy" remains unhealed, then the "leper" must be publicly banned from the community. Two possible interpretations of the meaning of such an exclusion present themselves here. If the earlier process described by Methodius is not ecclesial penance, then the first interpretation of this action is that it results from a public act of sin that sets in motion a formal postbaptismal penitential process.[54] In this way it would be the beginning of what has been designated as a direct coercive penance of isolation. The harmony with other third-century witnesses makes this interpretation attractive at first; yet it must be questioned, since indisputable evidence of its coercive purpose is lacking. Its connection with Leviticus 13 might be intended rather to highlight the absolute necessity of preserving the purity of the community.[55]

On the other hand, if the earlier process is a description of an actual experience of ecclesial penance and reconciliation, a second interpretation might see this exclusion as proof of the unrepeatabil-

---

the cause of sin, then the conversion experienced would be to lead one to continue to live out the Christian commitment, but at a new level. But if the process was penitential, that is, to reconcile a person after a particular sinful act, then the conversion would be to lead a person back to full ecclesial status and the possibility of living the Christian life, which sin had made impossible.

53. . . . *ei de epimenoi rhathymōn kai aphrontistōn, . . .ekballesthō tēs ekklēsias* (Bonwetsch, 460:11–461:1,3; trans. Van de Paverd, "Confession and Penance," II, p.64).

54. Even Van de Paverd, "Confession and Penance," II, p. 65, agrees that such a separation occurs not only as a result of the unconverted inner disposition of the sinner but also as a result of some public act of sin, based on *De lepra* VIII,1.

55. *Ibid.*, pp. 63–68. Van de Paverd does not see this exclusion from the Church as part of the penitential process but rather as a compulsory excommunication. In this way, exclusion results from Methodius's belief that it is sin itself that separates a person from the Church, even if the sin is unknown to the community (VIII,4). The ecclesial response of public exclusion only ratifies what has already happened.

ity of penance. Recidivists are to be excluded from the Church in
no uncertain terms and their salvation placed in doubt (X,2-3). Again,
the harmony with the custom of ecclesial penance being possible
only one time makes this theory favorable—at least until one recalls
that there is no witness to the practice in the East outside of Alexandria during the third century. As with the previous theory of interpretation, a definite decision regarding the meaning of the text
is impossible due to the indistinctness of the text itself.

In estimating the value of Methodius's witness to ecclesial penance, one cannot help but wonder if he has "adopted" a penance
of segregation, including the external actions associated with the
exomologesis, in order to teach that these ecclesial actions not only
reconcile those who have already committed grave postbaptismal
sin but also eradicate the very cause of sin, the personal desire to
act upon the temptation to sin before sin has actually been committed. What Methodius describes may have been the way sin is averted
as well as healed, a medicine that is preventative as well as restorative. If this is the case, then the use of the institutional elements
of the *paenitentia secunda* is singular to him. This may partially explain why a coercive penance of isolation found in other Eastern
Fathers is absent here. This lacuna in Methodius's witness to penance does not mean that the process of penance described earlier
is no longer operative by the very end of the third century; rather,
it only sets in relief those elements of the penitential practice that
could also be useful in a person's interior moral and spiritual
growth.[56]

Therefore, the uniqueness of the witness of Methodius lies in
his application of the process of penance rather than in the process
itself. His description of the penance of segregation is consistent with
the patristic witnesses who precede him, especially the *Didascalia*.
Though he never makes specific mention of the "grades" of penance found in the *Canonical Epistle* of Gregory Thaumaturgus, it is
not difficult to perceive in his account a description of the stage of
the "prostrators." The guilty party is considered to be within the

---

56. See above, n. 51. Perhaps because he is more interested in the interior and
ascetical development of the person, his descriptions of the ecclesial and public aspects
of penance are meager. See Farges, *Les idées morales*, p. 152.

boundaries of the community, and though he or she is excluded from the Eucharist, the community (represented by the bishop) is able to interact with him or her.[57] Whether one agrees that the witness of Methodius concerns a penitential process for those already guilty of grave postbaptismal sin or is only a process through which sin after baptism might be avoided, his testimony demonstrates that by the end of the third century, the elements of an order of penitents are institutionally well established.

CONCLUSION

In Syria and Asia Minor, the *Didascalia*, though paraenetically harsh, teaches that no sin is outside the possibility of pardon if one submits to the "hard medicine" of penance and to the healing skills of the bishop. The picture of the life and worship of the community reveals a well-ordered two-step process by which those guilty of grave postbaptismal sin are restored to full status in the community. The first step is the coercive penance of isolation seen already in the first two centuries. Though now directly imposed upon the sinner (resulting from the evolution of a monarchical episcopacy), penitents also appear to be less quantitatively isolated, having contact with members of the community who oversaw their personal penitential works. Even if this step in the penitential process is not explicitly mentioned by either Gregory Thaumaturgus or Methodius of Olympus, their implicit witness might nonetheless be present (at least in Gregory's *Canonical Epistle*).

---

57. Van de Paverd, "Confession and Penance," II, pp. 59–60, also sees the liturgical shape of the exomologesis in *De lepra* as similar to that penitential process found in the *Didascalia*, though he believes it to be comparable to the grade of the "listeners." His position, taken against Fendt, "Sünde und Busse," p. 39, is based on his view that the term "assembly" (*synagelazesthai*) in VII,6, may have a technical meaning referring to the gathering of the faithful after the dismissal of the catechumens (and so after the liturgy of the Word). However, the "prostrators" were also dismissed from the assembly after the liturgy of the Word. And their interaction with the community is more clearly sensed, especially in comparison with the grade of "listener," which, as has been stated previously, appears to have developed as a linking stage between isolation from, and segregation within, the community. For this reason, while admitting that the obliqueness of the text allows the position of Van de Paverd, we prefer to see in Methodius's description a reference to "prostrators."

An intervening stage of penance appears clearly for the first time in the *Didascalia*. Here penitents are once again brought into the life of the community, though without full status. This is a time of segregation, not only from the Eucharist but even geographically within the assembly. After a surprisingly brief duration, penitents are reconciled to God and to the community through the laying on of the hand and readmission to the Eucharist. The existential reality of being segregated within the community (that is, being part of the life and worship of the Church, though with limited status), is also to be found in Gregory's mysterious reference to "listeners" and "prostrators." Here the former stage appears as a "linking grade," incorporating both the marginal ecclesial status of those isolated from the community with at least one of the elements of the penance of segregation—being able to be present at the liturgical assembly for the liturgy of the Word. The second grade, that of "prostrators," could be said to involve more explicitly what appears in the *Didascalia* as the second step of penance, the penance of segregation. And though perhaps adapting the penitential process for the purpose of the spiritual growth of the Christian, Methodius, too, offers testimony to the external action of segregation.

II. ALEXANDRIA

A. CLEMENT († C. 215 A.D.)

Writing near the beginning of the third century, Clement of Alexandria preceded Origen as head of the influential Alexandrian catechetical school, an institution that brought the city to the center of Christian thought and philosophy. In his works he manifests an amazing knowledge of the Scriptures—Old and New Testaments—as well as Jewish and Greek philosophy.[58] His concern to construct a philosophic and scientific foundation for Christian faith has led later

---

58. Editions of Clement's works consulted include: O. Stählin and U. Treu (eds.), *Paedagogus*, GCS 12/3 (Berlin, 3rd ed., 1972); Stählin and L. Früchtel (eds.), *Stromata (Buch I–VI)*, GCS 15/3 (Berlin, 3rd ed., 1960); *id.*, *Stromata (Buch VII–VIII)*, *Eclogae propheticae*, *Quis dives salvetur*, *Fragmente*, GCS 17/3 (Berlin, 3rd ed., 1970). Direct citations will be indicated by GCS volume, page, and line number.

authors to describe him as an "orthodox Gnostic," an ironic epithet for one so fiercely committed to the refutation of the Gnostic heresy.[59]

Clement's writings on penance move back and forth between paraenetic rigorism and pastoral toleration. Those who have been baptized and who fall into sin will experience punishment from God (*Paed.* I,64,4–65,2) and will lose salvation (*Strom.* I,171,2-4; *Quis div. salv.* 39,1; *Frag.* 69). By such strong words Clement hopes to instill in his listeners that fear which is needed to convict oneself of sin and so come to true conversion (*Strom.* II,27,1; IV,27,3; 143,1; VI,109,1-6). Yet Clement is no rigorist. He speaks of a "second repentance" (*metanoian deuteran*) by which those who have fallen into sin after baptism may come to pardon (*Strom.* II,57,1).[60] He gives evidence that even the most serious sinners, dead through sin, can have life again if they are truly repentant: the adulterous (*Strom.* II,147,1-4), heretics (*Strom.* VII,102,2), and even murderers (*Quis div. salv.* 42,7).[61] Only those are lost who refuse to recognize their sin and do penance, those with impenitent hearts.[62]

---

59. Quasten, *Patrology* II, pp. 6–7; Hamell, *Handbook of Patrology*, pp. 60–62.

60. In *Strom.* II,58,1; IV,153,3–154,4, Clement appears to see baptism as the first and only remission (*aphesis*) of sin, while the second repentance only pardons (*syngnōmē*) sin after much torment and purification. Rahner, *Early Church*, p. 78, states that Clement is the first patristic author to make such a clear distinction, though the basis of such a difference might already be found in the *Shepherd of Hermas*, 31,3.

61. Poschmann, *PAS*, p. 63. See also E. Junod, "Un écho d'une controverse autour de la pénitence," *RHPR* 60 (1980) 153–160, who holds that Clement authored the story of the Apostle John and the robber chief (*Quis div. salv.*) as a polemic against the rigorists of his day.

62. Clement states (*Strom.* II,57-66) that only sins committed involuntarily (*akousiōs*) are pardonable through a second repentance, while those committed voluntarily (*hekousiōs*) are outside of pardon. There has been much discussion concerning the interpretation of Clement's meaning here, especially in light of the offered pardon to a murderer (*Quis div. salv.* 42). Poschmann, *Paenitentia Secunda*, pp. 233–239, states that only sins of pure malice, viz., sins committed by those who refused to recognize their sinfulness, were excluded from pardon. H. Karpp, "Die Busslehre des Klemens von Alexandrien," *ZNW* 43 (1950/51) 224–242, pp. 228ff., interprets all sin as involuntary, so that penance becomes a pedagogical device used by the true "Gnostic" to help the simple faithful to improve their conduct more and more. A. Mehat, "'Pénitence seconde' et 'péché involontaire' chez Clément d'Alexandrie," *VigChr* 8 (1954) 225–233, pp. 227ff., argues that such terminology points to the influence of Stoic philosophy on Clement and not to Clement's desire to limit the possibility of forgiveness (though in a later work, *Étude sur les 'Stromates' de Clément*

The contours of the practice of penance in the Alexandrian church are only obliquely related by Clement. He employs the term *exomologēsis* (or *exomologeomai*) in some nine texts throughout the *Stromata*.[63] Many of the references connote the necessity of confessing the name of Christ; however, the word is also used to extol the practice of confessing one's sins as spoken of in the Old Testament (*Strom.* II,59,3; VI,57,1; VII,105,4). In other passages the role of the true "gnostic" is to lead others to repentance and the confession of their sins (*Strom.* VII,78,3; 80,1). Both uses imply a confession of sin to God, though in the latter texts involvement on the part of the community might also be suggested.[64] The role of the Church in, and the liturgical setting of, exomologesis is not stressed as much in Clement as in some of the second-century writings previously examined. However, he does witness to the tradition of the sinner submitting himself or herself to "someone of God" who will pray, chastise, and correct the sinner and lead such a one to conversion (*Strom.* VII,80,1; *Quis div. salv.* 31,1; 32,4; 33,3; 40,6–41,7; *Eclog. proph.* 15,2). The tradition of a "director" of souls will flourish in the East, where one's relationship with God rather than the holding of ecclesial office made one fit for such a pastoral responsibility.[65]

There is a question as to whether Clement speaks of a separation of the sinner from the community. Certainly he is aware of the

---

d'*Alexandrie*, Patristica Sorbonensia 7 [Paris, 1966], pp. 317–319, n. 112, Mehat will move closer to Karpp's perspective). All these authors agree that such expressions do not limit the possibility of pardon in Clement but are an attempt by him to balance an appreciation of the power of sin with the free will of persons. This view is further echoed by Quasten, *Patrology* II, p. 33.

63. II,59,3; IV,56,1; VI,45,6; 46,3; 57,1; VII,7,6; 78,3; 80,1; 105,4. The term also appears in the *Protrepticus* 42,3; 73,1. O. Stählin, *Clemens Alexandrinus: Register*, GCS 39 (Leipzig, 1936), p. 399.

64. While disagreeing with Poschmann (*PAS*, p. 64) and Bernhard ("Excommunication et pénitence," pp. 66–67) that the term attests to a well-defined procedure, *Strom.* VII,80,1 does invite one to interpret Clement's usage as connoting some type of ecclesial involvement, perhaps including prayer and fasting, as evidenced in *Quis div. salv.* 42,15.

65. Von Campenhausen, *Ecclesiastical Authority*, pp. 199–201. He points out that even though Clement knew the work of Irenaeus and his theory of apostolic succession, no mention is made of it here. This highlights the fact that the clericalization of ecclesial leadership in the East followed a different line of development than in the West.

Pauline tradition (1 Cor 5:1-13) of sending the grave sinner out from the Church until such a one has repented of wrongdoing (*Paed.* I,10,6; *Strom.* III,106,3). This reflects Clement's justification of a present practice, even if he does not explicitly mention such a practice.[66] Also, there is an indication that ecclesial separation is one of the "chastisements" incurred in the correction of sin:

> For there exist partial corrections, which are called chastisements, under which many of us have fallen, being delivered up to transgression, going out from the Lord's people (*Strom.* VII,102,4).[67]

The question presents itself: Are the people who have transgressed by separating themselves from the Lord's people chastised? Or are the people who have transgressed chastised by being separated from the people of the Lord?[68] The text does not indicate a causal relationship between "transgressing" and "going out from the Lord's people"; rather, they are placed side by side, as if to indicate that transgressing automatically means being separated from the people of the Lord. Therefore, there is not enough textual evidence to know if this separation is indirect or coercive; indeed, the entire ecclesial dimension of the practice is obscure. All that is deducible is that Clement knows that grave sin fundamentally alters one's relationship with the Church in such a way that separation from the Church is the natural result.[69]

---

66. Poschmann, *Paenitentia Secunda*, pp. 252ff.; Karpp, "Die Busslehre," pp. 235ff. Clement also witnesses to the apostolic practice of avoiding contact with known sinners (*Paed.* II,1,10).

67. . . . *ginontai gar kai merikai tines paideiai, has kolaseis onomazousin, eis has hēmōn hoi polloi tōn enparaptōmati genomenōn ek tou laou tou kyriakou katolisthainontes peripiptousin* (17/3,72:16-8).

68. This is Mehat's contention (" 'Pénitence seconde'," pp. 232-233; *Étude sur les 'Stromata'*, pp. 320-321) against Karpp's protestations (*La pénitence*, p. 147, n. 1). It is interesting that Grotz does not treat the passage.

69. Grotz, *Busstufenwesens*, p. 327, is correct in saying that Clement speaks of ecclesial penance and pardon without ecclesial "excommunication." But the question remains: To whom does such a distinction apply? For certain sinners in the community, there seems to be no effective penance without some form of separation from the community, a separation reflecting the changed status of the offender due to the sin rather than a direct action by the Church. This point remains pivotal for the history of the order of penitents.

Clement makes no mention of an ecclesial act of reconciliation.[70] Once again, what is most important is the role of those charged with directing the correction of the sinner. The "true Gnostic" is to discipline transgressors so that they might improve (*Strom*. VII,3,1-4), but it is the Father alone who forgives sin (*Quis div. salv.* 39,5).[71]

Finally, as a consequence of the "second penance" that Clement has taken over from the *Shepherd of Hermas*, he, like the Shepherd, limits the practice to a single instance (*Strom*. II,56–57,2).[72] He condemns those who attempt "repeated penances" as making a pretense of true repentance (*Strom*. II,57,3-4).[73] Like *Hermas*, Clement bases his teaching on the unrepeatability of penance on pastoral grounds, though with greater emphasis on the free will of the person. To fall again after a second penance is a sign of one who is ruled by passion (*Paed*. I,64,4–65,2). As a result, the fate of the recidivist is questionable:

> . . . the frequent asking of forgiveness for faults committed often is an appearance of repentance and not repentance itself (*Strom*. II,59,1).[74]

B. Origen († 253 A.D.)

No Christian author of the third century can approximate the breadth of Origen's philosophical and theological scholarship. Following Clement as the head of the Alexandrian school and in-

---

70. This is one point on which scholars agree: Hoh, *Die kirchliche Busse*, pp. 94ff.; Poschmann, *Paenitentia Secunda*, pp. 256ff. (though holding that, in light of *Quis div. salv.* 42,15, Clement's familiarity with an ecclesial reconciliation cannot be doubted); Karpp, "Die Busslehre," pp. 235ff.; Von Campenhausen, *Ecclesiastical Authority*, p. 217.

71. *Quis div. salv.* 34,3 speaks of a practice of the laying on of hands, a reference here to the ancient rite of the anointing of the sick rather than to reconciliation. See Coppens, *L'imposition des mains*, p. 37, n. 4.

72. That the *Shepherd of Hermas* was a source for Clement is not disputed, even by those who wish to limit the scope of its influence (e.g., Mehat, *Étude sur les 'Stromates'*, p. 318, nn. 113, 114). See especially the passage preceding the teaching on a single postbaptismal repentance in which Clement directly refers to "the Shepherd" (*Strom*. II,55,1-4).

73. Grotz, *Busstufenwesens*, pp. 340ff., sees in this passage a repeatable ecclesial penance, operative without excommunication. See above, n. 69.

74. . . . *dokēsis toinyn metanoias, ou metanoia, to pollakis aiteisthai syngnōmēn eph' hois plēmmeloumen pollakis* (15/3, 144:20-22).

fluenced by Neoplatonism, he attracted many students and became known for his preaching and teaching in both the East and the West. When his career in Alexandria came to an end due to his conflict with the bishop Demetrius in 231, he went to Caesarea in Palestine and there founded a school, which he presided over until his death in 253.[75] Throughout his numerous works, he develops a systematic theology of penance and offers important descriptions of the penitential discipline, making a unique contribution to the Church's self-understanding of its approach to those guilty of postbaptismal sin.[76]

1. THE POSSIBILITY OF POSTBAPTISMAL PARDON

Upon a first reading of Origen's writings concerning penance, one might be tempted to label him a rigorist, refusing the possibility of ecclesial pardon to those who have committed grave sin.[77] However, it must be remembered that he is a theologian and a teacher rather than one engaged in daily pastoral concerns. As a result, his works tend to the paraenetic rather than the pastoral, the ideal rather than the concrete. Nonetheless, while compelled to write of the Church as the place where sin is overcome, he accepts the inescapable fact of sin present in the Church (*In Iesu Nave hom.* 21,1).[78] Even when he speaks of "sins unto death" (*mortale peccatum, peccatum ad mortem, hamartēma pros thanaton*), he is referring to those sins that cannot be pardoned by the mere prayer and sacrifice of the priest (*De orat.* 28,9-10; *In Lev. hom* 11,2; *In Evang. Ioan. comm.* XIX,14,84;

---

75. Quasten, *Patrology* II, pp. 37–40.

76. Editions of the texts consulted are to be found in the bibliography. For the sake of clarity, direct citations will be indicated by full references, including page and line numbers.

77. For a listing of authors who have interpreted Origen in such a way, or at least during his early writings, see Poschmann, *Paenitentia Secunda*, pp. 425–427.

78. Rahner, *Early Church*, pp. 250–251, believes that Origen was the first of the ancient authors to temper his enthusiasm for baptism, recognizing it as a beginning rather than a complete and total change. His famous passage on the seven ways through which sin might be forgiven is proof of his abiding awareness of the existence of sin in the Church (*In Lev. hom.* 2,4).

References to *In Jos. hom.* will be cited as *In Iesu Nave hom.* in deference to the witness of the oldest manuscripts. See A. Jaubert, *Origène: Homélies sur Josué*, SC 71 (Paris, 1960), pp. 90–91, n. 1.

In Exod. hom. 10,3). These sins need the hard and laborious penance during which the sinner, through the accomplishment of penitential works and accepting ecclesial discipline (including exclusion from the Church), receives healing and the restoration of baptismal grace (*In Lev. hom.* 2,4).[79] Even the much debated *De orat.* 28 does not reveal a rigorism that would not allow for the forgiveness of capital sins, such as murder, idolatry, and adultery. While not the remission of sin freely granted through baptism, the pardon resulting from penance is equally efficacious. Rahner states:

> . . . there is no longer any *aphesis* for mortal sins committed after baptism. This is because, on the one hand, the rite of baptism can no longer be considered appropriate for their forgiveness, and, on the other hand, they cannot be remitted by the immediate operation of the church's prayer and sacrifice. Rather, they must be expiated through the undergoing of punishment which they have deserved.[80]

In the tradition of the Letter to the Hebrews, Origen admits the incurability of sin in those persons who refuse to undertake penance (*De orat.* 28,8; *In Ier. hom.* 13,2). It is yet another indication of sin being unpardonable only because of the subjective stance of the sinner and not because of its objective gravity.[81]

---

79. Rahner, *Early Church*, pp. 252ff. Origen distinguishes between those sins that effect a complete loss of baptismal grace and those lighter sins that do not (*levis culpa, peccatum leve, minus peccatum, parvum peccatum, hamartēma mē thanatēphoron*) and can be remitted through prayer and sacrifice. There has been debate as to whether he makes a double distinction within the category of mortal sins (*In Lev. hom.* 15,2), but Rahner (pp. 259–261) rejects such a possibility.

The interpretation of Origen's teaching on "excommunication" of the sinner has been debated by modern authors, most notably Grotz, *Busstufenwesens*, pp. 262ff.; see below, n. 89.

80. Rahner, *Early Church*, pp. 258–259; 304–308; Poschmann, *Paenitentia Secunda*, pp. 453–460. In the passage from *In Lev. hom.* 2,4, only baptism, martyrdom, and ecclesial penance can be viewed as efficacious in the remission of grave sin. The other four ways, all of which are good works, are effective only against lighter, more common faults (G. Teichtweier, *Die Sündenlehre des Origenes* (Regensburg, 1958), pp. 328–336. Origen views martyrdom as efficacious only in conjunction with the prayer of the sinner (*Explan. super Ps. CXV* 8; *Exhort. ad mart.* 30). *Ibid.*, pp. 313–316.

81. Those modern authors who hold such an interpretation of Origen's penitential teaching include: d'Alès, *L'Édit*, pp. 252ff.; Galtier, *L'Église*, pp. 184ff.; Poschmann, mann, *Paenitentia Secunda*, pp. 427ff.; E. Latko, *Origen's Concept of Penance* (Quebec,

2. THE MINISTERS OF PENANCE

There is a certain ambiguity in Origen's comments concerning the role of the clergy in the penitential process. On the one hand, he holds that bishops who lack personal holiness no longer have the power to lead a sinner back to conversion (*In Evang. Matt. comm.* 12,14; *In Num. hom.* 10,1). In this regard, the power of the minister seems to be in direct correlation to a person's sanctity and has little to do with the possession of clerical office.[82] Further, the ministry to those guilty of postbaptismal sin can be exercised equally by a pious bishop or lay person. He emphasizes, in true Eastern tradition, the role of spiritual guides who serve as "doctors" for the sinners, advising them and exhorting them to do what is necessary for their healing (*Explan. super Ps.* XXXVII 2,6; *In Luc. hom.* 17,8).[83]

Yet on the other hand, Origen assigns a central role to the bishop and clergy in the care of sinners:

> It is then reasonable, according to his image, he who has given the priesthood to the Church, that the ministers and the priests of the Church also receive "the sins of the people" and they themselves, imitating their master, grant to the people the remission of sins (*In Lev. hom.* 5,3).[84]

In a manner reminiscent of the *Didascalia Apostolorum*, the bishop is to be both compassionate and stern, unafraid to impose the rigors

---

1949), pp. 160ff.; Grotz, *Busstufenwesens*, pp. 251ff.; Rahner, *Early Church*, pp. 261ff.; Von Campenhausen, *Ecclesiastical Authority*, p. 258; Teichtweier, *Die Sündenlehre des Origenes*, pp. 217ff.; H. Vogt, *Das Kirchenverständnis des Origenes*, BBK 4 (Cologne, 1974), p. 155; Vorgrimler, *Busse*, pp. 60ff.

82. Rightly, Poschmann, *PAS*, pp. 71–72, and Rahner, *Early Church*, pp. 319–320, vigorously oppose the position that Origen was a Donatist in his perception of ministry and ministerial office. His focus on the personal holiness of the minister was not to deny but to accentuate the office, to make those entrusted with the office more responsible in the execution of their ministry.

83. See Clement of Alexandria and his witness to the "someone of God" charged with directing souls, above, p. 145. In light of *In Evang. Matt. comm.* 13,31, it seems that a lay person could impose a private ban on a sinner as part of the process of the threefold correction of Mt 18:15-17 (Von Campenhausen, *Ecclesiastical Authority*, pp. 260–261).

84. "Consequens enim est, ut secundum imaginem eius, qui sacerdotium Ecclesiae dedit, etiam ministri et sacerdotes Ecclesiae 'peccata populi' accipiant et ipsi imitantes magistrum remissionem peccatorum populo tribuant" (M. Borret, *Origène: Homélies sur le Lévitique* I, SC 286 [Paris, 1981], 218:57-61).

of penance yet prepared to be pastorally lenient (*In Evang. Matt. comm.* 13,30; *In Iesu Nave hom.* 7,6).[85] To him alone is granted the formal power of the "keys" to bind and loose sin.[86] Nonetheless, it remains clear that Origen de-accentuates the bishop's role so as to highlight what is most important to the entire process of penance: the total conversion of the sinner. His stress on the penitential works of the penitent, the strong role of the community, and the pastoral role rather than the juridic acts of the bishop (guiding, admonishing, and praying) all point to "the moral and religious progress which the penitent actually makes under the minister's guidance."[87] While maintaining the ministerial structures of penance, Origen places more emphasis on the expiating work of the penitent and the ministry of the whole community than on the power of the bishop's office.[88]

3. THE PROCESS OF ECCLESIAL PENANCE

a) *Internal exclusion*

What is the process of ecclesial penance as outlined by Origen throughout his works? First and foremost, it necessarily involves an exclusion of the sinner from the Church.[89] While this separation

---

85. This is not to imply that Origen is dependent on the *Didascalia Apostolorum* or even knew of its existence. What is meant here is only that the picture of a monarchical episcopacy is similar in both the works of Origen and in the Syrian document.

86. Even Von Campenhausen, *Ecclesiastical Authority*, pp. 258ff., who does not find a sacramental reconciliation in Origen, upholds this. See Poschmann, *Paenitentia Secunda*, pp. 461ff.

87. Von Campenhausen, *Ecclesiastical Authority*, p. 261. While we agree with Von Campenhausen's interpretation, he goes too far in asserting the relative unimportance of the juridic act of pardon by the bishop. If it was so unimportant, how could Origen justify the rule of unrepeatable penance? See Latko, *Origen's Concept of Penance*, pp. 92–94.

88. Rahner, *Early Church*, pp. 266–279, denies that Origen is semi-Pelagian in his attitude toward the personal penance of the sinner. It is divine impulse in the first place that sparks one's desire for conversion, an impulse that takes the form of divine judgment of sin and flows from the sin itself. Penance, then, has the ontological effect of fundamentally reforming the person and leading him or her back to inner health. This is why Origen stresses the necessity of ecclesial penance even for secret sins (*In lib. Iudicum hom.* 2,5; *Explan. super Ps. XXXVII*, 2,6).

89. In the case of *levis culpa*, there was no exclusion (*In Iesu Nave hom.* 7,6). In certain other cases, where there was doubt about whether a mortal sin was

is necessarily external, to Origen's mind the nature of the sin itself so alters one's relationship with God that the exterior exclusion of the sinner only ratifies a previously realized internal split (*In Lev. hom.* 14,2; *In Ier. hom.* Fragment 48).[90] This sets in relief Origen's thinking regarding the ecclesiological reality that he describes as *mystērion*. The Church has both an external and an internal reality, with the external structures corresponding to a deeper, not totally revealed, internal existence of the eternal Logos. This internal ecclesial reality is pure Truth, which the external actions of the visible Church only partially disclose. While Origen recognizes that the internal reality does not always coincide with the external reality due to imperfection and sin, the two are never disconnected. All external ecclesial realities, including acts of penance, strive to bring the exterior Church into harmony with the fundamental internal truth.[91]

Only in light of Origen's ecclesiology can one begin to understand why there can be no question for him of allowing grave sinners to remain in the Church. To do so would be to make a mockery of the internal ecclesial reality, as if the falsehood of sin could coexist alongside the pure truth of Christ. Therefore, all serious sin necessitates some period of external exclusion from the Church. Such an exclusion is not merely a disciplinary rule of behavior for Origen but is the manifestation of a deeper, internal exclusion resulting from the sin itself.[92]

b) *A direct coercive penance of isolation*

For notorious sins or in cases where a sinner refuses to heed the private *correptio* of either the bishop or the "spiritual persons" to

---

involved, the *correptio* of the sinner would suffice if the sinner repented (*In Evang. Matt. comm.* 16,8; *In Iesu Nave hom.* 7,6; *In Lev. hom.* 3,2).

Grotz, *Busstufenwesens*, p. 262, takes exception to such a statement, maintaining his position that while every grave sin involved an "excommunication," not every "excommunication" was part of ecclesial penance.

90. J. Trigg, *Origen: The Bible and Philosophy in the Third Century Church* (Atlanta, Ga., 1948; reprinted 1983), p. 197.

91. Rahner, *Early Church*, pp. 247–250. For a fuller treatment of Origen's notion of "mystērion," see H. U. von Balthasar, "Le Mystérion d'Origène," *RSR* 26 (1936) 513–562; 27 (1937) 38–64; H. Crouzel, *Origène et la "connaissance mystique"* (Brussels, 1961), *passim*.

92. See below, n. 98.

change his or her life (*In Evang. Matt. comm.* 13,31), such a one must eventually be "cast away" (*abiciatur*) from the life of the community (*In Lev. hom..* 8,10). This is accomplished through a solemn *correptio* by the bishop, who publicly expels (*ekbalein, exire, abscindi, pellitur*) the sinner from the Church (*In Lev. hom.* 8,10; 14,2; *In Iesu Nave hom.* 21,1; *In lib. Iudicum hom.* 2,5; *In Ier. hom.* 12,5; Fragment 48).[93] This is done to preserve the purity of the community, but especially for the sake of the sinner. It is the hard "medicine" necessary to gain the possibility of recovering the life lost through sin. In Origen, the penance of isolation remains coercive, as in earlier writings, but the charge is no longer spoken indirectly to the community. It is now directly imposed upon the sinner.

Though the prescription by the bishop is harsh, it does not *a priori* permanently exclude the sinner from the community. Eventual readmission to the community is possible if the sinner decides to respond to the medicine offered by the Church. Outside the Church, the sinner is outside the sight of God and is considered dead (*Contra Celsum* 3,51).[94] Salvation depends on the acceptance of what is necessary for healing the separation that exists between the sinner and God/the Church. It is necessary that the sin be made known to the "doctors" responsible for the healing of those sick with postbaptismal sin. While the disclosure of one's sin is not an issue in cases of public scandal, when the sin is known to the entire community, such disclosure serves to express the necessary contrition of the sinner. In cases where the sin is secret, Origen pleads with

---

93. Rahner, *Early Church*, pp. 289–290. Karpp, *La pénitence*, p. 271, n. 1, sees the term *notare*, used in *In lib. Iudicum hom.* 2,5, as a technical term for a Roman censure adopted later by the Church as a technical term for the public exclusion, based on the principle of 2 Thess 3:14.

94. F. van de Paverd, "Disciplinarian Procedures in the Early Church," *Augustinianum* 21 (1981) 291–316, pp. 296–297, who sees in this passage proof of what he terms a "coercive excommunication." His phraseology is half right: it was surely a *coercive* action. However, we prefer the more precise "direct coercive penance of isolation" in order to continue to avoid altogether the term "excommunication," burdened as it is with so many later imposed meanings. Also, the term "isolation" implies an ongoing interaction (albeit negative) of two subjects: the sinner and the community, whereas "excommunication" only accentuates the judgment of the Church. Though the sinner is "dead" due to sin, the distant yet real concern of the community for the sinner continues.

sinners to be unafraid of revealing their sin to the Church so as to be able to receive the necessary medicine for sin and eventually be healed (*In Lev. hom.* 15,2; *Explan. super Ps. XXXVII* 2,1.6; *In Luc. hom.* 17,8). As in earlier patristic authors, confession of sin remains a necessary part of the penitential process, both as a sign of contriteness on the part of the sinner and to help the Church determine the appropriate exterior action to be taken.[95]

It remains unclear in the writings of Origen whether the confession of sin serves as a turning point in the movement toward readmission to the Church. For one who confesses spontaneously, it may be enough proof to the community of one's sorrow for sin, so that admittance into the penance of segregation and the exomologesis follow immediately.[96] Equally, in the case of notorious sinners who confess after a long period of neglecting the Church's invitation to do penance, further proof of their sorrow by external acts of penance may be required. Yet, even though "lepers," they are not isolated totally: the priests still must go out to them to observe their personal works of penance and to continue to admonish and correct them (*In Lev. hom.* 8,10).[97] They must work hard toward their eventual purification, performing personal penance so as to be judged worthy, as Lazarus was, of being "called from the tomb," though "with hands and feet still bound" (*In Evang. Ioan. comm.* 28,7,54-60).[98] Impelled by the power of the True Logos and with the

---

95. Karpp, *La pénitence*, p. 271, n. 1, who sees Origen's notion of confession as the same as Tertullian's (*De paen.* 9,2). This does not negate the possibility that some, aware of their sinfulness, might have already voluntarily excluded themselves from the Eucharist (*In Lev. hom.* 14,4).

96. Rahner, *Early Church*, pp. 289-290, 416-417, n. 315. Such a spontaneous confession could have been made publicly to the whole community or privately to either the bishop himself or a "spiritual guide." In the case of the latter, it was the spiritual guide who seems to have had the responsibility of recommending to the bishop whether or not the sin was grave enough (both subjectively and objectively) to warrant public exclusion. See *Explan. super Ps. XXXVII* 2,6.

97. Origen does not further specify how the isolated sinners were supervised by the Church. Rahner, *Early Church*, p. 417, n. 322, supposes that such a supervision might have resembled the process described by the *Didascalia Apostolorum* 80:20-26; 220:6-12.

98. Grotz, *Busstufenwesens*, pp. 304-306, sees in this passage Origen's distinction between sacramental reconciliation and the granting of the *communio*. The former was a mere canonical lifting of the ban of "excommunication" (being called from

direction of the priests, postbaptismal offenders are purified from sin by their own effort, and being thus purified, they prove to the community the genuineness of their conversion. They are now ready to enter the period proximate to the time of their full reconciliation.[99] This first stage of the entire process of penance involves the subjective response on the part of the sinner to the action taken by the Church and is best described as a direct coercive penance of isolation, rooted in, yet distinct from, the practice of the first two centuries.[100]

c) *The penance of segregation and the exomologesis*

When sinners are judged ready for the "divine altar," they are allowed to begin the immediate process leading up to full reconciliation and *communio*. In this way Origen witnesses to an intermediate stage of penance, following upon the coercive isolation and preceding the resumption of full ecclesial status. Though it is unclear how such a transition is marked, it may be that penitents are invited to make a formal petition to the community by those who have observed their external acts of contrition during the previous

---

the tomb), while the latter was being readmitted to the Eucharist (being loosed from the wrappings). Rahner, *Early Church*, p. 427, n. 436, opposes such an interpretation, stating that a mere external lifting of the "binding" word of exclusion was in contrast to Origen's overall ecclesiological perspective. This passage, then, is better understood as referring to two exclusions: the first (a direct coercive penance of isolation) leading to a second (a penance of segregation including exomologesis), which in turn led to full ecclesial reconciliation.

99. For a clear explanation of the distinction between the purification of sin that occurs through the personal effort of the sinner during this penance of isolation and the gift of the Holy Spirit given when the sinner is fully reconciled to the Church, see M. Borret, *Origène: Homélies sur le Lévitique II*, SC 287 (Paris, 1981), pp. 67–69, n. 1.

100. Perhaps it is the subjective response of the sinner that does not allow a completely airtight picture of postbaptismal penitential procedures to emerge from Origen. The very fluidity of his approach stresses the ascendancy of the individual over the process itself. The process was adapted to aid in the conversion of the sinner, which resulted in different cases being handled in different ways. It is this basis that allows Van de Paverd, "Disciplinarian Procedures," pp. 298–299, to distinguish the penance found in Tertullian and Origen from canonical penance of the fourth century, which tended to emphasize casuistical objectivity more than the sinner's subjective repentance.

time of their isolation from the Church.[101] They then enter into a new relationship with the Church, moving from being isolated from the entire life of the community to a more strictly liturgical exclusion from the Eucharist (*Contra Celsum* 3,51).[102] This new association between penitents and the Church is analogous to the relationship existing between the Church and those preparing for entrance into the catechumenate, and the catechumens themselves preparing for Christian initiation.[103] Though remaining marginally connected to the community in the previous coercive penance of isolation, now the penitent once again enters into the life of the Church, though with limited status. It is a process best described as a penance of segregation.

During this period penitents are expected to stay faithful to personal penitential works. They are excluded not just from the Eucharist but from the liturgy itself. References to *exire de coetu et congregatione Ecclesiae* (*In Lev. hom.* 14,2); *a conventu abscinderetur Ecclesiae* (*Explan. super Ps. XXXVII*, 1,1); and *eiciuntur ab oratione communi* (*In Matt. hom.* 89) make this clear. However, it must be stated again that Origen is not speaking here of a coercive penance of isolation. Rather, such references are based on the distinction, known to Origen, between the service of the Word and service of the *oratio*.[104] It is the latter that the penitents are excluded from, not the former. In such a case the penitents are segregated from the assembly by being assigned to a particular place in the Church but excluded after the preaching.[105]

---

101. H. Swete, "Penitential Discipline in the First Three Centuries," *JTS* 4 (1903) 321-337, pp. 335-336; Latko, *Origen's Concept of Penance*, p. 111. See also the *Didascalia Apostolorum* 52:10-20; 64:14-21; 76:20-78:9.

102. *Ibid.*, pp. 295-297. Of course, the one who spontaneously confessed before the community and asked for readmission might also have been allowed to begin the exomologesis, as seen above.

103. M. Dujarier, *Le parrainage des adultes aux trois premiers siècles de l'Église*, Parole et mission 4 (Paris, 1962), pp. 285-290; M. Borret, *Origène: Contre Celse II*, SC 136 (Paris, 1968), pp. 122-123, n. 1. Origen often compared those preparing for baptism to those preparing for reconciliation.

104. Rahner, *Early Church*, pp. 290, 417, n. 321, who cites Origen's *Fragment in I Cor* as proof that he knew such a distinction.

105. A possible reference could be in *In Lev. hom.* 11,2: there will be no *lacrimis locus* ("place of tears") for unrepentant adulterers. See also the end of *In Lev. hom.* 8,11. Again, this process is best described in the *Didascalia Apostolorum*.

Also within this time of close but limited association with the Church occurs the external action of the exomologesis. The term, as in other early writings, is used by Origen to convey the entire spectrum of its meanings.[106] He is surely cognizant of its penitential connotation, as the word seems to be employed in reference to a public penitential procedure for those who repent and confess their sin.[107] A description, matching an earlier one by Tertullian (*De paen.* 9), to be seen below, paints a harsh picture:

> . . . the humble man humiliates himself in a disgraceful and undignified manner, throwing himself headlong to the ground upon his knees, clothing himself in a beggar's rags, and heaping dust [ashes] upon himself (*Contra Celsum* 6,15).[108]

How often the exomologesis occurs remains obscure—either throughout the period of segregation or only at the end. It is obviously public and liturgical, evoking the prayer of the entire community. All the external actions of the period of segregation and exomologesis express the sinner's self-accusation in the face of his or her sin. They convince the bishop and the community that the penitent has truly "built the house" and "planted the garden" of conversion (*In Ier. hom.,* Fragment 48).

The duration of the total time of penance depends on the subjective stance of the sinner. Origen does explicitly state that the period of penance is to exceed the period of preparation for those who are coming into the community for the first time (*Contra Celsum* 3,51). Assuming that he, like Hippolytus, is aware of an extended catechumenal period, this would imply a similar timespan for the

---

106. See below, pp. 192–193. Origen himself admits a distinction of meaning for the term (*Selecta in Psalmos* CXXXV, 2).

107. Latko, *Origen's Concept of Penance,* pp. 90–91.

108. *Hama de dēloutai dia toutōn hoti ou pantōs ho tapeinophronōn aschēmonōs kai apaisiōs tapeinoutai, chamaipetēs epi tōn gonatōn kai prēnēs errimmenos, esthēta dystēnōn amphiskomenos kai konin epamōmenos* (M. Borret, *Origène: Contre Celse III,* SC 147 [Paris, 1969], 214:14-17; trans. H. Chadwick, *Origen: Contra Celsum* [Cambridge, 1953], p. 328). The "tears" and "burden" of penance are also spoken of in *Selecta in Psalmos* LXXIX,6; LXXXIV,3; CXIV,8; CXV,8.

Both Chadwick (p. 328, n. 2) and Borret (p. 215, n. 3) make reference to the Greek belief that prostration was a sign of grave superstition and was to be avoided at all costs (Theophrastus, *Charact.* 16; Plutarch, *Mor.* 166a). This would have made undertaking exomologesis doubly difficult for those whom Origen is addressing.

duration of the entire process of penance, including both the earlier coercive penance of isolation and the penance of segregation more proximate to reconciliation.[109] For those particularly zealous in undertaking personal works of penance as well as the difficult process of exomologesis, the time of their penance need not be extreme.[110] Yet it is the true conversion of the sinner and not mere time requirements that forms the ultimate criterion.

4. RECONCILIATION OF THE SINNER

Origen's ecclesiological perspective makes it clear that the reconciliation of the sinner is the work of the whole Church and not just of the bishops. It is the "saints" (hagioi), all Christians, who exercise the power (exousia) of loosing the sinner from sin, at least to the extent that they themselves are free from sin.[111] The prayers and works of the faithful, their martyrdom, and even their correptio of the erring brother or sister are described as delicta repropitiare and even remissionem peccatorum tribuere (In Lev. hom. 5, 3.4).[112] The internal unity of the Church as the Body of Christ cannot but be profoundly affected by the sin of one member. The Church, "having itself become sinful by the sin of its member, . . . expiates the sin together with the sinner" (Selecta in Ps. XXIV, 4; In Lev. hom. 7,1).[113]

---

109. While Hippolytus speaks specifically of a three-year catechumenate, Origen is never so explicit.

110. Origen interprets the incestuous man in 1 Cor 5:10-13 as the same man reconciled in 2 Cor 2:5-11 (In Ier. hom. 20:6; In Evang. Ioan. comm. 28,4). Therefore, a shorter time-lapse between the initial exclusion and reconciliation could be possible for those who remain faithful to penance. And nowhere in Origen is there evidence for a lifelong penance.

111. The power of the entire Church to reconcile the sinner is the focus of In Evang. Matt. comm. XII,10-14 as well as De orat. 14,6 (against Grotz, Busstufenwesens, pp. 218ff., who prefers to interpret these passages as referring only to those with clerical office).

112. As Rahner (Early Church, pp. 420–421, n. 370) points out, while this latter reference is to bishops, it is speaking of their power to reconcile fellow Christians, because they are homines spirituales and not because of their ecclesial office. Besides their unique role in the rite of reconciliation (see below, pp. 150–151), bishops could also offer sacrifice for sins, no doubt a reference to the actual liturgical sacrifice of the Eucharist (In Exodum hom. 4,8; De orat. 28,9; Adnot. in Lib. I Regum). Yet the last two passages make it clear that sacrifice alone does not suffice in the remission of mortal sins.

113. Ibid., p. 301.

Yet within the broader context of the role of all the "saints" in the pardon of sin, Origen witnesses to a unique rite by which those guilty of mortal sin and previously excluded are now reconciled to the community (*In Lev. hom.* 2,4). While he is never explicit concerning who has the authority to administer such a rite, he assigns too central a role to the bishop in the entire reconciling ministry of the Church to not have him in mind here.[114] Just as it is the bishop alone who has the *potestas ligandi*, the power to "bind" sin through the public exclusion of the sinner, it is he who certainly has the *potestas solvendi*, the power to "loose" the sinner from such a ban.

In speaking of the seventh and final way by which sins are remitted, Origen claims to quote from the Letter of James (5:14-15):

> If someone among you is sick, call for the presbyters of the Church, and let them impose the hand and anoint the sick one with oil in the name of the Lord. And the prayer of faith will save the sick, and if such a one has committed sins, they will be remitted (*In Lev. hom.* 2,4).[115]

It is interesting to note that Origen replaces the phrase "and let them pray over the sick one" found in the scriptural text with "and let them impose the hand." The imposition of the hand is an action receiving attestation in the third century as accompanying the reconciliation of penitents.[116] Therefore, in light of the context of this passage and Origen's insertion, there is reason to believe that Origen is describing here a rite of pardon for those who have completed adequate penance.[117]

The passage also raises the question of whether the rite of reconciliation in the East includes an anointing with oil. Such a practice is attested to by later patristic literature in the East from the fourth century onward.[118] Origen himself, later in the same work, refers

---

114. Rahner, *Early Church*, p. 302.

115. "Si quis autem infirmatur, vocet presbyteros Ecclesiae, et imponant ei manus ungentes eum oleo in nomine Domini. Et oratio fidei salvabit infirmum, et si in peccatis fuerit, remittentur ei" (Borret, SC 286, 110:63-66).

116. *Didascalia Apostolorum* 68:23-25; 114:10-16; Cyprian, *Epp.* 15,1; 16,2; 17,2; 18,1; 19,2; 20,3; 71,2; *De lapsis* 16.

117. Coppens, *L'imposition des mains*, pp. 41-42, n. 3, p. 374.

118. *Testamentum Domini* I,24; *Vita Porphyrii* 56,57; and in the works of Ephrem, John Chrysostom, Maruta of Maipherkat, and Aphraate. For precise references, see *ibid.*, pp. 377-379.

to the *olei imaginem* as signifying the grace of the Holy Spirit given to penitents who have been purified of their sins.[119] Therefore, it is within reason to see in Origen a first witness to the reconciliation of penitents through the imposition of the hand as well as an anointing with oil.

It may have been the practice that the imposition of the hand was often done as a sign of exorcism on those admitted to the penance of segregation and performing exomologesis. Given the connection between the laying on of the hand and exorcism, witnessed to by Hippolytus and Cyprian in their description of the catechumenate, and given the parallel Origen paints between the catechumenate and those experiencing the penance of segregation (*Contra Celsum* 3,51), it is possible to imagine this state of affairs. However, when the imposition of the hand occurs in conjunction with an anointing, it is a definitive communication of the Holy Spirit that restores the penitent to full *communio* with the Church.[120] In this way the rite of reconciliation of penitents liturgically parallels the rite of postbaptismal anointing (confirmation), which Origen knows also to be a definitive communication of the Holy Spirit (*De princip.* I,2,3; 3,7).[121] This is yet another example of the parallelism that Origen sees between the order of catechumens and the order of penitents.

---

119. Rahner, *Early Church*, p. 303, holds that Origen has in mind here an actual anointing, whereas Teichtweier, *Die Sündenlehre des Origenes*, p. 326, thinks he is speaking only in allegorical terms. The fact that Origen associates an anointing with oil with the reconciliation of penitents in both *In Lev. hom.* 2,4 and 8,11 at least makes plausible the argument that even if in the latter passage he uses the image metaphorically, there must have been an experience that recommended such a connection to his mind.

120. Rahner, *Early Church*, pp. 303–304. Given Origen's ecclesiological perspective of the unity between the external Church and the internal Logos, ecclesial reconciliation necessarily had a transcendent dimension, so that *communio* with the Church meant also divine pardon. Only in this sense can one speak of the sacramentality of Origen's teaching on penance. If the "binding" of sin, through the sinner's being excluded from the community, was no mere juridic action, then neither can the sinner, upon being "loosed" from such a ban, have merely an external reunion with the Church. See above, n. 98.

121. Coppens, *L'imposition des mains*, p. 289.

5. THE CONSEQUENCES OF ECCLESIAL PENANCE

a) *The custom of unrepeatable ecclesial penance*

Origen witnesses to the custom, passed down from Clement, of penance for grave sin being unrepeatable: "for the gravest crimes, a place of penance is only conceded one time" (*In Lev. hom.* 15,2).[122] He appears to assume that such an ecclesial discipline is a well-known rule of the Church, and so is not compelled to offer justification for its necessity. There is no explicit discussion of the fate of the recidivist. However, the question does put into relief the conflict between two themes found throughout Origen's works: God will not deny the genuine penance of a sinner, and the salvific importance of belonging to the Church. In allowing both themes to remain unreconciled, Origen maintains the tension between the radical connection of the Church with the True Logos and the inescapable fact that the Church is sinful. Since the ways of God are mysterious, all sinners, even recidivists, are left with hope.[123]

b) *The imposition of juridic restraints on the reconciled*

Origen is the earliest witness of certain limitations imposed on newly reconciled penitents that would affect their future life in the Church:

> . . . do not select those who have fallen after their conversion to Christianity for any office or administration in the Church of God, as it is called (*Contra Celsum* 3,51).[124]

He refuses to those who have experienced the exclusion and reconciliation of ecclesial penance the possibility of ever attaining to clerical office.[125] Later, in the fourth century, this teaching will become

---

122. "In gravioribus enim criminibus semel tantum paenitentiae conceditur locus . . ." (Borret, SC 287, 256:60-61).

123. Rahner, *Early Church*, pp. 310–311. One might argue that it was exactly in order not to leave the faithful without hope on this question that Origen outlined the seven ways sin could be remitted (*In Lev. hom.* 2,4).

124. . . . *eis oudemian archēn kai prostasian tēs legomenēs ekklēsias tou theou katalegontes tous phthasantas meta to proselēlythenai tō logō eptaikenai* (Borret, SC 136, 122,24:30-32; trans. H. Chadwick, *Origen: Contra Celsum*, p. 164).

125. This restraint will be imposed upon reconciled penitents at the beginning of the fourth century by Peter of Alexandria (*Epist. canon.* 10) and the Council of Nicaea (c. 10)

an intrinsic element of canonical penance, along with other juridic obligations demanded of the newly reconciled. The resultant stigmatization will force most persons to wait until they are dying before requesting admittance into the ranks of the penitents.[126] Origen, however, has no purely juridic notion in mind here. In his refutation of Celsus, he attempts to convey the seriousness of grave postbaptismal sin, standing in direct opposition to the internal reality of the presence of the eternal Logos in the Church. The stigma lies in the sin and not in the undertaking of penance.[127] Those who sin after baptism must accept the fact that their stigma, once removed by baptism, now remains with them, even after ecclesial reconciliation.[128]

6. SUMMARIZING ORIGEN'S ORDER OF PENITENTS

Origen is a fundamental witness to the development of the *ordo paenitentium* in the third century. His image of the Church as *mystērion* allows him to speak of a sinless internal reality, which is at the same time necessarily connected to the external structure. The reality of the external includes those who fall into grave sin after baptism. There is no sin objectively outside the possibility of pardon for those who are willing to undertake the hard and laborious work of penance. All persons in the community have a responsibility to minister to sinners, but only insofar as they themselves are not guilty of grave sin. There are particular persons, known for their holiness, who play a special role in this care of sinners, most especially the bishop, who alone can impose a solemn exclusion on grave

---

126. See below, pp. 249–251, the discussion in Chapter Five on the juridic restraints imposed upon the reconciled.

127. G. May, "Bemerkungen zu der Frage der Diffamation und der Irregularität der öffentlichen Büsser," *MThZ* 12 (1961) 252–268, pp. 255, 263–268.

128. It might be argued that since this imposed restraint of the reconciled appears only once in the works of Origen, and in one of his last works (*Contra Celsum* was most probably written in or near 248 A.D.), such a custom was unknown to him before. This receives support from *In Lev. hom.* 8,11 (written some eight to nine years earlier), where he speaks of sinners who have been purified and have received the Holy Spirit as those who *recipere priorem stolam et anulum possit et PER OMNIA reconciliatus Patri in locum filii reparari* (my emphasis). If Origen had reservations concerning the future status of the reconciled in the community, his emphatic remarks here seem inconsistent.

sinners and eventually decide when to reconcile them through the imposition of the hand and anointing with oil.

Origen speaks of three different exclusions of the sinner. The first is internal, resulting from the sin itself and having nothing to do with any external action taken on the part of the Church. This exclusion results from transgressing the internal reality of the Church as the expression of the True Logos.

The second exclusion is external and publicly pronounced by the bishop against the sinner. This exclusion is liturgical but also sociological, cutting the sinner off from all daily interaction with the Church. Yet the separated penitents remain under the supervision of the priests, who monitor their private penitential actions and determine the genuineness of their conversion. This exclusion is defined as a direct coercive penance of isolation, rooted in, yet developed from, the indirect coercive penance of isolation of the first two centuries.

A third exclusion brings the penitent into a closer but still limited association with the Church. It forms an intermediate stage between the time of coercive isolation and the resumption of full ecclesial status through reconciliation. It is a more strictly liturgical exclusion, during which the penitent undertakes the harsh action of the exomologesis. This exclusion is defined as a penance of segregation.[129]

The reconciliation of the penitent occurs at the end of the penitential process. It bestows the gift of the Holy Spirit, both reconciling the penitent to the community again and ending the time of exclusion from the Eucharist. After reconciliation the sinner is fully restored to *communio* with the Church, but with two conditions: (1) that ecclesial penance not be repeated; and (2) that the newly reconciled penitent never be admitted to clerical office.

C. DIONYSIUS († 265 A.D.)

Considered one of the most extraordinary students of Origen, Dionysius of Alexandria holds a prominent place in the history of

---

129. Rahner, *Early Church*, p. 410, n. 248; Borret, SC 287, pp. 230–231, n. 2.

the Eastern Church.[130] Born of pagan parents and knowledgeable of various schools of philosophy, he embraced the Christian faith through the influence of Origen. When Heraclas became bishop of Alexandria (c. 232), Dionysius succeeded him as head of the catechetical school there. Upon the death of Heraclas (c. 248), Dionysius succeeded him again, this time as bishop of Alexandria. The time of his episcopacy was full of hardship. During the Decian persecution he was arrested but was later rescued. He was banished during the persecution of Valerian (c. 257) and was unable to return to Alexandria for two or three years due to adverse political conditions as well as his own ill health. He died in Alexandria some few years later.[131]

Not as speculative as Origen and more directly involved with concrete pastoral situations due to his office, Dionysius proved himself to be both a thoughtful and practical shepherd. Eusebius records his constant efforts to maintain the unity of the Church, most especially during the Novatian schism and the question of the readmission of those who lapsed during the Decian persecution (VI,44–46; VII,4.7-9). Though an apologist, his letters are amicable in tone, even to Novatian himself (VI,45). Time and time again his genuine pastoral concern for those guilty of postbaptismal sin makes him one of the most attractive personalities of the period. This alone makes him an important witness to the developing penitential discipline in the East.[132]

Standing in opposition to the rigorism of Novatian, Dionysius holds that there are no sins outside the possibility of pardon. His position is gently driven home in a letter to Fabius, the bishop of Antioch, who, apparently sympathetic to Novatian's rigorist discipline, supported his spurious election as the bishop of Rome, in opposition to the legitimate election of Cornelius (VI,44,2-6).[133] After

---

130. Most of what is known of his life and works comes from the sixth and seventh books of Eusebius's *Ecclesiastical History* and the fourteenth book of his *Praeparatio Evangelica*. References in the text will be to the *Ecclesiastical History* unless otherwise indicated, while direct citations will be from the edition by Bardy (SC 41) and will be noted by SC volume and page number.

131. Salmond, *Fathers of the Third Century*, ANF 6, p. 78.

132. Poschmann, *Paenitentia Secunda*, pp. 471ff.

133. Nautin, *Lettres et écrivains chrétiens*, pp. 143–144.

recounting the glories of the martyrs of Alexandria (VI,41.42,1-4), all of which is to lend credibility to his "apologetical punch," Dionysius tells the story of Serapion, an old man close to death who had lapsed during the persecution. Though unable to obtain pardon in his life, he now sends his young nephew for the presbyter, who is unable to come due to the lateness of the hour and his own illness. Instead, the presbyter, acting upon explicit instruction given by Dionysius himself concerning the reconciliation of the dying, gives a small portion of the Eucharist to the boy who takes it to Serapion. The old man, upon consuming it, is able to die in peace. For Dionysius, Serapion dies clearly reconciled to the Church and to God:

> Was he not manifestly preserved and did he not continue [in life] until he could be absolved, and that, his sin having been wiped away due to the numerous good works he had done, could he not be acknowledged [as one who is Christian]? (VI,44,6)[134]

The story highlights the basic position of Dionysius in regard to penance: Salvation is possible for those who commit even sins unto death, and leniency toward the lapsed does not coincide with a soft, "martyrless" Church.[135]

Yet Dionysius's inclusion of the story of Serapion does not mean that the Alexandrian bishop does not know of a process of ecclesial penance seen in previous authors. In a fragment of his letter to Conon (Colon?), he echoes the witness of the *Canonical Epistle* of Gregory Thaumaturgus in speaking of penitential grades. Those guilty of apostasy must spend three years as "listeners" (*akroōmenoi*) and ten years as "prostrators" (*hypopiptontes*).[136] The authenticity

---

134. . . . *aph' ouk enargōs dietērēthē kai paremeinen, heōs lythē kai tēs hamartia exaleiphtheisēs epi pollois hois epraxen kalois homologēthēnai dynēthē* (41, 160). Bardy (in n. 1 on the same page) recognizes that this story does not reflect the normal way in which sinners were reconciled on their deathbed, which would include the presence of a presbyter. Dionysius tells this story to Fabius in hopes that an extreme case would move the Antiochene bishop toward a more moderate position.

135. W. Bienert, *Dionysius von Alexandrien zur Frage des Origenismus im dritten Jahrhundert*, PTS 21 (Berlin, 1978), pp. 183–185, stresses that this is a case of the more practical Dionysius applying the speculative theology of Origen, who held that pardon for sins unto death was theoretically possible.

136. This fragment (along with three other fragments on repentance attributed to Dionysius of Alexandria) was published by J. Pitra, *Iuris ecclesiastici graecorum historia*

of this passage remains a question; yet, if indeed it is to be ascribed to Dionysius, his must be considered one of the earliest testimonies to the penitential grades.[137]

There is nothing to suggest that Dionysius's usage of the technical terminology of the graded discipline of penance varies from the meaning already seen in Gregory. Those who are "listeners" must have been able to at least hear the proclamation of the Word, but are excluded from other liturgical or cultural participation in the community. They are on the very fringes of the community. During this time they perform personal penitential works so as to satisfy the bishop and the community of the sincerity of their conversion. At a certain time they are allowed to be "prostrators," who play a more active role in the liturgical life of the Church. In this stage they receive the prayers of the community after the liturgy of the Word while either kneeling or prostrating before the bishop.[138]

These two grades of penance are not as distinct from the direct coercive penance of isolation and the penance of segregation, including exomologesis, found in the *Didascalia Apostolorum* and in the writings of Origen, as they perhaps first appear. Though Dionysius does not directly indicate a penance of isolation of the sinner, the first stage of "listener," as with Gregory, could be said to link elements of separation from, and segregation within, the community. Penitents are on the outside margins of the Church, yet they are

---

et monumenta, Vol. I: *A primo p.c.n. ad VI saeculum* (Rome, 1864), pp. 545–546:20-28. While substantially the text of canon 12 of the Council of Nicaea, it is considered genuine by A. von Harnack, *Geschichte der altchristlichen Literatur bis Eusebius*, Bd. I,1 (Leipzig, 1893), p. 417, an assessment followed by Poschmann, *Paenitentia Secunda*, p. 471, n. 3; K. Hein, *Eucharist and Excommunication*, p. 337; and W. Bienert, *Dionysius von Alexandrien*, p. 54.

137. Against those who have argued for the authenticity of this text, Van de Paverd, "Confession and Penance," II, p. 59, n. 56, believes that Harnack is referring to other of the fragments listed by Pitra and so considers this text unauthentic. His position is further strengthened if one considers that there is no other witness to a casuist approach of the graded system, viz., the setting of strict time requirements for each stage, before the fourth century. However, the text is included here inasmuch as the question of its authenticity must still be considered an open one.

It is interesting that Grotz, in his concern to prove the existence of penitential stages in both the East and the West in his *Busstufenwesens*, does not refer to this fragment.

138. Poschmann, *Paenitentia Secunda*, pp. 472ff.

allowed to be present to hear the Word of God when the community gathers for the liturgy. When the bishop is satisfied that they
have purified themselves by their personal penance, they begin the
more specific period of segregation, being allowed to become "prostrators." Here they are no longer near the outer edges of the Church
but within it; the community (represented by the bishop) interacts
with them and acknowledges their presence. Yet they still have limited status within the Church, defined by the external actions associated with exomologesis, including continued exclusion from the
liturgy of the Eucharist, a segregated place in the assembly, and in-
tercessions and prostrations before the bishop. This intermediate
period occurs immediately prior to their full reconciliation with the
Church.[139]

If it is the case, and indeed it appears to be so, that Dionysius
knows of the traditional process of penance for those guilty of grave
postbaptismal sin, it is also true that what is most important for him
is the salvation of the sinner and not the process itself. His story
of Serapion is proof that one can be reconciled on his or her deathbed, necessarily bypassing the recognized stages of penance. This
is a genuine reconciliation, one that cannot be revoked if the person recovers unless the person falls into grave sin again.[140] From
the story it appears that readmittance to communion is effected without a prior laying on of the hand, so the reception of the Eucharist
takes on the character of reconciliation.[141]

---

139. This is the position of both Poschmann, *ibid.*, pp. 474–480, and Grotz, *Busstufenwesens*, pp. 400–408 (but only in reference to the similar canons in the *Canonical
Epistle* of Gregory Thaumaturgus).

140. See another of the penitential fragments ascribed to Dionysius as well as an-
notations by C. Feltoe, *The Letters and Other Remains of Dionysius of Alexander* (Cambridge, 1904), pp. 60–62. Its genuineness is again attested to by both Harnack,
Altchristlichen Literatur I,1, p. 417, and Bienert, *Dionysius von Alexandrien*, p. 54.

141. *Ibid.*, p. 181. It could be the case that the story highlights an older experience
of reconciliation of grave sins in which no separate rite was discernible (Irenaeus,
Clement of Alexandria). But there is no evidence to suggest that this continued to
be the common practice by late in the third century. Indeed, the heightened role
of the bishop in a rite of ecclesial pardon seen in the *Didascalia* and even in Origen
makes one hesitant to agree with Poschmann, *Paenitentia Secunda*, pp. 278–279, and
Hein, *Eucharist and Excommunication*, p. 341, who hold that a formal rite of reconciliation preceding readmission to the Eucharist was not essential. The situation of Serapion, who was reconciled on his deathbed without the presence of the bishop or

Another proof of the pastoral leniency of Dionysius comes in his willingness to allow the martyrs to retain an efficacious role in the forgiveness of sins (VI,42,5-6). After relating the courage of the martyrs (VI,41.42,1-4), he adds that in regard to those who have lapsed and have sacrificed during the persecution, the martyrs have taken it upon themselves to care for them. When it is observed that the lapsed are sincere in their conversion, the martyrs

> . . . received them, and gathered them, and were reunited with them again, and had fellowship with them in their prayers and feasts (VI,42,5).[142]

Dionysius then proceeds to ask Fabius if such a practice is acceptable or if the martyrs should be rebuked for their mercy. Such a rhetorical question seems to give implicit assent to the practice.

Finally, Dionysius does not give any explicit witness to the consequences of ecclesial reconciliation. Unlike the writings of his mentor, Origen, what is known of his writings contains nothing concerning any restraints imposed on those who have once been public penitents. However, in the fragment of the letter mentioned above, he does indicate that those who have been reconciled on their deathbeds, while fully reconciled, can be asked to undertake further penance if they recover. This is not so much a punitive measure as one undertaken for the good of both the sinner and the community. If they refuse to do penance, Dionysius indicates that

---

presbyter, must be considered a pastoral exception rather than normative experience (see above, n. 134). See also G. del Ton, "L'episodio eucaristico di Serapione narrato da Dionizi Alessandrino," *SCA* 70 (1942) 37-47, pp. 45-46.

142. . . . *eisedexanto kai synēgagon kai synestēsan kai proseuchōn autois kai hestiaseōn ekoinōnēsan* (41,152). The exact meaning of this text has been debated. Older authors, such as A. McGiffert, *Eusebius*, Nicene and Post Nicene Fathers 1 (New York, 1890; reprinted, Grand Rapids, Mich., 1979), pp. 285-286, n. 6, agrees with the interpretation of Valesius, found in his translation of the works of Eusebius (1659), that this was a reference to merely private fellowship granted by the martyrs and does not refer to full Eucharistic communion, granted only by the bishop. Other authors have refuted this view, seeing Dionysius as recognizing the power of martyrs to pardon sins (Bienert, *Dionysius von Alexandrien*, pp. 181-183), but not without the necessary stages during which they could judge their conversion (Feltoe, *Letters and Other Remains*, p. 18, n. on ln. 9). Still others simply leave the question open (Bardy, SC 41, p. 152, n. 6). The fact remains that at least during the times of persecution, martyrs could remit sins. See above, Chapter Two, p. 116, n. 170.

they are to be excluded a second time (*aphorismon deuteron*) from the community. Whether or not this implies a second reconciliation is not clear from the text; however, given the strong tradition in Alexandria of an unrepeatable penance by this time, this possibility seems unlikely.[143]

CONCLUSION

In Alexandria, the possibility of reconciliation exists for all sins as long as postbaptismal offenders are willing to express their contriteness through penance. While sinners are encouraged to confess their sin to a "spiritual person" in order to aid in their inner healing, the bishop takes on an increasingly central role in the process, having the authority to directly impose upon sinners an isolation for grave sins in order to coerce them back to the fold. As in the *Didascalia*, the care of these isolated penitents is entrusted to the presbyters, disclosing a closer relationship to them by the Church than in the previous two centuries. (This closer relationship is particularly evident in the development of the grade of "listener," which appears as what might be described as a linking grade incorporating elements of both isolation from, and segregation within, the community in the witness of Dionysius, if the relevant fragment is authentic). When the sincerity of their conversion is evident from the penitential works undertaken, they are admitted to an intermediate stage in the process, the penance of segregation, including the external actions of humiliation connected with exomologesis. The duration of this period is unknown, but it is followed by reconciliation, perhaps—if Origen's witness is to be accepted—through the laying on of the hand and anointing with oil, culminating with readmittance to the Eucharist. There is strong Alexandrian testimony to the custom of a single penance after baptism. And with Origen we have the first and only witness during the third century to juridic restraints being imposed upon penitents after reconciliation.

---

143. Feltoe, *Letters and Other Remains*, pp. 61–62.

CHAPTER SUMMARY

The testimony to an order of penitents in the East, when seen against the backdrop of the first two centuries, marks a development. The ascendancy of the bishop's role in the administration of the communities is reflected in the key part he plays in the pastoral care extended to grave postbaptismal sinners. However, the Eastern authors make it clear that the responsibility for the care of sinners is not the bishop's alone. Besides receiving the prayer of the whole community, penitents are to manifest their sin to "someone of God" who both directs and supports them on their journey toward full readmission to the Church. This emphasis on "spiritual direction," afforded to sinners within an ecclesial setting, will be retained throughout the later penitential tradition of the East. It will be a primary factor in preventing a movement toward undue severity and in allowing penitential practice to keep pace with concrete pastoral needs (unlike the later evolution of penance in the West).

Structural elements that recognize the different relationship between the sinner and God (and so the Church), and the altered status of the sinner within the Church, are explicitly in place, though not quite as defined as they appear in the West. For the first time an actual process appears, most especially in the witness of the *Didascalia* and Origen. Delineated moments in the movement toward reconciliation are discernible, proof that the informality of the first two centuries has given way to an established manner of dealing with the situation of those guilty of serious sin after baptism. Penitents now can be said to enter as an organized group into the conscious life and worship of the Church. It is these elements that emerge from the diverse witness of the East during the third century, elements which, taken together, lie at the heart of a developing order of penitents.

Chapter Four

THIRD-CENTURY WITNESSES IN THE WEST

Unlike the experience of the East, the development of the penitential discipline in the West during the third century was framed by controversy. The point of dispute centered on the very basic question: Who is to be reconciled? In Rome this question emerged as part of the stricter, more elitist ecclesiology of Hippolytus and Novatian. Both schismatics wanted a more demanding discipline for those guilty of postbaptismal sin. It was not a question of whether God could forgive sinners; God's great mercy is capable of embracing all persons, no matter their sin. Rather, the question was whether the Church should readmit such persons, even if they demonstrated sincere repentance. The perspective of Hippolytus and Novatian forced the local Churches to seriously reflect upon the meaning and effect of postbaptismal penance. The penitential witness of the Roman Church is examined in the first section of the chapter.

In North Africa, controversy was still the determinant in the evolution of penitential practice. The most celebrated case was that of Tertullian, whose turn toward Montanism gave the heresy its most eloquent spokesman. Tertullian shifted from his Catholic, more tolerant perspective of allowing the possibility of a *paenitentia secunda* for all repentant sinners to opposing this "indulgent" policy as a Montanist. Once again the Church was forced to be self-reflective concerning its penitential practice. Later, during Cyprian's day, controversy over penance arose due to the situation of the *lapsi*: Should they be readmitted to the Church? Cyprian's answer to this question was a watershed in the history of penance. Once and for all the question of the effectiveness of penance was resolved, but not before the North African Church was nearly torn asunder by immoderate elements on both sides of the issue. The dossier on penance in the North African Church is the subject of the second section of the chapter.

I. ROME

A. ANONYMOUS WRITING AGAINST ARTEMON = *ECCL. HIST.* V,28,8-12 (C. 230-240 A.D.)

The Church at Rome, from the last quarter of the second century until the first half of the third, was in the process of emerging as one of the largest and most representative centers of Christian life in the Roman Empire.[1] The Christian community there was as diverse as the number of races and traditions that congregated in the cosmopolitan capital of the empire, making it fertile ground for the formulation and crossbreeding of a variety of philosophies and practices. It is not surprising, then, that the most urgently felt problem in the young Roman Church was the question of unity. If it was to survive, it would do so, not by integrating the impossibly disparate pieces of belief and worship present in the community, but by the sheer force of disciplinary measures.[2] The development of a strong, centralized leadership, therefore, was necessary for the survival of the local church. By this time in history the monarchical form of the Roman episcopate was established and possessed the authority necessary to impose a uniformity of doctrine and practice within the boundaries of the Roman community. It was at the same time beginning to attempt to exert its influence on the life and worship of other local Churches.[3]

One of the consequences of the Roman quest for ecclesiastical unity and the rise in the power of the bishop was a tightening of the disciplinary norms relating to postbaptismal penance. The bishop

---

1. G. Lapiana, "The Roman Church at the End of the Second Century," *HThR* 18 (1925) 201-277, pp. 203-204. See also *id.*, "Foreign Groups in Rome During the First Centuries of the Empire," *HThR* 20 (1927) 183-203.

2. Lapiana, "The Roman Church," pp. 208-29.

3. *Ibid.*, p. 204; Von Campenhausen, *Ecclesiastical Authority*, pp. 236-237.

had evolved as the central figure charged with the responsibility of caring for those who, through some serious external action, had been unfaithful to their baptismal commitment. This is especially seen in the story of the confessor Natalius, who, Eusebius relates, fell into the false doctrine of one Theodotus the cobbler, a disciple of the heretic Artemon.[4] The act of schism on the part of the unfortunate Natalius is clearly accentuated; it is even said that he was paid to fulfill his function as bishop of the false sect (28,10). He came to his senses only after a miraculous encounter, being "scourged by holy angels an entire night" (28,10.12). The next morning

> [he] put on a sackcloth, covered himself with ashes, and going with great haste, while crying, before the bishop Zephyrinus, he prostrated himself at the feet not only of the clergy but also of the laity; he moved with his tears the merciful Church of the compassionate Christ; and, though using much supplication and showing the marks from the stripes he had received, he was only admitted into communion with difficulty (28,12).[5]

Besides the fact of the heightened awareness of the bishop's authority in the community that appears in the text, there are other reasons why this account is a significant witness to the development of an order of penitents. First, it stands as a reliable testament to the Roman practice of allowing for the possibility of heretics and apostates being reconciled and readmitted to communion.[6] As in

---

4. Though the account was written at a later date, Natalius is spoken of as a contemporary of Zephyrinus of Rome (c. 198–217 A.D.). Artemon, teaching in Rome at the end of the second or beginning of the third century, was associated with an Adoptionism that held that Christ was a mere man with divine power. He was eventually excommunicated by Zephyrinus (Deferrari, *Eusebius Pamphili*, p. 242, n. 1). There are differing opinions as to whether Hippolytus is the author of the work (Bardy, SC 41, p. 74, n. 1).

The text cited is found in Bardy's edition, SC 41, pp. 76–77.

5. ". . . *endysamenon sakkon kai spodon katapasamenon meta pollēs spoudēs kai dakryōn prospesein Zephyrinō tō episkopō, kyliomenon hypo tous podas ou monon tōn en klēro, alla kai tōn laïkōn, syngcheai te tois dakrysin tēn eusplangchnon ekklēsian tou eleēmonos Christou pollē te tē deēsei chrēsamenon deixanta te tous mōlōpas hōn eilēphei plēgōn molis koinōnēthēnai*" (41, 77).

6. Poschmann, *Paenitentia Secunda*, pp. 363–367. The story of Natalius is cited by Poschmann (and other commentators such as d'Alès, *L'Édit*, pp. 124–125) as one proof that the famous "edict of toleration," which allowed for the reconciliation of heretics, was neither innovative nor Roman.

the witness of the East, even objectively grave sins are not excluded from the chance of ecclesial pardon if the guilty one is willing to express sincere interior repentance through external acts of penance. Second, the penitential actions of Natalius fit almost exactly the description of exomologesis seen in Tertullian's *De paenitentia* 9–10. This points out a certain consistency in the external practice of post-baptismal penance for grave sins between the churches of Rome and Carthage.[7]

Finally, such external penitential actions, including prostrations, special dress, tears, intercession before the community, and being excluded from the Eucharist are all intended to reflect liturgically the relationship of sinners with the Church as a result of grave post-baptismal sin. Serious offenders in the community are no longer just quarantined outside the Church until they repent, as in the predominant witness of the first two centuries. With this brief story of Natalius, there is a clear testimony in the West of accepted symbolic penitential actions that not only afforded the sinners ecclesial readmission but also removed all ambiguity with regard to the status of such persons in the Church.

B. Hippolytus of Rome (c. 235 a.d.)

Of the ecclesial personages known from the ancient period, there is none whose character remains more irreconcilable than that of Hippolytus. As a defender of orthodoxy, he verged on heresy; as one who upheld the value of Church unity, he was elected an anti-pope; as an author who was both sarcastic and polemical, he is known for the breadth, if not the depth, of his scholarship.[8] Concerning his witness to the practice of ecclesial penance, there is little information offered that is not polemical. Yet, it is exactly his polemics that makes Hippolytus an impossible figure to ignore when studying the roots of the order of penitents.

---

7. Lapiana, ''The Roman Church,'' pp. 223–232, explores the numerous political and ecclesial connections between Rome and North Africa. The interpenetration of ecclesial discipline will especially become evident in Cyprian's correspondence with the leaders of the Roman Church.

8. G. Dix, *The Treatise on the Apostolic Tradition of St. Hippolytus of Rome* (London, 1937); reissued with additional material and corrections by H. Chadwick (London, 1968), pp. xiiff.

In his *Refutatio omnium haeresium* (also known as the *Philosophumena*), Hippolytus is angered by the policy of the Roman bishop Callistus, who seemingly made it a practice to offer reconciliation to any person guilty of serious sin (IX,12,20-26).[9] Not only were bishops guilty of grave sin allowed to keep their office and clerics who married more than once admitted to orders, but those guilty of severe sins of impurity and even of drug-induced abortions could have their sins remitted.[10] Hippolytus implies that Callistus began such indulgent practices himself, practices that up until that time were not permissible in Rome (IX,12,20). If that is true, Rome would have had a more rigorist attitude toward postbaptismal sin than appears in the East or in North Africa.

It must be remembered, however, that Hippolytus is no objective historian. Throughout the preceding chapters of the ninth book of the *Refutatio omnium haeresium*, he paints a completely unflattering picture of both Zephyrinus and his successor, Callistus, who became bishop of the Roman See instead of the better qualified Hippolytus.[11] It is apparent that since Hippolytus's own ecclesial ambitions were thwarted by Callistus, he would stop at nothing to tear down the reputation of the former slave.[12] His invectives against

---

9. Editions consulted include: M. Marcovich (ed.), *Hippolytus. Refutatio Omnium Haeresium*, PTS 25 (Berlin, 1986); G. Bonwetsch and H. Achelis, *Hippolytus Werke*, Vol. I: *Exegetische und Homiletische Schriften*, GCS 1 (Leipzig, 1897); B. Botte, *Hippolyte de Rome. La Tradition Apostolique d'après les anciennes versions*, SC 11 bis (Paris, 1968). Direct citations will be indicated by page and line numbers unless otherwise noted.

The discovery of the *Refutatio omnium haeresium* in 1850 led many modern authors to believe that it was also Callistus who had issued the famous "edict" that occasioned the writing of the *De pudicitia* by Tertullian. However, most contemporary scholars have now abandoned this view; see above, pp. 30-33.

10. Von Campenhausen, *Ecclesiastical Authority*, p. 235, n. 15, sees Hippolytus's reference to bishops guilty of grave postbaptismal sin retaining their office as proof that the power of the bishop comes no longer from his personal holiness or faithfulness to the gospel but solely from the office itself. This is further borne out in the prayer of consecration of a bishop in the *Traditio apostolica* III, 5, which recognizes the bishop's power to remit sin. See below, n. 19.

11. While Hippolytus does not explicitly refer to the story of Zephyrinus's readmittance of the schismatic bishop Natalius, it may be assumed that it is exactly such acts of indulgence about which he so bitterly complains. Also, his authorship of the Natalius story remains an open question; see above, n. 4.

12. For example, one of the actions of Callistus that Hippolytus takes issue with concerns the possibility of marriage between slave and free, a position taken by the

the lenient innovations existing in Rome originated more from his subjective perspective than from the objective historical situation he claims to describe.[13] This is in no way to say that Hippolytus was a singular anomaly in his cry for a more rigorist appreciation of sin after baptism; the very fact that he was later elected as a rival bishop to Callistus reflects the strong support he must have had within certain circles in the Church.[14] It is best to understand his accusations as another sign of the existence of rigorist elements in the Church, sometimes very strong, that coexisted alongside a more tolerant tradition in regard to grave postbaptismal sinners. Just as this was the situation in other local churches, so it also appeared in Rome.[15]

It is impossible to conclude from Hippolytus' writings that he actually refused ecclesial readmittance and pardon to grave sinners.[16] All that can be affirmed with certainty from his dispute over the indulgent practices of Callistus is that he perceives the Roman bishop as not adequately recognizing the altered relationship between the sinner and the Church due to postbaptismal transgressions. In this regard, Hippolytus accuses him of "not judging with whom to communicate [but] indiscriminately bringing communion to all" (IX,

---

Church against the laws and custom of the Empire (Quasten, *Patrology* II, pp. 206–207; Dix, *Apostolic Tradition*, pp. xvii–xviii). Hippolytus's stance is understandable in light of his attempt to bring out the more unseemly aspects of Callistus's past.

13. In this way the *modus operandi* of Hippolytus is similar to that of Tertullian, whose polemic against the *pontifex maximus* in the *De pudicitia* (as will be seen), results more from his turn toward Montanism than from the occurrence of a hereto unheard of action. Von Campenhausen, *Ecclesiastical Authority*, p. 221, n. 33, agrees that Hippolytus's debate with Callistus really does not center on penitential discipline.

14. Quasten, *Patrology* II, p. 164.

15. Dix, *Apostolic Tradition*, p. xvi. J. Daniélou and H. Marrou, *The Christian Centuries*, Vol. I: *The First Six Hundred Years*, trans. V. Cronin (London, 1964), pp. 144–151, hold that Hippolytus was a representative of the old Roman presbyterate who objected to the institutional progress of the Church made under the leadership of the more pragmatic Zephyrinus and Callistus.

16. Poschmann, *PAS*, p. 51, points out that it remains a question whether Hippolytus refused pardon to adulterers and so to idolaters and murderers, or if he simply wanted a greater penance imposed. Even if the former were the case (which may receive support from his harsh references to the fate of heretics in *Prouerbia fragmentum XXI*), it does not prove conclusively that he was outside acceptable ecclesial discipline. See especially Cyprian's *Ep.* 55.21, where he refers to certain African bishops who refused reconciliation to adulterers while remaining in communion with other more tolerant bishops.

12,26).[17] This is not acceptable, because the true tradition called for false teachers and heretics to be "ejected from the Church" (*ekblētoi tes ekklēsias*), "Church" here meaning Hippolytus and his followers (IX,12,21). This reference need not imply a permanent banishment from the community but could be interpreted as an indication by Hippolytus that certain grave sins demanded some sort of separation from the Eucharistic assembly.[18] Therefore, it is not a question of whether the bishop had the authority to readmit sinners back into the community. Hippolytus himself affirms that such authority is given to the bishop at his ordination (*Traditio apostolica* III,5).[19] His reproaches found in the *Refutatio omnium haeresium* center more on the fact that concrete penitential actions are necessary to adequately distinguish the status of the sinner due to his or her sin than on whether reconciliation is possible at all.

Outside his mention of the obligation of expelling sinners from the Church, Hippolytus provides little else by way of further testimony to penitential practices.[20] His references to exomologesis are not specific enough to view them as explicit allusions to a liturgical postbaptismal confession of sin.[21] Also, in describing the strange baptismal rites of the heretical Marcites, he alludes to an "imposition of the hand" (*epitithentes cheira*). Though the practice could have

---

17. . . . *mē diakrinon tisin (d)ei koinōnein, pasin (de) akritōs prospheron tēn koinōnian* (Marcovich, 356:141-142).

18. Grotz, *Busstufenwesens*, pp. 392ff., sees the penance practice of Callistus, which apparently did not include exclusion, as a more original form of ecclesial penance. Thus Hippolytus's insistence on a Eucharistic separation would be a later development.

19. . . . sp(irit)u[m] primatus sacerdotii habere potestatem dimittere peccata secundum mandatum tuum, dare sortes secundum praeceptu(m) tuum, soluere etiam omnem collegationem secundum potestatem quam dedisti apostolis (Botte, *La Tradition Apostolique*, pp. 44, 46).

20. In Hippolytus's condemnation of the second baptism allowed by Elchasai (*Refut. omn. haer.* IX,13,3-5; X,29), there is reference to adulterers and false prophets who wish to convert in order to obtain the remission of sin, the peace, and "a place/communion with the just" (*meros meta tōn dikaiōn*). The eschatological sense of the text prevents one from gleaning a witness to a penitential discipline.

21. See IV,48,1.3; VII,26,3.4. The reference of IV,48,1 is interesting: *auton de gony klinein / [kai] ektetakota amphoteras tas cheiras, hoionei peri hamartias exomologoumenon* (Marcovich,132:2-133:3). Though there is a comparison here between ritual actions and the confession of sin, it is likely that such actions were accomplished by the whole community rather than specifically reserved to grave sinners.

been adopted by the sect from the initiation rites of the Church, it cannot be construed as a reference to a reconciliation rite following upon ecclesial penance (VI,41,4).[22] The overarching concern of Hippolytus is to argue for a more rigorous approach to postbaptismal sin; to explicate exact pastoral measures concerning how sinners are to eventually be readmitted to the Church would stand at cross-purposes to his primary intention. He does not want to appear as indulgent as his opponent Callistus. No, the Church must never fail to recognize, through appropriate external actions, the fact that the relationship between God (and so the Church) and the sinner is fundamentally different due to sin. Though sin can be pardoned by the bishop, this necessarily requires firm disciplinary measures rather than the indulgence of one like Callistus.[23]

C. Novatian and Novatianism

1. novatian (c. 250 a.d.)

The Roman presbyter Novatian came into prominence shortly after the death of Hippolytus. Eusebius relates a letter by Cornelius (whose election as bishop of Rome was to set in motion the events leading up to Novatian's eventual schism with the Church), who states that Novatian was baptized at a moment in his life when he was ill to the point of death and who, even after his recovery, "never received the seal from the bishop."[24] Most likely it was the Roman bishop Fabian who ordained him "despite the opposition of all the

---

22. J. Dallen, "The Imposition of Hands in Penance: A Study in Liturgical History," *Worship* 51 (1977) 224–247, p. 225, sees a penitential intention in this action and credits Hippolytus with one of the earliest witnesses to a rite of reconciliation by the imposition of the hand. His position appears slightly more nuanced in *Reconciling Community*, pp. 36–37. The baptismal context of the reference makes it more likely that the sect copied a liturgical action connected with baptism and confirmation rather than appropriating the laying on of the hand to reconcile penitents, which is nowhere else mentioned by Hippolytus.

23. For a good appreciation of the conflict between Hippolytus and Callistus as well as an overview of the literature, see A. Hamel, *Kirche bei Hippolyt von Rome*, pp. 59ff.

24. *Eccl. Hist.* VI,43,5-22. The *sphragisthēnai hypo tou episkopou* must refer to confirmation. See Bardy, SC 41, p. 157, n. 15. Because of his bitter conflict with Novatian, the accuracy of Cornelius's account is subject to doubt.

clergy and even a great number of the laity" (VI,43,17).[25] Yet, in the face of such antipathy, when Fabian died a martyr's death at the height of the Decian persecution in January, 250 A.D., it was Novatian who emerged as the leader of the Roman clergy whose task it was to administer the community until the election of a new bishop.[26]

Among his extant works are three letters written to Cyprian of Carthage during the time Novatian served as spokesperson for the Roman *presbyterium*.[27] Here he outlines his own stringent position concerning the treatment of the *lapsi*, those who denied the faith during the Decian persecution. Whether such persons (the *sacrificati*) actually had offered sacrifice to the Roman gods or had obtained false documents stating that they had offered sacrifice when they in fact had not done so (the *libellatici*) made no difference to Novatian (*Ep.* 30.3.1-2). He is the "champion of the gospel" who must uphold the ancient "discipline" of the Roman Church.[28] Serious sinners must not be admitted to the "communion" of the Church nor be given the "fatal poison(s) of hasty reconciliation" (*properatae communicationis uenena*); otherwise, the Church's ancient tradition of faith gives way to laxity and the confession of the martyrs will have

25. . . . *hos diakōlyomenos hypo pantos tou klērou, alla kai laïkōn pollōn* . . . (Bardy, SC 41, p. 158).

26. The reasons for his ascent to a leadership position remain unclear. His work *De Trinitate*, probably written prior to 250 A.D., reveals, as do all his works, a man of learning and erudition, which may have enhanced his reputation in the Roman community. Even Cornelius admits this in his letter, although with sarcasm. There is also the question of whether he had been personally chosen by Fabian as his successor. See G. Diercks, *Novatiani Opera*, CCL 4 (Turnhout, 1972), p. ix.

27. The letters are nos. 30, 31, and 36 in the collected epistles of Cyprian. The first one Cyprian himself testifies to be from the hand of Novatian (*Ep.* 55.5.2), while the third is very similar in style and vocabulary. Letter 31 has been convincingly shown by B. Melin, *Studia in Corpus Cyprianeum* (Uppsala, 1946), pp. 43-67, to also be from Novatian, even though the Latin used is more "vulgarized."

Direct citations to Novatian's letters are from Diercks, *Novatiani Opera*, pp. 181-252, and will be indicated by page and line numbers.

28. C. Daly, "Novatian and Tertullian. A Chapter in the History of Puritanism," *IThQ* 19 (1952) 33-43, p. 36, n. 9; R. DeSimone, *Novatian*, FC 67 (Washington, D.C., 1974), pp. 180-181. Both authors maintain that the frequent use of *disciplina* by Novatian in the letters (five times), as well as the use of *severitas* (four times), *vigor* (six times) and *censura* (two times), not only manifests his rigorism but puts into relief Tertullian's influence on him.

been in vain (*Epp.* 30.3.3; 31.8.1-2; 36.1.3; 3.1). Prior to the election of the bishop who would decide further on the issue, the only concession to be made to the *lapsi* is that in their last moments prior to death, they can be given "proper care and solitude" (*demum caute et sollicite*), provided they show genuine signs of their repentance (*Ep.* 30.8).[29]

Novatian lauds the stand that Cyprian makes against those Carthaginian presbyters who have taken it upon themselves to reconcile the *lapsi* without first requiring them to undertake penance (*Epp.* 31.6.2; 36.1.2).[30] He agrees with the African primate that any decision regarding those who have denied the faith, even amid the storms of persecution, requires the collegial agreement of the bishop, presbyters, deacons, confessors, and those members of the laity who have remained faithful (*Epp.* 30.5.3; 31.6.2). It is apparent that while the words of Novatian certainly reveal a rigorist bent, at this point in his life he is not outside the tradition of offering the possibility of forgiveness to grave postbaptismal sinners (in this case, the *lapsi*) who are willing to undertake ecclesial penance.[31] He perceives the Church of Carthage as attempting to steer "a middle course" (*temperamenti moderamen*) in this matter, a course that the Roman Church also endeavors to follow (*Ep.* 30.8).

Novatian makes it clear that the *lapsi* must be willing to engage in a penance that is full of postponement and delays (*Ep.* 30.7.1),

---

29. Here Novatian is echoing the Roman policy indicated in a previous letter to the Carthaginian clergy (*Ep.* 8.3.1). Cyprian himself eventually adopted a similar policy (*Ep.* 20.3.2), but only after first mandating more stringent requirements (*Ep.* 18.1.2). See E. Amann, "Novatien et Novatianisme," *DThC* XI,1 (1931) 816–849, c. 834.

30. See Cyprian's letters to his presbyters and deacons (*Epp.* 16; 18; 19); to the laity (*Ep.* 17.2); and his letter to the Roman clergy to which Novatian is responding (*Ep.* 20.2.3).

31. In *Ep.* 30.8 he speaks of not wishing to introduce an *innouandum* (innovation) into the tradition before the election of the new bishop. This has been interpreted by some modern authors as proof of the Church's unwillingness to reconcile apostates prior to the time of Cornelius and Cyprian. However, the *innouandum* might well refer to reconciling apostates too quickly. They should be willing to do penance until the new bishop is elected; he would then determine the time of their readmittance. Taken in this sense, Novatian would be confirming the established practice of offering penance to all repentant sinners. See Daly, "Novatian and Tertullian," pp. 42–43.

one that gives those who have denied the faith time to prove their genuine sorrow (*Ep.* 36.3.3). But what is the process of ecclesial penance he has in mind? He offers no clear description, but there are indications that he is familiar with accepted penitential actions which recognized the changed relationship between the sinner and the Church:

> By all means let them beat at the doors but not so as to batter them down; let them approach the threshold of the Church, but not bound across it. Let them keep watch at the gates of the heavenly encampment but be armed with that sense of humility by which they acknowledge that they have been deserters. . . . As the envoys for their grief they should send forth tears, their advocates should be sighs drawn from the depths of their hearts, providing proof of the sorrow and the shame that they feel for the sin they have committed (*Ep.* 30.6.3).[32]

Though this passage speaks in metaphors, its similarity to other third-century witnesses allows one to apprehend a literal sense to the description of penance. Penitents could well have been isolated from the liturgical assembly outside of church, humbly entreating the community to pray for their pardon.[33] During this time the grief of the penitents is especially accentuated, expressed through tears and sighs.[34] In this way, through their sorrow along with "good works" (*operibus bonis*) and "words of genuine penance" (*paenitentiae . . . uerae sermonibus*), the honesty of their contriteness is witnessed by the whole community (*Ep.* 31.7.1). That the requirement

---

32. "Pulsent sane fores, sed non utique confringant. Adeant ad limen ecclesiae, sed non utique transiliant. Castrorum caelestium excubent portis, sed armati modestia qua intellegant se desertores fuisse. . . . Mittant legatos pro suis doloribus lacrimas, aduocatione fungantur ex intimo pectore prolati gemitus dolorem probantes commissi criminis et pudorem" (Diercks, CCL 4, 204:17-20; 205:27-29; trans. G. Clarke, *The Letters of St. Cyprian of Carthage*, Vol. II: *Letters 28–54*, ACW 44 (New York, 1984), p. 31.

33. Clarke, *Letters* II, pp. 129–130, n. 39. Tertullian also speaks of penitents being physically situated on the margins of the liturgical assembly. See *De paen.* 7,10; below, p. 193.

34. The term *luctibus* also appears in his *De bono pudicitiae* 13,4 to convey the necessity of showing some external sign of sorrow for sinful acts committed. As shall be seen, Cyprian will speak often of the necessity of the penitent to show sorrow through external acts of mourning.

of adequate penance for sin cannot be overlooked is emphasized by Novatian, especially when he states that the request by the *lapsi* for readmission to the Church "must be done within the sacred obligation, in accord with the regulation for the petition itself, after a fitting period of time" (7.1).[35] Though the exact meaning of his words remains unclear, Novatian does appear to indicate that not only does he know that penance must be done for sin (*Ep.* 36.3.3), but that it must be a specific discipline of penance, with accepted external actions. Even amid the special situation of the persecution, this specific discipline must be followed without deviation.[36]

Novatian is not explicit in his witness to an ecclesial rite of reconciliation. However, his use of the term *communicatio*, both negatively as exclusion from the Eucharist and positively as readmittance to communion, denotes that it is this action that is most determinant of the status of sinners within the Church. One cannot be said to possess full baptismal stature until one is readmitted to communion, and only one who has been readmitted to the Eucharist can be said to be pardoned (*Ep.* 36.1.3).[37] Pardon results from a sincere and humble undertaking of penance: "Let us pray that the effects of indulgence toward the fallen may also be accompanied by penance" (*Ep.* 30.6.2).[38] It is absolutely clear in his letters that unless one remained sinless in his or her baptismal commitment, or endured a long and laborious penance for denying one's baptism in the face

---

35. "Sed hoc totum in sacramento, sed in ipsius postulationis lege temporis facto temperamento . . ." (Diercks, 205:5-7).

36. *Sacramentum* is difficult to translate: a technical term for an obligation? (Clarke, *Letters* II, p. 124, n. 16; p. 130, n. 41); a direct reference to a penitential discipline? (Desimone, *Novatian*, p. 193, n. 9). See also J. De Ghellinck, *et al.*, *Pour l'histoire du mot "sacramentum,"* SSL 3 (Louvain, 1924), pp. 201-202, who affirms that the term connotes the "dispositions de la loi" necessary to be accomplished for one to receive reconciliation.

37. H. Vogt, *Coetus Sanctorum. Der Kirchenbegriff des Novatian und die Geschichte seiner Sonderkirche*, Theophaneia 20 (Bonn, 1968), pp. 118-119, rightly points out that even though Cyprian witnesses to a double rite of reconciliation (the prayer of the bishop/presbyter with the laying on of the hand *and* readmittance to the Eucharist), Novatian only indicates the latter in referring to the reconciliation of the sinner.

38. "Oremus ut effectus indulgentiae lapsorum subsequatur et paenitentia" (Diercks, 204:10-11). It must be admitted that the corruptness of the text makes it uncertain if the *indulgentia* granted is God's or the Church's. See Clarke, p. 129, n. 37.

of persecution, only then could one have life in Christ, expressed in the partaking of his Body and Blood.

2. NOVATIANISM

a) *Schism and radical rigorism*

In the spring of 251 A.D., the Roman *presbyterium* elected Cornelius as the successor to Fabian. Though the reasons for their choice are lost, it meant that Novatian and his rigorist perspective were left without a mandate, in favor of a more tolerant approach toward the *lapsi* advocated by Cornelius. With the aid of Novatus, a Carthaginian presbyter living in Rome, the disillusioned Novatian gathered together a group of his supporters and was ordained a bishop, an antipope to the Roman See.[39] This incipient act of schism taken by Novatian and his followers brought into existence the Cathari, a puritanical sect, which flourished in both the East and West until the end of the sixth century.[40]

By the middle of 251 A.D., when Cyprian and the Carthaginian church recognized Cornelius as the legitimate bishop of Rome and refused even to hear arguments in favor of Novatian's claim to the Roman See, the antipope became more hostile and recalcitrant.[41] On the question of the reconciliation of grave postbaptismal sinners, the orthodox rigorism expressed by him prior to his act of schism developed into a heretical doctrine of radical severity.[42] Those guilty of apostasy were now required to undertake a lifetime of penance; yet, due to the seriousness of the sin, ecclesial reconciliation could never be given. Though God might forgive them, the Church could not; otherwise the purity of the Church itself would be endangered, and the power of the Holy Spirit, given at the time of baptism, left in doubt.[43]

---

39. Daly, "Novatian and Tertullian," pp. 34–35. According to Eusebius, Novatian (though he confuses the name with Novatus) and his adherents were later excommunicated from the Church by a Roman synod (*Eccl. Hist.* VI,43,2).

40. Amann, "Novatien et Novatianisme," *DThC* 11,1 (1931) 841–849.

41. Due to rumors concerning Cornelius's reputation, it may not have been until early summer before enough reliable evidence from Rome reached Carthage for the North African Church to affirm his legitimate election. See Clarke, *Letters* II, pp. 223–224.

42. Cyprian, *Epp.* 15; 16; 17; 19; 55,28-29; Eusebius, *Eccl. Hist.* VI,43; 45.

43. Vogt, *Coetus Sanctorum*, pp. 136–138.

There is a certain familiarity about the story of Novatian and the Novatianists. In the position of the orthodox Novatian, one is reminded of the strident tone of Hippolytus, who opposed Callistus exactly because of his perception of the latter's leniency toward sinners. Further, the intransigent position of the Novatianists toward the *lapsi* is reminiscent of the position taken by the Montanists with regard to those guilty of adultery and grave carnal sins (which, as will be seen, appears most prominently in Tertullian's *De pudicitia*).[44] One might be led to remark that the rigorism of Novatian is at the same time incongruous with, and not foreign to, existing tradition.

The discipline proposed by Novatian and the later Novatianists was yet another attempt by a small, though seemingly ever-present, contingent of Christians desiring to sift the Church of sinners and establish it as an elite community of saints. This ecclesiological perspective grew up alongside of, and provided a constant challenge to, the more dominant tradition of offering reconciliation to all post-baptismal sinners, provided they were repentant and undertook external acts of penance, in whatever form demanded by a particular time and place. At moments in the history this challenge went beyond even the broad bounds of acceptable ecclesial discipline of the primitive Church, as in the case of Montanism and Novatianism. Yet these more extreme cases inform us that the rigorist element remained viable within the mainstream of the life of the Church; otherwise there is no adequate explanation of why such radical positions were able to receive the wide support that they did.

However, Cyprian will serve as a terminus point of the uneasy marriage between rigorist Christians and those more willing to accept the reality of sin after baptism. He will clarify the role and the

---

44. Daly, "Novatian and Tertullian," *passim*, while recognizing that Novatianism and Montanism had different origins and distinct organizations, brings forth internal evidence from Novatian's letters and his later works to prove that he took as a model the puritanism of the Montanist Tertullian. Yet, even authors from as early as the fourth century, such as Jerome and Pacian, noted the similarity between the two. Philostorgius, in his *Ecclesiastical History*. VIII,15, went so far as to write that Novatian, like Montanus, was Phrygian by birth and grew up familiar with the tenets of Montanism. While this view has been totally dismissed by modern historians, it reveals that a similarity between the two sects was already perceived by the Church Fathers. See Diercks, *Novatiani Opera*, p. viii.

authority of the episcopal office in the reconciliation of sinners in such a way that the process of ecclesial penance will become, at the same time, more institutionalized and more effective. And those who, like Novatian, yearn for a sinless community of saints and the exclusion of sinners, are themselves pushed to the margins of a Church where the tradition of an order of penitents has become unequivocally established.[45]

b) *The anonymous tract* Ad Novatianum

Conserved in seven of the nine manuscripts of Novatian's work *De bono pudicitiae* is the anonymous pamphlet known as *Ad Novatianum*.[46] It dates from 254–257 A.D., and though it was originally published among the works of Cyprian, many modern authors contend that it is of Roman origin.[47] It is a polemical work against the rigorism of Novatian and his followers and a strong apologetic in favor of a more tolerant policy toward the *lapsi*, such as the one taken by both Cyprian and Cornelius.

The tract is of interest to the study of the roots of the order of penitents, if for nothing else than to serve as a further confirmation of the existence of accepted penitential practices in the Roman Church. In refuting Novatian's claim that the penance of the lapsed is done in vain, the author claims that if the heresiarch had known Ezek 33:12, which reads that the righteous are not saved by their righteousness when they err, just as the sinful are not condemned by their sinfulness when they repent, then

> . . . he who is always opposed to penitents would have long ago put on the ashes of repentance; [he] who works more readily in the ruin of structures which are standing than in the building up of those [ruins] which are prostrate . . . (13,10).[48]

As in Novatian's own letter cited above, the metaphorical imagery of the passage reveals a literal basis: the use of ashes and prostra-

---

45. Von Campenhausen, *Ecclesiastical Authority*, pp. 264–292.

46. Direct citations from Diercks, *Novatiani Opera*, pp. 137–152.

47. See the discussion on the difficult question of authorship in Diercks, *Novatiani Opera*, pp. 134–135.

48. . . . iam olim in cinere paeniteretur, ille qui semper paenitentibus aduersatur, qui in ruina facilius aedificatorum stantium operatur quam in structione iacentium ruinarum . . ." (Diercks, 147:21-24).

tion is vividly reminiscent of the story of the penance and difficult readmission of the schismatic bishop Natalius (*Eccl. Hist.* V,28,8-12). Not only is the accomplishment of penance effective in restoring the former baptismal status of sinners, but the liturgical action of penance has become more established.

CONCLUSION

In Rome, the impetus for the development of a penitential discipline was not so much the pastoral situation of sinners but the controversies spawned from dissonant ecclesiological perspectives. With Hippolytus and Novatian, the desire to keep beyond doubt the clear-cut boundaries of the Church impelled them to defend a rigorist approach (with regard to the readmission of grave postbaptismal sinners) against the more tolerant overtures of Callistus and Cornelius. That the dissidents found support for their stringency signals that both rigorist and lenient elements were still existing side by side in the local Churches. Certainly sinners could be reconciled— that much is clear. But all of them? And through what means, and with how much difficulty? These were the key questions to which answers much too tolerant were a factor in leading both figures into schism and, in Novatian's case, toward a radical elitism that allowed for no ecclesial readmission after grave postbaptismal sin.

Yet the story of the schismatic bishop Natalius brings to light the fact that an accepted liturgical penitential discipline was emerging at Rome. This is further confirmed, albeit with sparse witness, by Novatian and the anonymous tract *Ad Novatianum*. These writings are not explicit in their testimony to an intermediate stage of segregation within the community; however, the existence of a monarchical episcopacy makes it possible to infer a parallel existence of a more developed penitential process, more than just the coercive isolation of the first two centuries. Also, the liturgical actions described match the actions found in the witness of Tertullian, where an intermediate stage of penance is clearly in evidence. Indeed, from this appropriate juncture in the testimony of the Roman Church, it is now time to turn to the translucid witness of North Africa, where the external activity connected with postbaptismal penance, and the development of an order of penitents are most perceptible.

II. NORTH AFRICA

A. Tertullian († 220–225 a.d.)

It might be argued that to place Tertullian behind the witness of the patristic authors previously examined is to miscast him within the entire dossier of ecclesial penance in the third century. Certainly it is true that among all writers during the first three hundred years of the life of the Church, Tertullian holds a place of prominence in the development of the Church's penitential practice.[49] He is the first writer to offer a specific description of an ecclesial process undertaken by those who committed grave postbaptismal sin. What is only vaguely alluded to in authors such as Irenaeus and Clement of Alexandria becomes clearer with Tertullian, most especially through his two works *De paenitentia* and *De pudicitia*. Although he wrote the former while still a "Catholic" and the latter as a Montanist, together they offer important information concerning the early development of the order of penitents.[50] The significance of his witness is undeniable; it is exactly for this reason that he is placed at the present location in this study. He is the missing link in the story who, if discovered too early, would make the plot appear less complex than it is, and if too late, would fail to tie together the disparate threads of the fragile though sure testimony to the early history of the order of penitents.

---

49. As seen throughout Chapter One, the interpretation of Tertullian has been the linchpin in contemporary theories concerning the origin of ecclesial penance.

50. The *De paenitentia* was composed probably around 203 a.d. and certainly before 207 a.d., when Tertullian began to show some support for Montanist ideas (Quasten, *Patrology* II, p. 299). The *De pudicitia* was written after 212/213 a.d., when he broke totally with the Catholics, and perhaps even as late as 217 a.d. (Le Saint, *Treatises on Penance*, p. 52).

Direct citations are from the editions by P. Borleffs, *De paenitentia*, in *Tertulliani Opera*, Vol. IV, CSEL 76 (Vienna, 1957), pp. 127–170; and E. Dekkers, *De pudicitia*, in *Tertulliani Opera*, Vol. II: *Opera Montanistica*, CCL 2 (Turnhout, 1954), pp. 1279–1330, and will be indicated by page and line numbers.

Other editions consulted include: C. Munier, *Tertullien. La pénitence*, SC 316 (Paris, 1984); and E. Dekkers, *Ad Martyres* (pp. 3–8); *Apologeticum* (pp. 85–171), both in *Tertulliani Opera*, Vol. I: *Opera Catholica, Adversus Marcionem*, CCL 1 (Turnhout, 1954).

1. THE POSSIBILITY OF POSTBAPTISMAL PARDON

In the *De paenitentia*, Tertullian is clear that there are no sins that are objectively excluded from pardon, since there exists a *paenitentia secunda* that allows for remission of sin after the "first penance": baptism.[51] Constantly, through his interpretation of select parables, he demonstrates God's great mercy and compassion toward sinner's. Believers are not to be lost to the "shipwreck of sin" but saved by the "plank" of baptism and penance (*De paen.* 7,5; 12,9). Postbaptismal sin must be submitted to a defined penitential process—the exomologesis—while lesser sins are pardoned by the sinner's own individual works of penance, including prayer, fasting, and works of mercy.[52]

After his turn to Montanism, Tertullian himself admits that there is a definite shift in his teaching concerning the possibility of pardon for sins:

> This book, therefore, will also be directed against the Sensualists. It will, moreover, oppose an opinion which I formerly held while in their company. Let them, on this account, upbraid me all the more with the accusation of inconstancy. To break with a group is never an antecedent proof of guilt (*De pud.* 1,10).[53]

The pastoral sensitivity and orthodoxy of the *De paenitentia* are replaced by sectarian rigorism and the acrimonious tone of the *De pudicitia*. Here Tertullian, enraged over the "peremptory edict" that he claims goes against the *disciplina* of the Church in offering reconciliation to adulterers, proceeds to exegete copious references from the Scriptures to prove that certain sins are reserved to God's judgment alone.[54] He sets up a distinction between remissible and ir-

---

51. Chapters 7–12 of the *De paenitentia* describe the process for pardon of postbaptismal sin. Since the work is addressed to catechumens, Tertullian admits his hesitancy to speak of a "second hope" for sin (7,2).

52. Chapters 9-11 of the *De paenitentia* give a description of exomologesis, while chapter 12 exhorts sinners to personal works of penance as well. For a fuller treatment of the process of exomologesis, see below, pp. 192–193.

53. "Erit igitur et hic aduersus psychicos titulus, aduersus meae quoque sententiae retro penes illos societatem, quo magis hoc mihi in notam leuitatis obiciant. Numquam societatis repudium delicti praeiudicium. Quasi non facilius sit errare cum pluribus, quando ueritas cum paucis ametur" (Dekkers, 1282:41-45; trans. W. Le Saint, *Treatises on Penance*, p. 55).

54. See above, pp. 30–33, on the debate of the authorship of the famous edict.

remissible sins.[55] First, there are those unnatural sexual acts that are *non delicta, sed monstra*, for which permanent expulsion from the community is the only response (4,5). Then there are capital sins, such as adultery, murder, and apostasy, for which sinners must undertake lifelong penance, including exomologesis, but due to the objective gravity of the sin, not receive *venia* from the Church (1,20 and *passim*).[56] There are those lesser sins that also involve exomologesis, but only temporarily, and end with ecclesial pardon (7,14-16,20).[57] Finally, there are the *delicta cotidianae incursionis*, which seem to entail personal rather than ecclesial penance (19,23ff.).[58]

Throughout the *De pudicitia*, Tertullian claims that to reconcile adulterers would be inconsistent with the Catholic tradition of refusing pardon to all who are guilty of capital sin. If the bishop who issues his edict shows toleration toward adulterers, he must also show the same toward apostates and murderers (5,8-15 and *passim*). There have been countless interpretations concerning Tertullian's claim that up until the time of his writing, no ecclesial pardon was

---

55. Le Saint, *Treatises on Penance*, p. 197, n. 35, points out that it is necessary to remember that Tertullian speaks often in *De pudicitia* of two separate realities: sins that are either *remissibilia* or *irremissibilia/inconcessibilia* and the objective gravity of sins, expressed by a variety of terms (*maxima, capitalia, mortalia, exitiosa, maiora, gravia, mediocria, modica,* and *leviora*). One cannot easily determine the correspondence between the gravity of a sin and whether it may be pardoned.

56. Tertullian is ambiguous as to which sins are to be designated as *capitalia*. Besides the usual triad, he also lists blasphemy, fornication, false witnessing, and fraud (*De pud.* 19,25). Lists of such sins also appear at other places in his works: *De pud.* 7,5; *De orat.* 3,1; *Adv. Marc.* IV,9,6.

57. Not all contemporary authors would agree with such a division. Galtier, *L'Église*, pp. 272ff., for example, interprets the reference in 7,20 to *peccata mediocria* as proof of a less grave but serious sin that was normally remitted by a private form of penance, spoken of by Tertullian as *castigatio* or *correptio*. On the other hand, Le Saint, "*Traditio* and *Exomologesis* in Tertullian," SP 7 [=TU 93] (1969) 414-419, p. 417, and M. Mügge, "Der Einfluss des juridischen Denkens auf die Busstheologie Tertullians," ThGl 68 (1978) 426-450, pp. 438ff., follow a long line of historians of penance in maintaining that there is no distinction in the form of ecclesial penance in either the *De paenitentia* or the *De pudicitia*. The only difference lies in which sins can be remitted by ecclesial reconciliation and which ones are left solely up to the mercy of God.

58. Munier, *La pénitence*, pp. 69 and 95, n. 33. For the various meanings that have been assigned to this term, as well as a lucid discussion of the different classifications of sin in the *De pudicitia*, see Le Saint, *Treatises on Penance*, pp. 220-223, n. 198.

offered for certain grave sins.[59] As seen previously, it is more comprehensive of the reality to admit a tension between tolerant and rigorist expressions in the local Churches concerning postbaptismal sin.[60] The experience of certain local Churches highlights this struggle more than that of others. Tertullian, in the *De paenitentia*, defends the more mainline and stronger tradition of leniency toward sinners, while as a Montanist in the *De pudicitia*, he chooses to cast his lot with the rigorists on the basis of the new revelation of the ''Paraclete.''[61]

2. THE MINISTERS AND THE EFFICACY OF ECCLESIAL PENANCE

The bishop plays a definite role in Tertullian's witness to the penitential process, indicative of the growing institutionalization of the organizational structures of the Church.[62] It is he, along with the presbyters, who decides who is to be excluded from the Church, who cares for the sinner throughout the time of the exomologesis, and who decides when reconciliation with the Church is to be extended to the repentant sinner.[63] Yet pastoral responsibility for the penitent does not fall solely upon his shoulders or the shoulders

---

59. See the appropriate discussion in Chapter One, where both liberal Protestant and Catholic authors, especially at the beginning of this century, raged in debate over the origin of ecclesial penance and the Church's use of the ''power of the keys.''

60. This is the position of both B. Botte in his review of C. Daly's study in *BTAM* 6 (1950–53) 104–105, p. 104, and of Von Campenhausen, *Ecclesiastical Authority*, p. 218, n. 21. H. von Soden's position (as found in Von Campenhausen, p. 219, n. 22), that murder and apostasy happened so exceptionally that there was no set policy for them, is also well taken. This goes against Poschmann, *Paenitentia Secunda*, pp. 321ff., who holds that these sins were only pardonable on a person's deathbed.

61. Botte, *BTAM*, pp. 104–105. F. Cardman, ''Tertullian on Doctrine and the Development of Discipline,'' SP 16 [= TU 129] (1975) 136–142, pp. 138–139, states that Tertullian, throughout his works, is unclear as to the relationship between doctrine and discipline. For example, his treatment of postbaptismal sin in the *De pudicitia* is an example of a discipline he lived becoming a doctrine he came to believe. Also, see above, pp. 184–185.

62. See below, n. 77.

63. C. Chartier, ''L'Excommunication ecclésiastique d'après les écrits de Tertullien,'' *Antonianum* 10 (1935) 301–344, 499–536, pp. 310–313, 521–522. Tertullian's reference to the bishop's *in praesidentis officio* in *De pud.* 14,16 points clearly to the centrality of the bishop's ministry.

of the clergy; they are joined by the prayer of the whole community. This notion of the community interceding on behalf of the sinner is constant in the patristic witness and finds no less expression in Tertullian (*De paen.* 9,4; 10,5-6; *De pud.* 19,28).[64] Along this same line is the strong role that Tertullian assigns to the martyrs in interceding for the pardon of penitents (*Ad martyres* I,4-6). His later negative witness in *De pud.* 22 will signal the heightening of the controversy concerning the proper role of martyrs in the reconciliation of sinners, a controversy that will remain unresolved until Cyprian's day.[65]

The question of the prayer of the bishop and the community proves that the African is no Pelagian. As important and necessary as the penitential works accomplished during the exomologesis are, alone they do not earn pardon for the penitent. It is the prayer of the bishop and the community, joined with the efficacious prayer of Christ, that reconciles the sinner to the Church and so to God. Thus Tertullian is the first patristic author to lay a dogmatic framework for the action of ecclesial reconciliation.[66] Certainly he draws a distinction between the pardon of sin at baptism and the forgive-

---

64. Rahner, *Early Church*, p. 140, who states: "Even though he [the bishop] has received it [the power to absolve] as a special power through the apostolic succession . . . he can exercise it nevertheless as a power within the Church, that is, as an authority that is only at all thinkable and meaningful because the holy community of the redeemed exists in Christ. Thus the application of this power involves a participation in that Spirit which is the essential life of the Church and which cannot be received apart from the Church. In this sense it can be said: the Church forgives as a whole."

65. Le Saint, *Treatises on Penance*, pp. 290–292, n. 669; Vokes, "Penitential Discipline in Montanism," pp. 74–75; above, Chapter Two, n. 169. The mention of the martyrs' role here points to the influence of persecution on the development of the order of penitents, at least in creating a situation in which the Church had to do *something* about the sin of those who denied the faith during persecution. See Karpp, *La pénitence*, p. XIX.

66. Poschmann, *PAS*, p. 48, who asserts: "He teaches in the *De paenitentia* (10,6) and takes for granted in the *De pudicitia*, that the prayer of the Church is the prayer of Christ, who pleads before the Father—*exorator Patris*—and pronounces forgiveness. By thus identifying it with Christ's prayer, Tertullian attributes to the prayer of the Church that formed part of the exomologesis a kind of sacramental efficacy. He is thus the first writer to provide a dogmatic basis for the procedure of public penance."

ness attained through the *paenitentia secunda* (7,10).[67] Nonetheless, it is a constant theme throughout his writings that the intercessory prayer of the bishop joined with that of the entire community of the faithful is an efficacious prayer always heard by God. The "second penance" is equal to baptism in effecting the remission of sin. It restores one to the Church and reconciles one to God. The only question for Tertullian (in the *De pudicitia*) concerns for which sins such an efficacious prayer can be uttered.[68]

3. THE PROCESS OF ECCLESIAL PENANCE

a) *The exomologesis (the penance of segregation)*

Tertullian most proves his worth as an early witness to the origins of an order of penitents in his description of the external process necessary before the granting of *paenitentia secunda*—the exomologesis. Though the term has been previously encountered in other writings from the first three centuries, especially Irenaeus, Clement of Alexandria, and Origen, it is first with the writings of Tertullian that it emerges as a specified term for the ecclesial penitential process.[69] As has been seen, exomologesis communicates many meanings in the early patristic writings, all in reference to the accomplishment of particular religious acts. Throughout the writings previously examined, at least four basic meanings are distinguishable: (1) to speak praise publicly to God; (2) to confess one's sins to God; (3) to confess one's sins to an ecclesial community; (4) to undertake public penitential acts within an ecclesial process lead-

---

67. Le Saint, *Treatises on Penance*, pp. 164–165, n. 120. As *ignoscentia* is the only Latin word used for forgiveness, here it is employed to signify both the *aphesis* of baptism and the *syngnōmē* of ecclesial penance.

68. Rahner, *Early Church*, pp. 141–144, who agrees with Galtier and others (against Poschmann) that throughout the work Tertullian never abandons the ancient orthodox belief that to reconcile sinners to the Church is to reconcile them to God. The granting of the *pax Ecclesiae* and *communio* effect such a reconciliation and are not just the lifting of the juridic ban from the Eucharist as a necessary precondition to divine pardon.

69. The term is found in *De paenitentia* eleven times as well as in *De orat.* 7,1; 9,2 and *De patientia* 10,13. Though the term is not used at all in the *De pudicitia*, the two instances where the process of ecclesial penance is described (5,14; 13,7) fit the descriptions of exomologesis in the *De paenitentia*.

ing to the granting of reconciliation to grave postbaptismal sinners.[70] Because of the close relationship between the last three meanings, it is difficult to isolate which one is primarily intended within a given text. Generally Tertullian uses the term with one of these meanings, so that one contemporary commentator has been led to believe that exomologesis became for him a "technical term to describe the complexus of penitential acts performed before the Church as works of satisfaction for postbaptismal sin."[71] The nature of those acts must now be examined.

First and foremost, the exomologesis involves at least temporary exclusion of the sinner from the Eucharist. Tertullian speaks of penitents *conlocati in vestibulo* (*De paen.* 7,10) and being *pro foribus ecclesiae* (*De pud.* 3,5; 5,14). Also, as a Montanist, he admits that remissible sins might for a time put one *extra gregem* (*De pud.* 7,16).[72] These passages show that penitents, once admitted to penance, are segregated from the community by being barred from the reception of the Eucharist. Yet they remain in relationship with the community, although marginally, by the very fact of their remaining *in vestibulo* rather than not being admitted to the church at all. Their association with the Church is made even clearer when Tertullian speaks of them being led into the church (*in ecclesiam inducens*), perhaps to some designated place, in order to benefit from the *exorandam fraternitatem*.[73]

---

70. See G. Mead, "Exomologesis," in *DCA* I (London, 1875), pp. 644–650; Le Saint, *Treatises on Penance*, pp. 171–172, n. 151; J. Mühlsteiger, "Exomologèse," *ZKTh* 103 (1981) 1–32, 129–155, 257–288, pp. 6–13. For a survey of patristic use of the term, see Lampe (ed.), *A Patristic Greek Lexicon*, pp. 499–500.

71. Le Saint, *Treatises on Penance*, p. 171, n. 151. See also W. Teeuwen, *Sprachlicher Bedeutungswandel bei Tertullian*, SGKA 14,1 (Paderborn, 1926), pp. 32, 75–79. It is for this reason that the term is used synonymously with what has been designated here as a penance of segregation. As will be seen in the following examination of Cyprian's witness, Tertullian's more generic use of the term differs from Cyprian's use, which is more circumscriptive.

72. Le Saint, *Treatises on Penance*, pp. 219–220, n. 193. In *De pud.* 7,16 *extra gregem datus est* could either mean a separation from the Eucharist due to the sin itself (*ipso facto*) or due to judicial sentence.

73. That Tertullian witnesses to a segregated location of the penitents within the assembly of the faithful has been ascertained by most modern scholars, beginning with the fundamental studies by H. Koch, "Die Büsserentlassung in der alten abendländischen Kirche," *ThQ* 82 (1900) 481–534; "Die Büsserplatz im Abendlande," *ThQ*

Once admitted into the church, penitents are segregated not only by location but also by dress and action in the performance of the penitential acts associated with the exomologesis:

> Exomologesis, then, is a discipline which leads a man to prostrate and humble himself. It prescribes a way of life which, even in the matter of food and clothing, appeals to pity. It bids him to lie in sackcloth and ashes, to cover his body with filthy rags, to plunge his soul into sorrow, to exchange sin for suffering. Moreover, it demands that you know only such food and drink as is plain; this means it is taken for the sake of your soul, not your belly. It requires that you habitually nourish prayer by fasting, that you sigh and weep and groan day and night to the Lord your God, that you prostrate yourself at the feet of the priests and kneel before the beloved of God, making all the brethren commissioned ambassadors of your prayer for pardon (De paen. 9,3-4).[74]

Such works of penance are not punitive measures taken against the sinner nor juridical penalties imposed as proof of the sinner's good intention. Rather, they are genuine acts of compensation, acts assigned to the penitent by the bishop in order to eventually lead such a one to the *pax Ecclesiae*. Of themselves, they are private acts of penance. But as compensatory acts and as part of that which makes the penance of segregation exactly that—segregated—they are a necessary part of the process of the exomologesis.[75]

---

85 (1903) 254-270. See the archeological description of the *domus ecclesiae* of the early third century and its bearing on this question in Munier, La pénitence, pp. 59-62, 75.

74. "Itaque exomologesis prosternendi et humilificandi hominis disciplina est conversationem iniungens misericordiae inlicem, de ipso quoque habitu atque victu: mandat sacco et cineri incubare, corpus sordibus obscurare, animum maeroribus deicere, illa quae peccant tristi tractatione mutare; ceterum pastum et potum pura nosse, non ventris scilicet sed animae causa; plerumque vero ieiuniis preces alere, ingemiscere, lacrimari et mugire dies noctesque ad dominum deum tuum, presbyteris advolvi, [et] aris dei adgeniculari, omnibus fratribus legationem deprecationis suae iniungere" (Borleffs, 163:8-18; trans. Le Saint, *Treatises on Penance*, pp. 31-32).

This description is repeated throughout *De paen.* 9-11 and is also found in *De pud.* 5,14; 13,7. The latter reference also includes *omnium vestigia lambentum*, a possible indication that kissing the feet of the faithful might have at times been part of the penitential action.

75. Rahner, *Early Church*, p. 132, sees these acts as solely private, done in addition to ecclesial penance. In this he is correct only from the perspective of viewing these works outside their connection with exomologesis. Their accomplishment within the period of the exomologesis gives them a more formal and liturgical sense. Not

b) *A coercive penance of isolation?*

Does the witness of Tertullian to this "new" process of segregated penance within the life of the community mean that the earlier practice of coercive isolation of the sinner has passed from the scene? In an earlier work and while still a Catholic, he makes reference to what he describes as a *censura divina* for very grave crimes that would bar one from *communicatione orationis et conventus et omnis sancti commercii (Apol.* 39,4). This procedure, to which he also refers in other places in his works, seems different from the description of the exomologesis seen above.[76] It is not a matter of exclusion from the Eucharist within the context of a continued, clear connection with the community; rather, it is a total separation, resulting from the serious nature of the sin itself and the unrepentant attitude of the sinner.

Recalling that Tertullian, in his Catholic period, does not hold any sin as objectively able to permanently separate the contrite sinner from the Church, his words in this context strike one as suggestive of the earlier practice of isolating the sinner for the sake of impressing upon him or her the serious obligation of repentance. Yet now it is the Church that perceives itself as having the power to directly impose the isolation upon the guilty party. This is a definite shift from the more indirect procedure common in the first two centuries. The rise of a distinct, professional clergy and the appearance of a monarchical episcopacy lead to more direct influence over the sinner by the Church. No longer does the Church, as a small, sectarian, charismatically led community, merely exert control over its faithful members, directing them to isolate sinners by stepping back away from them. With Tertullian, as with later authors of the third century, a larger, more structured, hierarchically led Church

---

just any works are acceptable, but only those that have been received in the tradition. See below, pp. 200–201, the discussion of Le Saint's application of Tertullian's distinction between *traditio* and *traditiones* to the *paenitentia secunda*.

76. See also *Ad uxorem* II,3,1. Van de Paverd, "Disciplinary Procedures," pp. 294–295, argues that Tertullian's use of *damnatio* in *De pud.* 2,12-13 also is in reference to a total separation of the sinner from the community.

perceives itself as having the power to expel from its midst those guilty of grave postbaptismal sin.[77]

It is then left to the sinners themselves to decide whether to respond to this measure taken by the Church—a measure that leaves them outside the possibility of salvation—and undertake some external manifestation of their internal repentance. Only this will serve as conclusive proof to the community of the sincerity of their conversion.[78] This external manifestation appears most vividly when the sinner confesses his or her sin before the community. This not only expresses internal contrition but a desire on the sinner's part to begin the exomologesis leading up to readmission to full communion with the Church:

> This external act, rather expressively designated by the Greek word for it in common use, is the exomologesis. Herein we confess our sin to the Lord, not as though he were ignorant of it, but because satisfaction receives its proper determination through confession, confession gives birth to penitence, and by penance God is appeased (*De paen.* 9,2).[79]

Tertullian has in mind here more than an individual confession of faults before God alone. Sin is to be confessed *coram Ecclesia* as an

---

77. Von Campenhausen, *Ecclesiastical Authority*, pp. 234–237, believes it is with Tertullian that the conscious recognition of the power of ecclesiastical officeholders over sin first makes its appearance: ''. . . the claim to decide whether a sinner should be excommunicated or readmitted was from now on based essentially not on the concrete authority of spiritual power or direct illumination, but simply on the possession of a spiritual office to which one had been regularly appointed. The stress is on the office as such'' (p. 235).

78. Van de Paverd, ''Disciplinarian Procedures,'' *passim*, uses the term ''censure-procedure'' to describe this action of what he calls ''coercive excommunication.'' See above, Chapter Three, p. 153, n. 94.

79. ''Is actus, qui magis Graeco vocabulo exprimitur et frequentatur, exomologesis est qua delictum nostrum domino confitemur, non quidem ut ignaro, sed quatenus satisfactio confessione disponitur, confessione paenitentia nascitur, paenitentia deus mitigatur'' (Borleffs, 162–163:4-8; trans. Le Saint, *Treatises on Penance*, p. 31.

Throughout both works Tertullian often uses juridic terms and concepts. M. Mügge, ''Der Einfluss des juridischen Denkens,'' *passim*, makes the case that his entire ecclesiological understanding flows from his juridical categories. One example of Tertullian's overriding legalism in his approach to faith is his use of *satisfacere*. See A. Beck, *Römisches Recht bei Tertullian und Cyprian* (Halle, 1930), pp. 67–69; E. Langstadt, ''Some Observations on Tertullian's Legalism,'' SP 6 [= TU 81] (1959) 122–126, p. 123.

expression of the sinner's contrition and willingness to undertake the necessary penitential practices leading to ecclesial reconciliation.[80] The degree of publicity of such a confession cannot be determined from Tertullian, though if a sin is particularly notorious and known to the whole community, public confession would be redundant. Sins that are not a matter of common knowledge most probably would be confessed before the bishop and/or his delegate, with perhaps a more generic confession made before the entire community.[81] The more private confession could occur sometime prior to or after the liturgy during which the sinner makes his or her public confession. The bishop or his delegate then decides the *castigatio* of the penitent, which varies according to the sin and the fervor of the penitent, but which always includes the exomologesis.[82] For Tertullian, therefore, the confession of sin stands as the hinge that both ends a period of isolation (if the situation of the sinner warrants such) and begins the period of the exomologesis (the penance of segregation). It could well separate the two stages by being made by the penitent before the doors of the church (expressing isolation), which is followed by the sinner being led in (*in ecclesiam inducens*) to begin the exomologesis (expressing segregation).[83]

In the age previous to Tertullian, only two stages of the penitential process are indisputably comprehensible: the coercive penance of isolation, followed by readmission of the sinner once the Church is assured of the sincere repentance of the guilty person. What is most significant is that adequate penance be done to show this, not a specific penance. Now, Tertullian witnesses to a designated process of penance that includes an intermediate element between iso-

---

80. Le Saint, *Treatises on Penance*, pp. 172–173, n. 152.

81. Munier, *La pénitence*, p. 63, argues that since the entire process of exomologesis was public, so must have been the confession of sin.

82. Rahner, *Early Church*, pp. 130–132. In *De pud.* 2,13, *castigatio* refers to beginning the process of exomologesis, including the penance of segregation and eventually leading to ecclesial reconciliation. For the Montanists, this is distinguished from permanent exclusion from the Eucharist (*damnatio*), during which the sinner must still perform penance (*poena*) in order to at least hope to be reconciled with God. Obviously, this interpretation flies in the face of Galtier, who sees *castigatio* as a reference to a milder, nonsegregated penance, whereas *damnatio* referred to the full process of exomologesis. See above, n. 57.

83. Poschmann, *Paenitentia Secunda*, pp. 316ff.; Rahner, *Early Church*, p. 133.

lation and readmission: the segregation of the penitent within the community during the period of the exomologesis.[84] It is closely related to the penance of isolation in that both express the altered relationship between the sinner and the Church due to the sin. Both are ultimately medicinal, and both exclude the sinner from the Eucharist. Yet, while the intention of the isolation is to coerce the sinner to recognize the gravity of the sin and to convince such a one to do penance, the exomologesis (the penance of segregation) offers a clear-cut liturgical process through which the penitent remains within the Church during the time of penance and is led back to the *pax Ecclesiae*. It is a transitional experience, connecting the isolation of the sinner with his or her eventual readmission to the Eucharist. As such, it is comprehensible only when joined to these earlier remedies for grave postbaptismal sin, out of which it has been born.[85]

4. RECONCILIATION AND READMITTANCE TO THE EUCHARIST

If Tertullian offers testimony for the existence of an ecclesial rite of reconciliation coming at the end of the exomologesis, he does so almost cautiously and with hesitancy. Certainly he is the first to witness to the practice of *veniam ab episcopo*, at least for "light sins" as defined from the Montanist perspective.[86] His use of the terms

---

84. Van de Paverd, "Disciplinary Procedures," pp. 314–315.

85. As previously noted, there has been much debate as to whether the "excommunication" of the sinner was always a constituent part of ecclesial penance. Throughout this study the position of Grotz, *Busstufenwesens*, pp. 350ff., has been examined; he has argued that it was only after the influence of Montanism that ecclesial penance was connected with the practice of excommunication. Other authors, such as Galtier (*L'Église, passim*) and C. Daly ("The Sacrament of Penance in Tertullian—III," *IER* 70 (1948) 731–746, pp. 742ff.) also see the existence of an ecclesial penance which did not include "excommunication" and which developed due to the different gravities of sin. Yet, the majority of modern interpreters of Tertullian's witness to Eucharistic exclusion, including Chartier, Poschmann, Von Campenhausen, Rahner, Le Saint, and Vorgrimler, while making a clear distinction between what we have termed a coercive penance of isolation and a penance of segregation, have defined exclusion from the Eucharist as a necessary part of the process of ecclesial penance. See the overview of the key terms employed by some of these authors in Van de Paverd, "Confession and Penance" II, pp. 45–51.

86. In fact, Tertullian's objection over the reconciliation of adulterers by the Church would make little sense if this did not include some sort of official act by the bishop. His polemic of *De pud.* 21, where he draws a distinction between *potestas* and *disci-*

absolvere and *restituere* in the *De pudicitia* (19,6 and *passim*) might be interpreted to be technical or juridical references to what happens to the penitent who has successfully fulfilled the rigorous requirements of ecclesial penance. Yet there remains a question as to whether the African specifically witnesses to a public rite of reconciliation that restores the sinner to communion. In exhorting those guilty of grave sin after baptism, he asks: "Is it better to be condemned in secret than to be absolved in public?" (*De paen.* 10,8).[87]

Palam absolvi has been cited both positively and negatively concerning Tertullian's testimony on a rite of reconciliation. The vagueness of the term makes an indisputable decision impossible. However, Tertullian's distinction between remissible and irremissible sins, and the fact that the *paenitentia secunda* is allowable only once, being analogous to the *paenitentia prima*, which ends with a public act by the bishop (baptism), point to the process of the exomologesis having some definite point of termination. Nonetheless, what liturgical actions might have accompanied the ending of the period of penance and readmittance to communion remain unknown.[88]

5. THE CONSEQUENCES OF ECCLESIAL PENANCE

Since the effect of the *paenitentia secunda* on the person parallels the effect of baptism, it, like baptism, must be unrepeatable:

> He has placed in the vestibule a second penitence so that it may open the door to those who knock; only once, however, because

---

plina, is meant exactly to prove that the bishops only had the right to pass on the essentials of faith and did not share in the personal power given to the apostles to forgive sins. Such a power was given at God's discretion only, though, for Tertullian, God had bestowed it upon the Montanist prophets. See E. Langstadt, "Tertullian's Doctrine of Sin and the Power of Absolution in '*De pudicitia*,' " SP 2 [= TU 64] (1955) 251–257, pp. 253ff.

87. "An melius est damnatum latere quam palam absolvi?" (Borleffs, 165:28-29; trans. Le Saint, *Treatises on Penance*, p. 33.

88. *Ibid.*, pp. 179–182, n. 179. Here, in an excellent exposition of the reasons pointing to the presence of ecclesial reconciliation in the *De paenitentia* as well as in the *De pudicitia*, Le Saint sees an explicit reference to a public rite of reconciliation. Nonetheless, his is not the only view: see E. Fruetsaert, "La réconciliation ecclésiastique vers l'an 200," NRTh 57 (1930) 379–391, pp. 388–389; Daly, "The Sacrament of Penance—I," IER 69 (1947) 693–707, p. 703; Vokes, "Penitential Discipline in Montanism," p. 64.

it is already a second time; never again, however, because the last
time was in vain (*De paen*. 7,10).[89]

Here Tertullian echoes the ancient tradition, known at least from
the time of *Hermas*, that ecclesial penance can never be repeated;
otherwise it is a penance without fruit.[90] It is interesting that Tertullian argues on pastoral grounds against the possibility of more
than one penance after baptism, an indication that the custom still
does not have the force of a juridic regulation. Also, the fact that
only one penance is allowable makes it reasonable to conclude that
not only does Tertullian have in mind some defined end to the time
of the exomologesis, as seen above, but that the fate of the recidivist
is solely in the hands of God. The Church does not have the authority to offer its pardon again.[91]

6. *TRADITIO* AND *TRADITIONES* IN THE EVOLUTION OF TERTULLIAN'S ORDER OF PENITENTS

Finally, it may be asked how the practice of the exomologesis
(the penance of segregation), first indisputably witnessed to by Tertullian, developed as an established remedy for postbaptismal sin.
One answer might be found in Tertullian's own distinction between
traditio and *traditiones*. The former is definable as all that the apostles
received from Christ and what they, in turn, handed on to the
Church, both orally and in writing. *Traditiones*, on the other hand,
would refer more to ecclesial customs which came to life in the
Church for a long period but for which no apostolic teaching can
be cited.[92] Applied to Tertullian's witness to the penitential discipline, what is essential to the apostolic *traditio* is that the hope of
pardon be offered to all guilty of postbaptismal sin who subsequently

---

89. ". . . conlocavit in vestibulo paenitentiam secundam, quae pulsantibus
patefaciat, sed iam semel quia iam secundo, sed amplius numquam quia proxime
frustra" (Borleffs, 159:35-38; trans. Le Saint, *Treatises on Penance*, p. 29).

90. The *Shepherd of Hermas* 29,8; 31,6. On Tertullian's attitude toward the supposed leniency of *Hermas*, see De Labriolle, *La crise Montaniste*, pp. 421–422.

91. Le Saint, *Treatises on Penance*, p. 167, n. 122.

92. See *De corona* 3–4 for how Tertullian distinguishes between *traditio* and *traditiones* in the many practices connected with baptism and the Eucharist. However,
nowhere in his works does he make such a distinction with regard to the practices
involved in the exomologesis.

repent. True contrition demands penance, usually externally expressed through the basic features of the coercive penance of isolation: exclusion from the community/Eucharist (either directly imposed on the sinner or indirectly practiced by the community), confession of sin, penitential works, and eventual readmittance to the community with full baptismal status.[93] These express the fundamental relationship of the sinner to the Church, altered due to grave sin, and the response of the Church, confirming this new relationship and wishing to lead the sinner back to life.

Yet the accepted pattern of how these penitential actions are accomplished within a local church might account for the further development of the intermediate stage of the exomologesis (the penance of segregation), which includes liturgical rites, specific penitential works and dress, and designated places within the community. These may have begun as ecclesial *traditiones*, important to the life of a local community, yet secondary in their development to what is essential to the apostolic *traditio* concerning the pardon of sinners. Even so, at a certain moment in the history, they are adopted from community to community as part of the received and accepted tradition of the liturgical actions connected with the accomplishment of postbaptismal penance. As has been seen, the expression of these *traditiones* will vary from church to church, though it is with a surprising consistency that elements found in Tertullian's witness are also found in the witness of other third-century authors. The fact remains that the testimony of Tertullian affords us the first clear picture of all the constituent elements of an order of penitents: the coercive penance of isolation (in certain notorious cases), confession of sin leading to an intermediate stage of the exomologesis (the penance of segregation), and reconciliation/readmission to the Eucharist.[94]

---

93. M. Mügge, "Der Einfluss des juridischen Denkens," pp. 449–450.

94. The application of the distinction between *traditio* and *traditiones* in Tertullian's witness to the exomologesis is made by Le Saint in his insightful article "*Traditio* and *Exomologesis* in Tertullian," *passim.*

B. Cyprian of Carthage († 258 a.d.)

Some years following the passionate vacillations of Tertullian, there appeared in the North African Church the strong and resolute figure of Cyprian.[95] He became bishop of Carthage in 248 a.d., leading his fellow Christians through the hardships of the Decian persecution before he himself died a martyr's death during the persecution of Valerian in 258 a.d. His numerous surviving letters and works not only paint a vivid picture of the crises that seemed to fill the years of his episcopate but are a rich font of information concerning the penitential practice of the North African Church in the middle of the third century. Due to the rigors of the Decian persecution, Cyprian was forced to deal more extensively with the question of penance for grave postbaptismal sinners than any other author of the first three centuries.[96]

1. HISTORICAL AND ECCLESIOLOGICAL PRESUPPOSITIONS

a) *The historical situation of the Decian persecution*

In order to understand Cyprian's writings on ecclesial penance, it is necessary to situate his work historically. Fabian, the bishop of Rome, died in January, 250 a.d., the first known Christian martyred for refusing to offer sacrifice to the ancient Roman gods, an act of homage decreed for all citizens of the empire by Emperor Decian.[97] This was the beginning of a persecution against those who

---

95. A complete biographical sketch of Cyprian's life would take us far afield from our purpose here. Biographical details will be supplied only to better understand his references to penance. The reader is referred to one of the many works on the life of Cyprian, including the classic work by W. Benson, *Cyprian, His Life, His Times, His Work* (New York, 1897), and a more recent study by M. Sage, *Cyprian*, Patristic Monograph Series 1 (Cambridge, Mass., 1975).

For earlier works on Cyprian's penitential discipline, see Poschmann, *Paenitentia Secunda*, p. 369, and for later works, see Rahner, *Early Church*, pp. 364–365, n. 2, and Vorgrimler, *Busse*, p. 43.

96. The rebaptism controversy between Cyprian and Stephen might also be said to form part of Cyprian's witness to ecclesial penance and reconciliation. However, it is a separate question and touches on the development of the rites of initiation, specifically confirmation. Therefore, our study will confine itself, with few exceptions, to the period during and immediately following the Decian persecution.

97. The following survey of the events of the Decian persecution is taken from Cyprian's letters (as noted) and from G. Clarke, *The Letters of St. Cyprian of Carthage*,

refused to obey the imperial decree due to their singular adherence to Christ. The religious suppression was so fierce that Cyprian himself was forced into hiding until the spring of the following year (*Epp.* 14; 20).[98]

In the face of imminent danger, Christians who, unlike Cyprian, were not able to remain "underground," were faced with three choices: (1) to publicly confess their faith and refuse to sacrifice, suffering imprisonment, torture, and sometimes martyrdom; (2) to acquiesce to the demands of the emperor and perform temple sacrifice (known as the *sacrificati*); or (3) to stoop to bribery in order to obtain a certificate (*libellus*) claiming one had offered sacrifice when, in fact, one had not done so (known as the *libellatici*).[99] Those choosing one of the latter two options were referred to as the *lapsi*, because they had committed the grievous sin of apostasy, which *ipso facto* excluded them from the life of the Church and placed their very salvation in serious doubt. From Cyprian's perspective, until the matter could be discussed by a plenary council when the persecution ended, their only hope was to perform the necessary penance in order to be reconciled to the Church and come again to life with God (*Epp.* 17.3.2; 19.1,2.2; 20.3.3). Though such a solution to the precarious situation of the *lapsi* seemed reasonable to Cyprian, in perfect accordance with the ancient tradition of the Church, it proved unsatisfactory to some of the *lapsi* who were anxious to be reconciled but not at all anxious to undertake the rigors of public penance. Their plight was heard by certain members of the Carthaginian clergy, who began offering the *pax Ecclesiae* to the *lapsi* without the necessary penance (*Epp.* 16; 17.2.1).[100] To make mat-

---

Vol. I: *Letters 1–27*, ACW 43 (New York, 1984), pp. 21–39. One of the earliest witnesses to the events of the persecution is Dionysius of Alexandria, as reported by Eusebius *Eccl. Hist.* VI,39–42.

98. References to the letters of Cyprian will normally be to number, chapter, and verse. Direct citations will be taken from L. Bayard, *Saint Cyprien: Correspondance*, 2 vols. (Paris, 1925), and will be further indicated by volume and page number.

99. See above, p. 179. *Ep.* 55.2.1 also refers to the *thurificati*, those who burn incense at the temple rather than sacrifice. See Clarke, *Letters* I, pp. 135–136, n. 149.

100. From the moment of his election as bishop, Cyprian had to contend with an opposition faction among the Carthaginian clergy, led by one Felicissimus (*Epp.* 41–43), who were eventually excommunicated and condemned by the Council of 251 A.D. (*Ep.* 45.4) for their refusal to follow Cyprian's directives on the *lapsi*.

ters worse, large numbers of the *lapsi* claimed to be in possession of certificates (*libelli*) which proved that they had been granted reconciliation by certain imprisoned confessors about to go to their martyrdom, a practice based on the ancient tradition of the "martyr's privilege" (*Ep.* 20.3.1). Finally, there was the special situation of *lapsi* who had faithfully undertaken penance but were now close to death without having received the *pax* (*Epp.* 18.1.2; 19.2.1).

In the midst of such a mélange of ecclesial life, it fell upon Cyprian to balance the demand of an uncompromised gospel with his pastoral responsibility to seek out the lost. What emerges is a clear teaching concerning the inseparable connection between penance and the granting of the *pax Ecclesiae*, as well as the clearest description thus far of what it means for one to do "full penance" (*paenitentia plena*).[101] There are two basic sources for Cyprian's teaching on penance: (1) his letters, both those written and received during the persecution and afterward, including the relevant decrees from the Councils of Carthage in 251 and 252 A.D.;[102] and (2) the tract *De lapsis*, written in the spring of 251 A.D., when the persecution was drawing to a close, which summarizes Cyprian's own position with regard to the situation of the *lapsi*.[103]

b) Cyprian's ecclesiology

What has been often assumed and implicit in the writings of previous Christian authors is stated clearly and dogmatically by Cyprian: *Extra Ecclesiam nulla salus* (*Epp.*. 4.4.3; 55.24.1; 69.3.1;

---

101. In attempting to "walk the middle ground," Cyprian is opposed not only by his own presbyters (see preceding note) for what they perceived as his rigorist stance with regard to the *lapsi* but also by Novatian and his followers after the persecution for his willingness to reconcile apostates at all. The situation of the *lapsi* as well as groups on both sides of the issue continually forced Cyprian to develop his own thinking on penance both during and after the Decian persecution.

As will be seen below, *paenitentia plena* is a term often employed by Cyprian in describing the process of ecclesial penance.

102. The chronology of the letters remains a necessary point of study, even with the thorough work by L. Duquenne, *Chronologie des lettres de S. Cyprien. Le dossier de la persécution de Dèce*, SH 54 (Brussels, 1972).

103. References to Cyprian's *De lapsis* will be by chapter. Direct citations will be taken from M. Bévenot, "*De lapsis*," in *Sancti Cypriani Episcopi Opera*, CCL 3,1 (Turnhout, 1972), pp. 221–242, and will be further indicated by page and line numbers.

73.21.2). While not a new concept in the tradition of the first centuries of Christianity, what is new about Cyprian's perspective is the emphasis he places on the structures and institutions through which the concrete Church is recognizable.[104] The Church is a corporate body, governed by those divinely appointed as bishops, without whom there could be no Church (*Epp.* 59.6.2; 66.8.3). The office of the bishop is accentuated in his writings. This is especially evident in the bishop's sacramental and liturgical functioning: it is the juridic authority of his office that enables him to baptize, to celebrate the Eucharist, and to administer penance and reconciliation to those who sin after baptism.[105]

Above all, the bishop must preserve the unity of the Church. This requires that he admonish those in his own diocese who breach the teachings and discipline set down from the apostles, even among the clergy (*Epp.* 41-43). Yet, he himself, especially in times of persecution and crisis, must be able to act alone, even to infringe upon customary laws if need be, and only later justify his action to the whole Church (*Epp.* 55.7.1; 64.1.2).[106] The responsibility of his flock is ultimately his alone; therefore, in his pastoral decisions and actions, it is he alone who is ultimately responsible before God.[107]

Yet while administering his local church, the bishop must also preserve the unity of the Church universal. Von Campenhausen states:

> It is a fundamental principle with Cyprian that the bishop never stands alone, and the universal interrelationship of the one catholic Church is crucial for the whole of his ecclesiological thought . . . what is distinctively Cyprianic is simply the way in which

---

104. Von Campenhausen, *Ecclesiastical Authority*, p. 282, n. 71. See his chapter "Cyprian and the Episcopate" (pp. 265-292) for a more complete treatment of Cyprian's ecclesiological perspective.

105. M. Bévenot, *Cyprian: De Lapsis and De Ecclesiae Catholicae Unitate* (Oxford, 1971), p. xvii; Von Campenhausen, *Ecclesiastical Authority*, pp. 270-272.

106. The requirement of justifying his action to the Church reminds one that Cyprian does not see the power of the bishop as absolute but rather speaks often of the importance of acting "in counsel" with the clergy and people (*Ep.* 14.4.1). See Von Campenhausen, *Ecclesiastical Authority*, pp. 274-275, and Clarke, *Letters* I, p. 268, n. 13.

107. M. Bévenot, "A Bishop Is Responsible to God Alone (St. Cyprian)," *RSR* 39 (1951) 397-415, pp. 400-401, 414.

> this primitive Christian belief in the unity and spiritual cohesion
> of the Church is given a strictly and exclusively official form, and
> thus defined in concrete terms.[108]

One can perceive in Cyprian the intense desire to act in harmony with his fellow bishops in order to preserve the unity of the concrete Church. Due to the situation of the *lapsi*, he writes his *De Ecclesiae catholicae unitate*, developing a dogmatic basis for this unity against those who would divide the bishops on this question, specifically the laxity of Felicissimus (see note 100, p. 203) on the one hand, and the rigorism of Novatian on the other.[109]

Having set the context through this brief sketch of the historical situation of the Decian persecution and Cyprian's own ecclesiological presuppositions, we must now turn to the focus of the present study: the penitential discipline as described by Cyprian of Carthage.

2. THE POSSIBILITY OF POSTBAPTISMAL PARDON

In his pre-Decian work *Ad Quirinum*, Cyprian writes simply: "It is not possible for the Church to forgive one who has transgressed against God" (III,28).[110] A similar thought is expressed later in *De lapsis*, when he states that it is "only the Lord who can grant mercy" to sinners.[111] Such sentiments expressed by the African bishop have touched off endless debate: (1) Was Cyprian throughout his life a rigorist with regard to certain postbaptismal sins? Or (2) did he move away from rigorism due to the special situation created by the persecution, and so become the first to reconcile apostates? Or (3) could it be that he was not a true rigorist at all but made paraenetically intolerant statements against those who refused to repent of their sin?[112]

---

108. Von Campenhausen, *Ecclesiastical Authority*, p. 275. See *Epp.* 55.1.1; 59.14; 60.1.2; 68.3.2; 73.26.2.

109. Bévenot, *De Lapsis and De Unitate*, p. xi.

110. "Non posse in ecclesia remitti ei qui in Deum deliquerit" (R. Weber, "*Ad Quirinum,*" in CCL 3,1, pp. 1–179, 122:1-2). The work, commonly called the *Testimonia*, is referred to here as *Ad Quirinum* in deference to the simple address found in the manuscripts. See p. liii.

111. ". . . solus Dominus misereri potest" (Bévenot, CCL 3,1, 230:337-238).

112. The task of accumulating the major positions of the various interpreters of Cyprian has already been accomplished by P. Fraenkel, "*Solus dominus misereri potest*: St. Cyprien, *De lapsis*, ch. XVII, et le problème de son interprétation," SP 10 [= TU

On the side of those who interpret rigorist leanings in Cyprian toward grave sinners, there is evidence beyond these statements that postbaptismal reconciliation was not allowed in certain local churches. Cyprian himself knew of certain bishops in the region who refused the *pax* to adulterers, yet who themselves remained in communion with their fellow bishops (*Ep.* 55.21.1).[113] Also, the extreme protestations of Novatian over the decision to reconcile the *lapsi* at all may in fact indicate some existing custom against the readmittance of apostates, at least in certain local communities.[114] Finally, there appears to be an admission by Cyprian himself that he shifted from a position of rigorism to one of tolerance. In writing to Antonianus, a brother bishop of Numidia, Cyprian felt obligated to justify his position to reconcile the *lapsi* against the rigorist position of Novatian, for which Antonianus appears to have had sympathy:

> I must vindicate both my person and my cause before you lest anyone should think that I have withdrawn lightly from my purpose and that, although I defended evangelical vigor at first and at the beginning, afterward I seem to have turned my mind from discipline and from my earlier judgment to think that peace should be made easy for those who have stained their conscience with certificates or have engaged in nefarious sacrifices. But neither of these things was done by me without a long-deliberated and well-pondered reason (*Ep.* 55.3.2).[115]

107] (1967) 71–76, pp. 71–73, whose own position would tend to regard such statements by Cyprian as paraenetic rather than expressions of Church policy. To the positions he examines, we add Clarke, *Letters* I, pp. 276–277, n. 12; 293–294, n. 9, who agrees with Bévenot and others that a definite development of thought on the issue is discernible in Cyprian's writings.

113. This exemplifies Cyprian's belief that a bishop was responsible to God alone in the pastoral care of his flock, even if it meant that there might result a diversity of disciplinary customs. The deeper *communio* of the Church remained intact. See Matellanes Crespo, "Communicatio," pp. 359ff.

114. It is clear from *Ep.* 55.24 that Cyprian first and foremost opposes Novatian because of the disunity brought about by his illegitimate election as the Roman antipope rather than his rigorism.

115. ". . . mea apud te et persona et causa purganda est, ne me aliquis existimet a proposito meo leuiter recessisse, et cum euangelicum uigorem primo et inter initia defenderim, postmodum uidear animum meum a disciplina et censura priore flexisse, ut his qui libellis conscientiam suam maculauerint uel nefanda sacrificia commiserint laxandam pacem putauerim. Quod utrumque non sine librata diu et

It is futile to deny the existence of certain factions within the early Church who refused reconciliation for at least some cases of grave postbaptismal sin. The fact that elements of such a disciplinary position are found in the writings of Cyprian must not blind one from seeing the strong tradition of offering the *pax Ecclesiae* to those who performed adequate penance, no matter how objectively grave their sin.[116] Rigorist elements were present because rigorists were present in the Church.

It is Cyprian's insistence on the power of the bishop over the penance and reconciliation of the sinner that constructs the dogmatic basis which confirms that those who refuse ecclesial readmission of truly repentant sinners infringe upon the divinely appointed ministry of the bishop. Therefore, they no longer remain in communion with the "Church of Christ" and must be driven out (*Ep.* 55.28-29). Because their rigorism departs from the apostolic tradition of which the bishops are guardians, they themselves, rather than the repentant sinners, are cast out of the Church.[117] Whether Cyprian demonstrates his own personal development of thought on the issue or whether he is only applying an already accepted principle in a new way due to the special circumstances of the persecution does not ultimately make a difference. What is most clear is that he offers the possibility of ecclesial reconciliation to all who are willing to undertake adequate penance for their sin:

> I pardon all things. I ignore many things in the zeal and pledge
> of gathering together the brotherhood. Even those things which

---

ponderata ratione a me factum est" (Bayard, II:132-133; trans. R. Donna, *Saint Cyprian Letters*, FC 51 [Washington, D.C., 1964], p. 135). It has been pointed out by J. Taylor, "St. Cyprian and the Reconciliation of Apostates," *TS* 3 (1942) 27-46, pp. 42-43, that this passage can only be properly interpreted within its context. The position of Cyprian has shifted, not from rigorism to leniency with regard to grave sinners, but from prohibiting the reconciliation of the *lapsi* during the persecution (except for the dying) now to providing for the immediate reconciliation of the *libellatici*, following the decision of the Council of Carthage in 251 A.D.

116. It appears that Cyprian, unlike Tertullian, does not maintain a strict classification of sins, so that it is always possible to say which sins were "sins against God" and so required the *paenitentiam plenam*. He seems to follow the general principle that the punishment must suit the crime (*De lapsis* 17;28;35). See Bévenot, *De Lapsis and De Unitate*, pp. xvii; 27, n.3.

117. See above, pp. 184-185.

have been committed against God, I examine not with the full judgment of religion. I myself am almost negligent in remitting sins much more than I ought. I embrace with prompt and full love those returning with repentance, confessing their sin with simple and humble satisfaction (*Ep.* 59.16.3).[118]

3. THE MINISTERS OF ECCLESIAL PENANCE

The preceding reflections already make it apparent that it is the bishop who plays a central role in the care of those who have committed grave postbaptismal sin. Cyprian is not at all vague on this point: Those who too hastily reconcile the *lapsi* deny that any "satisfaction is to be rendered to God through the bishops and presbyters" (*Ep.* 43.3.2). By their wrong actions, it is as if "penance has been abrogated and no confession of sin made," because "bishops have been despised and tread underfoot" (*Ep.* 59.13.8).[119] Even if the bishop reconciles someone on his or her deathbed who subsequently recovers, or someone who has not fulfilled all the obligations of penance, the *pax*, once given, remains (*Epp.* 55.13.1; 64.1.2), since the decision by the bishop concerning who is to be admitted to penance is all-important (*Ep.* 59.16.3). The bishop is responsible to exhort and help sinners to make penance (*Ep.* 55.19), and it is through the bishop, joined with the clergy, that the *pax Ecclesiae* is given (*Epp.* 55.29.1; 57.4.1; *De lapsis* 29) through the laying on of the hand (*Epp.* 15.1.2; 16.2.3; 17.2.1; *De lapsis* 16). Since obedient presbyters and deacons share the ministry of the bishop (*Epp.* 3; 16.1.2), they may be delegated by him to reconcile dying penitents if proof of repentance is provided and the bishop himself is unavailable (*Epp.* 18.1.2; 19.2.1). But reconciliation without the presence of the bishop is conceded only in the exceptional situation caused by the persecution and can hardly be seen as a regular occurrence.[120]

---

118. "Remitto omnia, multa dissimulo studio et uoto colligendae fraternitatis. Etiam quae in Deum commissa sunt non pleno iudicio religionis examino. Delictis plus quam quod oportet remittendis paene ipse delinquo. Amplector prompta et plena dilectione cum paenitentia reuertentes, peccatum suum satisfactione humili et simplici confitentes" (Bayard, II:186; trans. R. Donna, *Saint Cyprian*, p. 189).

119. *Ep.* 43.3.2: ". . . nec per episcopos et sacerdotes Domini satisfiat" (Bayard, II:106); *Ep.* 59.13.5: "sublata paenitentia nec ulla exomologesi criminis facta, despectis episcopis adque calcatis . . ." (Bayard, II:182).

120. Cyprian is the only witness during the first three centuries to deacons' having the authority to reconcile sinners, even if under emergency circumstances. How-

One of the points of controversy that arose from the dire situation of the *lapsi* centered on the role of the martyrs and confessors in granting the *pax* to grave sinners.[121] The existence of the so-called "martyr's privilege"—the right of martyrs, due to their suffering, to play a part in the reconciliation of sinners—is observed by a smattering of second- and third-century witnesses.[122] It might be possible to infer from such witnesses that the martyrs played a more independent role in the reconciliation of sinners at an earlier moment in the Church's history, or, at the very least, that their role is left undefined, coexisting alongside the role of the bishop. With Cyprian, any thought of an authoritative equality between martyr and bishop with regard to the ministry to penitents is vigorously refuted. In addressing the martyrs and confessors, he reminds them that those to whom they have granted certificates of peace must keep them until the end of the persecution, when a decision by the bishop might be made:

> They should keep your petitions and requests for the bishop, awaiting the seasonable time [when peace has been restored] for granting the peace which you request. The mother needs first to receive peace from the Lord and then the question of peace for her sons can be considered, in the way in which you desire (*Ep.* 15.2.2).[123]

---

ever, in the next century the Council of Elvira will decree the same action in emergency circumstances when the bishop or priest is unavailable (can. 32). See V. Saxer, *Vie liturgique et quotidienne à Carthage vers le milieu du IIIe siècle*, SAC 29 (Rome, 1969), pp. 174–175; Poschmann, *Paenitentia Secunda*, p. 421; Clarke, *Letters* I, pp. 298–299, n. 7.

121. There has been much discussion over Cyprian's use of the terms "martyr" and "confessor." Either could refer to one who has died or is near to death for the sake of the faith, or to one who has suffered for the faith but is not in danger of death. See E. Hummel, *The Concept of Martyrdom According to St. Cyprian of Carthage*, StCA 9 (Washington, D.C., 1946), pp. 14–33.

122. Examples previously examined include the letter from the Churches of Lyons and Vienne (*Eccl. Hist.* V,1,45-46,48; 2,5); Dionysius of Alexandria (*Eccl. Hist.* VI,42,5-6); Tertullian, *Ad martyres* I,4-6; *De pud.* 22. Poschmann, *PAS*, p. 80, is correct in saying that the occurrence of the practice was only sporadic in the first centuries and could not be considered normative.

123. "Petitiones et desideria uestra episcopo seruent, ad pacem uobis petientibus dandam maturum et pacatum tempus expectantes, ut a Domino pacem mater prior sumat, tunc secundum uestra desideria de filiorum pace tractetur" (Bayard, I:44; trans. G. Clarke, *Letters* I, p. 91). Similar sentiments are expressed in *Epp.* 22.2.2; 26; *De lapsis* 18;20;36.

The martyrs themselves agree to the decisive role of the bishop in the process (*Ep.* 23), and even the Roman Church, while seemingly not faced with the problem, recognizes in principle that the final word of peace must be spoken by the bishop (*Ep.* 36.2). Nonetheless, Cyprian is anxious to maintain the independence of the bishops in this matter: the bishops are not the mere "executive functionaries" of the martyrs, as if they are obligated to honor any martyr's certificate presented to them (*Epp.* 27.3.1; 33.1.2/2.2).[124] The bishops have the duty to make the decision to grant the peace based on the genuine conversion of the penitents, expressed in their willingness to perform penance. The certificates of the martyrs might be figured in as a factor in this decision, but they do not absolve the bishops from their duty to make this judgment themselves.[125]

As for the role of the entire community in the penitential process, it might be said that Cyprian is not as explicit on the matter as other early authors. Yet it must be remembered that the disciplinary confusion of the time forced him to accent the authority of the bishop in the administration of ecclesial penance; the role of the community, though often not expressed, seems to be assumed. In this way, the task of the bishop to care for sinners is always in conjunction with, rather than to the exclusion of, the community. In point of fact, in the decision to admit sinners to the process of penance, Cyprian reports that it is the people who are most annoyed with the tolerance of their bishop: "With difficulty I persuade the people—indeed, I must force them—to allow these to be admitted" (*Ep.* 59.15.3).[126] Yet, the people care for them, even if they know full well that the penance of particularly difficult cases is not genuine (*Ep.* 59.15.3-4). Therefore, not only do the people have a say about the ecclesial policy concerning what is to be required of the *lapsi* in order to be readmitted to the Church (*Epp.* 14.1.2; 14.4; 16.4.2; 17.3.2; 19.2.2), but the granting of the *pax Ecclesiae* in particular cases must include their consent and must not go against the *petitu et con-*

---

124. Clarke, *Letters* II, pp. 147–148, n. 6.
125. Swann, *Relationship*, p. 254.
126. "Vix plebi persuadeo, immo extorqueo, ut tales patiantur admitti" (Bayard, II:185).

scientia plebis (Ep. 64.1.1).[127] Though in the background, the role of the entire Church in the reconciliation of sinners is present.

4. THE PROCESS OF ECCLESIAL PENANCE

a) *Cyprian's order of penitents*

It would be grossly understated to say that Cyprian uses a variety of terms in making reference to the process of ecclesial penance in his letters and in *De lapsis*.[128] *Paenitentia (paenitere)* is the most frequently used term, but its intended meaning is nearly impossible to assess in every instance. In the most general sense, it refers to a disposition of repentance necessary for past sin on the part of the sinner. This disposition might be expressed either internally, involving an intense interior contrition over past sinful behavior, and/or externally, involving active and objective penitential acts expressive of an internal sense of contriteness.[129] The externally expressive side of *paenitentia* is often referred to as *satisfactio (satisfacere)*, used in the legal sense of compensation or reparation for something owed. Here Cyprian employs a vocabulary similar in meaning to Tertullian's, having a basis in the Roman legal tradition, to indicate that external acts of penance serve as reparation for the debt owed due to sin.[130] Inasmuch as any payment of a debt has to be considered adequate by the one who is owed, so *satisfactio* necessarily implies a judgment on the part of the bishop (and clergy) as to whether the acts of penance are compensation enough for the debt of sin, opening the way for a sinner's readmission to the Church. Therefore, external works of *paenitentia* done to make *satisfactio* for grave postbaptismal sin are ecclesial rather than solely personal actions, having as their aim the *pax Ecclesiae*.[131]

---

127. The Council of Carthage in 251 A.D. included the presence of the laity along with bishops, confessors, and presbyters. However, it seems the process was that "the clergy may proffer counsel, the people may voice consent, but the bishop decides" (Clarke, *Letters* I, p. 268, n. 33).

128. In the two sections that are to follow, we admit our indebtedness to Swann, *Relationship*, Chapters Three and Four (pp. 151–459), for his precise philological analysis of Cyprian's penitential vocabulary.

129. *Ibid.*, pp. 154–176, 312–318.

130. Especially *Ep.* 15.4; Beck, *Römisches Recht bei Tertullian und Cyprian*, pp. 145–148.

131. Swann, *Relationship*, pp. 232–256, 323–329.

But the term's meaning is far from exhausted. More than merely indicating a general sense of internal contrition for sin and its consequent external manifestation, *paenitentia* is also utilized to denote a formal and definite process of ecclesial penance, involving delineated stages (*Epp.* 15.1.2; 18.1.2; 19.1.2; 20.3.1; 71.2.2; 74.1.2; 74.3.1).[132] Similar in usage is the phrase *paenitentiam agere (paenitentiam plenam agere, paenitentiam ueram agere, paenitentiam uere agere)*, which is used by Cyprian synecdochically as a command to the *lapsi* to perform either the whole process of this definite *ordo paenitentiae* or to undertake the necessary penance that forms the initial phase of the process. What are the steps of penance according to the witness of Cyprian? We cite one of some six instances in the letters and *De lapsis*:

> For in the case of less serious sins, not committed directly against God, a man does penance for an appropriate period; the penitent then must make public confession after his life has been examined; and nobody can be admitted to communion without first having had hands laid on him (*manus fuerit inposita*) by the bishop and clergy. It follows that in the case of these most serious and grievous of sins we must comply with every observance, with all the greater reserve and restraint, in conformity with the discipline of the Lord (*Ep.* 17.2.1).[133]

Speaking literally, then, the whole order of *paenitentia* involves three stages: *paenitentia satisfactionis*, the exomologesis, and the granting of the *pax Ecclesiae*. For Cyprian, to do "full penance" (*paenitentiam plenam*) means more than some sort of piecemeal accomplishment of the necessary *satisfactio*: the step-by-step process itself is of key significance.[134]

---

132. Swann, *Relationship*, pp. 177–185.

133. "Nam cum in minoribus delictis quae non in Deum committuntur paenitentia agatur iusto tempore et exomologesis fiat inspecta uita eius qui agit paenitentiam, nec ad communicationem uenire quis possit nisi prius illi ab episcopo et clero manus fuerit inposita, quam magis in his grauissimis et extremis delictis caute omnia et moderate secundum disciplinam Domini obseruari oportet" (Bayard, I:49; trans. G. Clarke, *Letters* I, p. 97). See also *Epp.* 4.4.1; 15.1.2; 16.2.3; 59.13.5; *De lapsis* 16.

Throughout the entirety of the present study, *manus* is translated in the singular, as it appears in the texts, rather than in the more common but less literal plural.

134. Swann, *Relationship*, pp. 206, 269. There has been much discussion over whether in fact the first "stage" of the penitential process in Cyprian was solely pri-

i) *The* paenitentia satisfactionis

When Cyprian speaks of the works of penance required before one guilty of apostasy can be readmitted to communion, usually what is intended are penitential actions to be accomplished during the first stage of his order of penitents.[135] These actions appear throughout his letters and the *De lapsis,* and include the performance of personal works of penance, such as the giving of alms, fasting, prayer, and other charitable works (*Ep.* 15.3.1; *De lapsis* 29). These are born out of the overriding attitude of intense sorrow for sin that the penitent must express, a theme Cyprian highlights often through a variety of terms (*ingemescere, gemitus, lacrima, lamentari/lamentatio).*[136] Penitents can be found knocking on the doors of the church (*Epp.* 19.2.3; 59.1.1) and are to be admitted only to the vestibule (*ad ecclesiae limen—Epp.* 57.3.1; 59.16.2), where they entreat (*rogare*) the community for help and prayers and eventually petition (*prex*) to be readmitted to the church. They wear distinctive garb, dressing in sackcloth as a sign of their mourning and wearing ashes, and are notable by their bodily positions of kneeling and prostration, a sign of profound self-abasement (*De lapsis* 35). Though described by Cyprian as *longa et plena* (*De lapsis* 16), there is no set time frame for this stage of doing penance. The *aestimato tempore* is determined by the bishop (*Ep.* 4.4.1).[137]

---

vate works of penance, after which the penitent was admitted to what was proper to truly ecclesial penance: the exomologesis. This is the position of Grotz, *Busstufenwesens,* pp. 96ff., who prefers to call this first stage an "exkommunikationsbusse." Both Rahner, *Early Church,* pp. 73ff. and Hübner, "Kirchenbusse und Exkommunikation," pp. 71ff., disagree with Grotz, maintaining that this stage was not purely private but was carried out under the observation and with the support of the Church; see below, n. 135.

135. Grotz is correct to point out the necessary distinction between the "works" of the *paenitentia satisfactionis* and the act of the exomologesis. However, his differentiation is too black and white (see above, n. 134). It might be best to say that the *paenitentia satisfactionis* was both personal and ecclesial, with the strong emphasis on the personal, while the liturgical act of the exomologesis was also both personal and ecclesial, with the strong emphasis on the ecclesial. See L. Landini, "Drop-Off in Confession: The Epistles of St. Cyprian of Carthage," *AER* 169 (1975) 133–142, pp. 136–137.

136. Swann, *Relationship,* pp. 299–308, 341–342.

137. Clarke, *Letters* I, p. 179, n. 34.

Though segregated from the community by the requirements of this stage of ecclesial penance, most especially by being unable to partake of the Eucharist, the penitent is not totally isolated from the Church. The passage cited above concerning the role of the bishop and the community in the care of sinners makes it clear that the penitential works accomplished are done under the supervision of the clergy (*Ep.* 59.15.3-4). It is the bishop in consultation with the whole community who makes the final decision with regard to the adequate completion of the *paenitentia satisfactionis*; therefore, it is reasonable to assume that the actions of the penitents are closely observed in order that a judgment might eventually be made. As to how much contact is necessary or even allowable between ministers and penitents, Cyprian is not clear. However, it may be the case that penitents are allowed to remain in the vestibule of the church for the liturgy of the Word and excluded before ''the prayer and the offering'' (*De lapsis* 25).[138] Thus the stage of the *paenitentia satisfactionis* includes all the elements that have been described as a penance of segregation.

ii) *The exomologesis*

From the texts cited as proof of Cyprian's indication of a three-stage process of penance, *exomologesi facta* appears as a separate external action, functioning as a middle term between the *paenitentia satisfactionis* and readmittance to the Eucharist.[139] Even in the passages where Cyprian admits a ''mitigated'' penance for particular pastoral circumstances (to be examined below), so that the time requirement of the *paenitentia satisfactionis* is reduced, the necessity of the exomologesis always remains, preceding and being clearly distinct from the laying on of the hand and reconciliation (*Epp.* 4.4.1; 18.1.2; 19.2.1; 20.3.1). Unfortunately, Cyprian is never explicit as to what the term actually connotes; he seems to assume an understanding on the reader's part. Yet, given the numerous times he

---

138. Bévenot, *De Lapsis and De Unitate*, p. 39, n. 1, believes that Cyprian's unusual use of *mixta cum sanctis* is to underscore the fact that one guilty of grave sin was allowed to be present for the ''prayer'' instead of being dismissed (even in the case of an infant) with the other penitents after the liturgy of the Word.

139. See above, n. 133; Swann, *Relationship*, pp. 259–262, 329–331.

uses the terms *delictum* and *crimen* as the object of the action implied by exomologesis (*Epp.* 15.1.2; 18.1.2; 50.13.6; 59.14.1), and given the fact that Tertullian employs a similar usage with the verb *confiteri* rather than exomologesis, "it seems safe to conclude that the basic meaning of *exomologesis/exomologesin facere* is the acknowledgment or confession of sin."[140]

In attempting to further specify the nature of the action of the exomologesis and to come to a more satisfying picture of the entire *ordo* as presented by Cyprian, one must keep in mind an often confused point: the confession of sin implied by the use of exomologesis does not necessarily refer to an initial action by the sinner at the beginning of the *paenitentia satisfactionis*.[141] Inasmuch as the actions of the penitents would be scrutinized by the bishop and the community during the first stage of doing penance, in order that they might make a judgment as to whether adequate satisfaction has been accomplished, a previous knowledge of their sin is presumed. Therefore, a detailed confession of sin at the end of the *paenitentia satisfactionis* would be redundant. More probably the exomologesis is a more ritualized confession of fault in the presence of the entire Christian assembly (seen in the *in ecclesia* of *Ep.* 59.13.5), followed immediately by the ritual act of the imposition of the hand. As such, the exomologesis functions as a liturgical "summing up" of the more personal sorrow and contrition expressed during the time of the *paenitentia satisfactionis*. Understanding the exomologesis as a liturgical and ritual action rather than one that is informative or disclosive best respects the step-by-step *ordo* as outlined by Cyprian.[142]

While this may be the predominant meaning of the term, it seems that Cyprian also employs the word to indicate an initial, more personal and detailed confession of sin in the presence of the bishop and clergy:

---

140. Swann, *Relationship*, p. 266; see also pp. 263–265.

141. For example, J. Dallen, "The Imposition of Hands in Penance," pp. 227ff. He reconfirms his position in *Reconciling Community*, pp. 38–40.

142. This is the position of most modern commentators on Cyprian's penitential system, including Poschmann, *Paenitentia Secunda*, pp. 419ff.; Grotz, *Busstufenwesens*, pp. 144ff.; Saxer, *Vie liturgique et quotidienne*, pp. 169ff.; Rahner, *Early Church*, pp. 153ff.; Swann, *Relationship*, pp. 269ff.; Clarke, *Letters* I, pp. 179–180, n. 35.

Accordingly, how much greater is the faith and more salutary the fear of those who, though they have committed no crime of sacrifice or certificate, yet because they have merely thought of doing so, confess even this to the priests of God simply and contritely, and manifest their conscience to them. They get rid of the burden on their minds and seek treatment for their wounds, light and superficial as they are, knowing that it is written: God is not mocked (*De lapsis* 28).[143]

This text appears to be a testimony to some regular custom of personal confession, even for sins that may not require *paenitentiam plenam*. This confession, unlike the ritualized exomologesis that forms the second step of Cyprian's *ordo*, is disclosive in character and aids the bishop in deciding what satisfaction is to be required from the penitent for the fault committed. On the part of the sinner, it involves the recognition of sin and a willingness to submit to the judgment of the Church.[144]

Finally, it is further noted that Cyprian, like Tertullian, utilizes the term "exomologesis" in two instances to indicate the entire process of the *paenitentia satisfactionis* leading up to the laying on of the hand and ecclesial reconciliation (*De lapsis* 31).[145] His rare usage

---

143. "Denique quanto et fide maiore et timore meliore sunt qui, quamvis nullo sacrificii aut libelli facinore constricti, quoniam tamen de hoc vel cogitaverunt, hoc ipsum apud sacerdotes Dei dolenter et simpliciter confitentes exomologesin conscientiae faciunt, animi sui pondus exponunt, salutarem medellam parvis licet et modicis vulneribus exquirunt, scientes scriptum esse: Deus non deridetur" (Bévenot, CCL 3,1, 236-237:548-554).

While Galtier, *L'Église*, pp. 285-286, interprets this text as proof of a private discipline of penance evident in Cyprian's works, most modern authors, such as Rahner, *Early Church*, p. 155, see it only as an indication of a detailed and perhaps private confession.

144. Swann, *Relationship*, pp. 331-332. Other texts employ the term *confessio* or *delicta intellegere* in the same way (*De lapsis* 29; 33). Also, the distinction between *confessio* and *exomologesis* in *Ep.* 55.29.2 may also highlight the different intended meanings (*ibid.*, pp. 264-265). The question might be raised as to whether one's penance might not "count" if done prior to this initial confession (the implication of Clarke, *Letters* II, p. 150, n. 14, in his interpretation of *Ep.* 33.2.1). However, one must be careful to suppose any hint of an "enrollment" consciousness on Cyprian's part. This confession probably took place outside the Eucharistic gathering, and penance done prior to its occurrence would have been taken into account by the bishop.

145. That Cyprian intends a penitential interpretation of exomologesis in this text from Dan 1:7 is obvious from the context, though most probably this is not the origi-

points to a genuine development in the meaning of the term itself and in the process of ecclesial penance as a whole. Tertullian uses the word in a technical sense for all the acts required of the sinner who undertakes the *paenitentia secunda*, and so makes no distinction between the exomologesis and what has been defined as the penance of segregation. However, with Cyprian the terminology becomes much more specific. He also employs "exomologesis" in a technical sense but clearly delineates it from the *paenitentia satisfactionis*, which has been seen to involve all the requirements of the penance of segregation. Exomologesis stands on its own as a liturgical and ritual act of confession of sin always and immediately preceding the imposition of the hand. It forms the basis of a sacramental encounter between the penitent and the forgiveness of Christ, expressed through his Church. That is why even if the doing of personal works of penance (the first step of Cyprian's *ordo*) is reduced for the penitent, the exomologesis is never disposed of. Nor is there any witness by Cyprian, in using the term to refer to a specific moment in the process of ecclesial penance, of the exomologesis occurring without being followed by the granting of the *pax Ecclesiae*. Whereas the witness of Tertullian joins together the exomologesis and the penance of segregation, with Cyprian the penance of segregation is clearly separate from and precedes the exomologesis.[146]

b) *Mitigated forms of penance*

As mentioned earlier, Cyprian testifies to forms of penance that seem to mitigate his three-step *ordo*. Generally these are "emergency" procedures necessitated by the unique situation of the Decian persecution. Nonetheless, they witness to one fact with extreme clarity: Cyprian is no casuist. As much as he insists on the necessity of adequate penance before reconciliation, the person and not the process always takes precedence, even if it means the adaptation of his three-step order of penitents. This is testimony not only

---

nal sense of the text. See Bévenot, *St. Cyprian: The Lapsed; The Unity of the Catholic Church*, ACW 25 (Westminster, Md., 1957), p. 95, n. 153.

146. Swann, *Relationship*, pp. 272–273.

to the African's pastoral concern but also to a certain fluidity in the young penitential process.[147]

i) *The penance of the dying*

Recognizing the desperate situation of the *lapsi* struck with mortal illness before adequate penance is accomplished, Cyprian advises that after the exomologesis (even in the absence of the bishop and with only a presbyter or deacon), the hand should be laid upon them in forgiveness and the *pax Ecclesiae* given (*Epp.* 18.1.2; 19.2.1). The one condition for such a concession is that the *lapsi* must be in possession of a *libellus* from one of the martyrs, which would serve as proof of the sinner's conversion in lieu of the *plenum tempus* ("full time") of the *paenitentia satisfactionis*.[148] However, in light of the Roman practice of granting the peace to any of the gravely ill *lapsi* who "are doing penance for their action and are anxious for communion" (*Ep.* 8.3.1), it seems that Cyprian is ready to moderate his demand and no longer require the martyr's certificate (*Ep.* 20.3.1).[149] At least, it is the more moderate policy that appears later in his letters (*Ep.* 55.5.2,13.1). Though a streamlined demand for penance is required for the dying, the elements of personal penance, exomologesis, and the laying on of the hand remain intact and are effective, even if the dying penitent should recover from the illness (*Ep.* 55.13.1).[150]

---

147. Saxer, *Vie liturgique et quotidienne*, pp. 173–175.

148. Throughout his works, Cyprian indicates the importance of the temporal element in the accomplishment of *paenitentia plena* (*Epp.* 33.2.1; 64.1.1). Therefore, here, as in all expressions of a mitigated ecclesial penance, it is not that he waives entirely the requirement of doing penance but that he only allows for a reduction in the time during which it was done. See J. Köhne, "Die Bussdauer auf Grund der Briefe Cyprians," *ThGl* 29 (1937) 245–256; Swann, *Relationship*, pp. 384–385.

149. ". . . agant paenitentiam facti sui et desiderent communionem" (Bayard, I:20; trans. G. Clarke, *Letters* I, p. 69). The Roman practice is cautiously confirmed later by Novatian (*Ep.* 30.8).

This interpretation of Cyprian's action is taken by both Bévenot, in a review of Duquenne's *Chronologie des lettres de S. Cyprien*, VC 28 (1974) 156–158, and by Clarke, *Letters* I, p. 296, against the chronology suggested by Duquenne (pp. 114–120), namely, that Letter 8 was received by Cyprian prior to writing 18 and 19, and so was the stimulus of Cyprian's policy toward the dying *lapsi* in the first place. See n. 29 above.

150. The Church's position toward reconciliation of the dying will be definitely canonized by the Council of Nicaea, can. 13, which upheld the general principle that the Eucharist should be granted to any who are dying and who desire it.

ii) The penance of confessors

In responding to the question asked of him by the bishop Caldonius concerning the status of *lapsi* who are imprisoned for publicly confessing their faith (*Ep.* 24), Cyprian agrees that no further penance is required of them (*Ep.* 25.1.1). This may hint at the fact that *lapsi* who do not succumb to schism but submit to the required penance can be assured of the *pax Ecclesiae* without ecclesiastical intervention if they subsequently become confessors.[151]

iii) The penance of the libellatici and the sacrificati

By decision of the Council of Carthage in 251 A.D., the *libellatici* are to be reconciled "at the present time" (*interim*), while the *sacrificati* are to be "aided at the time of death" (*in exitu subueniri*: *Ep.* 55.17.3).[152] The following year a second council decides to offer the peace to the latter group, due to fears of a renewed persecution by Gaius, provided that in the intervening time they have remained faithful to works of penance (*Ep.* 57.1.2). While neither decision specifies that this is to be accomplished through the exomologesis and the laying on of the hand, the context of both texts leads one to such a conclusion. Though mitigated, the essential elements of the penitential *ordo* remain operative, inasmuch as both groups are engaged in the *paenitentia satisfactionis* at the time of their restoration.

iv) The penance for everyday sins

One of Cyprian's recurring themes is the necessity of performing good works, giving alms, and praying as satisfaction for daily sins (*De dom. orat.* 12; 22; *De opere et eleemosynis* II). It is through these works of charity that a just person is constantly formed and reformed

---

151. Swann, *Relationship*, pp. 376–377.

152. There has been discussion of the passage, particularly surrounding the meaning of *interim*. See H. Koch, *Cyprianische Untersuchungen*, AK 4 (Bonn, 1926), pp. 264–266; Poschmann, *Paenitentia Secunda*, pp. 381ff. The position of Poschmann and Bévenot, *De Lapsis and De Unitate*, p. 107, n. 1, correctly points out that Cyprian is saying that the *sacrificati* are to receive the "peace" of the Church on their deathbeds if they have not received it previously. Their penance is to be long, certainly longer than that of the *libellatici*, but not necessarily for a lifetime.

in the likeness of Christ.[153] While these works are also part of the *paenitentia satisfactionis* required of *lapsi*, clearly Cyprian is not advocating the same remedy for both everyday and grave postbaptismal sins. These actions are to be done by all Christians serious about living lives centered on the gospel and cannot be equated with the unique process of ecclesial penance.[154]

c) *A coercive penance of isolation?*

Can anything of a coercive penance of isolation be discerned in the works of Cyprian? This question invites one to recall the dialectical yet interpenetrative poles of Cyprian's ecclesiology: the complete authority of the individual bishop in the care of his flock, and the preeminent importance of the unity of the catholic Church. The former affirmation leaves little room for doubt that Cyprian envisions the authority of the bishop over the penitential process to be central. The office of bishop has reached such a point of institutional development that the bishop need no longer plead with his small community to avoid the erring brother or sister. Any action to isolate the sinner is directly imposed on the offender.[155] Yet when one examines Cyprian's witness to the total isolation of a sinner from the community, it is the second pole of his ecclesiology that comes to the foreground. Only for the shocking sin of disobedience to the teaching of the bishop, which in Cyprian's mind is the cause of all ecclesial disunity and schism, is one totally excluded without recourse to ecclesial penance. It is the sign of a willful disposition against Christ himself, inasmuch as the bishop, legitimately elected and himself free from doctrinal error, is entrusted with the solemn function of *iudex uice Christi* (*Ep.* 59.5.1). He acts *in persona Christi* in upholding the genuine truth of the gospel. To be at odds with such an authority demands a total exclusion, which can be taken unilaterally by an individual bishop (*Ep.* 4.4.1) or collegially by a

---

153. Bévenot, *St. Cyprian*, ACW 25, pp. 97–98, nn. 170 and 171; H. Pétré, *Caritas. Étude sur le vocabulaire latin de la charité chrétienne*, SSL 22 (Louvain, 1948), pp. 260–262; Rahner, *Early Church*, pp. 171–173.

154. The "lesser sins" of *Ep.* 17.2.1, though not apostasy, require the process of ecclesial penance and so must be distinguished from the everyday sins. See Clarke, *Letters* I, pp. 293–294, n. 9.

155. Von Campenhausen, *Ecclesiastical Authority*, pp. 283ff.

council of bishops (*Epp.* 41.6; 57.1.1), even if they are but ratifying the voluntary separation of the schismatic (*Ep.* 43.1.3). Such persons cannot be admitted to penance because theirs is the sin of unrepentance, a crime even more grievous than that of the *lapsi*:

> This crime is a greater one than that which the lapsed, admittedly, have committed; but these, becoming penitents for their crime, are at least calling upon God's mercy by making satisfaction for it to the full. In their case the Church is being sought and appealed to, in the other the Church is repudiated; in the first likely enough there was coercion, in the second the will persists in its guilt (*De Eccl. cath. unitate* 19).[156]

And if they should die a martyr's death, it is to no avail, so total is their separation from God and the Church (*Ep.* 55.29.3; *De Eccl. cath. unitate* 19).

For Cyprian, the isolation of those disobedient to the bishops is solely a punishment inflicted to preserve the unity of the Church. They have to be excised because they threaten the one holy Church itself. It is not a coercive penance of isolation. In fact, nowhere does the African bishop make explicit mention of such an act of ecclesial discipline being inflicted in hopes of helping a grave sinner to repent and return to the Church. Rather, what we find in Cyprian, for the first time, is a genuine penal excommunication, done for the sake of the Church rather than for the sake of the sinner. It is purgative, not to preserve the purity of the Church but to maintain its unity. While the action might be temporary (indeed there seems to be evidence that those who are so excluded have the possibility of being admitted to penance if there is not undue scandal involved and if they manifest adequate contrition for their crimes—*Ep.* 59.15.2), its length is not predetermined. It is a punitive action rather than a penitential one, and cannot be said to be part of Cyprian's process of ecclesial penance.[157]

---

156. "Peius hoc crimen est quam quod admisisse lapsi uidentur, qui tamen in paenitentia criminis constituti Deum plenis satisfactionibus deprecantur. Hic ecclesia quaeritur et rogatur, illic ecclesiae repugnatur; hic potest necessitas fuisse, illic uoluntas tenetur in scelere . . ." (Bévenot, CCL 3,1, 263:463-467; trans. M. Bévenot, *De Lapsis and De Unitate*, p. 89. See also *Epp.* 34.3.2; 35.1.2; 55.17.2; 57.3.1.

157. Though he employs terms we wish to avoid for the sake of clarity, M. Chartier has made this point in "La discipline pénitentielle d'après les écrits de saint Cyprien,"

5. ECCLESIAL RECONCILIATION AND READMISSION TO THE EUCHARIST

The reconciliation and readmission of the penitent to the Eucharist are the terminus points in the process of ecclesial penance, the *fructus paenitentiae* (*Ep.* 55.17.2). Whether defending the effectiveness of penance against the rigorism of the Novatianists (*Ep.* 55.24-29) or reprimanding Felicissimus and his followers for too hastily reconciling the *lapsi* who had yet to do *paenitentiam plenam* (*Epp.* 15-20), Cyprian teaches that there is to be no reconciliation without adequate ecclesial penance, and there is to be no ecclesial penance without the hope of reconciliation. As has been seen, the moment of reconciliation is not the decision of the penitent but is ecclesially mediated by the bishop in judging the sufficiency of the conversion and repentance of the sinner, externally expressed through the *paenitentia satisfactionis*. It is a judgment based on the criterion of the successful completion of the assigned penance, balanced with the specific need of particular penitents to be readmitted to the Eucharist (as in cases of the sick or those about to undergo the trials of persecution).

As with his terminology for penance, Cyprian uses a diversified vocabulary in describing the act of ecclesial reconciliation of the penitent. On the part of the sinner, it is a returning to the Church (*ad Ecclesiam redire*), and from the Church's perspective, it is the admittance (*admittere*) and reception (*suscipere*) of the sinner (*Epp.* 4.4.1; 55.11.2,29.2). To be reconciled is to be given the peace (*pax/pacem dare*) of the Church, expressing both the ruptured and now healed relationship of the sinner with the Church. Sinners are once again allowed to share in the life of the community (*Epp.* 18-20; *De lapsis* 15;16). Reconciliation is communion (*communicare/communicatio*) with the Church, given as a sign of authentic interior conversion and repentance (*Epp.* 15.4.1; 56.1.1,2.1).[158] Through ecclesial reconcilia-

---

Antonianum 14 (1939) 17-42, 135-156, pp. 155-156. While both groups were excluded from the Eucharist, those who were admitted to ecclesial penance remained in relationship with the Church, unlike those who were schismatic and unrepentant.

158. Grotz, *Busstufenwesens*, pp. 154ff., believes that the distinction between the *communicatio* and the *pax* lies in the fact that the former ended the time of *paenitentiam agere* and excommunication (not properly ecclesial penance for Grotz), while the latter term denoted the real reconciliation with God and the Church that occurred after the exomologesis (the only action of genuine ecclesial penance). His position

tion the penitent is once more allowed to come to the Eucharistic banquet (*eucharistiam dare—Epp.* 15.1.2; 16.2.3,3.2; 17.2.1; 57.2.2,4.2; *De lapsis* 15;25-26).[159]

Amid the nuances of meaning that Cyprian assigns to such vivid expressions, it appears in these texts that he especially wishes to draw a distinction between the act of reconciliation and readmittance to the Eucharist. In fact, following upon the ritual action of the exomologesis, a three-step liturgical process that leads a penitent back into full life with the community is discernible: the laying on of the hand by the bishop and clergy, the offering of the Eucharist on behalf of the penitents, and readmission to the Eucharist.[160]

a) The laying on of the hand by the bishop and clergy

In the texts cited above in which Cyprian outlines the *ordo* of ecclesial penance, the exomologesis is immediately followed by the *manus ab episcopo et clero in paenitentiam inposita*. His is the first witness in the West to the imposition of the hand at the moment of reconciliation and, as such, the first witness to a clearly delineated rite of ecclesial reconciliation. It is obviously liturgical, occurring within the church (except in cases of the dying), and, at least in two texts, is the action that opens the way to readmission to the Eucharist (*Epp.* 16.2.3; 17.2.1). This subtle distinction between reconciliation through the laying on of the hand and the readmission to the Eucharist makes it possible to observe that this action forms the final stage of the procedure of ecclesial penance. It seals and ratifies the true conversion of the sinner, but it only opens up the possibility of full reconciliation, which is not effected until the reception of the Eucharist. Therefore, it is an action necessary in order to be readmitted to the Eucharist but incomplete without it.[161]

The origin of the laying on of the hand as a sign of ecclesial reconciliation continues to be a debated question. Is it based on 1 Tim

---

has been attacked by most contemporary authors, especially Matellanes Crespo, *El tema de la "Communicatio" en los escritos penitenciales*, pp. 59-70, who prefers to see in the two terms Cyprian's use of a stylistic pleonasm.

159. Swann, *Relationship*, pp. 357-451, *passim*.

160. Two texts (*Epp.* 34.1.1; 57.2.2) do not include all three elements in reference to reconciliation. Yet between the two passages all three steps are mentioned.

161. Swann, *Relationship*, pp. 435, 454-455.

5:22, assuming this to be a reference to the restoration of sinners?[162] Does it develop as a parallel rite to the postbaptismal anointing, a gesture that signifies the communication of the Holy Spirit?[163] Or is it likened to the catechumenal exorcisms, which also are administered amid penitential works by those preparing for initiation?[164] The question is further confused by the rebaptism controversy between Cyprian and Stephen, with the latter insisting that heretics are not to be rebaptized, but only that *manus illis inponatur in paenitentiam* (*Ep.* 74.1.2). Though Stephen claims to be appealing to the ancient tradition of penance as the basis for his position (*Ep.* 71.4.1; 73.3.1), his theologizing on the issue appears to make the laying on of the hand on repentant heretics a completion of their baptism by the granting of the Holy Spirit (*Epp.* 69.10.1; 74.5; 75.8).[165]

Perhaps all that can be said with certainty is that due to its obscure origins, the action is grounded in ancient, pretheologically reflective roots, the existence and meaning of which are not witnessed to in the West until Cyprian.

b) *The offering of the Eucharist on behalf of the penitents*

After the laying on of the hand, the newly reconciled faithful remain for the *oratio* in which they are commemorated individually at the offering of the Eucharist (*offerre pro illis*—*Epp.* 15.1.2; 16.2.3,3.2; 17.2.1; *De lapsis* 16). That Cyprian knows the practice of remembering, in a specific way, certain persons or groups of persons is evident from his letters (*Epp.* 62.4.2, donors; 1.2.1, the dead; 12.2.1, martyrs). Further, it is customary that those who are to partake of the Eucharist be present for the liturgy unless prevented by serious circumstances. As to whether this offering on behalf of the peni-

---

162. See above, p. 80.

163. That both actions communicate the Spirit is more obvious in the *Didascalia Apostolorum* 68:23-25; 114:10-16; 117:4-5, and in Origen's *De Lev. hom.* 2,4. This is the position of Coppens, *L'imposition des mains*, pp. 387–392.

164. Rahner, *Early Church*, pp. 167–171. Rahner is correct to point out that Cyprian's connection of the imposition of the hand with the other elements of ecclesial penance might indeed make it more credible that it was an action primarily purgative (like the exorcisms) rather than communicative (like confirmation).

165. *Ibid.*, pp. 160–166; Dallen, "The Imposition of Hands," pp. 226–228.

tents means that they are also the ones who provide the sacred elements remains an open question.[166]

c) *Readmission to the Eucharist*

After being commemorated at the prayers, the newly reconciled are once again allowed to partake of the Eucharist. It is the "final and definitive act by which the sinner's reunion with the Lord and his Church is signified and effected."[167] In the passages cited above, and especially in *De lapsis*, it is evident that Cyprian views the *eucharistiam dare* as the ultimate goal of the process of ecclesial penance and reconciliation. In the variety of terms he uses to speak of reconciliation, particularly where he refers to *pax* and *communicatio*, a close relationship with the eventual readmission of the penitent to the Eucharist is revealed. It is the source and the summit of Christian life and must not be profaned under any circumstances (*Epp.* 15.1.2; 64.1.2; *De lapsis* 25;26).[168] That is why only those who have fulfilled all the requirements of ecclesial penance and received the laying on of the hand are judged worthy of its reception. They who were once separated are now fully restored.

Cyprian's stress on the sinner's reconciliation and readmission to the Eucharist, resulting from ecclesial penance, puts into relief two questions: (1) What is the relationship between re-membership in the Church and divine forgiveness? and (2) Which action is ultimately effective for ecclesial reconciliation—the *paenitentia satisfactionis* of the sinner or the *pax Ecclesiae* granted by the bishop?

The first question has been debated by contemporary authors, who rightly perceive in Cyprian's writings both a juridic and effective action of forgiveness in the rite of reconciliation and readmission to the Eucharist, and a constant acknowledgment of the ultimate independence of God from human action.[169] No doubt Cyprian is within the patristic tradition of allowing that sins are forgiven by

---

166. Clarke, *Letters* I, pp. 277–278, n. 14.

167. Swann, *Relationship*, p. 434.

168. Hein, *Eucharist and Excommunication*, pp. 374–383.

169. D. Capelle, "L'absolution sacerdotale chez S. Cyprien," *RThAM* 7 (1935) 221–234; C. Daly, "Absolution and Satisfaction in St. Cyprian's Theology of Penance," SP 2 [= TU 64] (1955) 202–207.

God alone. In an eschatological sense, it is God who has the final say concerning the ultimate salvation of all, particularly those guilty of postbaptismal sin. Yet the Church, as the legitimate *mater* of those joined to Christ through baptism, can be assured that the judgment of God will not contradict its own judgment. Therefore, those who are the recipients of the Church's reconciliation receive the "necessary precondition" for reconciliation with God (*Epp.* 18.1; 20.3; 55.29).[170] While it is he alone who will forgive, the final outcome of his judgment is less doubtful if the sinner has first been readmitted to the Church.

As for the second question regarding the relationship between the performance of ecclesial penance and being granted ecclesial reconciliation by the action of the bishop, at first sight Cyprian appears to contradict himself. On the one hand, there can be no ecclesial restoration without the necessary performance of penance by the sinner; on the other hand, the performance of penance means nothing without the necessary intervention by the bishop to restore the sinner. Which actually is effective for reconciliation? The problem is brought toward a resolution if it is recalled that throughout the process of ecclesial penance, the sinner remains in constant relationship with, and under the constant care of, the Church. Though the penitential action is the work of the sinner, it is mediated and given meaning by the Church. In fact, it is the Church that defines and interprets such personal penitential actions in terms of "satisfaction" for sin. While there is no reconciliation without penance, effective penance is done only in relationship with the Church. Therefore, Cyprian cannot properly be labeled semi-Pelagian. The action of the bishop at the moment of reconciliation only confirms, and is in continuity with, the previous action of the Church on behalf of the sinner.[171]

---

170. Rahner, *Early Church*, pp. 191-199; Poschmann, *PAS*, pp. 58–60; Swann, *Relationship*, pp. 368, 399–400. This is against the position of Bévenot, "The Sacrament of Penance," pp. 191ff., and *St. Cyprian*, ACW 25, pp. 98–99, n. 174, who feels that there is "no reason for separating God's forgiveness from the reconciliation with the Church, as if the latter were only something provisional" (ACW 25, p. 99).

171. Rahner, *Early Church*, pp. 189-191, 200–205, who points out that the decision to undertake the rigors of ecclesial penance was already the work of the Spirit and not just the sole action by the sinner. See also Amann, "Pénitence," c. 785–786.

6. THE CONSEQUENCES OF ECCLESIAL PENANCE

Cyprian does not explicitly testify to the now familiar practice of ecclesial reconciliation being unrepeatable as a consequence of penance. Only one text might be cited as a reference to this disciplinary practice, so well attested to by his "master," Tertullian. In a letter to Pomponius, in which the delicate situation of consecrated virgins sleeping with deacons is discussed, it is laid down that if such virgins break off these relationships, do penance, and are found to still be in possession of their "technical" virginity after examination by the midwives, then

> . . . they should be received into the Church and admitted to communion—with this warning, however, that if at a later date they return to these same men or if they dwell with them in the same house and under the same roof, they will be censured more severely and will be cast out, and will not be easily readmitted to the Church for any such misconduct in the future (*Ep.* 4.4.1).[172]

Though the penance necessary for the virgins is mitigated (as opposed to the *paenitentiam plenam* which the letter goes on to prescribe for those virgins who actually had intercourse with the men), a second penance and reconciliation are not considered to be likely, or at least not easy.[173] Inasmuch as Cyprian is aware of certain African bishops who do not offer the *pax* for certain grave sins, it hardly seems possible that other local sees would offer *carte blanche* a number of possibilities for ecclesial penance and reconciliation. It is more likely that the custom of a single penance is well established in the tradition of the African Church from Tertullian. Given the situation of persecution and the disciplinary confusion over what is necessary for a first postbaptismal repentance, perhaps few situations would arise that would occasion comment on the practice by Cyprian.[174]

---

172. ". . . accepta communicatione ad ecclesiam admittantur, hac tamen interminatione, ut si ad eosdem masculos postmodum reuersae fuerint aut si cum isdem in una domo et sub eodem tecto simul habitauerint, grauiore censura eiciantur nec in ecclesiam postmodum tales facile recipiantur" (Bayard, I:11; trans. Clarke, *Letters* I, p. 60).

173. Clarke, *Letters I*, p. 178, n. 32.

174. Rahner, *Early Church*, p. 208.

It might further be argued that another consequence of penance, to which Cyprian more clearly testifies, is the disciplinary rule that clerics who become schismatic but who later return to the Church and are admitted to penance can only be reconciled and allowed *vel laico communicare* and can no longer hold clerical office (*Epp.* 55.11.3; 64.1.1; 67.6.3; 72.2.1).[175] However, this requirement appears more likely as part of the necessary penance for those once entrusted with Church leadership who later became instruments for ecclesial disunity. As such, for this particular group, it is an addition to rather than a consequence of the process of penance. No other restraints upon the reconciled are mentioned by Cyprian. Those who have been reconciled and readmitted to the Eucharist possess full baptismal status in the life and worship of the community.[176]

7. SUMMARIZING CYPRIAN'S ORDER OF PENITENTS

It is evident that the testimony of Cyprian of Carthage on ecclesial penance and reconciliation is the most lucid and also the most significant witness of the first three centuries. The clarity of his attestation arises from the disciplinary confusion resulting from the dire situation of the Decian persecution. His pastoral reflection on the plight of the *lapsi* highlights the two dialectical poles of his ecclesiology that influence his teaching on penance: the complete authority of the bishop in the care of the flock entrusted to him, and the necessity of the unity of the universal Church, manifested through the unity of its bishops. While it is possible that ecclesial penance could be successfully undertaken for any sin (even sins against God, such as apostasy), it is the bishop who determines the requirements of the *paenitentia satisfactionis*, who cares for the sin-

---

175. The one exception might be Maximus, the Roman presbyter, whom Cornelius says was able "to resume his former position" after seeing through the heresy of Novatian and returning to the Church. However, it does not appear that Maximus or his companions were reconciled through ecclesial penance but were simply restored to their former status due to the generous sympathy of Cornelius and the assembly. See L. Greenslade, *Schism in the Early Church* (London, 1964), p. 149.

176. Rahner, *Early Church*, p. 207, against Von Campenhausen, *Ecclesiastical Authority*, p. 290. A distinction must be drawn between Cyprian's witness and that of Origen (*Contra Celsum* 3,51), who imposes as a juridic restraint the holding of clerical office upon any who have been reconciled through ecclesial penance.

ner throughout the time when satisfaction is accomplished, and who judges, in consultation with the entire community, the sincerity of the sinner's conversion and the time when such a one is ready to be reconciled through the laying on of his hand.

It is possible to discern a three-step process of ecclesial penance in Cyprian: the *paenitentia satisfactionis* (which we have referred to as a penance of segregation), the exomologesis, and reconciliation with the Church/readmission to the Eucharist. The first (which may have commenced upon a personal confession of sin) includes personal works of penance under the supervision of the community. The latter two are liturgical-ritual actions celebrated when it is judged that the penitent has successfully completed the necessary satisfaction. Cyprian allows for mitigated forms of penance, such as penance to the dying, but even these forms of penance, if they are truly ecclesial and not undertaken for everyday sins, maintain the three-step process, though temporally streamlined. There does not seem to be testimony to the postapostolic action of a coercive penance of isolation of the sinner. Rather, schismatics are totally excluded, apparently without recourse, in order to restore and preserve the unity of the Church. It is a punitive action, rather than an act of penance, taken by the bishop, who exercises direct authority over the sinner.

The rite of reconciliation of the penitent can also be seen to have three moments: the laying on of the hand, the offering of the Eucharist on behalf of the penitent, and readmission to the Eucharist. All the terms used by Cyprian to describe these actions *in toto*, especially *pax* and *communicatio*, connect the doing of penance with its ultimate goal, readmission to the Eucharist. Ecclesial reconciliation forms the necessary precondition for the forgiveness of God, whose ultimate independence Cyprian is careful to maintain. Finally, there is only vague reference to the custom of a single penance, and no witness to any further disciplinary obligations being imposed on those who have already been reconciled.

CONCLUSION

The experience of the North African Church forms the crux of the development of an order of penitents. Tertullian's witness to the technical procedure of exomologesis is the first unclouded affirmation of a formal process of ecclesial penance. It is an intermediate step of segregation within the community, seen already in some of the writings from the East, and one which signals that the entire action of penance is now a defined process. Penitents not only have the obligation to accomplish penance before being readmitted to the Church, but they have the obligation to accomplish a specific action of penance—the exomologesis. This experience organizes them as a defined group who had an impact upon the conscious life and worship of the community. Only in his oblique references to a rite of reconciliation does Tertullian fail us as a source; otherwise, even his later shift to the elitist rigorism of Montanism does not cloud the importance of his witness. In truth, the vehemency of his Montanist argumentation will serve to sharpen the Church's reflection concerning the appropriate response to those guilty of grave post-baptismal sin.

Yet Tertullian is soon replaced by Cyprian as the premier witness to an order of penitents. It is Cyprian, struggling over the situation of the *lapsi*, who propels penitents, as a distinct class of persons, into the center of the Church's life. Opposing those who would refuse ecclesial readmittance to sinners, as well as those who would grant it too easily, Cyprian plays the role of a practical pastor. He knows that penance is *the* effective means in leading the erring believer back to Christ and his Church. It bears fruit, the fruit of the *pax Ecclesiae*. On the other hand, the real effect of sin can only be healed through a gradual process rather than in a single moment. Therefore, specific procedures are established to reflect the altered relationship between the sinner and God (and so the Church), and the altered status of such a one within the Church. Only when accomplished step-by-step are these procedures effective. The penitential practice that appears in these writings from North Africa offers the most solid evidence seen heretofore upon which to posit the existence of an order of penitents during the third century.

CHAPTER SUMMARY

As stated in the introduction to this chapter, the dossier on ecclesial penance in the third-century West is marked by controversy.

It is here that the struggle between rigorists and those advocating leniency for those guilty of serious sin after baptism came to its climax. The result was a penitential process that attempted to combine the best elements from both perspectives. Reconciliation with the Church (and with God) was possible for any offense, even those most objectively grave, through effective penance. Yet effective penance required a necessary process by and through which one was led to genuine conversion. The process that evolved also manifested the Western concern for an ecclesial unity achieved through external discipline (a perspective distinct from the Alexandrian view, whose authors tended more to emphasize the internal reality of unity). This need for external unity in the West resulted from the confusion created by the persecutions, as well as from the influence of a wide spectrum of false teachings and schismatic activities. These contributed to the establishment of a strong monarchical episcopacy and were ultimately the reason why the more rigorist elements could no longer find a place in the mainstream of ecclesial life. Diversity in practice signaled not pluriformity but heterodoxy.

Nonetheless, the process of penance remained a process, a journey made by the penitent and involving the entire community. More clearly than in the East, delineated stages were in evidence, at least in the witness of the North Africans. Being reformed in the image of the gospel demanded time and a willingness to seek out the prayer of the whole Church. Though in actuality the exomologesis (used in the Tertullianist sense of the entire penitential procedure) was required in only a very few situations, no person in the community remained untouched by the process. Penitents remained part of the Church, living symbols of the need for conversion in all the baptized and of the reconciling ministry in which all the baptized partake.

Chapter Five

DISCOVERING AND REDISCOVERING
THE ORDER OF PENITENTS

The working hermeneutic of this study has been to reopen the thorny dossier of penance during the first three centuries in order to throw light upon two separate but related issues. The first concerns the origin of the order of penitents that emerges in the witness of the patristic writers beginning in the fourth century. The external liturgical actions that give shape and definition to this *ordo* are by then inseparable from the institution of canonical penance. In other words, from the fourth century there is no liturgical expression of an order of penitents outside the wider practice of canonical penance. It is consolidated with the other characteristic elements that made up this ecclesial discipline, especially its consequent unrepeatability and the imposition of juridic restraints upon the reconciled. The preceding three chapters have examined the external procedures of the first three centuries, in hopes of uncovering the existence of an order of penitents that predates its being subsumed within the smothering embrace of the later canonical penance.[1] The results of our examination are included in the first section of this chapter.

The second issue that has formed our working hermeneutic concerns the present pastoral situation of the sacrament of reconciliation. It has been described as being in the midst of a crisis due to

---

1. In continuity with the definition proposed in Chapter One, "canonical penance" is used here in the strict temporal sense of the penitential practice after the Peace of Constantine.

decreasing numbers of practicing Catholics who avail themselves of it.[2] Many contemporary authors insist that new forms of the sacrament must be allowed to develop in order for the practice of penance and reconciliation within the Church to be renewed.[3] One form that has come under experimentation by some parish communities in the United States is being described as a restored order of penitents. After uncovering the early history of penance, and in light of the present situation of the Church, the study must ask the question: On what basis might the order of penitents be restored today? A response to this question is formulated in the chapter's second section.

I. THE ORDER OF PENITENTS PRIOR TO ITS FOURTH-CENTURY CANONIZATION

A. The Existence of an Order of Penitents in the Third Century

1. TOWARD A DEFINITION OF *ORDO*

The term *ordo* ("order") has a variety of root meanings. Its most basic definition evokes a sense of "rank" or "alignment" of concrete objects. In a more abstract usage, it suggests "succession" or "norm" or a "rule" over a range of diverse objects or persons. In Roman law the term was used in a technical sense to speak of an "organized group" or "college," often coming to be applied to the "governing body," whether administrative or legislative. *Ordo* also distinguished different "classes" within Roman society, such as the "order of the equestrian," which were organized around particu-

---

2. We point only to the study by A. Greeley, W. McCready, K. McCourt, *Catholic Schools in a Declining Church* (Kansas City, Mo.,1976), p. 162, who offer the results of the National Opinion Research Center in the United States showing a decrease in the number of Catholics confessing monthly from thirty-eight percent in 1964 to seventeen percent in 1974. Other more recent studies confirm this view, J. Gremillion and J. Castelli, especially *The Emerging Church: the Notre Dame Study of Catholic Life since Vatican II* (San Francisco, 1987), pp. 145-148.

3. See especially Ramos-Regidor, "Reconciliation in the Primitive Church," p. 88; M. Hellwig, *Sign of Reconciliation and Conversion*, pp. 102-103; Orsy, *The Evolving Church and the Sacrament of Penance*, pp. 148ff.; Martos, *Doors to the Sacred*, pp. 362-363; Dallen, *Reconciling Community*, pp. 355ff.

lar functions and had set regulations. Later the term was applied more generically to whole professions and groups within society, such as the *ordo scribarum* or the *ordo publicanorum*, which only shared common characteristics rather than being tightly organized. The word also had a military usage, evolving metonymically from connoting "rank" to the commandment issued from a particular rank. Finally, in the realm of religion, *ordo* was used to refer to those persons who functioned as representatives of the divinity they represented (*ordo sacerdotum*). These formed a "hierarchy," which also developed as an acceptable meaning of *ordo*.[4]

The specific application of the term to structures of the Church in the writings of the early patristic writers is slight and reveals no set pattern of usage. In the Latin, the first author to employ the term is Tertullian, though he might have taken it over from the Greek terms *taxis* and *tagma*. Clement of Rome and Irenaeus had earlier assigned an ecclesial meaning to these secular terms in speaking of either the class of, or functions by, the hierarchy.[5] Tertullian, then, given his propensity for juridic vocabulary and perhaps being influenced at least by Clement, adopts *ordo* in the same way. His references to an *ordo ecclesiae* (*De monogamia* 8,4; 11,4) or an *ordo ecclesiastica* (12,2; *De exhortatione castitatis* 13,4) speak of the hierarchical class within the Church that had a governing function. Of highest importance within this class was a select group, the *ordo sacerdotalis* (*De exhortatione castitatis* 7,2-3; *De idololatria* 7,3).[6] Yet Tertullian also indicates, at least implicitly, other groups that had a specific place in the structure of the Church: an *ordo* of widows (*Ad uxorem* 7,4) and virgins (*De virginibus velandis* 9,2), both of which are found among those listed in *De exhortatione castitatis* 13,4. In these usages Tertullian mirrors the variety of contemporary meanings associated with the term. At the same time, it can connote "hierarchy,"

---

4. P. van Beneden, *Aux origines d'une terminologie sacramentelle: Ordo, Ordinare, Ordinatio dans la littérature Chrétienne avant 313*, SSL 38 (Louvain, 1974) 1–4.

5. Clement's *Epistle to the Corinthians* 37,3; 40,1; Irenaeus's *Adv. haer.* III,11,11; IV,8,3.

6. Van Beneden, *Ordo, Ordinare, Ordinatio*, pp. 13–14. Of course, this does not negate the fact that the Greek term *klēros*, by the time of the postapostolic writers, had already assumed the technical meaning of "clergy."

"group," or "class." By the beginning of the third century, there is no technical Christian meaning assigned to *ordo*.[7]

Without specifically mentioning the term, other authors also refer to specific classes or groups that had distinct functions within the Church. They formed part of its structure and were distinguishable from the larger body. As seen in the writings examined in the previous chapters, first among these were the clergy, who exercised a specific leadership function. Though in the beginning they possessed a prophetic function, it was their hierarchical role that emerged as their most distinguishing mark by the third century.[8] They were the governing body of the communities. This body was further "ordered" to include bishops, presbyters, and deacons as well as other groups that had more specifically liturgical functions, such as subdeacons, readers, acolytes, exorcists, and porters.[9] Also distinguishable within the community were other groups whose function was more prophetic than governmental or liturgical. Tertullian's mention of widows and virgins has already been noted; to these we add martyrs and confessors.[10]

Beyond these, there were certain nonfunctionary classes of persons distinguishable within the Church. In fact, it might be said that these groups were distinctive, not because of an established posi-

---

7. Van Beneden, *Ordo, Ordinare, Ordinatio,* pp. 16–44. Van Beneden goes on to point out that Cyprian, though borrowing other concepts and terms employed by his "master" Tertullian, does not apply *ordo* to ecclesial structures (pp. 45–49).

8. The institutionalization of ecclesial office and its connection with the development of penitential discipline has been a recurring theme throughout the present study, inspired by the fundamental work by Von Campenhausen, *Ecclesiastical Authority.*

9. The earliest lists of such a structuring of groups in the Church are from Hippolytus's *Apostolic Tradition* (chs. 1–14) and from a letter by bishop Cornelius of Rome, related by Eusebius, *Eccl. Hist.* VI,43,11. A more in-depth examination of the evolution of the hierarchical orders goes beyond the bounds of the present study. See P. Fransen, "Orders and Ordination," in *Sacramentum Mundi* 4 (New York, N.Y., 1969), c. 305–327; P. De Clerck, "Ordination, ordre," in *Catholicisme hier aujourd'hui demain,* 10/44 (Paris, 1983), c. 162–206.

10. Hippolytus's reference to a *klēros* of confessors is seen by Lods, *Confesseurs et martyrs,* p. 71, n. 4, as only an honorific title rather than the designation of a separate ecclesial status. However, this only highlights one of the many meanings of *ordo.* It cannot take away from the fact that the martyrs and confessors are distinguishable from the larger body of the Church by the simple fact of their confession of faith before the civil authorities. See Nautin, *Lettres et écrivains,* p. 57, n. 1.

tion in the community, but exactly because of their transitory rank, which limited their ecclesial functioning. The first among these appears in the witness of Hippolytus and other writers of the third century, who speak of a specific body of persons in the process of becoming fully initiated Christians—the catechumens.[11] One can perceive a dialectic as to the stature of these persons in the Church. Negatively, catechumens, having not yet celebrated the liminal events of baptism and Eucharist, were in a different relationship with God and with the fully initiated. For a limited time they had a limited status within the community, expressed in their being assigned specific places and being restricted to participating in only the liturgy of the Word during the liturgical assembly.[12] Positively, they were not outcasts but formed a part of the Church, in process toward that day when their relationship with God and the community would come to its fullest expression through baptism and Eucharist. Theirs was a transitory "order" in the truest sense.

A second group paralleling the transitional *ordo catechumenorum* with regard to their ecclesial stature were those guilty of grave post-baptismal sin—the penitents.[13] Though already fully initiated, their sin reduced them to the status they formerly possessed as catechumens. They must be treated like those who had never experienced baptism or the Eucharist. Yet, as we have seen, a dialectic exists here as well concerning the standing of such persons in the Church. Negatively, they were in an estranged relationship with God and the fully initiated. As in the case of the catechumens, this was brought home to them by their limited status within the community, expressed in their exclusion from the Eucharist. Positively, the penitents were not considered outside the Church but remained a part of the community, in process toward the day when they would be readmitted to the Eucharist and come once more to their full bap-

---

11. M. Dujarier, *A History of the Catechumenate*, trans. E. Haasl (New York, N.Y., 1979), pp. 48ff. It is with the *Apostolic Tradition* of Hippolytus that catechumenal stages are clearly delineated. However, a process of preparation for those entering the Church has earlier roots in the *Didache*, the *Shepherd of Hermas*, and Justin Martyr's *Apologiae*.

12. Dujarier, *The Rites of Christian Initiation*, trans. K. Hart (New York, N.Y., 1979), pp. 59–62.

13. As has been seen, Origen makes an explicit comparison between the status of catechumens and penitents (*Contra Celsum* 3,51). See above, pp. 157–158.

tismal status. Their "order," like that of the catechumens, was also one of transition.

Though they are not technically so designated, the existence of "orders"in the third-century Church cannot be denied. Certain groups or classes of persons were distinguishable from the larger body of the community, either due to established governmental, liturgical, or prophetical functions, or because of a period of transition. This period expressed a specific relationship and status and resulted from not yet possessing, or being dispossessed of, full baptismal stature. In both hierarchical and transitional orders, a certain fluidity was evident, though by the fourth century both groups took on a more absolute character. In the case of penitents, this development would evince the loss of the transitional character of the order, leading to the limited status of those in the penitential class being made pemanent, even after their ecclesial reconciliation. The resulting effect would be the stigmatization of canonical penance.

a) A transitional ordo reflected in "relationship between"

The early Church reflected upon itself as an *ordo*, taken in its broadest possible sense as a class of persons distinguishable from the rest of society. The salvific event of Christ has redeemed the whole world, and the community of believers, upon whom the Holy Spirit has been poured out, was entrusted with the task of spreading the good news of salvation. Their identity as a community in a new relationship with God, a relationship established through Christ and by the power of the Holy Spirit, was recalled and made present each time they gathered to retell the stories of Jesus and to celebrate, through accepted symbolic action, his continued presence at work in the world. These early symbols, water baptism and the gathering together to break bread and share the cup in memory of the Lord, formed their distinguishing mark. These actions were normative, necessary for one's identity as a follower of Jesus and expressive of the relationship that bonded the members of the Church to God and one to another.[14]

In a negative way, this is seen in the case of grave sin. The ac-

---

14. B. Cooke, *Sacraments and Sacramentality* (Mystic, Conn., 1983), pp. 68–72.

tion of sinning was interpreted by the Church as denying the gift of the Spirit given at baptism, *ipso facto* making one unfit to enter into the Lord's presence at the Eucharist. It was a rejection of the distinctive mark of the Christian "order" and effected a fundamental alteration in the relationship between the sinner and God, and so with the Church.[15] Such an alteration had to be recognized, either through voluntary self-exclusion on the part of the sinner or through the indirect or direct imposition of isolation by the leaders of the community. The sinner was counted among the dead and his or her salvation placed in serious doubt, possible only through the generous love of a merciful God.

Yet if such a one, through divine initiative, was brought to a sincere desire for repentance, then all hope was not lost. True repentance demanded both an interior conversion of the heart and the exteriorization of deep sorrow for sin, expressed in the accomplishment of concrete works of penance. These works were not done merely in the hope that the sinner's relationship with God would be rectified in the world to come; no, they were ecclesial actions, having the effect of reordering and reforming all the sinner's relationships. Though still excluded from the most distinguishing mark of Christian life, the Eucharist, and segregated from the fully initiated in the liturgical assembly, the penitents remained in relationship with the community. Sin altered the relationship, while ecclesial penance acknowledged that the relationship still existed, though obviously in a different way.

Once it was judged by the Church that the conversion of the penitent was complete, a judgment based on fidelity to penitential actions that served as an external gauge of the internal transformation process, then the relational reformation of the penitent was celebrated by his or her being readmitted into full relationship with the community and allowed once more to partake of the Eucharist. The

---

15. Given the patristic belief of the inseparable connection between God and the Church, so that the action of the Church was disclosive of God's will, to speak of the sinner's relationship with God being altered due to grave postbaptismal sin assumes that the same relational reality exists between the sinner and the community of believers. When this reality is externally expressed by the isolation and/or segregation of the sinner from the Eucharist, the Church is only confirming what already exists.

period of transition was complete. Certainly this did not *a priori* symbolize the complete restoration of one's relationship with God. But the rehabilitation of the relationship between penitent and fully initiated believers was, at the very least, the necessary precondition for the reestablishment of one's relationship with God.[16]

The order of penitents was distinguishable due to the alteration of the internal relationship between the sinner and God, manifested by the external isolation from and/or segregation within the Church. Its purpose was to provide for the transitory process of transformation of the sinner's relationship with the believing community, celebrated in readmission to the Eucharist. This action opened the way for the same transformation to be effected in the sinner's relationship with God.

b) *A transitional* ordo *reflected in "status within"*

For the early Christians, the experience of full initiation into the Church was the most self-defining event of the life of faith. It incorporated one into the priesthood of all believers. As members of Christ's Body, they had certain responsibilities for the life of the community as a result of their common profession of faith: to share *koinōnia*, to exercise ministry, to confess the faith, perhaps even to the point of martyrdom. In short, the life of the entire community was maintained through the full living-out of the experience of initiation by each of the members. The wellspring of baptismal life was the Eucharist, partaking of the one bread and the one cup when the community gathered to make present the living memory of Jesus. Just as the relationship between the sinner and God (and so the Church) was fundamentally altered due to sin, so also was the ecclesial status of one guilty of grave postbaptismal sin. No longer was full interaction with the community possible. To overcome the sickness of sin and to preserve the health of those who still walk in grace, the sinner must be quarantined, isolated from the Church. What

---

16. For the early authors, there is no question that it is God alone who forgives, and his ultimate freedom to do so must be preserved. However, inasmuch as the Church acted on God's behalf, the readmission of the penitent was not solely a disciplinary action but also affected the sinner's relationship with God. God would not refuse the sincere prayer of his people.

was gained at the time of initiation is now forfeited. This was poign-antly signified by the penitent's no longer being able to partake of the saving food from the Eucharistic table with fellow Christians. Exclusion from the Eucharist was the ultimate symbol of the loss of full baptismal stature.

When and if the action of isolation led a sinner to undertake the journey of penance, it was apparent that the penitent had not be-come an ecclesial "zombie," having no real existence in the Church. Rather, though the stature of such a one had been radically changed, the sinner still possessed a particular status within the life of the community. While continuing to be excluded from communion and segregated within the liturgical assembly, penitents were allowed certain other prerogatives, such as being present for the liturgy of the Word and receiving prayers of intercession from the commu-nity. Their new, though circumscribed, status can be spoken of as an *ordo*, inasmuch as it distinguished penitents from the larger body and formed a time of transition from limited to full baptismal stature.

The decision on the part of the Church to readmit the penitent to the Eucharist, based on the sincerity of his or her conversion, celebrated the transformation of status of the penitent within the community, effected through the process of conversion. In other words, readmission to the Eucharist symbolized that the penitent once more shared in the full baptismal stature of all Christians. The status of penitent, with all of its attendant distinguishing charac-teristics, was exchanged for the distinctive mark of the fully initiated Christian—partaking in the breaking of the bread and sharing of the cup. During the third century the status of newly reconciled peni-tents was fully restored.[17] Except in cases where grave sin was com-mitted again (and here only in those local Churches in which the custom of an unrepeatable penance was normative), the future of their life within the Church did not differ from that of other fully initiated Christians. They were free to live out their baptismal life by engaging themselves in all aspects of the community's life and worship.

---

17. The one exception is Origen's restriction of former penitents from holding clerical office (*Contra Celsum* 3,51). See below, pp. 161–162.

The order of penitents was distinguishable due to the altered status of the sinner within the Church, manifested by the isolation from, and/or segregation within, the Church. Its purpose was to provide for the conversion journey back to full initiatory status, celebrated through readmission to the Eucharist. This action freed the penitents to undertake again the living-out of baptismal commitment through full participation in all aspects of the Church's life.

2. EXCLUSION FROM THE EUCHARIST AS THE FIRST SIGN OF AN
ORDER OF PENITENTS

From what has been reflected in the patristic sources and further developed in the discussion above, we have seen that the enduring sign of the presence of an order of penitents in the first three centuries was the sinner's exclusion from the Eucharist. More consistently than any other external penitential action, Eucharistic exclusion most clearly affirmed that there existed a different relationship between the penitent and God (and so the Church), and that the status of the penitent within the Church was radically altered. Given the central place of the Eucharist in the life of the community, seen already by the middle of the second century in the witness of the *Didache*, to be excluded from this distinctive act that "ordered" the Christian community was an action in itself indicative of an "ordering."

It has not been the intention here to make a definitive judgment as to the absolute connection between exclusion from the Eucharist and ecclesial penance during these first centuries. As already noted, this question has been justifiably raised by Grotz and answered by many of his critics, most especially Rahner. It does appear from the early writings that true ecclesial penance, undertaken for grave post-baptismal sin (as opposed to personal penitential acts of penance for slight faults), always included some form of Eucharistic exclusion; however, an apologia in defense of this position goes beyond our purpose here. Rather, our perspective has been to demonstrate that when exclusion from the Eucharist did occur, it resulted from the grave sin of a member of the Christian community.[18] It is only

---

18. This is so clear by the fourth century. See. T. Van Bavel, "Eucharistie en zondenvergeving," *Tijdschrift voor liturgie* 61 (1977) 87–102, pp. 95–96, who stresses

in this sense that there is justification for the statement previously made: It was the very fact of exclusion that was most expressive of the new relationship and status of the penitent vis-à-vis the Church. In other words, exclusion from the Eucharist was the premier sign of an order of penitents before the fourth century.

At the same time, it must be said again, even to the point of repetition, that exclusion, either voluntarily undertaken or indirectly or directly imposed upon the sinner, was in no way a punitive action. It merely recognized externally what had occurred already due to the sin: the alteration of the relationship between the sinner and God (and so the community of the faithful).[19] In the case of an imposed isolation, it was the hope of the Church that expressing the internal reality in an exterior way would lead the sinner to see the effects of sin and do something about it, namely, repent. Thus the isolation of the sinner from the community was a coercive action, meant to induce heartfelt contrition and a willingness to undertake penance. In the image of the early writers, it was a "hard medicine"; nonetheless, it remained a medicine rather than a punishment.[20]

In the third-century experience of the penance of segregation, the exclusion was strictly liturgical; yet it continued to have a medicinal value. It aided the sinner to see the seriousness with which penance was accomplished if it was to be efficacious. Reconciliation was no magical action. It was won only through God's grace and the hard, though effective, penance of the sinner. Exclusion from the Eucharist, then, in the history of penance examined here, was both a realistic expression of the effect of sin and a medicinal action to induce sinners to begin, and aid them during, the journey toward readmittance to full communion.[21]

Augustine's conviction of the fundamental incompatibility ("onverenigbaarheid") between grave postbaptismal sin and partaking in the Eucharist.

19. See above, n. 15. Even secret sins do not escape this. Both Origen and Cyprian remark that even if one is able to escape the judgment of the Church, the reality of sin remains.

20. Eastern authors most often use medical imagery to speak of the healing effect of genuine penance. This has previously been seen in the penitential witness of the *Didascalia*, Methodius of Olympus, and Origen.

21. In this case the exception is Cyprian, who does not speak of the coercive purpose of the isolation of false teachers. See above, pp. 221–222.

3. A DELINEATED TRANSITIONAL PROCESS AS THE SECOND SIGN OF AN ORDER OF PENITENTS

The present discussion has attempted only to establish a basis upon which one can distinguish an *ordo* of penitents in the early Church from the larger body of the fully initiated, based on the distinctive mark of Eucharistic exclusion. Taken in this sense, the term *ordo* is used more generically, referring to a distinctive group of persons, while making no decision whether such persons were themselves organized. They were bound together solely because of their life situation rather than because of any action taken by the group itself or imposed upon it. While this definition has precedent in the history of the term's usage (viz., the *ordo scribarum* in Roman society), such a generic distinction of people guilty of postbaptismal sin is hardly a sufficient basis to legitimately speak of an order of penitents before the fourth century. If this were the case, then it would be possible to claim the existence of an order of penitents in New Testament times. One need only look at 1 Cor 5:1-13 to see an example of a person guilty of serious sin being distinguished from the larger community. A further question must then be raised: What is the element of self-organization that stimulates the Church to be conscious of penitents as a distinctive class of persons?

The most patent yet perhaps the most overlooked answer lies in the process of penance itself. During the first two centuries the procedure for grave sinners was hardly elaborate. If a member of the community erred, he or she was to be corrected. In cases of unrepentance, the sinner was isolated from (and by) the community until such a one came to admit the error of his or her ways and sought reconciliation with the Church. If the expressed contrition was genuine, gauged by external acts of penance, the sinner appears to have been directly admitted back into the assembly.[22] The procedure is informal, neither framed by attendant liturgical rites nor expressive of a gradual process of conversion on the part of the sinner. Though the individual transgressor was distinguishable from the larger body of the faithful due to the isolation, the sources do

---

22. The exception here may be Irenaeus, whose use of "exomologesis" might imply a more developed process of penance by the end of the second century. See above, pp. 109-113.

not indicate that sinners were organized as a group or even had emerged in the consciousness of the community as a distinct class of persons.

With Tertullian and a more technical use of the term "exomologesis," the first indication of grave postbaptismal sinners having an organized life in the Church emerges. The situation was not as informal as in the earlier period, with normative penitential actions coming to be part of the penitent's movement back toward ecclesial reconciliation. An important development in the Church's recognition of penitents as a class was the rise in institutional office, which played a key role in this further structuring of ecclesial penance. Bishops had an increasingly central part as overseers of the penitential procedures. The shift from the informal practice of the first two centuries to the assigned penitential actions that occur in the third century cannot be properly understood without being cognizant of this evolution.

For the first time it is acceptable to use the image of "journey" in speaking of the penitential actions of the third century. In the most serious cases, sinners were in transit from being isolated from the community, to being segregated within the community, to being readmitted to the Eucharist. With the first witness of the segregation of penitents within the assembly comes the first testimony of a delineated "process" of penance. The sinner journeyed in stages, from the outer reaches of isolation back home toward the reestablishment of full baptismal status. The "process" model of ecclesial penance is echoed by several third-century sources, most especially the *Didascalia* and the writings of Gregory Thaumaturgus, Origen, Tertullian, and Cyprian. Indeed, Cyprian is a unique witness. His testimony makes it especially clear that the "how" of penance was inseparable from the "fact" of penance; that is, the step-by-step process of penance itself (*paenitentia satisfactionis*, exomologesis, reconciliation/readmission to the Eucharist) was as necessary as which penitential works were actually accomplished.

While it is the exclusion from the Eucharist that points to the existence of a generic *ordo* of penitents in the early Church, it is the testimony to a delineated transitional process of penance in the third century that further specifies the picture of an order of penitents. The process itself is testimony to a self-organization that evinces a consciousness on the Church's part of the existence of penitents as a distinct class of persons. It stands as the conclusive proof that prior to the inception of the liturgical expression that marked the order of penitents in the fourth century, it had a distinguishable life within the Church.

4. THE ORDER OF PENITENTS AND THE DESIGNATED TERMINOLOGY

Throughout this study the terms "indirect (or direct) coercive penance of isolation" and "penance of segregation" have been employed in order to move toward a new terminology about the history of an order of penitents in the first three centuries. This has been done so as not to further confuse an already obscure period of the history of ecclesial penance, which, as seen in the first chapter, has already borne the heavy burden of ambiguous terminology. These terms have emerged on their own, after a careful examination of the available documentation. Without making the history neater than it actually is, they are able to encompass the wide spectrum of penitential experiences of the local communities from both East and West. Certainly, like all descriptive vocabulary, they are limited in their ability to penetrate the experiences they attempt to describe. For this reason they can only stand for the most common experiential denominator, still making indispensable the study of the specific witness of individual patristic authors.

What is most appealing about these terms is the immediate sense they convey of the particularity of the sinner's situation, or to parallel what has been said above, the *ordo* of the penitent. The words "isolation" and "segregation" offer an image of what was most fundamental to the ecclesial response to grave postbaptismal sin: exclusion from the Eucharist. Further, the terms suggest a delineated process, so that one senses that there was a transition from being "isolated," to being "segregated," to being reconciled/readmitted to the Eucharist. In short, the terms make it apparent that it is possible to speak of an order of penitents in the third century.

It may be objected that the use of the term "penance" in connection with these actions is to read too much into practices that were solely disciplinary. Yet, it is penance that opens these disciplinary practices to a meaning beyond the action itself. By definition, penance is not something done for its own sake; it is undertaken to achieve a greater good, the conversion of the sinner.[23] A present moment of penance combines both the past and the future: expiation for past wrong and a pledge to abstain from future transgressions. In the early Church, when a sinner was isolated from, or segregated within, the community, it was done for the sinner's sake—to lead such a one back to the full life of grace. To be sure, such actions were also didactic (to inform others in the community of the serious effects of postbaptismal sin) and purgative (to keep the purity of the Church intact). But from the majority of the writings examined, these purposes were not the central reasons for the exclusion of the sinner from the Eucharist. It was to lead the lost to undertake sincere penance so as to have the possibility of life with God reopened to them.

By the fourth century—indeed, already in the testimony of Cyprian —the medicinal purpose of the discipline of isolation will begin to be less evident, so that the action can no longer be observed to be coercive or penitential. Later the practice became disconnected from penance altogether, being transformed into a disciplinary sanction imposed as an ecclesial punishment. In this sense, it rightly takes on the designation of an "excommunication."[24] The fourth-century order of penitents is in fact what has been designated here as a penance of segregation. Yet in the first three centuries (with the exception of Cyprian), both isolation from, and segregation within, had as their end purpose, the penance of the sinner. It is for this reason that there is a certain appropriateness to the simple yet descriptive designations "coercive penance of isolation" and "penance of segregation."

B. The Disconnection Between the Order of Penitents of the Third Century and the Consequences of Canonical Penance

During the fourth century, those who were enrolled into the order of penitents and eventually reconciled to the Church were saddled with certain lifelong consequences, imposed simply because

---

23. Adnès, "Pénitence," in *DicSp* 12,1, c. 1006–1007.

24. J. Gaudemet, "Notes sur les formes anciennes de l'excommunication," *RevSR* 23 (1949) 64–77; Poschmann, *PAS*, p. 112.

of their previous penitential status. These consequences were two-fold: ecclesial penance could never be repeated, and certain juridic restraints were to be undertaken by the newly reconciled penitents. In particular, these later-imposed restraints developed into extremely harsh and inhumane restrictions and became the rose window through which later generations of Christians have looked back upon the early experience of penance. It is necessary to examine the roots of the connection (or disconnection) between these consequent obligations and that process of ecclesial penance of the third century which is termed an order of penitents. Are the consequences, even at this early period, inseparable from the process?

1. THE CONSEQUENCE OF THE UNREPEATABILITY OF PENANCE

The writings on penance from the West during the first three centuries witness to the widespread custom of the unrepeatability of penance. Beginning with the testimony of the *Shepherd of Hermas* and continuing through the writings of Tertullian and Cyprian (though to a lesser extent), reconciliation after penance was to be granted only once by the Church. The strength of this early teaching is seen in the writings of numerous Latin Fathers from the fourth century on, especially Ambrose, Jerome, Pacian, Augustine, Leo, and Gregory the Great, all of whom testify to the unrepeatability of ecclesial penance as an accepted disciplinary norm of the Church. At least in the West, therefore, the consequence of the possibility of penance being efficacious only one time appears as part of the very early tradition of postbaptismal penance.[25]

However, as we have had occasion to see, there was a different story in the East. Only in Alexandria, in the testimony of Clement and Origen, both of whom are familiar with the *Shepherd of Hermas*, is there mention of the custom of ecclesial penance being a one-time affair. In other Eastern third-century witnesses, though there is obviously knowledge of a penitential process, there does not seem to be knowledge that readmittance to the Church after penance can happen only once. This is especially true in the *Didascalia*, where

---

25. Certainly recidivists were expected to undertake the rigors of penance in order to preserve the faint hope of future salvation, even though the pardon of the Church could not be given.

a developed and organized witness to an order of penitents is found. Indeed, the brevity of the time of segregation within the community mentioned in the document suggests that the practice could be undertaken more than once.[26] In any event, as stated previously, there is just as much reason to believe that it is the Alexandrian witness in the East, with its testimony to a single penance, that is the anomaly here, rather than vice-versa. Though both the West and East witness to a penitential *ordo*, the custom of an unrepeatable penance may have gained only a small foothold in the practice of the East.[27]

The conclusion to be drawn is obvious: Though the connection between the process of penance in the first three centuries and the consequence of a single penance was strong, it was not universal. The two practices were not inseparable, so that one did not exist without the other. This will only be the case once the custom of the unrepeatability of penance becomes an inflexible juridic obligation in the fourth century. At that time, in an effort to brace up the ancient penitential discipline in the face of mass conversions after the Peace of Constantine, and to make clear its absolute parallel with baptism, there could be no compromise as to the practice of a single penance. The very institutionalization of the Church was at stake.

However, during the earlier period the unrepeatability of penance had much more to do with inner conversion than external regulation. It was meant to encourage the sincere repentance of the sinner so that he or she would not fall a second time. As in the case of the *Didascalia* and other Eastern documents from the third century, the sinner's conversion was also of tantamount importance but was encouraged through exhortations and prayer rather than the custom of a single penance. Therefore, at least in some instances, the order of penitents could, and did, have an existence without the consequence of the unrepeatability of penance.

2. THE CONSEQUENCE OF IMPOSED JURIDIC RESTRAINTS
UPON THE RECONCILED

We saw earlier that upon readmittance to the Eucharist, peni-

---

26. Rahner, *Early Church*, pp. 240ff.
27. See above, p. 128.

tents came once again into full baptismal status, so that they could engage in all aspects of the community's life and worship. However, after the third century this was no longer the case. Imposed upon newly reconciled penitents were certain juridic restraints that affected not only their future ecclesial life but also their personal life. Though the intention of these restraints was pastoral, intended to further encourage the deep inner conversion of the penitent, it was not long before they became more sanctionary than medicinal measures.

As has been seen, the first evidence of sanctions taken against the reconciled comes from Origen, who recommends that those who have fallen should not be admitted to clerical office (*Contra Celsum* 3,51).[28] In the fourth century this same restriction is first mentioned in a letter by the Roman bishop Siricius and receives further testimony from a host of other fourth- and fifth-century authors and councils.[29] Examples of other restraints include prohibitions against the holding of public office, engagement in military service or in public commerce, and the resumption of marital relations.[30]

It is difficult to pinpoint exactly why such juridic restraints became so connected with postbaptismal penance. Perhaps they were an attempt after the Peace of Constantine to stem the tide of half-converted neophytes flooding into the Church once it became socially advantageous to be a Christian. Due to such great numbers of candidates for baptism, the institution of an extended catechumenate broke down, and the understanding of baptism shifted from being a faith commitment to a kind of eschatological insurance policy.[31] It may have been the hope of Church leaders that a more

---

28. See above, pp. 161–162. It has already been noted that similar references by Cyprian concern only those who were once clerics, having more to do with their unique penance than being intended as a general rule applicable to all penitents. See above, p. 229.

29. See Poschmann, *PAS*, p. 105, n. 180, for a listing of these later witnesses.

30. *Ibid.*, pp. 105–106. For a presentation of the early sources of such juridic restraints, see May, "Bemerkungen zu der Frage der Diffamation," pp. 254–263, who sees these imposed sanctions resulting not so much from ecclesial penance as from the sin committed (pp. 263–268). Yet the outcome remains the defamation of the penitent.

31. Dujarier, *A History of the Catechumenate*, pp. 107–109.

stringent practice of penance could make up for what was lacking in a person's preparation for Christian initiation, and so deepen his or her interior conversion.[32] But it was a misplaced hope as the restraints themselves became a key factor as to why canonical penance ceased to be an effective instrument of reconciliation in the life of the Church. They, along with the juridic law of a single penance, are the most obvious reasons why more and more people put off ecclesial penance until the end of their life. Indeed, it may even be said that the imposition of postpenitential juridic restraints helped to sound the deathknell for canonical penance.[33]

Except for the reference in Origen, there is no allusion to any imposition of sanctions upon newly reconciled penitents during the third century.[34] The process of penance ends definitively once a person is readmitted to communion. The dossier of the witnesses speaks much with silence on this point: the process predated the consequence. If, therefore, the order of penitents is harshly judged for its excessive postpenitential requirements (as it has been by later generations), the process of penance that exists during the third century must be exempt from such a valuation. Even more clearly than in the consequence of unrepeatability, the order of penitents, as it appears prior to the fourth century, could, and did, have an existence without the consequence of imposed juridic restraints upon the reconciled.

CONCLUSION

It is possible to speak of an order of penitents in the Church during the third century, though not with the same liturgical defini-

---

32. Berrouard, "Le pénitence publique," pp. 116–119.

33. Poschmann, *PAS*, p. 106, who states: "The origin of these obligations, which added such a heavy burden to penance, is to be explained by the legalistic tendency of the Roman mind. What was earlier a mere matter of counsel gradually took on the character of a rigid law, much in the same way as the rule of one penance which originally was based only on moral and psychological grounds. These excessive demands, more than anything else, were the shoals on which the system of canonical penance would inevitably be wrecked."

34. Unless, of course, one includes the restriction of a single penance in the West and in Alexandria.

tion as will be seen in the fourth century, especially with its specified rite of enrollment. Yet it is just as real, demarcated by the fundamental experience of exclusion from the Eucharist and the fact that, by the third century, a delineated process is discernible. These realities have been designated by the terms "coercive penance of isolation" and "penance of segregation," which allow one to perceive that the relationship between the sinners and God (and so the Church), as well as their status within the Church, is manifestly altered due to sin. Though such persons are distinguishable from the larger body of fully initiated Christians, they remain a part of the Church. They form a transitional *ordo*, distinctive and organized. The rites of the fourth century, particularly the rite of enrollment as a penitent, will only be an objectification of what already in some way existed.

This third-century experience of an order of penitents is further distinguished from the later discipline of canonical penance by being divorceable from the consequences of ecclesial penance: the unrepeatability of penance and the imposition of juridic restraints upon the newly reconciled. It may even be maintained that there is a certain characteristic leniency to the early practice that is lost after the fourth century.[35] Certainly the transitional character of the order was better maintained before the fourth century, at which point the imposition of these consequences made permanent the circumscribed status of penitents in the community. In any event, it is possible to speak of a process of penance as having a life apart from the stigmatizing consequences of canonical penance.

In light of this picture of an order of penitents, a picture that has emerged from the previous examination of the sources, a foundation is laid to make a clear distinction between the experience of penance during the third century and the experience of canonical penance after the Peace of Constantine. It is a genuine process, one that is not to be confused with the rigidity and harshness that followed it. Though the earlier order of penitents will be subsumed by the suffocating hold of canonical penance, and so become much

---

35. Morin, *Commentarius historicus de paenitentiae*, Book V, c. 20, finding no evidence of the juridic restraints upon the reconciled in the first three centuries, arrives at this same conclusion—just three hundred years ago!

more liturgically specified, it has a life that predates this later development. Therefore, taking as our starting point the third-century experience of an order of penitents that is distinguishable from canonical penance, it is now time to turn our attention to the second part of our working hermeneutic: On what basis might the order of penitents be restored today as a new form of the sacrament of reconciliation?

II. THE BASIS FOR THE RESTORATION OF
THE ORDER OF PENITENTS

A. Recent Discussion Concerning a Restored Order of Penitents

On October 5, 1983, Cardinal Joseph Bernardin of Chicago presented a written intervention during the international Synod of Bishops, which had as its theme: "Reconciliation and Penance in the Church's Mission."[36] In this text Cardinal Bernardin suggested that "consideration be given to a new rite of penance—not in place of those which now exist, but as a further option which has merit of its own." The "new rite" suggested is a restoration of the "order of penitents" that was "practiced in the penitential discipline of the ancient Church." It is modeled on the process of conversion developed in the Rite of Christian Initiation of Adults (RCIA), described as "a kind of microcosm of the life of conversion to which the entire Church is called," a ritual that both respects the witness of Church tradition and allows for a gradual journey of conversion for those inquiring into faith.[37] The process of the RCIA recommends itself as a suitable model upon which a new form of sacramental reconciliation might be based.

Cardinal Bernardin outlined a four-stage process, delineated by appropriate liturgical rites: the confession of sins, doing penance,

---

36. J. Bernardin, "New Rite of Penance Suggested," *Origins* 13 (1983) 324–326. His proposal was previously mentioned in the Introduction. It originated from a work-group of the North American Academy of Liturgy, which is in the process of studying a contemporary expression of the order of penitents. See J. Dallen, "Church Authority and the Sacrament of Penance: The Synod of Bishops," *Worship* 58 (1984) 194–214, p. 209.

37. Bernardin, "New Rite," pp. 324–325.

the celebration of the sacrament, and the prolongation of the sacramental experience. These stages are extended over an undetermined period of time, depending on the lived experience of the penitent. They accentuate the role of the community in the ministry of reconciliation and respect the divine initiative of grace in a person's conversion. Finally, the stages model a sacramentology that emphasizes not only the sacramental event but the process preceding it and the reflection following from it. In this way it becomes possible to relish the full experience of a sacramental encounter.[38]

The recommendation submitted by Cardinal Bernardin has received support from some recent authors, who echo his plea for a new form of the sacrament, not as a substitute for the other three forms established in the *Rite of Penance* of 1973, but in response to the need for a sacramental rite that more adequately reflects a process model of conversion.[39] This plea has also emerged from the experience of several parish communities in the United States; they are presently experimenting with a pastoral process of reconciliation that is being presented as a restored order of penitents.[40] Therefore, to raise the question about the restoration of an order of penitents is not merely an academic endeavor; it touches on the present pastoral experience of the Church. It is a timely subject, one that merits serious reflection, rooted in the historical study of the preceding chapters. As the pastoral need emerges for a rite of reconciliation that more adequately reflects the model of sacramental process, it is necessary to examine, from a historical perspective, the basis for the present restoration of an order of penitents.

---

38. Bernardin, "New Rite," pp. 325–326.

39. W. Lentzen-Deis, *Busse als Bekenntnisvollzug*, Freiburger Theologische Studien 86 (Freiburg, 1969) *passim*; J. Slattery, "Restore the Ordo Poenitentium? Some Historical Notes," *The Living Light* 20 (1984) 248–253; J. Lopresti, "RCIA and Reconciling the Alienated," *Church* 1 (1985) 11–16; Dallen, *Reconciling Community*, pp. 390–395.

40. In 1984 the North American Forum on the Catechumenate (Washington, D.C.) listed eight parishes engaged in this pastoral endeavor. Recently the subject of a restored order of penitents was included as part of a national workshop at the University of Notre Dame entitled: "Reconciliation: The Continuing Agenda," sponsored by the Notre Dame Center for Pastoral Liturgy. Also, the study of the adaptation of a restored order of penitents is the purpose of a two-year grant given to the North American Forum on the Catechumenate.

B. The Necessary Circumscription of Terms in the Discussion of a Restored Order of Penitents

The popular consciousness of the history of penance in the early Church links the practice of reconciling sinners with harsh and fanatical procedures. Indeed, the judgment of history cannot overlook the unreasonable expectations demanded of those guilty of grave postbaptismal sin by the institution of canonical penance. At the very least, these demands trapped penitents in a permanent debilitating order, making them second-class citizens of the Church; at most, they signaled the loss of the compassionate approach of Jesus, who ate and drank with sinners. If at one time canonical penance served a pastoral purpose, it did so no longer, as the lived experience of believers outgrew it. It became lifeless and had to be buried, being replaced by other expressions of penance and reconciliation that more adequately reflected the experience of sin and forgiveness in the lives of Christian people.[41]

Given the inseparable connection between the order of penitents and canonical penance from the fourth century, it is understandable that talk of a restored order of penitents would evoke a negative first reaction by modern persons. Proven by history to be incapable of responding to the pastoral needs of the Church, the discipline of canonical penance should not be resurrected by the present age, as if the mere fact of its antiquity is proof of a consummate wisdom. If canonical penance is to stay in the grave, it is reasoned, so must the order of penitents; otherwise the same forces of elitism and severity could be unleashed upon the contemporary Church. How could an institution already proven to be pastorally ineffective renew the sacrament of penance today, so that it will once again come into contact with the broken and unreconciled lives of Christian persons? Would not a restored order of penitents only serve to inflict a death-dealing blow to the ecclesial experience of sacramental reconciliation, already pushed to the margins of Christian life and worship?

---

41. Hellwig, *Sign of Reconciliation and Conversion*, pp. 41–42, who admits that the experience of conversion and the role of the community were better modeled in the ancient rite.

From the discussion in the first section of this chapter, it should be patently obvious that the present study draws a distinction between an earlier experience of a transitional order of penitents and the liturgical expression found during the fourth century. This distinction is based on the presence of the distinguishing characteristics of exclusion from the Eucharist and a clearly delineated transitional process of penitential stages. It was an experience of a transitional *ordo*, having a life independent of the constricting consequences of canonical penance. The result of this distinction is that the language used to speak of a restored order of penitents must be extremely circumscriptive, so as to avoid needless confusion and unnecessary negativity.

Let the order of penitents be restored, but let the present Church have the historical acumen to know what is being restored. It must be a transitional order, respecting the exigencies of conversion as it leads a penitent out of the marginalization resulting from sin, back to the loving embrace of Christ, sacramentally experienced in the Church. It must be an order that allows for the full participation of all the baptized in the ministry of reconciliation. Formed around the nuclei of the liturgy of the Word and the presence of clearly delineated penitential stages, it must be historically grounded in the experience of the Church in the third century. Yet it is this very fact that will give to a restored order the fluidity necessary to meet the pastoral situation of the present Church. Its transitional character will highlight the place of penitents in the life and worship of local communities without stigmatizing them by undue publicity and severity. Being in touch with the historical roots of the third-century experience of an order of penitents will both allow for the pastoral effectiveness of a restored order of penitents and act as a safeguard against future aberration.

C. The Foundations of a Restored Order of Penitents

Cardinal Bernardin's intervention at the 1983 Synod makes it obvious that a restored order of penitents is not intended to replace the present forms of sacramental reconciliation; rather, it draws attention to the fact that, in certain pastoral situations, a restored order would further enrich the celebration of the sacrament.[42] Not only would it better respect the process of conversion, but it would allow for the entire community to take up a shared ministry of reconciliation. Indeed, it is upon these two foundational principles in the experience of forgiveness that the call to restore the order of penitents is given impetus.[43]

1. THE EXIGENCIES OF CONVERSION

There is no definition or approach that can encompass all aspects of the experience of conversion.[44] At its most fundamental level, it has been described by one contemporary author as

> the successful negotiation of crisis or change . . . a form of "passage" or "transition" whereby a person may pass through a new lease on life and enter into a new set of relationships with himself, the world around him, and with life itself.[45]

Moments of crisis or change are occasioned either by a particular trial in a person's life or perhaps by a general unsettledness with one's present life situation. These are invitatory moments, to which a person is free to respond or not. Response leads one out of the security of one's created world with all its accepted values and relationships toward what is a less sure, yet a new level of, existence. It involves a movement through specific experiences: the crisis itself, a transitional period during which the experience of crisis is given meaning, and finally surrender to a truth beyond one's own making, a truth of what is "really real," the Truth of a transcen-

---

42. Indeed, the very recognition by the Church that several forms of the sacrament can exist makes it conceivable that a fourth form might eventually be admitted, especially in the face of sound historical reflection and serious pastoral need. In addition, there is nothing in the present forms that prohibits the restoration of an order of penitents.

43. This is not to imply that the present forms of the rite are totally inadequate in this regard. In many cases a more compressed and individualized experience of the conversion process is sufficient. However, there are other cases where the present rite falls short. See below, pp. 262–263. For an appreciation of the benefits and deficiencies of the present forms, see Dallen, *Reconciling Community*, pp. 367ff.

44. For an appreciation of the many sides from which the experience of conversion can be addressed, see W. Conn (ed.), *Conversion: Perspectives on Personal and Social Transformation* (New York, 1978).

45. M. Searle, "The Journey of Conversion," *Worship* 54 (1980) 35–55, p. 36.

dent God. Translated into Christian terms, conversion is initiated by the divine initiative of the indwelling Spirit. It is the Spirit who invites the person to the response of grace through historical events, an invitation that one is free to embrace or reject. Embracing the invitation leads one toward a closer relationship with Jesus as one enters more deeply into his paschal mystery. It is a willingness to die to self-security in order to "have life, and have it to the full" (Jn 10:10).[46]

Conversion, then, is an ongoing experience, a process that involves an extended temporal period. Time is necessary to the whole experience, in order that a person might be able to experience, interpret, and celebrate the entire transition from crisis or change (death) to a new level of existence (life).[47] It is a process that occurs in stages, so that the entire movement of conversion is imaged as a journey. It does not happen in a single moment nor only once in a person's life.

If the sacraments are to touch the lived experience of believing persons, then the experience of the conversion journey must be expressed by Christian signs and ritual. Sacraments can celebrate the passages in a person's life, enabling one who is experiencing the sometimes unintelligible and terrifying journey of conversion to encounter the paschal mystery of Jesus. Just as with conversion, sacramental experiences lead one from a time of crisis, through a period of transition when a new meaning is assimilated, and finally to the moment of celebration of a new existence.[48] In short, sacraments are experiences of dying and rising to new life. This sacramental process is a model for all the Christian sacraments and is most evident in the RCIA. The journey toward full Christian initiation is marked by stages that respect the exigencies of conversion. The

---

46. Searle, "Journey of Conversion," pp. 36–45.

47. W. Freburger, "Ongoing Conversion—A Process," in *The New Rite of Penance, Background Catechesis*, Federation of Diocesan Liturgical Commissions (Pevely, Mo., 1974), pp. 16–22.

48. Searle, "Journey of Conversion," pp. 45–49. Searle utilizes the work of the anthropologist Arnold van Gennep, *The Rites of Passage* (Chicago, Ill., 1960), who identifies three stages in the structure of ritual: *separation* from an existing state of affairs, a *liminal* or in-between period necessary for transition, and *aggregation* to a new state.

RCIA allows for an adequate temporal duration, during which persons seeking faith have the time to reflect on the experience of crisis or change, interpret their life story through the Christian story, and celebrate moments of passage along the entire journey of their faith development.[49]

However, when one attempts to locate this sacramental process, reflective of the conversion journey, within the structure of the present forms of sacramental penance and reconciliation, a certain disparity emerges. Unquestionably, the revised *Rite of Penance* gives emphasis to the continual task of conversion to which the people of God are called (nos. 3,4,6). Unlike the experience of penance following upon the Counter-Reformation, which overemphasized the juridical efficaciousness of priestly absolution, the present rite insists that sacramental absolution is the completion of the process of the "inner conversion" of heart (no. 6). Contrition and forgiveness must first be experienced by the penitent before they can be celebrated by the liturgy.[50] But it is exactly at this point that the disparity appears. The rites provide only for the end of the process, the celebration of sacramental reconciliation, without giving adequate liturgical recognition and support to the process that precedes, and follows from, the celebration. The revised forms compress the process of conversion into a single historical moment rather than allowing for the temporal extension of the ritual that would better reflect the exigencies of conversion.[51]

This leads to the heart of this discussion on conversion as being one of the foundation stones of a restored order of penitents. A restored order of penitents would allow for the span of time necessary for the entire journey of conversion. It would respect the fact

---

49. T. Guzie, *The Book of Sacramental Basics* (New York, 1981), pp. 79–80. Guzie observes that the celebration of sacraments is bound up with consciousness. Sacraments do not make present something that was absent but celebrate something that one is now conscious of through a process of conversion, namely, the abiding and loving presence of God. On this basis he presents his plea for a sacramental process in the celebration of all the sacraments. For other reflections on the process of conversion in the RCIA, see R. Duggan (ed.), *Conversion and the Catechumenate* (New York, 1984).

50. Guzie, *Sacramental Basics*, pp. 19–20, 87–88.

51. Dallen, "Church Authority," pp. 211–213; *Reconciling Community*, p. 255.

that the movement away from patterns of serious postbaptismal sin is not overcome in a single experience but requires the gentle progression of time. The passage from crisis and change, through the transition period of interpretation, when one's personal story is linked with the Christian story, to the celebration of a new level of relationship with Christ and the Church—all find expression in the delineated process of the order of penitents. Therefore, based on the exigencies of the conversion process, there are historical, liturgical, and pastoral reasons for the restoration of the order of penitents.

a) *From the historical perspective*

A restored order of penitents would historically recall the experience of the early Christians, who took seriously the relational effects of sin and the hard work of repentance and conversion. Exclusion from the Eucharist, as expressed in both the coercive penance of isolation and the penance of segregation, recognizes the fundamental connection between approaching the table of the Lord and one's willingness to enter into the paschal mystery of Jesus Christ. Christian life and worship are a constant movement from death to life. Dying to sin requires that one realize, through coercive isolation, the stark reality of a life isolated from God. This is the crisis that leads persons to confess their sin and undertake adequate works of penance. This begins a time of segregation within the community, a period of transition during which penitents reinterpret their lives through the Christian message of forgiveness. Finally, the process of conversion is completed when the person is readmitted to the Eucharist, a sign that the penitent has passed to a new level of relationship with Christ and the Church. The local third-century churches, through an order of penitents, respected the cycle of the conversion process: crisis, a period of transition, entering a new level of existence. The reconciliation of the penitent is a rite of passage into the dying and rising of Jesus.

Further, as seen in the early sources, there is a historical connection between the two transitional orders in the third century: the catechumenate and the order of penitents. It was during this period that a flourishing catechumenate existed alongside an order of penitents, one that still maintained its transitional character. Indeed, it was only when the catechumenate began to fade from the life and worship of the Church during the fourth and fifth centuries that the order of penitents also lost its pastoral vigor, becoming entwined in the death-grip of canonical penance and suspending persons in a permanent inferior class.

As mentioned earlier, the present restored catechumenate is beginning to have more and more impact on the life of the Church, moving the Christian initiation of adults away from a short-term catechetical experience toward a process-centered model of conversion. In this light, the historical moment has again arrived for a restored order of penitents to image the transitional process of the catechumenate and to move away from a short-term juridical experience of forgiveness. In specific cases where baptized persons are seeking to respond to the crisis of sin and fragmentation in their lives, a restored order of penitents, like the restored order of the catechumenate, must respect the exigencies of conversion.[52]

b) *From the liturgical perspective*

A restored order of penitents would liturgically provide for the development of rites of passage celebrating the entire process of a penitent's conversion rather than just the climaxing event of sacramental absolution. These rites would give ritual expression to the altered relationship existing between the penitent and the Church, and his or her different status within the community. At the same time, they would strengthen the penitent during the difficult journey of conversion. Liturgical rites would clearly delineate the stages of an order of penitents, marking the entire movement from crisis, through the period of transition, and leading to the celebration of a new level of relationship. In this sense, the process itself becomes as necessary as its end result, a sign of the Church's recognition that a genuine experience of conversion is not to be expected in a single sacramental moment.[53]

---

52. For an example of how a process-centered order of penitents might be comparable to the initiation process of the RCIA, see the Appendix following this chapter.

53. Lopresti, ''RCIA,'' pp. 14–15, who suggests liturgical moments of passage for the ''truly alienated'' based on the conversion process and paralleling the rites of the RCIA.

c) *From the pastoral perspective*

A restored order of penitents would pastorally reflect a caring stance toward those who have experienced fragmentation and alienation in their lives. Particular cases come to mind where a restored order would be pastorally effective. A primary example is the situation of those who, having drifted apart from the Church, experience a crisis or malaise that leads them to reflect on the direction of their life and on the need for a renewed ecclesial expression of their faith. Their own sense of isolation and alienation may be so strong that a gradual process of care and personal healing is necessary before a meaningful experience of sacramental reconciliation can be celebrated.

Other examples might be those who have significantly altered previous life commitments, such as those divorced and remarried outside the Church, or resigned priests. These "more delicate issues" are given special attention by Pope John Paul II in his postsynodal exhortation *Reconciliatio et Paenitentia*.[54] Such persons may sense a need to explore more deeply the pain of their past within an ecclesial setting in order to move toward a new sense of personal integration. A restored order of penitents would provide the setting for such a time of transition and would also be a sign of the Church's willingness to embrace even those who find themselves in juridically irregular situations.

Finally, there may be the situation of active members of Christian communities who, for whatever reason, sense a deep need to deal with the guilt and pain resulting from traumatic experiences in the past, such as wartime actions, unfaithfulness to one's marital or religious commitments, or abortion. A restored order of penitents would better reflect what has been learned through the work of other

---

54. *Reconciliatio et Paenitentia: Postsynodal Apostolic Exhortation*, December 2, 1984 (English translation by the United States Catholic Conference, Washington, D.C., 1984), pp. 134–136. Unfortunately, Pope John Paul II does not allow for the possibility of sacramental reconciliation in these cases, inasmuch as such persons "are not at the present moment in the objective conditions required by the Sacrament of Penance." However, if the sacrament of penance is to be pastorally effective and touch the lived experience of hurting people today, the real question is whether it can enable genuine conversion and not simply be maintained in its former juridic structure.

disciplines, especially the findings of psychology and sociology. Deep personal scars need a climate of trust, gentle personal interaction, and time to be healed.[55] If the sacramental process allows for this, then the moment of sacramental reconciliation will more truly reflect the movement of divine grace and peace in a person's life.

In all the cases cited, a restored order of penitents would provide a process through which penitents are led on the gradual journey back toward wholeness and integration. To avoid stigmatizing publicity, a strong "conversion catechesis" would have to be undertaken in the local communities so that members of the Church would better understand the process of conversion, and be empowered to support the penitents on their journey. The whole community would need to recognize that no one is free from the relational effects of sin; therefore, the experience of the penitents is, to some degree, the experience of the whole Church. This awareness would free penitents from being caught by an ecclesial consciousness that would look upon them as second-class citizens and allow for the process to be truly transitional, respective of their conversion. A restored order of penitents, though appropriate in only certain pastoral situations, could be a factor in the renewal of the entire experience of sacramental reconciliation. It could well effect a shift from sacramental reconciliation being perceived solely as a juridical obligation to becoming a genuine experience of conversion that gives meaning to, and celebrates, the lived encounters of believing persons.

2. THE ROLE OF THE COMMUNITY

The previous discussion concerning the "conversion catechesis" of the entire Church brings us into contact with the second principle of reconciliation upon which a case for the restoration of an order of penitents is built: the role of the community. In actuality, the presence of the community cannot be separated from the experience of conversion. Only within the context of relationship can one successfully negotiate the crises or changes in life, leading one

---

55. One need only look at the success of the numerous "twelve step" groups who recognize the absolute need for process if persons are to be liberated from a controlling dependency in their lives.

to personal growth and deeper contact with transcendent reality. Conversion and community are separated here only for the sake of presentation, in order to specify how a restored order of penitents might amply reflect these two foundational principles in the experience of healing and reconciliation.

The *Rite of Penance* stresses the role of the community in the ministry of reconciliation:

> The whole Church, as a priestly people, acts in different ways in the work of reconciliation that has been entrusted to it by the Lord. Not only does the Church call sinners to repentance by preaching the word of God, but it also intercedes for them and helps penitents with a maternal care and solicitude to acknowledge and confess their sins and to obtain the mercy of God, who alone can forgive sins (no. 8).[56]

This emphasis on the community in the reconciliation process is a far cry from the Counter-Reformation stress on the central role of the bishop/priest in the Church's penitential discipline. In the renewed rite, while the bishop/priest continues to have a key role in the ministry to penitents, his ministry is to be enhanced by the ministry of the community. Of particular importance is the intercession of the Church to aid the penitents in undertaking the difficult journey of repentance and conversion.

One concrete result of this new emphasis on the role of the community has been the popularity of communal penance services, usually celebrated under the second form of the rite.[57] These services highlight the reality that no person in the community is ex-

---

56. Since the promulgation of the new *Rite of Penance*, a plethora of publications have appeared on the role of the community in the process of reconciliation. See the copious bibliography in T. Fleming, *The Second Vatican Council's Teaching on the Sacrament of Penance and the Communal Nature of the Sacrament*, published dissertation, The Pontifical University of St. Thomas Aquinas (Rome, 1981), pp. 199ff. Two references of note omitted by Fleming include G. Pinckers, "Le rôle de la communauté dans le sacrement de pénitence," *PeL* 5 (1973) 419–426; B. Scienczak, *Partecipazione dei fedeli al sacramento della penitenza. Il contributo della Chiesa del periodo dei Padri nel contesto dell'attuale riforma penitenziale*, published doctoral dissertation excerpt, Pontifical Gregorian University (Rome, 1974).

57. Dallen, *Reconciling Community*, pp. 374ff., makes the point that though canonically restricted, the third form of the rite (communal confession and absolution) is the only fully communal form.

empt from the experience of sin. The Church is a Church of sinners, who rely on the mercy of God for forgiveness. In the same way, sacramental reconciliation is not just a sign of God's forgiveness of the sinner; it also "entails reconciliation with our brothers and sisters who remain harmed by our sins" (*Rite of Penance*, no. 5). Communal services of penance remind the assembly that just as there is a commonality of sinfulness among them, so also a new bond of reconciliation is established through the celebration of the sacrament.

However, these penitential celebrations of the sacrament do not fully express the reconciling ministry of the community, provided for by the rite itself. They tend only to give emphasis to the common link of sinfulness. The role of the community, interceding for sinners and leading them to repentance, is minimized in the structure of the celebration.[58] Also, the ministry of the bishop/priest continues to take center stage. This is especially evident in the retention of the "indicative" formula of absolution, as opposed to the more historically attested "deprecative" formula. The latter would de-emphasize the singular "power" of the clergy, thus accentuating the participation of the whole Church in the reconciliation of the sinner.[59] The resultant picture of the community is one of passivity rather than active ministerial function. The new rite, for all its accentuation on the role of the community in reconciliation, lacks appropriate forms that respect and enhance this role.

This leads us back to the discussion concerning the restoration of an order of penitents. A restored order of penitents would allow the community to claim the ministry of reconciliation to which they are rightfully called by the new rite itself. The celebration of the sacrament would involve a multiplicity of ministerial roles to the penitents, including, but not exclusively, the ministry of the bishop/

---

58. Though Vatican Council II specifically calls for the Church to intercede on behalf of sinners (*Sacrosanctum Concilium*, no. 109).

59. G. Diekmann, "Reconciliation Through the Prayer of the Community," in N. Mitchell (ed.), *The Rite of Penance. Commentaries*, Vol. 3: *Background and Directions* (Washington, D.C., 1978) 38–49, p. 48, who indicates that though there were strong supporters of the deprecatory formula during the process of the revision of the rite, the indicative formula was retained. A more detailed explanation of how the debate over the absolution formula figured in the whole process of the rite's revision is provided by Dallen, *Reconciling Community*, pp. 209–215.

priest. While the "indicative" formula of absolution could still be retained, the intercessory prayer of the community would have an equally prominent place in a restored discipline. Therefore, based on the community's role in the process of sacramental reconciliation, there are historical, liturgical, and pastoral reasons in favor of the restoration of an order of penitents.

a) From the historical perspective

A restored order of penitents would recall a pivotal belief and practice of the local churches during the first three centuries: all members of Christ's Body are called to be reconcilers. In the New Testament and postapostolic writings, the practice of fraternal correction was the normative way of handling the situation of serious sin within the community. As the communities grew and ecclesial offices developed, those charged with leadership in the communities assumed a more direct and central role in the ministry to grave postbaptismal sinners, but never to the exclusion of the rest of the community. It was the community, in conjunction with the ministry of the bishop, that cared for penitents during the time of their isolation and/or segregation, exhorting them to be faithful to penance and guiding them through their prayer.

In the East, the tradition of the penitents' submitting their sins to "someone of God," chosen because of holiness of life rather than the possession of an ecclesial office, was an example of lay persons in the community exercising a direct ministry to postbaptismal sinners. In the West, it was only with Cyprian that the absolute priority of the bishop's authority over the ecclesial penitential discipline clearly emerged. Before him, confessors and martyrs played a more prominent role in the reconciliation of penitents. Even Cyprian himself, in the tradition of other early authors, witnessed to the necessity of having to secure the agreement of the community before a penitent was admitted to penance and later readmitted to the Eucharist.[60]

---

60. Diekmann, "Reconciliation Through the Prayer of the Community," pp. 43–48, recalls that even the great Latin Fathers of the fourth century—Ambrose, Jerome, and especially Augustine—witness to the role of the community in the decision to readmit penitents to the Eucharist.

The early writings are also unanimous in their testimony to the intercessory prayer uttered on the behalf of penitents by the entire community. Penitents are pictured as beseeching the community to pray for them, an action often accompanied by sighs and tears. This not only manifested the intensity of the sinner's sorrow but demonstrated how important the prayer of the community was to the successful completion of the penitential process. It was their prayer, uttered in conjunction with the prayer of the bishop, that was efficacious in the reconciliation of the penitent.[61] One could not exist without the other. The community always acted and prayed alongside those who, by virtue of their office, had a mandate to minister to penitents.

A restored order of penitents would confirm that the historical moment has arrived to rediscover the reconciling ministry of all Christians, carried out in conjunction with, rather than subordination to, the ministry of bishops and priests. The present model of the sacrament of reconciliation would gradually be informed and transformed by a new, truly communal model of all members of the Church sharing in the one ministry of sacramental reconciliation.[62] It is a sharing that would be expressed not only theologically but structurally, allowed for by the rite itself. The reconciling ministry of all baptized persons to those seeking sacramental forgiveness would be joined by the distinctive ministry of the bishop/priest. The absolving prayer of the whole Church would be joined harmoniously with the prayer of absolution uttered by the bishop/priest. Thus the historical roots of a restored order of penitents would help the Church rediscover the fullness of its sacramental sign of reconciliation.[63]

---

61. It is Tertullian who first gives explicit stress to the efficaciousness of the prayer of the whole Church. The Church's prayer is heard by the Father because it is necessarily joined to the prayer of Christ, her spouse (*De paen.* 10.6; *De pud.* 1,8). See above p. 45, n. 137; p. 191, nn. 64 and 66.

62. J. Lescrauwaet, "Kerkelijke Zondenvergeving in de Historie," in N. Tromp, J. Lescrauwaet, A. Scheer, *Geroepen tot vrede: over zonde en vergeving,* Van exegese tot verkondiging 13 (Boxtel, 1973), p. 57, makes the point that for all the liabilities of the ancient discipline of penance, the reconciling role of the entire community continued to be a central feature.

63. Diekmann, "Reconciliation Through the Prayer of the Community," p. 49; Dallen, *Reconciling Ministry,* pp. 300–304.

b) *From the liturgical perspective*

A restored order of penitents would lead to the development of appropriate liturgical rituals that would enable the assembly to assume its proper role in the reconciling ministry to penitents. Above all, the season of Lent, with its penitential themes expressed in the Scriptures and the ritual prayers, would serve as the most suitable period in the liturgical formation of the penitents. Especially during this season the entire community would support the penitents through designated liturgical action. Penitents might be enrolled during the Ash Wednesday celebration, after having made a prior personal confession. Throughout the Lenten season, as they are engaged in penitential works, they would be prayed over and dismissed (along with the catechumens) after the liturgy of the Word. During one of the liturgies of Holy Week (the Liturgy of the Lord's Supper on Holy Thursday seems most appropriate), and prior to the Easter Vigil, penitents would have the hand of the bishop/priest laid upon them in the celebration of sacramental absolution. This would be followed by readmission to the Eucharist.[64] Such liturgical rites would allow for the intercessory prayer of the community throughout the entire process of reconciliation, strengthening the penitents throughout the journey of conversion.

c) *From the pastoral perspective*

A restored order of penitents would pastorally involve the community in a variety of ministries which, taken together, would form a complete picture of the Church's care for the penitent. Using the process provided by the "Rite of Reconciliation for Individual Penitents" (*Rite of Penance*, nos. 15–20), members of the community, including the priest, root their ministry to penitents always within the context of personal prayer (no. 15). It is here that they humbly realize their own sinfulness, which allows them to stand in solidarity with those to whom they will minister. Certain persons in the com-

---

64. The enrollment of penitents on Ash Wednesday and their reconciliation on Holy Thursday are liturgical practices found in the eighth-century Gelasian Sacramentary, but most likely reflect the practice in Rome by the fifth century. See J. Jungmann, *Die Lateinischen Bussriten*, pp. 5–44; A. Chavasse, *Le sacramentaire Gélasien*, BTh 4, Histoire de la théologie 1 (Tournai, 1957), pp. 147–153.

munity would have the task of welcoming the penitent, especially if such a one has been away from the Church for a long time (no. 16). 'Welcoming'' could extend over weeks and months, assuring the penitents of the commitment by the community to listen to and share the burden of their pain and to walk along with them during the conversion journey.

Members of the assembly would be ministers of the Word, allowing the Scriptures themselves to re-form the penitents (no. 17). Breaking open the Word for the penitents would prepare their hearts for the event of their sacramental reconciliation and readmission to the breaking of the bread. Ministry of the Word would involve catechesis, aiding penitents to find expression of their personal story within the Christian story. Throughout the time of their penance, penitents would be encouraged and supported by the prayer of the entire assembly (no. 18). Besides the unique ministry of the bishop/priest, the support of the Church would be expressed through a variety of ministries that would emerge throughout the entire process: counselors, sponsors, mentors, catechists, and spiritual directors, to name a few. It would be this multiplicity of ministerial responsibilities that would give flesh to the statement previously cited from the *Rite of Penance*: ''The whole Church, as a priestly people, acts in different ways in the work of reconciliation which has been entrusted to it by the Lord.''[65]

CONCLUSION

Recent discussion has raised the possibility of the restoration of the ancient order of penitents as a fourth form of the present *Rite of Penance*, based on the necessity of specific pastoral situations. Parish communities are now beginning to experiment with a restored order, one having an analogous structure to the sacramental process modeled in the RCIA. This makes the present investigation of the historical roots of the order of penitents imperative, so as to enable parish communities to discern what exactly is being restored. It must be made absolutely evident that canonical penance is not

---

65. Lopresti, ''RCIA'', pp. 15–16.

being resurrected from the grave. The order of penitents connected with this institution was no longer a transitional order but one that trapped penitents in a permanent second-class ecclesial status. No, the order of penitents to be restored today has its historical roots in the third century, free from stigmatizing snares of canonical penance (as seen in the first section of the chapter). As such, it remains a truly transitional order, with enough fluidity for pastoral adaptation yet grounded in historical tradition.

The foundation for the restoration of the order of penitents rests on the fact that it respects and enhances the two basic principles of a genuine sacramental experience of reconciliation: the exigencies of conversion and the reconciling ministry of the community. A restored order would offer a process through which a penitent would be able to negotiate the journey of conversion, moving from crisis or change, to a time of transition, when one's personal story is linked with the Christian story, to the celebration of a new existence. In short, it would enable a person to enter into the dying and rising of Jesus. This is seen in the historical experience of the early Church (seen in the previous chapters), in the liturgical rites that would clearly delineate stages throughout the entire process, and in the specific pastoral situations that would make a restored order of penitents an effective instrument of healing and integration.

A restored order of penitents would also transform sacramental reconciliation from being a juridic action solely within the domain of the clergy to being an experience in which the whole community exercises its rightful call to be ministers of reconciliation. This is seen in the historical experience of the early Church, where the intercession of the entire assembly on behalf of the penitent is of equal efficacious effect as the prayer uttered by the bishop. It would be seen in the development of liturgical rites that would allow for the intercession of the Church throughout the entire process of sacramental reconciliation. And it would be clearly evident in the variety of ministries that would evolve to care for the penitent during the journey toward forgiveness. The prayer and ministry of the entire Church would not replace the distinct ministry of the bishop/priest in the sacramental process but would join with it, through a multiplicity of ministerial roles, to enhance the sacramental experience of reconciliation.

CHAPTER SUMMARY

A crucial lesson to be learned from the history of ecclesial penance is that the lived experience of believing persons, rather than traditional structures, allows one to answer the question: Is the Church's sacramental practice of penance and reconciliation pastorally effective? The structures of penance are secondary to the fundamental experiences of conversion and reconciliation. When the structures fail to be flexible enough to enable these experiences, they must be renewed by more adaptable and suitable forms. The situation of accepted penitential practice not adequately touching the pastoral needs of people is a familiar one, intermittently appearing throughout the history of penance. It is nowhere more clearly perceived than in the fate of canonical penance. Once it was no longer connected with the lived reality, it became hollow, an empty practice that was replaced by more pastorally effective penitential forms. The movement from crisis to new institutional forms of penance, which has framed the Church's practice throughout the centuries, allows accepted ecclesial structures to be instruments through which the abiding offer of the Lord's forgiveness is experienced amid the broken and fragmented lives of God's people.

The sacramental experience of penance is once again at a critical juncture. If the practice of sacramental reconciliation is in the midst of crisis today, as is claimed, it is a crisis inviting the Church to once again examine the effectiveness of its penitential discipline. The experience of the past must inform the present and transform the future. That has been the motivation of this study: to bring to light the wisdom of the Church's tradition in order to enable it to speak to the situation of the Church today. The moment has come for the restoration of the order of penitents. Nothing less than the pastoral effectiveness of sacramental reconciliation is at stake. The ritual modeling of the conversion process by a restored order of penitents would be a positive movement toward the conversion of the sacramental practice itself. The historical roots have been uncovered, the future pastoral possibilities underscored. The restoration of the order of penitents stands at the brink of the present realizable moment.

APPENDIX

A Comparison of the Process of Christian Initiation Modeled in the RCIA With a Suggested Process of Sacramental Reconciliation Modeled in a "Restored" Order of Penitents

	RCIA	EXPERIENTIAL PROCESS	ORDER OF PENITENTS	
1st Period	Precatechumenate/ Inquiry	Crisis Event/Situation of Change		
Stage I	Rite of Becoming a Catechumen	Personal Story Questions of Meaning	Evangelization Welcoming Confession of Sin	1st Period
2nd Period	Catechumenate		Rite of Becoming a Penitent	Stage I
Stage II	Rite of Election	Linking Personal Story with Christian Story	Lenten Conversion and Penance	2nd Period
3rd Period	Enlightenment/ Illumination	Deepening in Faith	Rite of Reconciliation	Stage II
Stage III	Baptism/Confirmation/ Eucharist	New Level of Conversion and Personal Integration Growth in the Sacramental Life	Postreconciliatory Reflection	3rd Period
4th Period	Mystagogia	Entry into Active Ministry		

BIBLIOGRAPHY

I. PRIMARY SOURCES

A. LEXICA

Lampe, G. (ed.), *A Patristic Greek Lexicon*, Oxford, 1961
Lewis, C., and Short, C. (eds.), *A Latin Dictionary*, Oxford, 1879.
Liddell, H., and Scott, R. (eds.), *A Greek-English Lexicon*, 9th ed., Oxford, 1968.
Moulton, H., and Holly, D. (eds.), *The Analytical Greek Lexicon*, London, 1977.

B. TEXT EDITIONS

*(Text editions that include a translation and/or commentary
are marked with an asterisk.)*

Postapostolic Writers

Audet, J., *La Didachè. Instructions des Apôtres*, Paris, 1958.*
Bihlmeyer, K., *Die Apostolischen Väter. Bd. I*, Tübingen, 1924; 2nd. ed., 1956.
Camelot, P., *Ignace d'Antioche, Polycarpe de Smyrne: Lettres, Martyre de Polycarpe* (SC 10), Paris, 1969.*
Fischer, J., *Die Apostolischen Väter*, Darmstadt, 1956; 2nd ed., 1970.*
Guerrier, L., and Grébaut, S., *Le Testament en Galilée de Notre-Seigneur Jésus Christ* (PO 9), Paris, 1913.*
Jaubert, A., *Clément de Rome. Epître aux Corinthiens* (SC 167), Paris, 1971.*
Prigent, P., and Kraft, R., *Epître de Barnabé* (SC 172), Paris, 1971.*
Rordorf, W., and Tuilier, A., *La doctrine des douze Apôtres (Didachè)*—(SC 248), Paris, 1978.*
Schmidt, C., and Wajnberg, I., *Gespräche Jesu mit seiner Jüngern nach der Auferstehung* (TU 43), Leipzig, 1919.*

274

The *Shepherd of Hermas*

Joly, R., *Hermas le Pasteur* (SC 53 bis), 2nd ed., Paris, 1968.*
Whittaker, M., *Die Apostolischen Väter I. Der Hirt des Hermas* (GCS 48), Berlin, 1956; 2nd ed., 1967.

Irenaeus of Lyon

Rousseau, A., et al., *Irénée de Lyon. Contre les Hérésies, Book IV* (SC 100), Paris, 1965.*
————, Doutreleau, L., and Mercier, C., *Irénée de Lyon. Contre les Hérésies, Book V* (SC 152-153), Paris, 1969.*
————, and Doutreleau, L., *Irénée de Lyon. Contre les Hérésies, Book III* (SC 210-211), Paris, 1974.*
————, *Irénée de Lyon. Contre les Hérésies, Book I* (SC 263-264), Paris, 1979.*

The *Ecclesiastical History* of Eusebius of Caesarea

Bardy, G., *Eusèbe de Césarée. Histoire ecclésiastique, Livres I-VII* (SC 31, 41), Paris, 1952, 1955.*

The *Didascalia Apostolorum*

Achelis, H., and Flemming, J., *Die syrische Didaskalia* (TU 25), Leipzig, 1904.*
Tinder, E., *Didascaliae apostolorum, Canonum ecclesiasticorum, Traditionis apostolicae versiones latinae* (TU 75), Berlin, 1963.
Vööbus, A., *The Didascalia Apostolorum in Syriac with Translation* (CSCO 401-402 407-408), Louvain, 1979.*

Gregory Thaumaturgus

Phouskas, M., "Gregoriou Thaumatourgou he kanonike epistole. Eisagoge-kritike ekdosis keimenou-metaphrase-scholia," *Ekklesiastikos pharos* 60 (1978) 736-809.

Methodius of Olympus

Bonwetsch, G., *Methodius (GCS 27)*, Leipzig, 1917.

Clement of Alexandria

Stählin, O., *Clemens Alexandrinus. Stromata Buch I-VI* (GCS 15), Leipzig, 1906; 3rd ed., L. Früchtel (ed.), Berlin, 1960.
————, *Clemens Alexandrinus. Stromata Buch VII-VIII. Eclogae propheticae—Quis dives salvetur—Fragmente* (GCS 17), Leipzig, 1909; 3rd ed., L. Früchtel (ed.), Berlin, 1970.
————, *Clemens Alexandrinus. Paedagogus* (GCS 12), Leipzig, 1909; 3rd ed., U. Treu (ed.), Berlin, 1972.

Origen

Baehrens, W., *Homilien zu Samuel I, zum Hohenlied und zu den Propheten, Kommentar zum Hohenlied in Rufins und Hieronymus' Übersetzung* (GCS 33), Leipzig, 1925.

_____, *Homilien zum Hexateuch in Rufins Übersetzung* (GCS 30), Leipzig, 1921.

Blanc, C., *Commentaire sur Saint Jean* (SC 157), Paris, 1970; (SC 290), 1982.*

Borret, M., *Contre Celse* (SC 136), Paris, 1968; (SC 147), 1969.*

_____, *Homélies sur le Lévitique* (SC 286, 287), Paris, 1981.*

_____, *Homélies sur l'Exode* (SC 321), Paris, 1985.*

Jaubert, A., *Homélies sur Josué* (SC 71), Paris, 1960.*

Klostermann, E., *Jeremiahomilien; Klageliederkommentar; Erklärung der Samuel-und Königsbücher* (GCS 6), Leipzig, 1906; 2nd ed., P. Nautin (GCS 6/2), 1983.

_____, and Benz, E., *Origenes Matthäuserklärung I; Die griechisch erhaltenen Tomoi* (GCS 40), Leipzig, 1935.

_____, *Origenes Matthäuserklärung II; Die lateinische Übersetzung der commentariorum Series* (GCS 38), Leipzig, 1933; 2nd ed., U. Treu (GCS 38/2), 1976.

Koetschau, P., *Buch V-VIII Gegen Celsus; Die Schrift vom Gebet (GCS 3)*, Leipzig, 1899.

_____, *De principiis* (GCS 22), Leipzig, 1913.

_____, *Die Schrift vom Martyrium; Buch I-IV Gegen Celsus (GCS 2)*, Leipzig, 1899.

Migne, J.-P., *Adnotationes in Librum I Regum* (PG 17), Paris, 1857.

_____, *Selecta in Psalmos* (PG 12), Paris, 1862.

Nautin, P., *Homélies sur Jérémie* (SC 238), Paris, 1977.

Rauer, M., *Die Homilien zu Lukas in der Übersetzung des Hieronymus und die griechischen Reste der Homilien und des Lukas-Kommentars* (GCS 49), Leipzig, 1959.

Dionysius of Alexandria

Pitra, J., *Iuris ecclesiastici graecorum historia et monumenta*. Vol. I. *A primo p.c.n. ad VI saeculum*, Rome, 1864.

Hippolytus

Bonwetsch, G., and Achelis, H., *Hippolytus Werke*. Vol. I. *Exegetische und Homiletische Schriften* (GCS 1), Leipzig, 1897.

Botte, B., *Hippolyte de Rome. La Tradition Apostolique d' après les anciennes versions* (SC 11 bis), Paris, 1968.*

Marcovich, M., *Hippolytus. Refutatio Omnium Haeresium* (PTS 25), Berlin 1986.

Novatian

Diercks, G., *Novatian. Opera* (CCL 4), Turnhout, 1972.

Tertullian

Bulhart, V., and Borleffs, P., *De paenitentia*, in *Tertulliani Opera*. Vol. IV (CSEL 76), Vienna, 1957, pp. 127-170.

Dekkers, E., *Ad Martyres* and *Apologeticum*, in *Tertulliani Opera*. Vol. I: *Opera Catholica, Adversus Marcionem* (CCL 1), Turnhout, 1954, pp. 3-8; 85-171.

_____, *De pudicitia*, in *Tertulliani Opera*. Vol. II: *Opera Montanistica* (CCL 2), Turnhout, 1954, pp. 1279-1330.

Munier, C., *Tertullien. La pénitence* (SC 316), Paris, 1984.*

Cyprian of Carthage

Bayard, C., *Saint Cyprien. Correspondance.* 2 vols., Paris, 1925.*

Bévenot, M., *De lapsis* and *De ecclesiae catholicae unitate*, in *Sancti Cypriani Episcopi Opera* (CCL 3), Turnhout, 1972, pp. 221-242.

C. TRANSLATIONS AND COMMENTARIES

(Translations in the text have been made by the author unless otherwise cited.)

Postapostolic Writers, The *Shepherd of Hermas*, and Irenaeus of Lyon

Coxe, A. (ed.), *The Apostolic Fathers with Justin Martyr and Irenaeus* (ANF 1), Edinburgh, 1885; reprint, Grand Rapids, Michigan, 1979.

Crombie, F., *The Pastor of Hermas* (ANF 2), Edinburgh, 1885; reprint, Grand Rapids, Michigan, 1979, pp. 3-58.

Dibelius, M., *Der Hirt des Hermas*, Tübingen, 1925.

Glimm, F., Marique, J. and Walsh, G., *The Apostolic Fathers* (FC 1), Washington, D.C., 1947; 4th ed., 1969.

Goodspeed, E., *The Apostolic Fathers. An American Translation*, London, 1950.

Kleinst, J., *The Epistles of St. Clement of Rome and St. Ignatius of Antioch* (ACW 1), Westminster, Maryland, 1946.

_____, *The Didache, The Epistle of Barnabas, The Epistles and The Martyrdom of St. Polycarp, The Fragments of Papias, The Epistle to Diognetus* (ACW 6), Westminster, Maryland, 1948.

Richardson, C., et al., *Early Christian Fathers* (The Library of Christian Classics 1), London, 1953.

Schoedel, W., *Ignatius of Antioch* (Hermeneia), Philadelphia, 1985.

The *Ecclesiastical History* of Eusebius of Caesarea

Deferrari, R., *Eusebius Pamphili. Ecclesiastical History. Books I-V* (FC 19), Washington, D.C., 1965.

McGiffert, A., *Eusebius* (Nicene and Post-Nicene Fathers, 1), New York, 1890; reprint, Grand Rapids, Michigan, 1979.

The *Didascalia Apostolorum*

Connolly, R., *Didascalia Apostolorum. The Syriac Version Translated and Accompanied by the Verona Latin Fragments*, Oxford, 1929.

Funk, F., *Didascalia et Constitutiones Apostolorum*. Vol. I, Paderborn, 1905.

Gregory Thaumaturgus

Salmond, S., *Fathers of the Third Century* (ANF 6), Edinburgh, 1861; reprint, Grand Rapids, Michigan, 1978.

Clement of Alexandria

Wilson, W., *Clement of Alexandria* (ANF 2), Edinburgh, 1885; reprint, Grand Rapids, Michigan, 1979, pp. 165–605.

Origen

Chadwick, H., *Origen: Contra Celsum*, Cambridge, 1953.

Jay, E., *Origen's Treatise on Prayer*, London, 1954.

Mehat, A., *Homélies sur les Nombres* (SC 29), Paris, 1951.

Menzies, A. (ed.), *Recently Discovered Additions to Early Christian Literature; Commentaries of Origen* (ANF 5), Edinburgh, 1860; reprint, Grand Rapids, Michigan, 1978.

Oulton, J., and Chadwick, H., *Alexandrian Christianity* (The Library of Christian Classics 2), London, 1954.

Dionysius of Alexandria

Feltoe, C., *The Letters and Other Remains of Dionysius of Alexandria*, Cambridge, 1904.

Salmond, S., *Fathers of the Third Century* (ANF 6), Edinburgh, 1861; reprint, Grand Rapids, Michigan, pp. 81–124.

Hippolytus

Dix, G., *The Treatise on the Apostolic Tradition of St. Hippolytus of Rome*, London, 1937; reissued by H. Chadwick, 1968.

MacMahon, J., *Hippolytus: The Refutation of All Heresies* (ANF 5), Edinburgh, 1885; reprint, Grand Rapids, Michigan, 1978, pp. 9–162.

Novatian

De Simone, R., *Novatian* (FC 67), Washington, 1974.

Wallis, R., *Novatian and Appendix* (ANF 5), Edinburgh, 1869; reprint, Grand Rapids, Michigan, 1978, pp. 607–650, 657–663.

Tertullian

De Labriolle, P., *Tertullien. De paenitentia, De pudicitia*, Paris, 1906.

Le Saint, W., *Tertullian. Treatises on Penance: On Penance and Purity* (ACW 28), Westminster, Maryland, 1959.

Rauschen, G., *Tertullianus, Quintus Septimus Florens: De paenitentia et De pudicitia recensio nova* (Florilegium Patristicum 10), Bonn, 1915.

Thelwall, S., *Tertullian: On Repentance* (ANF 3), Edinburgh, 1885; reprint, Grand Rapids, Michigan, 1978, pp. 657–668.

Cyprian of Carthage

Bévenot, M., *St. Cyprian. "The Lapsed" and "The Unity of the Catholic Church"* (ACW 25), Westminster, Maryland, 1957.

_____, *Cyprian. De Lapsis and De Ecclesiae Catholicae Unitate*, Oxford, 1971.

Carey, H., *The Epistles of St. Cyprian* (Library of the Fathers 17), Oxford, 1844.

Clarke, G., *The Letters of St. Cyprian of Carthage*. 2 vols. (ACW 43/44), New York, 1984.

Donna, R., *Saint Cyprian. Letters* (FC 51), Washington, 1964.

II. SECONDARY SOURCES

A. PUBLICATIONS PRIOR TO 1900

Alexandre, N., *Historia ecclesiastica*, Paris, 1699.

Aquinas, St. Thomas, *Summa Theologiae*, Blackfriars Edition. Vol. 60: *Penance*, introduction and translation by R. Masterson and T. O'Brien, London, 1966.

Arnauld, A., *De la fréquente communion*, in *Oeuvres de Messire Arnauld*. Vol. XXVII, Paris, 1779, pp. 181–673.

Aubespine, G. de l', *De veteribus Ecclesiae ritibus Observationum*. Vol. II, Paris, 1623.

Benson, E., *Cyprian. His Life, His Time, His Work*, London, 1897.

Boudinhon, A., "Sur l'histoire de la pénitence à propos d'un livre récent," *RHLR* 2 (1897) 306–344, 496–524.

Döllinger, J., *Hippolytus und Kallistus, oder die römische Kirche in der ersten Hälfte des dritten Jahrhunderts*, Regensburg, 1853.

Francolini, B., *De disciplina poenitentiae*. Vol. III, Rome, 1708.

Funk, F., *Kirchengeschichtliche Abhandlungen und Untersuchungen*. Vol. I, Paderborn, 1897.

Gieseler, J., *Lehrbuch der Kirchengeschichte*, 4th ed., Bonn, 1844.

Harnack, A. von, *Geschichte der altchristlichen Literatur bis Eusebius*. Vol. I: Die Überlieferung und der Bestand, Leipzig, 1893.

_____, *History of Dogma*. Vol. II, translated by N. Buchanan, London, 1896.

Harent, S., "La Confession," *Études* 80 (1899) 577–605.

Huygens, G., *Methodus remittendi et retinendi peccata*, Louvain, 1674.

Lea, H., *A History of Auricular Confession and Indulgences in the Latin Church*. Vol I: *Confession and Indulgence*, Philadelphia, 1896.

Leutbrewer, C., *Industria spiritualis in qua modus traditur praeparandi se ad confessionem aliquam plurimorum annorum*, Cologne, 1639.

Luther, M., *Disputatio pro declaratione virtutis indulgentiarum* (D. Martin Luthers Werke. Kritische Gesamtausgabe 1), Weimar, 1883.

Mead, G., "Exomologesis," in *DCA* 1 (1875) 644–650.

Morcelli, A., *Africa christiana*. Vol. II, Brescia, 1817.

Morinus (Morin), J., *Commentarius historicus de disciplina in administratione sacramenti paenitentiae*, 2nd ed., Antwerp, 1682.

Neercassel, J. van, *Amor poenitens, sive de divini amoris ad poenitentiam necessitate et recto clavium usu*, Emmerich, 1683.

Orsi, Cardinal, *Dissertatio historica qua ostenditur catholicam Ecclesiam*, Milan, 1730.

Petavius (Pétau), D., *De poenitentia et reconciliatione veteris ecclesiae moribus recepta diatriba ex notis in Synesium*, in *Opus de theologicis dogmatibus*. Vol. VI, F. Zachariae (ed.), Venice, 1757, pp. 243–335.

_____, *De poenitentiae vetere in Ecclesia ratione diatriba*, in *Opus de theologicis dogmatibus*. Vol. VI, F. Zachariae (ed.), Venice, 1757, pp. 211–242.

_____, *De poenitentia publica et praeparatione ad communionem*, in *Opus de theologicis dogmatibus*. Vol. VI, F. Zachariae (ed.), Venice, 1757, pp. 336–342.

Rolffs, E., *Das Indulgenz-Edict des römischen Bischofs Kallist* (TU 11), 3rd ed., Leipzig, 1893.

_____, *Urkunden aus dem Antimontanistischen Kampfe des Abendlandes* (TU12), 4th ed., Leipzig, 1895.

Rossi, J. de, "Esame archeologico e critico della storia dei S. Callisto narrata nel libro nono dei Filosofumeni," *Bulletino di archeologia cristiana* 4 (1866) 1–33.

Sirmond, J., *Historia paenitentiae publicae*, Paris, 1651.

Suarez, F., *Opera Omnia*. Vol. XXII: Commentarii et Disputationes, C. Berton (ed.), Paris, 1861.

Thomassin, L., *Ancienne et nouvelle discipline de l'Église*. Vols. I and II. Paris, 1725.

Tournely, H., *Praelectiones theologicae*, Paris, 1728.

Vacandard, E., "Le pouvoir des clefs et la confession sacramentelle. À propos d'un livre récent," *Revue du clergé français* 18 (1899) 142–157.

B. PUBLICATIONS AFTER 1900

Acta Synodalia Sacrosancti Concilii Oecumenici Vaticani II. Vol. II, Part 1, Rome, 1962.

Adam, K., *Der Kirchenbegriff Tertullians* (FCLD 6,4), Paderborn, 1907.

_____, *Das sogenannte Bussedikt des Papstes Kallistus* (Veröffentlichungen aus dem Kirchenhistorischen Seminar München 4,5), Munich, 1917.

_____, *Die kirchliche Sündenvergebung nach dem hl. Augustin* (FCLD 14,1), Paderborn, 1917.

_____, ''Die abendländische Kirchenbusse im Ausgang des christlichen Altertums. Kritische Bemerkungen zu Poschmanns Untersuchung,'' *ThQ* 110 (1929) 1–66.

Adler, N., ''Die Handauflegung im NT bereits ein Bussritus? Zur Auslegung von I Tim. 5,22,'' in J. Blinzler, O. Kuss, and F. Mussner (eds.), *Neutestamentliche Aufsätze* (Festschrift J. Schmid), Regensburg, 1963, 1–6.

Adnès, P., ''Les fondements scripturaires du sacrement de pénitence,'' *Esprit et Vie: L'ami du clergé* 93 (1983) 305–310, 385–392, 497–508.

_____, ''Pénitence,'' in *DicSp* 12,1 (1984) 943–1010.

Alès, A. d', *La théologie de Tertullien*, Paris, 1905.

_____, *L'Édit de Calliste*, Paris, 1914.

_____, ''Zéphyrin, Calliste ou Agrippinus?,'' *RSR* 3–4 (1920) 254–256.

_____, *La théologie de saint Cyprien*, Paris, 1922.

_____, *Novatien. Études sur la théologie Romaine au milieu du IIIe siècle*, Paris, 1925.

Altaner, B., *Patrologie*, Freiburg, 1938; 8th ed. with A. Stuiber, 1978.

Alszeghy, Z., *De paenitentia Christiana*, Rome, 1961.

Amann, E., ''Pénitence-Sacrement,'' in *DThC* 12,1 (1903) 747–845.

_____, ''Novatien et Novatianisme,'' in *DThC* 11,1 (1931) 816–849.

_____, ''Pénitence,'' in *DThC* 12,1 (1933) 749–845.

Anciaux, P., *The Sacrament of Penance*, London, 1962.

Anderson, W., *Jus Divinum and the Sacrament of Penance in Two Tridentine Theologians: Melchior Cano and Ruard Tapper*, published doctoral dissertation: The Catholic University of America, Washington D.C., 1979.

Arranz, M., ''La liturgie pénitentielle juive après la destruction du Temple,'' in *Liturgie et rémission des péchés* (Bibliotheca Ephemerides Liturgicae Subsidia 3), Rome, 1975, pp. 39–56.

Audet, J., ''La penitenza christiana primitiva,'' *Sacra Doctrina* 46 (1967) 153–177.

Bainvel, M., ''Note sur la confession sacramentelle dans les premiers siècles de l'Église,'' *RSR* 3–4 (1920) 212–224.

Balthasar, H. U. von, ''Le mystérion d' Origène,'' *RSR* 26 (1936) 513–562; 27 (1937) 38–64.

Bardenhewer, O., *Patrologie*, 3rd ed., Freiburg, 1910.

Bardy, G., ''L'édit d'Agrippinus,'' *RevSR* 4 (1924) 1–25.

_____, *Clément d'Alexandrie* (Les moralistes chrétiens, F. Gabaldi ed.), Paris, 1926.

_____, *La conversion au Christianisme durant les premiers siècles* (Théologie 15), Paris, 1947.

_____, *La vie spirituelle d'après les pères des trois premiers siècles*, Paris, 1935; revised, 1968.

Barnes, T., "Eusebius and the Date of the Martyrdoms," in *Le Martyrs de Lyon (177). Colloques internationaux du centre national de la recherche scientifique. Septembre, 1977*, Paris, 1978, pp. 137–141.

―――――, *Tertullian. A Historical and Literary Study*, Oxford, 1971.

Barnett, C., *A Commentary on the Second Epistle to the Corinthians* (Black's New Testament Commentaries), London, 1973.

Bartlet, J., *Church-Life and Church-Order during the First Four Centuries, with Special Reference to the Early Eastern Church-Orders*, C. Cadoux (ed.), Oxford, 1943.

Batiffol, P., "L'Edit de Calliste d'après une controverse récente" *BLE* 10 (1906) 339–348.

―――――, *Études d'histoire et de théologie positive*, Paris, 1902; 7th ed., 1926.

Baus, K., *From the Apostolic Community to Constantine*, Vol. I: *Handbook of Church History*, H. Jedin and J. Dolan (eds.), New York, 1965.

Bausch, W., *A New Look at the Sacraments*, Notre Dame, 1977; revised, 1983.

Bavel, T. Van, "Eucharistie en Zondenvergeving," *Tijdschrift voor Liturgie 61 (1977)* 87–102.

Bayard, C., *Tertullien et Saint Cyprien*, Paris, 1930.

Beauchamp, P., "Un évêque du IIIᵉ siècle aux prises avec les pécheurs: son activité apostolique," *BLE* 50 (1949) 26–47.

Beck, A., *Römisches Recht bei Tertullian und Cyprian*, Halle, 1930.

Behm, J., "*Metanoeo, metanoia*," in *TDNT* IV, G. Kittel (ed.), translated by G. Bromiley, Grand Rapids, Michigan, 1967, pp. 975–1008.

Beneden, P. van, *Aux origines d'une terminologie sacrementelle: ordo, ordinare, ordinatio dans la littérature chrétienne avant 313* (SSL 38), Louvain, 1974.

Benko, S., *The Meaning of Sanctorum Communio* (Studies in Historical Theology 3), London, 1964.

Benoit, A., *Le baptisme chrétien au second siècle. La théologie des Pères*, Paris, 1953.

Bernhard, J., "Excommunication et pénitence-sacrement aux premiers siècles de l'Église," *RDC* 15 (1965) 265–281, 318–330; 16 (1966) 41–70.

Bernardin, J., "New Rite of Penance Suggested," *Origins* 13 (1983) 324–326.

Berrouard, M.-F., "La pénitence publique durant les six premiers siècles," *MD* 118 (1974) 92–130.

Bethune-Baker, J., *An Introduction to the Early History of Christian Doctrine to the Time of the Council of Chalcedon*, London, 1903; 2nd ed., 1962.

Bévenot, M., "A Bishop Is Responsible to God Alone (St. Cyprian)," *RSR* 39 (1951) 397–415.

―――――, "The Sacrament of Penance and St. Cyprian's 'De Lapsis,' " *TS* 16 (1955) 188–213.

―――――, "Review of L. Duquenne's Chronologie des lettres de S. Cyprien. Le dossier de la persécution de Dèce," *VC* 28 (1974) 156–158.

Bienert, W., *Dionysius von Alexandrien zur Frage des Origenismus im dritten Jahrhundert (PTS 21)*, Berlin, 1978.

Blond, G., *L'hérésie encratite vers la fin du IVe siècle* (SRTR 2), Paris, 1944.

Bonwetsch, G., *Grundriss der Dogmengeschichte*, 2nd ed., Munich, 1919.

————, *Die Theologie des Irenäus*, Gütersloh, 1925.

Bornkamm, G., "Die Binde- und Lösegewalt in der Kirche des Matthäus," in G. Bornkamm and K. Rahner (eds.), *Die Zeit Jesu* (Festschrift H. Schlier) Freiburg, 1970, pp. 51–62.

Borobio, D., "Sacramental Forgiveness of Sins," *Concilium* 184 (1986) 95–112.

Botte, B., "Review of C. Daly's The Sacrament of Penance in Tertullian," *BTAM* 6 (1950–1953) 104–105.

Bourque, E., *Histoire de la pénitence-Sacrement*, Quebec City, 1947.

Braun, R., *Deus Christianorum. Recherches sur le vocabulaire doctrinal de Tertullian*, Paris, 1977.

Brightman, F., "Terms of Communion and Ministration of the Sacraments in Early Times," in H. Swete (ed.), *Essays on the Early History of the Church and the Ministry*, London, 1921.

Brink, J., van den Bakhuizen, "Reconciliation in the Early Fathers," SP 13 [= TU 116] (1971), 90–106.

————, "Tradition and Authority in the Early Church," SP 7 [= TU 92] (1963) 3–22.

Brown, R., *The Gospel According to John.* 2 vols. (AB 29, 29A), New York, 1966, 1970.

————, *The Epistles of John* (AB 30), New York, 1982.

Bruders, H., "Matt. 16.19; 18.18 und Jo. 20.22-3 in frühchristlicher Auslegung," *ZKTh* 34 (1910) 659–677; 35 (1911) 79–111, 292–346, 466–481, 690–713.

Brulin, M., "Orientations pastorales de la pénitence dans divers pays," *MD* 117 (1974) 38–62.

Bultmann, R., *The Johannine Epistles* (Hermeneia), translated by R. O'Hara, Philadelphia, 1973.

Buonaiuti, E., "The Ethics and Eschatology of Methodius of Olympus," *HThR* 14 (1921) 255–266.

Burgess, J., *A History of the Exegesis of Matthew 16:17-19 from 1781 to 1965*, Ann Arbor, Michigan, 1976.

Bussini, F., "L'intervention de l'assemblé des fidèles au moment de la réconciliation des pénitents, d'après les trois 'postulations' d'un archdiacre romain du V-VIe siècle," *RevSR* 41 (1967) 28–38.

Campenhausen, H. von, *Ecclesiastical Authority and Spiritual Power in the Church of the First Three Centuries*, translated by J. Baker, Stanford, California, 1969.

Capelle, B., "L'introduction du catéchuménate à Rome," *RThAM* 5 (1933) 129–154.

————, "L'absolution sacerdotale chez S. Cyprien," *RThAM* 7 (1935) 221–234.

Cardman, F., "Tertullian on Doctrine and the Development of Discipline," SP 16 [= TU 129] (1975) 136–142.

Cavallera, F., "La doctrine de la pénitence au IIIᵉ siècle," *BLE* 30 (1929) 19–36; 31 (1930) 49–63.

Chartier, M., "La discipline pénitentielle d'après des écrits de saint Cyprien," *Antonianum* 14 (1939) 17–42, 135–156.

————, "L'excommunication ecclésiastique d'après écrits de Tertullian," *Antonianum* 10 (1935) 301–344, 499–536.

Chavasse, A., *Le sacrementaire Gélasien* (BTh 4, Histoire de la Théologie 1), Tournai, 1957.

Cochrane, C., *Christianity and Classical Culture. A Study of Thought and Action from Augustus to Augustine*, New York, 1977.

Conn, W. (ed.), *Conversion. Perspectives on Personal and Social Transformation*, New York, 1978.

Cooke, B., *Ministry to Word and Sacraments*, Philadelphia, Pennsylvania, 1976.

————, *Sacraments and Sacramentality*, Mystic, Connecticut, 1983.

Coppens, J., *L'imposition des mains et les rites connexes dans le Nouveau Testament et dans l'Église ancienne*, Wetteren, 1925.

Cothenet, È., "Sainteté de l' Église et péchés de chrétiens. Comment le N.T. envisage-t-il leur pardon?," *NRTh* 96 (1974) 449–470.

Courtney, F., "The Administration of Penance," *Clergy Review* 46 (1961) 10–27, 85–98.

————, "Preliminary Considerations on the Sacrament of Penance," *Clergy Review* 40 (1955) 513–519.

Crehan, J., "The Prayer After Absolution," *Clergy Review* 48 (1963) 95–101.

Crichton, J., *Christian Celebration. The Sacraments*, London, 1973.

————, *The Ministry of Reconciliation*, London, 1974.

Crouzel, H., *Origène et la 'connaissance mystique,'* Brussels, 1961.

————, *Grégoire le Thaumaturge, Remerciement a Origène suivi de la lettre d'Origène a Grégoire* (SC 148), Paris, 1969.

————, *Bibliographie critique d'Origène* (Instrumenta Patristica 8), Steenbrugge, 1971; supplément I, 1982.

Dallen, J., "The Imposition of Hands in Penance. A Study in Liturgical Theology," *Worship* 51 (1977) 224–247.

————, "Church Authority and the Sacrament of Penance. The Synod of Bishops," *Worship* 58 (1984) 194–214.

————, "Reconciliatio et Paenitentia. The Postsynodal Apostolic Exhortation," *Worship* 59 (1985) 98–116.

————, *The Reconciling Community*, New York, 1986.

Daly, C., "The Sacrament of Penance in Tertullian," *IER* 69 (1947) 693–707, 815–821; 70 (1948) 731–746, 832–848; 73 (1950) 156–169.

_____, "Novatian and Tertullian: A Chapter in the History of Puritanism," *IThQ* 19 (1952) 33–43.

_____, "Absolution and Satisfaction in St. Cyprian's Theology of Penance," SP 2 [= TU 64] (1955) 202–207.

_____, "The Edict of Callistus," SP 3 [= TU 78] (1959) 176–182.

Daniélou, J., and Marrou, H., *The First Six Hundred Years*. Vol. I: *The Christian Centuries*, translated by V. Cronin, New York, 1964.

Dassman, E., *Sündenvergebung durch Taufe, Busse und Martyrerfürbitte in den Zeugnissen frühchristlicher Frömmigkeit und Kunst* (MBTh 36), Münster, 1973.

Dauvillier, J., *Les temps apostoliques, Ier siècle* (Histoire du droit et des institutions de l'Église en Occident 2), Paris, 1968.

De Clerck, P., "De la confession à la réconciliation," *PeL* 55 (1973) 143–153.

_____, "Ordination, ordre," in *Catholicisme hier aujourd 'hui demain* 10/44 (1983) 162–206.

De Ghellinck, J., et al., *Pour l'histoire du mot "sacramentum"* (SSL 3), Louvain, 1924.

De Labriolle, P., *La crise Montaniste*, Paris, 1913.

_____, *Les sources de l'histoire du Montanism* (Collectanea Friburgensia 15), Fribourg, Switzerland, 1913.

_____, *La réaction païenne. Étude sur la polémique antichrétienne du Ier-VIe siècle*, Paris, 1934.

Delahaye, K., *Ecclesia mater chez les Pères des trois premiers siècles* (Unam Sanctam 46), Paris, 1964.

Del Ton, G., "L'episodio eucharistico di Serapione narrato da Dionisi Alessandrino," *SCA* 70 (1942) 37–47.

Deniau, F., and Dye, D., "Recherches sur la pénitence publications Françaises, 1960–1975," *MD* 124 (1975) 111–139.

De San, L., *De Poenitentia*, Bruges, 1900.

Dibelius, M., and Conzelmann, H., *The Pastoral Epistles* (Hermeneia), translated by P. Buttolph and A. Yarbro, Philadelphia, Pennsylvania, 1972.

Didier, J.-D., "D' une interprétation récente de l'expression 'lier-délier,' " *MSR* 9 (1952) 55–62.

Diekamp, F., "Ueber den Bischofssitz des hl. Märtyrers und Kirchenvaters Methodius," *ThQ* 109 (1928) 285–308.

Diekmann, G., "Reconciliation through the Prayer of the Community," in *The Rite of Penance. Commentaries*. Vol. 3: *Background and Directions*, N. Mitchell (ed.), Washington, D.C., 1978.

Dirksen, H., *The New Testament Concept of Metanoia* (CUAT 34), Washington, D.C., 1932.

Dodd, C., *Historical Tradition in the Fourth Gospel*, Cambridge, 1963.

Dölger, F., "Ante absidem. Der Platz des Büssers beim Akt der Rekonziliation," *AuC* 6 (1950) 196–201.

Donfried, K., *The Setting of Second Clement in Early Christianity* (SuppNT 38), Leiden, 1974.

Dooley, C., "Devotional Confession. A Historical and Theological Survey," unpublished doctoral dissertation, Katholieke Universiteit Leuven, 1982.

Doskocil, W., *Der Bann in der Urkirche. Eine rechtgeschichtliche Untersuchung (MThS 11)*, Munich, 1958.

Duggan, R., (ed.), *Conversion and the Catechumenate*, New York, 1984.

Dujarier, M., *Le parrainage des adultes aux trois premiers siècles de l' Église* (Parole et Mission 4), Paris, 1962.

—————, *A History of the Catechumenate*, translated by E. Haasl, New York, 1979.

—————, *The Rite of Christian Initiation*, translated by K. Hart, New York, 1979.

Duquenne, L., *Chronologie des lettres de S. Cyprien. Le dossier de la persécution de Dèce* (SH 54), Brussels, 1972.

Emerton, J., "Binding and Loosing—Forgiving and Retaining," *JThS* 13 (1962) 325–331.

Ercole, G. D', *Penitenza canonico-sacramentale dalle origini alla pace Costantiniana*, (Communio 4), Rome, 1963.

Esser, G., *Die Busschriften Tertullians "De paenitentia" und "De pudicitia" und das Indulgenzedikt des Papstes Kallistus*, Bonn, 1905.

—————, "Nochmals das Indulgenedikt des Papstes Kallistus und die Busschriften Tertullians," *Der Katholik* 8–9 (1907) 184–204, 297–309; 1–2 (1908) 12–28, 93–113.

—————, *Der Adressat der Schrift Tertullians "De pudicitia" und der Verfasser des römischen Bussedikts*, Bonn, 1914.

Exeler, A., et al., *Zum Thema: Busse und Bussfeier*, Stuttgart, 1971.

Eynde, D. van den, *Les norms de l'enseignement chrétien dans la littérature patristique des trois premiers siècles*, Paris, 1933.

—————, "Notes sur les rites latins d'initiation et de la réconciliation," *Antonianum* 33 (1958) 415–422.

Faivre, A., "Le 'système normatif' dans la lettre de Clément de Rome aux Corinthiens," *RevSR* 54 (1980) 129–152.

—————, "Bibliographie de Cyril Vogel," *RDC* 34 (1984) 390–395.

Farges, J., *Les idées morales et religieuses de Méthode d' Olympe*, Paris 1929.

Fendt, L., "Sünde und Busse in den Schriften des Methodius von Olympus," *Der Katholik* 3 (1905) 24–45.

Fleming, T., *The Second Vatican Council's Teaching on the Sacrament of Penance and the Communal Nature of the Sacrament*, published doctoral dissertation, The Pontifical University of St. Thomas Aquinas, Rome, 1981.

Forkman, G., *The Limits of the Religious Community. Expulsion from the Religious Community within the Qumran Sect, within Rabbinic Judaism, and within Primitive Christianity* (Coniectanea Biblica 5), Lund, 1972.

Fraenkel, D., "Solus dominus misereri potest. Saint Cyprian, 'De Lapsis' ch. XVII, et le probléme de son interprétation," SP 10 [= TU 107] (1967) 71–76.

Fransen, P., *Faith and Sacraments* (Aquinas Papers 31), London, 1958.

————, "Orders and Ordination," in *Sacramentum Mundi* 4 (1969) 305–327.

Franses, D., "Das 'Edictum Callisti' in der neuern Forschung," in *Studia Catholica* 1 (1924) 248–259.

Freburger, W., "Ongoing Conversion—A Process," in *The New Rite of Penance, Background Catechesis* (Federation of Diocesan Liturgical Commissions), Pevely, Missouri, 1974.

Fruetsaert, E., "La réconciliation ecclésiastiques vers l'an 200," *NRTh* 57 (1930) 379–391.

Funk, F., "Das Indulgenzedikt das Papstes Kallistus," *ThQ* 88 (1906) 541–567.

————, *Histoire de l'Église*. Vol. I, translated by M. Hemmer, Paris, 1911.

Funke, F., "Survey of Published Writings on Confession over the Past Ten Years," *Concilium* 61 (1971) 120–132.

Furnish, V., *II Corinthians* (AB 32A), New York, 1984.

Galtier, P., "Le rémission des péchés moindres dans l'Église du troisième au cinquième siècles," *RSR* 13 (1923) 97–129.

————, *De paenitentia. Tractatus dogmatico-historicus*, Paris, 1923; 10th ed., Rome, 1956.

————, *L'Église et la rémission des péchés*, Paris, 1932.

————, "La date de la Didascalie des Apôtres," *RHE* 42 (1947) 315–351.

————, "Les canons pénitentiels de Nicée," *Gregorianum* 29 (1948) 288–294.

————, *Aux origines du sacrement de pénitence*, Rome, 1951.

————, "La réconciliation des pécheurs dans la première épître a Timothée," *RSR* 39 (1951) 317–320.

Garrigou-Lagrange, R., *Reality: A Synthesis of Thomistic Thought*, translated by P. Cummins, St. Louis, Missouri, 1950.

Gaudemet, J., "Note sur les formes anciennes de l'excommunication," *RevSR* 23 (1949) 64–78.

————, *L'Église dans l'empire romain. IVᵉ–Vᵉ siècle* (Histoire du droit et des institutions de l'Église en occident 3), Paris, 1958.

————, *La formation du droit séculier et du droit de l'Église aux IVᵉ et Vᵉ siècles* (Institut de droit romain de l'université de Paris 15), 2nd ed., Paris, 1979.

Geerard, M., *Patres Antenicaeni* (Corpus Christianorum Clavis Patrum Graecorum 1), Turnhout, 1983.

Giet, S., "L'Apocalypse d'Hermas et la pénitence," SP 3 [= TU 78] (1959) 214–218.

————, "De trois expressions: 'Auprès de la tour, la place inférieure, et les premiers murs', dans le Pasteur d'Hermas," SP 8 [= TU 93] (1963) 24–29.

————, *Hermas et les pasteurs. Les trois auteurs du Pasteur d'Hermas*, Paris, 1963.

————, "Les trois auteurs du Pasteur d'Hermas," SP 8 [= TU 93] (1963) 10–23.

————, "Pénitence ou repentance dans le Pasteur d'Hermas," *RDC* 17 (1967) 15–30.

————, *L'énigme de la Didachè* (Publications de la faculté des lettres de l'université de Strasbourg 149), Paris, 1970.

González, S., "Los penitenciales del Concilio de Elvira," *Gregorianum* 22 (1941) 191–214.

Greeley, A., McCready, W., and McCourt, K., *Catholic Schools in a Declining Church*, Kansas City, Missouri, 1976.

Gremillion, J., and Castelli, J., *The Emerging Parish: The Notre Dame Study of Catholic Life since Vatican II*, San Francisco, 1987.

Griffe, E., "Un example de pénitence publique au Ve siècle," *BLE* 59 (1958) 170–175.

Greenslade, S., *Schism in the Early Church*, London, 1964.

Groupe de la Bussière, Pratiques de la confession. Des pères du désert à Vatican II. Quinze études d'histoire, Paris, 1983.

Grotz, J., *Die Entwicklung des Busstufenwesens in der vornicänischen Kirche*, Freiburg, 1955.

Gula, R., *To Walk Together Again. The Sacrament of Reconciliation*, New York, 1984.

Gülzow, H., *Cyprian und Novatian* (BHTh 48), Tübingen, 1975.

Gunstone, J., *The Liturgy of Penance* (Studies in Christian Worship 7), London, 1966.

Guzie, T., *The Book of Sacramental Basics*, New York, 1981.

Gy, P.-M., "Histoire liturgique du sacrement de pénitence," *MD* 56 (1958) 5–21.

————, "Penance and Reconciliation," in A. Martimort (ed.), *The Church at Prayer*. Vol. III: *The Sacraments*, Collegeville, Minnesota, 1988, 101–115.

Hall, S., "Repentance in I Clement," SP 8 [= TU 93] (1963) 30–43.

Hamel, A., *Kirche bei Hippolyt von Rom* (BFT 49), Gütersloh, 1951.

Hamelin, L., *Reconciliation in the Church*, translated by M. O'Connell, Collegeville, Minnesota, 1980.

Hamman, A., "La signification de *sphragis* dans le Pasteur d'Hermas," SP 4 [= TU 79] (1959) 286–290.

Hargreaves, K., *Cornelius Jansenius and the Origins of Jansenism*, published doctoral dissertation, Brandeis University, Waltham, Massachusetts, 1974.

Harnack, A. von, *The Constitution and Law of the Church in the First Two Centuries*, translated by Pogson, London, 1910.

_____, *Die Mission und Ausbreitung des Christentums in den ersten drei Jahrhunderten.* Bd. II, Leipzig, 1906; 4th ed., 1924.

Harrison, P., *Polycarp's Two Epistles to the Philippians*, Cambridge, 1936.

Haslehurst, R., *Some Account of the Penitential Discipline of the Early Church in the First Four Centuries*, London, 1921.

Hebblethwaite, M., and Donavan, K., *The Theology of Penance* (Theology Today 20), Dublin, 1979.

Hein, K., *Eucharist and Excommunication: A Study in Early Christian Doctrine and Discipline* (European University Papers XXIII/19), Frankfurt, 1973.

Hellwig, M., *Sign of Reconciliation and Conversion. The Sacrament of Penance for Our Times* (Message of the Sacraments 4), Wilmington, Delaware, 1982; 2nd ed., 1984.

Hoh, J., *Die kirchliche Busse im zweiten Jahrhundert* (BSHTh 22), Breslau, 1932.

Holstein, H., "L'Exhomologèse dans 'l'Adversus Haereses' de Saint Irénée," *RSR* 35 (1948) 282–288.

Hornschuh, M., *Studien zur Epistula Apostolorum* (PTS 5), Berlin, 1965.

Houssiau, A., *La christologie de S. Irénée* (UCLDiss 3,1), Louvain, 1955.

Hübner, S., "Kirchenbusse und Exkommunikation bei Cyprian," *ZKTh* 84 (1962) 49–84, 171–215.

Hünermann, F., *Die Busslehre des heiligen Augustinus* (FCLD 12,1), Paderborn, 1914.

Hummel, E., *The Concept of Martyrdom According to St. Cyprian of Carthage* (StCA 9), Washington, 1946.

Jacquin, M., "Bulletin d'histoire des doctrines chrétiennes," *RSPTh* 1 (1907) 368–369; 2 (1908) 383–387; 7 (1913) 331–337; 9 (1920) 269–282; 10 (1921) 272–273.

Janini Cuesta, J., "La penitencia medicinal desde la Didascalia Apostolorum a S. Gregorio de Nisa," *RET* 7 (1947) 337–362.

John Paul II, *Reconciliatio et Paenitentia. Postsynodal Apostolic Exhortation*, United States Catholic Conference, Washington, D.C., 1984.

Joly, R., "La doctrine pénitentielle du Pasteur d'Hermas et l'exégèse récente," *RHR* 147 (1955) 32–49.

_____, "Note sur *metanoia*," *RHR* 140 (1961) 149–156.

Jouassard, G., "Le rôle des chrétiens comme intercesseurs auprès de Dieu dans la chrétienité Lyonnaise au second siècle," *RevSR* 30 (1956) 217–229.

Joyce, G., "Private Penance in the Early Church," *JThS* 42 (1941) 18–42.

Jungmann, J., *Die lateinischen Bussriten in ihrer geschichtlichen Entwicklung* (Forschungen zur Geschichte des innerkirchlichen Lebens 3–4), Innsbruck, 1932.

_____, *The Early Liturgy to the Time of Gregory the Great* (Liturgical Studies 6), translated by F. Brunner, Notre Dame, Indiana, 1959.

Junod, E., "Un echo d'une controverse autour de la pénitence," *RHPR* 60 (1980) 153–160.

Jurgens, W., *The Faith of the Early Fathers*, Collegeville, Minnesota, 1970.

Karpp, H., "Die Busslehre des Klemens von Alexandrien," *ZNW* 43 (1950/1951) 224–242.

————, (ed.), *La pénitence. Textes et commentaires des origines de l'ordre penitentiel de l'Église ancienne* (Traditio Christiana 1), translated by A. Schneider, W. Rordorf, and P. Barthel, Neuchâtel, 1970.

Kelly, J., *Early Christian Doctrine*, San Francisco, California, 1970.

————, *A Commentary on the Pastoral Epistles* (Black's New Testament Commentaries), London, 1963; 2nd ed., 1972.

Kirk, K., *The Vision of God*, London, 1932.

Kirsch, J., *Handbuch der allgemeinen Kirchengeschichte*. Vol. I: *Die Kirche in der antiken Kulterwelt*, Freiburg, 1911.

Kirsch, P., *Zur Geschichte der katholischen Beichte*, Würzburg, 1902.

Koch, H. "Die Büsserentlassung in der alten abendländischen Kirche," *ThQ* 82 (1900) 481–534.

————, "Der Büsserplatz im Abendland," *ThQ* 85 (1905) 254–270.

————, "Die Sündenvergebung bei Irenäus," *ZNW* 9 (1908) 36–46.

————, *Kallist und Tertullian*, (Sitzungsberichte der Heidelberger Akademie der Wissenschaften, Philosophie-historische Klasse 10), Heidelberg, 1919.

————, *Die Bussfrist des Pastor Hermä*, in K. Holl (ed.), *Festgabe von A. von Harnack*, Tübingen, 1921, 173–182.

————, *Cyprianische Untersuchungen* (AK 4), Bonn, 1926.

Koch, R., "La rémission et la confession des péchés selon l' Ancien Testament," *Studia Moralia* 10 (1972) 219–247.

Köhne, J., "Die Bussdauer auf Grund der Briefe Cyprians," *ThGl* 29 (1937) 245–256.

————, "Zur Frage der Busse im Christlichen Alterum," *ThGl* 35 (1943) 26–36.

Kraft, H., "Die lyoner Märtyrer und der Montanismus," in *Le Martyrs de Lyon (177). Colloques internationaux du centre national de la recherche scientifique, Septembre, 1977*, Paris, 1978, 233–244.

Landini, L., "Drop-Off in Confession. The Epistles of St. Cyprian of Carthage," *AER* 169 (1975) 133–142.

Langstadt, E., "Some Observations on Tertullian's Legalism," *SP* 6 [= TU 81] (1959) 122–126.

————, "Tertullian's Doctrine of Sin and the Power of Absolution in 'De pudicitia,'" *SP* 2 [= TU 64] (1955) 251–257.

La Piana, G., "Foreign Groups in Rome during the First Centuries of the Empire," *HThR* 20 (1927) 183–203.

————, "The Roman Church at the End of the Second Century," *HThR* 18 (1925) 201–277.

Latko, E., *Origen's Concept of Penance*, Quebec, 1949.

Lebreton, J., "La développement des institutions ecclésiastiques à la fin du IIe siècle et au debut du IIIe siècle," *RSR* 24 (1934) 129-164.

Leclercq, H., "Martyr" in *DACL* 10,2 (1932) 2359-2511.

Lefèvre, A., "Péché et pénitence dans la Bible," *MD* 55 (1958) 7-22.

Leijssen, L., *Penance and the Anointing of the Sick,* unpublished course notes, Katholieke Universiteit Leuven, 1980.

Leitzmann, H., *History of the Early Church.* Vol. 2: *The Foundation of the Church Universal,* translated by B. Woolf, 2nd ed., London, 1961.

Lentzen-Deis, W., *Busse als Bekenntnisvollzug. Versuch einer Erhellung der sakramentalen Bekehrung anhand der Bussliturgie des alten Pontificale Romanum* (Freiburger Theologische Studien 86), Freiburg, 1969.

Le Saint, W., "Traditio and Exomologesis in Tertullian," SP 7 [= TU 93] (1969) 414-419.

Ligier, L., "Le sacrement de pénitence selon la tradition orientale," *NRTh* 89 (1967) 940-967.

Lipinski, E., *La liturgie pénitentielle dans la Bible* (Lectio Divina 52), Paris, 1969.

Lods, M., *Confesseurs et martyrs. Successeurs des prophètes dans l'Église des trois premiers siècles* (CTh 41), Neuchâtel, 1958.

Loisy, A., *The Gospel and the Church,* B. Scott (ed.), translated by C. Home, Lives of Jesus Series, Philadelphia, 1976.

Loofs, F. *Leitfaden zum Studium der Dogmengeschichte,* Halle, 1906.

Lopresti, J., "RCIA and Reconciling the Alienated," *Church* 1 (1985) 11-16.

Marcen Tihista, A., "Liturgias penitenciales en el Antiguo Testamento," in *El sacramento de la Penitencia, XXX Semana española de teología, Madrid, 1970,* Madrid, 1972, pp. 85-104.

Markus, R., *Christianity in the Roman World,* New York, 1974.

Marliangeas, B., "Aperçu sur l'histoire des formes liturgiques de sacrement pénitence," *Parole et Pain* 7 (1970) 139-148.

Martinez, F., *L'ascétisme chrétien pendant les trois premiers siècles de l'Église,* Paris, 1913.

Martos, J., *Doors to the Sacred,* Garden City, New Jersey, 1981.

Matellanes Crespo, A., *El tema de la 'Communicatio' en los escritos penitenciales y bautismales de San Cipriano de Cartago* (UCLDiss 41), Louvain, 1965.

————, "Communicatio. El contenido de la comunión eclesial en San Cipriano," *Communio* 1 (1968) 19-64, 347-401.

May, G., "Bemerkungen zu der Frage der Diffamation und der Irregularität der öffentlichen Busser," *MThZ* 12 (1961) 252-268.

McAuliffe, C., "Absolution in the Early Church. The View of St. Pacian," *TS* 6 (1945) 51-61.

————, "Penance and Reconciliation within the Church," *TS* 26 (1965) 1-39.

McNeill, J., and Gamer, H., *Medieval Handbooks of Penance* (Records of Civilization 29), New York, 1938.

Mehat, A., *Études sur les 'Stromates' de Clément d'Alexandrie* (Patristica Sorbonensia 7), Paris, 1966.

———, "Pénitence seconde et péché involontaire chez Clément d'Alexandrie," *VigChr* 8 (1954) 225–233.

Melin, B., *Studia in Corpus Cyprianeum*, Uppsala, 1946.

Metzger, M., "La pénitence dans les Constitution Apostoliques," *RDC* 34 (1984) 224–234.

Michel, O., "*Homologeō, exomologeō, anthomologeomai, homologia, homologoumenōs*," in TDNT V, G. Friedrich (ed.), translated by G. Bromiley, Grand Rapids, Michigan 1968, pp. 199–220.

Mitchell, N., "The Many Ways of Reconciliation. An Historical Synopsis of Christian Penance," in *The Rite of Penance. Commentaries*. Vol. 3: *Background and Directions*, N. Mitchell (ed.), Washington, D.C., 1978, pp. 20–37.

Monceaux, E., *Histoire littéraire de l'Afrique chrétienne*. Vol. I: *Tertullien et les origines*, Paris, 1906.

Mortimer, R., *The Origins of Private Penance in the Western Church*, Oxford, 1939.

Mügge, M., "Das Bussverständnis in der Theologie des Irenäus," *ThGl* 67 (1977) 393–405.

———, "Der Einfluss des juridischen Denkens auf die Busstheologie Tertullians," *ThGl* 68 (1978) 426–450.

———, "Entwicklung und theologischer Kontext der Busstheologie Karl Rahners," in H. Vorgrimler (ed.), *Wagnis Theologie. Erfahrungen mit der Theologie Karl Rahners*, Freiburg, 1979, pp. 435–450.

Mühlsteiger, J., "Exomologese," in *ZKTh* 103 (1981) 1–32, 129–155, 257–288,

Munier, C., "Discipline pénitentielle et droit pénal ecclésial," *Concilium* 107 (1975) 23–32.

———, (ed.), *Les Statuta ecclesiae antiqua* (Bibliothèque de l'Institut de Droit Canonique de l'Université de Strasbourg 5), Paris, 1960.

Murphy-O'Connor, J., "Péché et communauté dans le Nouveau Testament," *RB* 74 (1967) 161–193.

Musurillo, H., *The Acts of the Christian Martyrs*, Oxford, 1972.

———, and Debidour, V.-H., *Méthode d' Olympe. Le Banquet* (SC 95), Paris, 1963.

Nautin, P., *Lettres et écrivains chrétiens des IIe et IIIe siècles* (Patristica 2), Paris, 1961.

Nicolau, M., *La reconciliacion con Dios y con la Iglesia en la Biblia y en la historia*, Madrid, 1977.

Oakley, T., *English Penitential Discipline and Anglo-Saxon Law in Their Joint Influence* (Studies in History, Economics, and Public Law 107), New York, 1923.

O'Donnell, J., *Penance in the Early Church with a Short Sketch of Subsequent Development*, Dublin, 1907.

O'Hagan, A., "The Great Tribulation to Come in the Pastor of Hermas," SP 4 [= TU 79] (1959) 305–311.

Orsy, L., *The Evolving Church and the Sacrament of Penance*, Denville, New Jersey, 1978.

Palmer, P., "Jean Morin and the Problem of Private Penance," *TS* 6 (1945) 317–357; 7 (1946) 281–308.

————, *Sources of Christian Theology*. Vol. II: *Sacraments and Forgiveness*, Westminster, Maryland, 1959.

Parker, H., *A History of the Roman World from A.D. 138 to 337*, London, 1958.

Pavan, V., "Battesimo e Incorruttibilità nella II Clementis, catechesi ai neofiti," *VC* 14 (1977) 51–67.

Paverd, F. van de, "The Meaning of *ek metanoias* in the Regula fidei of St. Irenaeus," *OCP* 38 (1972) 454–466.

————, "Paenitentia secunda in Methodius of Olympus," *Augustinianum* 18 (1978) 459–485.

————, "Confession (*Exagoreusis*) and Penance (*Exomologesis*) in De lepra of Methodius of Olympus," *OCP* 44 (1978) 309–341; 45 (1979) 45–74.

Pelikan, J., *Historical Theology: Continuity and Change in Christian Doctrine*, London, 1971.

Pellegrino, M., "Le sens ecclesial du Martyre," *RevSR* 35 (1961) 151–175.

Percival, H., *The Seven Ecumenical Councils of the Undivided Church* (Nicene and Post Nicene Fathers 14), Edinburgh, 1899; reprint, Grand Rapids, Michigan, 1979.

Pétré, H., *Caritas. Étude sur le vocabulaire latin de la charité chrétienne* (SSL 22), Louvain, 1948.

Pinkers, G., "Le rôle de la communauté dans le sacrement de pénitence," *PeL* 5 (1973) 419–426.

Pius X, *Actes de S. S. Pie X*. Vol. *III*, Paris, 1905–1910.

Pohle, J., *Lehrbuch der Dogmatik in sieben Büchern*. Vol. III, Paderborn, 1905.

Poschmann, B., "Die kirchliche Vermittlung der Sündenvergebung nach Augustinus," *ZKTh* 45 (1921) 497–526.

————, *Kirchenbusse und correptio secreta bei Augustinus*, Braunsberg, 1923.

————, *Die abendländische Kirchenbusse im Ausgang des christlichen Altertums* (Münchener Studien zur historischen Theologie 7), Munich, 1928.

————, "Review of Galtier's L'Église," *ThRv* 7 (1933) 263–267.

————, *Paenitentia Secunda*, Bonn, 1940.

————, *Penance and Anointing of the Sick*, translated by F. Courtney, New York, 1964.

Preuschen, E., "Die Kirchenpolitik des Bischofs Kallist," *ZNW* 10 (1910) 134–160.

Quacquarelli, A., "Libertà, peccato e penitenza secundo Tertulliano," *Rassegna di science filosofiche* 2 (1948) 16–37.

Quasten, J., *Patrology*. 3 vols., Utrecht, 1953.

Rahner, K., *Tractatus historico-dogmaticus. De paenitentia*, 2nd ed., Innsbruck, 1952.

———, *Theological Investigations*. Vol. 15: *Penance in the Early Church*, translated by L. Swain, London, 1983.

Rambaux, C., *Tertullien face aux morales des trois premiers siècles*, Paris, 1979.

Ramos-Regidor, J., "Reconciliation in the Primitive Church and Its Lessons for Theology and Pastoral Practice Today," *Concilium* 1 (1971) 76–88.

Rauschen, G., *L'Eucharistie et la pénitence*, translated by M. Decker and E. Ricard, Paris, 1910.

Recheis, A., "Das Fragment De paenitentia," *Traditio* 9 (1953) 419–420.

Riga, P., "Penance in St. Ambrose," *EeT* 4 (1973) 213–252.

Rigaux, B., "Lier et Délier—Les ministères de réconciliation dans l'Église des temps apostoliques," *MD* 117 (1974) 86–135.

Rite of Penance, English translation prepared by the International Commission on English in the Liturgy, Collegeville, Minnesota, 1975.

Rivas, S., *La penitencia en la primitiva iglesia española*, Salamanca, 1949.

Rondet, H., "Esquisse d'une histoire du sacrement de pénitence," *NRTh* 80 (1958) 561–584.

———, *The Grace of Christ*, translated by T. Guzie, New York, 1966.

Rordorf, W., "La rémission des péchés selon la Didachè," *Irénikon* 46 (1973) 283–297.

Russo, A., "Excommunicatio e anathema nella letteratura Cristiana antica," *Asprenas* 8 (1961) 240–251.

Ruysschaert, J., "Les 'martyrs' et les 'confesseurs' de la Lettre des Églises de Lyon et de Vienne," in *Colloques internationaux du centre national de recherche scientifique, Septembre, 1977*, Paris, 1978, pp. 155–164.

Sabourin, L., "La rémission des péchés: Ecriture Sainte et pratique ecclésiale," *SE* 32 (1980) 299–315.

Sage, M., *Cyprian* (Patristic Monograph Series 1), Cambridge, Massachusetts, 1975.

Saint-Palais D'Aussac, F., *La réconciliation des hérétiques dans l'Église Latine* (Études de science religieuse 2), Paris, 1943.

Saxer, V., *Vie liturgique et quotidienne à Carthage vers milieu du IIIe siècle* (SAC 29), Rome, 1969.

Schepelern, W., *Der Montanismus und die Phrygischen Kulte*, Tübingen, 1929.

Schmitt, J., "Contribution à l'étude de la discipline pénitentielle dans l'Église primitive à la lumière des textes de Qumran," in *Les manuscripts de la Mer Morte. Colloque de Strasbourg, Mai 1955*, Paris, 1957.

Schmöle, K., "Gnosis und Metanoia. Die anthropologische Sicht der Busse bei Klemens von Alexandrien," *TThZ* 82 (1973) 304–312.

Schroeder, H., (ed.), *Disciplinary Decrees of the General Councils*, St. Louis, Missouri, 1937.

Schwartz, E., "Busstufen und Katechumenatsklassen" in *Gesammelte Schriften*, Vol. 5: *Zum Neuen Testament und zum frühen Christentum*, Berlin, 1963 (reprint of 1911 publication).

Scienczak, B., *Partecipazione dei fedeli al sacramento della penitenza. Il contributo della Chiesa del periodo dei Patri nel contesto dell'attuale riforma penitenziale*, published doctoral dissertational excerpt, Pontifical Gregorian University, Rome, 1974.

Searle, M., "The Journey of Conversion," *Worship* 54 (1980) 35–55.

Seeberg, R., *Lehrbuch der Dogmengeschichte*. Vol. I: *Die Anfänge des Dogmas im Nachapostolischen und alt katholischen Zeitalter*, 2nd ed., Leipzig, 1908.

Sirinelli, J., *Les vues historiques d'Eusèbe de Césarée durant la période prénicénienne*, Paris, 1961.

_____, and Places, E. des, *Eusèbe de Césarée. La préparation évangélique. Book I* (SC 206), Paris, 1974.

Slattery, G., "Restore the Ordo Poenitentium?—Some Historical Notes," *The Living Light* 20 (1984) 248–253.

Stählin, O., *Clemens Alexandrinus. Register* (GCS 39), Leipzig, 1936.

Steinruch, J., "Busse und Beichte in ihrer geschichtlichen Entwicklung," in *Dienst der Versöhnung* (TThS 31), Trier, 1974, pp. 45–65.

Stirnimann, J., *Die Praescripto Tertullians im Licht des römischen Rechts und der Theologie*, Freiburg, 1949.

Stufler, J., "Die Sündenvergebung bei Origenes," *ZKTh* 31 (1907) 193–228.

_____, "Die Bussdisziplin der abendländischen Kirche bis Kallistus," *ZKTh* 31 (1907) 433–473.

_____, "Die Sündenvergebung bei Irenäus," *ZKTh* 32 (1908) 488–497.

_____, "Zur Kontroverse über das Indulgenzedikt des Papstes Kallistus," *ZKTh* 32 (1908) 1–42.

_____, "Einige Bemerkungen zur Busslehre Cyprians," *ZKTh* 33 (1909) 232–247.

Swann, W., *The Relationship between Penance, Reconciliation with the Church, and Admission to the Eucharist in the Letters of the 'De Lapsis' of Cyprian of Carthage*, published doctoral dissertation, The Catholic University of America, Washington, D.C., 1980.

Swanson, H., "Penance and the History of Penance," *New Blackfriars* 50 (1969) 754–759.

Swete, H., "Penitential Discipline in the First Three Centuries," *JThS* 4 (1903) 321–337.

Taylor, J., "St. Cyprian and the Reconciliation of Apostates," *TS* 3 (1942) 27–46.

Taylor, M., *The Mystery of Sin and Forgiveness*, New York, 1971.

Teetaert, A., "Doctrine de Saint Thomas d'Aquin au sujet du sacrement de pénitence et de la confession aux laïques." *Miscellania Tomista. Etudis Franciscans* 34 (1924) 302–325.

_____, *La confession aux laïques dans l'Église latine depuis le VIIIe jusqu'au XVIe siècle*, Bruges, 1926.

Teeuwen, W., *Sprachlicher Bedeutungswandel bei Tertullian* (SGKA 14), Paderborn, 1926.

Tefler, W., *The Forgiveness of Sins*, London, 1959.

Teichtweier, G., *Die Sündenlehre des Origenes*, Regensburg, 1958.

Tentler, T., *Sin and Confession on the Eve of the Reformation*, Princeton, New Jersey, 1977.

Thomas, F., *Textbook of Roman Law*, Amsterdam, 1976.

Thyen, H., *Studien zur Sündenvergebung im Neuen Testament und seinen alttestamentlichen und jüdischen Voraussetzungen* (FRLANT 96), Göttingen, 1970.

Tixeront, J., *Le sacrement de pénitence dans l'antiquité chrétienne*, (Questiones théologiques 691), Paris, 1914.

_____, *History of Dogmas*, Vol. I: *The Antenicene Theology*, translated by H.L.B., St. Louis, Missouri, 1930.

Trigg, J., *Origen. The Bible and Philosophy in the Third Century*, Atlanta, Georgia, 1949; reprint, 1983.

Tromp, N., Lescrauwaet, J., and Scheer, A., *Geroepen tot vrede: over zonde en vergeving* (Van exegese tot verkondiging 13), Boxtel, 1973.

Vacandard, E., *La confession sacrementelle dans l'Église primitive* (SR 224), Paris, 1903.

_____, *La pénitence publique dans l'Église primitive* (SR 223), Paris, 1903.

_____, "Absolution des péchés au temps des Pères," in *DThC I,1* (1903) 145–161.

_____, "Confession du I^e au XIIIe siècle," in *DThc III* (1908) 838–894.

Valton, E., "Excommunication," in *DThC* 2 (1913) 1735.

Vanbeck, A., "La pénitence dans les premières générations chrétiennes," *RHLR* 1/new series (1910) 436–465.

Vaux Saint-Cyr, B. de, *Revenir à Dieu. Pénitence, conversion, confession* (CTT 26), Paris, 1967.

Vellico, A., "Episcopus episcoporum in Tertulliani libro De pudicitia," *Antonianum* 5 (1930) 25–56.

Verheul, A., "Le sacrement de la réconciliation à travers les siècles," *QL* 58 (1977) 27–49.

Viller, M., *La spiritualité des premiers siècles chrétiens* (BCSR 32), Paris, 1930.

Vogel, C., *La discipline pénitentielle en Gaule des origines à la fin du VIIe siècle*, Paris, 1952.

_____, "Le péché et la pénitence. Aperçu sur l'évolution historique de la discipline pénitentielle dans l'Église latine," in P. Delhaye (ed.), *Pastorale du péché* (BTh II, Théologie Morale 8), Tournai, 1961, pp. 147-236.

_____, *Le pécheur et la pénitence dans l'Église ancienne* (CTT 15), Paris, 1966.

_____, "Vacua manus impositio. L'inconsistance de la chirotonie absolue en Occident," in *Mélanges liturgiques offerts au B. Botte*, Louvain, 1972, 511-524.

_____, "Laïca communione contentus. Le retour du presbytre au rang des laïcs," *RevSR* 47 (1973) 56-122.

Vogt, H., *Coetus Sanctorum. Der Kirchenbegriff des Novatian und die Geschichte seiner Sonderkirche* (Theophaneia 20), Bonn, 1968.

_____, *Das Kirchenverständnis des Origenes* (BBK 4), Cologne, 1974.

Vokes, F., "The Opposition of Montanism from Church and State in the Christian Empire," SP 4 [= TU 79] (1959) 518-526.

_____, "Penitential Discipline in Montanism," SP 14 [= TU 117] (1971) 62-76.

Vööbus, A., *Liturgical Traditions of the Didache*, Stockholm, 1968.

Voorvelt, G., "L'Amor Poenitens de Neercassel," in *Jansénius et la Jansénisme dans les Pays-Bas* (EThL 56, T. Van Bavel and M. Schrama, eds.), Louvain, 1982, pp. 66-92.

Vorgrimler, H., "Matthieu 16, 18 s. et le sacrement de pénitence," *Théologie* 56 (1963) 51-62.

_____, *Busse und Krankensalbung* (HDg 4, 3, M. Schmaus, et al., eds.), Freiburg, 1978.

Walgrave, J., *Unfolding Revelation. The Nature of Doctrinal Development* (Theological Resources), London, 1972.

Watkins, O., *A History of Penance*. Vol. I: *The Whole Church to A.D. 450*, London, 1920.

Wilhelm-Hooijbergh, A., *Peccatum. Sin and Guilt in Ancient Rome*, published doctoral dissertation, Rijksuniversiteit te Utrecht, Groningen, 1954.

Windisch, H., *Taufe und Sünde im ältesten Christentum bis auf Origenes*, Tübingen, 1908.

Worden, T., "The Remission of Sins," *Scripture* 9 (1957) 65-79, 115-127.

Xiberta, B., *Clavis Ecclesiae*, Rome, 1922.

Index

Authors cited in the Index are those whose names and words appear within the text or who are named and quoted (or paraphrased) in the notes.

Authors not cited in the Index but who are listed as sources within the notes are fully cited in the Bibliography.